The Data and Analytics Playbook

The Data and Analytics Playbook

Proven Methods for Governed Data & Analytic Quality

Lowell Fryman
Collibra, USA

Gregory Lampshire
K2 Solutions, USA

Dan Meers
K2 Solutions, USA

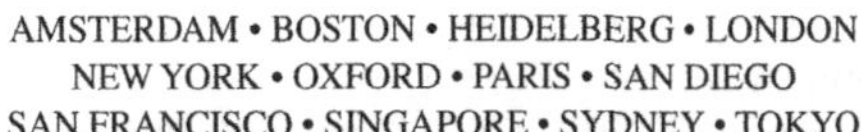
AMSTERDAM • BOSTON • HEIDELBERG • LONDON
NEW YORK • OXFORD • PARIS • SAN DIEGO
SAN FRANCISCO • SINGAPORE • SYDNEY • TOKYO

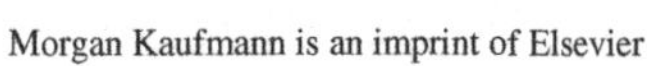
Morgan Kaufmann is an imprint of Elsevier

Morgan Kaufmann is an imprint of Elsevier
50 Hampshire Street, 5th Floor, Cambridge, MA 02139, United States

Library of Congress Cataloging-in-Publication Data
A catalog record for this book is available from the Library of Congress

British Library Cataloguing-in-Publication Data
A catalogue record for this book is available from the British Library

ISBN: 978-0-12-802307-5

For information on all Morgan Kaufmann publications visit our website at https://www.elsevier.com/

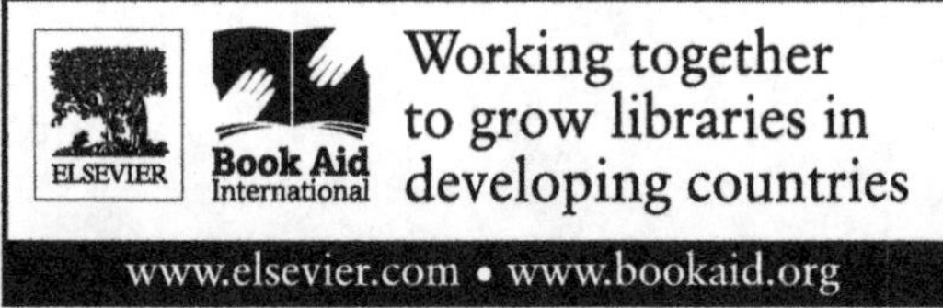

Publisher: Todd Green
Acquisition Editor: Todd Green
Editorial Project Manager: Amy Invernizzi
Production Project Manager: Priya Kumaraguruparan
Designer: Greg Harris

Typeset by TNQ Books and Journals

To our partners in crime at Knightsbridge Solutions and all its successors—from the founders to the support staff, Knightsbridge was a great company because it had great vision (thanks founders!), culture (thanks Rod!), and people. We miss it still!

Lowell Fryman

To my wife, Elizabeth, who after three decades still challenges me to be the best man I can be, but lets me have the room to make my own mistakes, as well as accomplishments. There is never enough time, but love never fails to fill the gaps.

Gregory Lampshire

To my wife, Laura, and sons, Jared and Nathan, who put up with my crazy schedule, sales pursuits, and jobs over the years. They take me to school every day.

Dan Meers

For my Father, Patrick James Meers, whose insightful guidance, love, and support prepared me for this work and my loving family who supports my growth, as I support theirs, thanks forever to my T, H, and S!

Contents

Author Biographies

Lowell Fryman is responsible for directing thought leadership and advisory services in the customer success practice of Collibra. He has been a practitioner in the data management industry for three decades and is recognized as a leader in data governance, analytics, and data quality, having hands-on experience with implementations across most industries. Lowell is a coauthor of the book *Business Metadata; Capturing Enterprise Knowledge*. Lowell is a past adjunct professor at Daniels College of Business, Denver University, a past president and current VP of Education for DAMA-I Rocky Mountain Chapter (RMC), a DAMA-I charter member, and member of the Data Governance Professionals Organization. He is also an author and reviewer of the *DAMA-I Data Management Book of Knowledge* (DMBOK). He focuses on practical data governance practices and has trained thousands of professionals in data governance, data warehousing, data management, and data-quality techniques. You can read his data governance blogs at https://www.collibra.com/blog/

Gregory Lampshire has started and led consulting practices and product development efforts in multiple industries including financial services, healthcare, life sciences, telecommunications, and energy. His work in playbook development and deployment extends to multiple data sprints addressing complex financial crimes detection and prevention solutions in large financial services institutions. He has a strong background in advanced sales and marketing strategy and analytics and sales and marketing processes including strategic and operational segmentation, targeting, acquisition, and retention. He has built and deployed multiple front-line CRM applications. His clients and companies have won a variety of innovation awards for bringing analytics to customer touchpoints.

Dan Meers serves as the President of K2 Solutions LLC and manages the Reston, VA-based consultancy, solving complex data-centric problems with asset-based consulting services. He has over 25 of experience with clients in financial, retail, manufacturing, government, and other markets. Dan regularly addresses enterprise risk issues including information assurance and security, antimoney laundering and broader financial crime detection and prevention, and integration of social-media data. Dan has worked with Bill Inmon and John Zachman in the development and application of Corporate Information Factory and other models for global firms including Shell Oil Services, BP, Target, and others.

Acknowledgments

Dan Meers

Cary Martin, who taught me to be a client-centered consultant and team player while supporting my passion for innovation, Bill Inmon, who taught me how to reuse data, innovate continuously, and give back to the industry—here you go, Bill. Mark DeLong, who taught me the meaning and importance of a "controls conscious management" as well as how to audit and improve financial institutions, and Rod Walker, who taught me how to lead by example.

The teachers who gave me the guidance, room, and challenges I needed to learn how to learn, starting with Eileen (life), then Korby (faith) and Ed (science), and many others who have followed.

The partners who share their knowledge and opportunities, especially Bill Inmon, Derek Strauss, Genia Neushloss, Charlie DeFelice, Gregory Lampshire, Lowell Fryman, Eric Vaughn, Balu Kadiyala, Vin Siegfried, Rohit Tandon, Sanjiv Tandon, Barry Smith, and my first and best business partner, my brother Tom "Gus" Meers.

The clients who have shared so much knowledge and experience along the way, especially Marv Adams, Carl Gerber, John Carrow, Michael Nicosia, Rich Strader, Derek Strauss, Claire LeBlanc, Dave Jeska, Stuart Gray, Lanette Beatty, and Randy Parker.

And, of course my team of Pirates at Freddie Mac Enterprise Architecture—consistent leaders in thought and practice.

This book required tremendous support from Cecily Dennis, Jessie Bur, and Sara Raab. Cecily Dennis is an exemplary program and project manager who also provided data governance support for clients while managing to get this book off the ground. Jessie Bur is a journalist and editor whose work on more the half the book content as an editor and graphics director was critical to our success. Sara provided invaluable support to authoring and editing.

Lowell Fryman

Dan Meers and I will acknowledge many of the same individuals that have been great influencers and supporters of our careers over the years. Having been in this profession for over 30 years there are far too many to acknowledge and thank.

First, I want to acknowledge Dan Meers whom has been a wonderful peer, influence, mentor, partner, and friend for 13 years now. This book is an acknowledgment of his vision and drive to educate. Cheers, my friend.

To W. H. (Bill) Inmon who has given so much to the technology industry and cared about the people who showed passion and desire to further the data industry. Bill, thanks for inviting me in, inspiring me to write, and being the great partner you have been for two decades.

Many warm thanks to John Zachman for his steadfast dedication to keeping us all reminded that we provide enabling technology to the business and must maintain that understanding and alignment for the business to be successful. To me the Zachman Framework is the equivalent of the Rosetta Stone for data governance and analytics. Many warm thanks and blessings to John and his family.

To my many partners and peers at Knightsbridge Solutions; to Derek Strauss, Genia Neushloss, and my friends at Gavroshe; many thanks for the long-term partnership with Bruce Gallager and team at Synechron, as well as all the clients that have been part of my professional life for three decades.

Finally to my very excellent current family at Collibra. Congratulations to Stijn, Benny, Pieter, Felix, and Dieter (as well as 100 others) for the vision and passion to bring data governance practices, techniques, and technology to so many. Keep fighting the good fight to get the right people to do the right activities on the right data for all the right reasons.

Keep calm and allow your data governance program to prosper.

Gregory Lampshire

I have been fortunate over the years to work with such wonderful people who have taken the time to help me learn and grow professionally and personally. Their commitment to providing me feedback has helped me be better. From the time spent at Shell Offshore as a geophysicist to Thinking Machines, MRJ, PwC, Siemens, Knightsbridge, Launchpoint, Solariat, and K2 Solutions, I have learned how to listen, be helpful, and lead.

I would like to thank my coauthors, Dan and Lowell, for putting up with me writing this book (my first, but their second, third, and so on).

I would also like to thank all those that I have spoken with and turned to for advice over the years. You know who you are! If I ever asked for help, asked you to teach me something, wanted your opinion, or asked for your guidance, know that I listened carefully and integrated it into what I was working on and was very thankful.

Introduction

THE VALUE OF INFORMATION, DELIVERED

We focus on the union of data and analytics as the combination of supply and demand. Executives who rely upon this union often refer to it as information delivery.

> Information about money has become almost as important as money itself.
>
> **Walter Wriston**

Data was recognized as an asset over three decades ago, and it was accompanied by an executive mandate to treat certain assets, such as those associated with critical physical assets, with critical care.

Walter Wriston, Chairman of Citicorp from 1970 to 1984 and pioneer of negotiable certificates of deposit and the automated teller machine (ATM) networks, was no stranger to assets or the value streams of data they produced. He was the beneficiary of mass computerization of the banking, investment, and related industries, so data was his stock in trade. His realization is more applicable today than ever, because our ability to deliver data for specific uses and outcomes has advanced so far, so fast.

Mr. Wriston also said, "Capital goes where it is welcome and stays where it is well treated." It might be fair to think of critical data as a form of capital; we've certainly seen all manner of financial and commodity traders use data to improve their performance just as they would use cash and credit. So, by extension, we might start thinking about data governance as more than data control; it really should be a way to ensure an environment where critical data is well treated.

Our experience with industry leading clients suggests a new perspective based on Mr. Wriston's insight: leading institutional performance increasingly requires leading data performance. Therefore this book focuses on empowering sustainable data leadership.

> Thirty years ago we were producing data from transactions almost as fast as they occurred and capturing it for operational activities. The ATM network relied on extending the "memo posting" technology of the mainframe to make people's money on deposit continuously available. Ensuring withdrawals were immediately posted and deducted from available funds calculations was the key data-processing enhancement. This process began with branch banking but had to scale to thousands of real-time interfaces for the ATM network.
>
> In this example, data is produced at thousands of locations and must be delivered to central processing centers to provide real-time balance updates. The data flows are critical as well as the timeliness, accuracy, and completeness of the data they contain. Data was traditionally governed by the applications that produced and consumed it because their interfaces were dedicated and highly defined.

Data delivery channels are expanding without consistent controls. In fact, they often source from local and external channels with very little control over their creation or operation. This multitude of data channels creates a need to produce, apply, and maintain effective, control-based governance for critical business data. Only effective control-based governance results in quality, attestable data. The other impact of data channel multiplicity is the construct of "enterprise data." Our approach provides a simple way to determine what enterprise data is, thus shaping which data is subject to enterprise governance. Enterprise data is subject to shared use either inside the enterprise, outside the enterprise, or both. The emerging goal, and in some cases, requirement for enterprise data governance programs, is the movement toward data outcomes with a balance of controls and business objectives.

DATA DELIVERY, VALUE DELIVERY

Now that we have a benefit-based context to frame data governance, we can really focus on governing data delivery. This is an applied governance function to ensure delivered data satisfies user requirements appropriately. In this context, we are governing the way data it is delivered, including the choice of source and delivery method. A standard architectural construct is the use of a "system of record" to denote sources of book entries for transactions, master and reference data values, and other primary systems the business uses to capture events, changes, and statuses. The other commonly standardized source is often referred to as an "authoritative data source," or ADS.

We recognize that data governance, particularly business-owned and operated data governance, is a critical set of capabilities for all businesses. This delivery focus moves us another step forward into the business value arena. Data governance as a control function is still a difficult business case to make since the cost/benefits take time to balance out and lines of business all have their own workarounds and a sense of ownership. The use of capability-based models, usually centered on maturing key data capabilities across an enterprise, has resulted in some movement from local to common or enterprise controls.

"Capability" is a term that many people use but seldom define. Our definition of capability is the simple combination of ability and capacity, meaning that it is a given, measurable level of ability in a specific process. A data capability is a measurable level of performed process. This Playbook therefore addresses the need to capture, catalog, communicate, use, and improve standard processes that create enterprise data capabilities.

Over time, the scope of these capabilities has grown in size just as the array of delivery needs and vehicles has grown. Our process recognizes the different levels of activity that must occur to provide program-level governance as well as workflow and data-element-level stewardship. Communicating the importance of stewardship activities as well as governance functions is critical to engaging members of the business in a sustainable way.

Delivering data to closed-loop analytics that automate decisions about supply chain or customer retention actions adds a new level of requirements for timeliness, accuracy, and completeness. Thus the discipline of data governance has grown in both scope and importance. Sharing experience, insights, and practices has proven to be one of the best ways to advance the discipline of business data governance—hence this book.

Our approach uses a business focus on "governed enterprise data quality," which explicitly requires governance support for both change and quality controls and outcomes. The value of governance is variable, since the value of governed data is change- and quality-controlled and is specifically measurable through conditions and outcomes. This makes governed data foundational to data leadership.

"Data leadership" is the term clients in the forefront of data-intensive industries and regulation now use to identify the integration of data capabilities, practices, and outcomes into their overall enterprise strategy and processes. Data leadership is not a new concept, but very few practitioners have yet accepted this level of responsibility for their various efforts. Consultants often tout the need for data governance, data quality and master data management, Big Data and analytics, and so on. They sell engagements to establish a strategy, roadmap, and business case to do the work. These efforts, in the absence of a clearly articulated focus on leading with data, are all too often seen as another attempt to mature the data and some of the activities around it. For a long time, our business and funding models have been focused on what is clearly application leadership, from ERP to cloud computing. As a result, the resources and sponsorship look to applications to solve their problems and scale their business. Data is an afterthought. Consider this book a challenge to the data and application communities to rebalance the approach we take to both components. We should be focusing on data much more comprehensively across both the application and data management domains.

We have been challenged repeatedly to support initiatives that are on the "run the business" side of the equation where the sponsor expects a "change or improve the business" outcome with data. These outcomes range from permanent improvements in data controls, quality, and timeliness to attestability. This last term, "attestability," is used to differentiate types of critical data, such as regulatory reporting, financial results, and customer data, which all require executive attestation. You will not find data attestability in standard industry publications, because it is a business term arising from increased regulatory requirements. It is used in risk management, compliance, and audit areas of businesses in industries including financial services, healthcare, manufacturing, and others.

Executives understand attestation very well; they are required be personally accountable for their company reports and the information they use to produce them. Company financial statements as well as many other regulatory and public filings require their formal attestation as well as that of their accounting firm. Critical data is much more important when an executive is committed to its accuracy. This accountability causes executives to increasingly ask the chief data officer and his/her organization to meet specific levels of quality, control, and protection. This ensures the executive attestations are appropriate and supportable enough to withstand the test of time—and auditing!

Data initiatives ranging from new data programs to full enterprise data organization design and development are increasingly using the term "data leadership" to describe their contribution to the enterprise and its partners. Data leadership councils (DLCs) are seen to have a more forward looking, offensively positioned, and organizational approach than the old data governance councils and committees. These DLCs balance competitive data outcomes, such as advanced customer and competitive analytics, with operational governance, quality, and attestability outcomes. The ability to tie market-facing delivery of data-driven outcomes back to data governance, quality, and controls has been the central challenge of first-generation data resource- and asset-based governance approaches. Now we are able to focus on generating returns from these data assets through the services we develop to deliver consistently advanced data outcomes. The solid foundation that data resource management programs, disciplines, and methods have provided supports this advanced approach.

The overall scope of governance includes the stewardship-based application of controls over the change and quality of enterprise data. The data leadership cycle completes when a measurement of impacts is taken and communicated to support ongoing improvements.

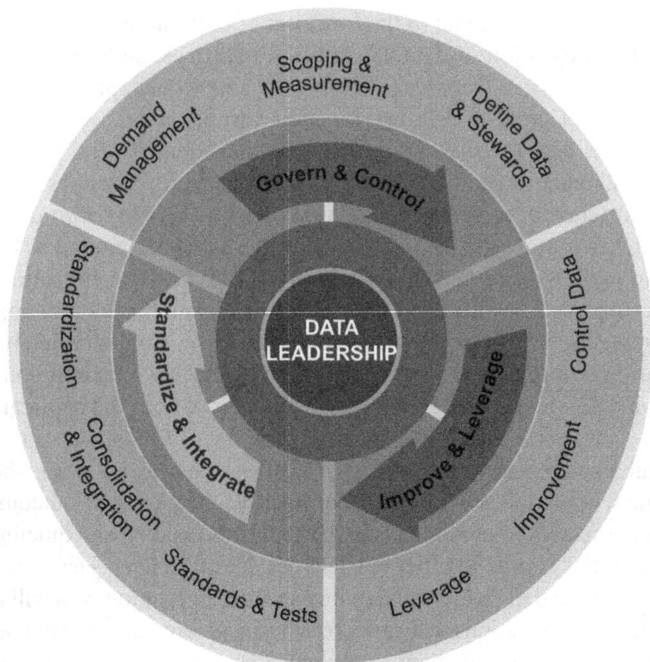

The data leadership cycle

Data leadership has been defined by William H. "Bill" Inmon, father of the data warehousing industry, as "leverage." We spoke with Bill about this as part of our research and he was clear about this challenge. Leaders leverage data using data governance, integration, and warehousing disciplines to support massive reuse of quality-controlled data across enterprise and time horizons. Data reuse enables many industry leaders to compete on analytics and run their operations efficiently. Inmon continues to prove that principle with his Big Data integration methods, showing that leverage knows no bounds when it comes to enterprise data assets.

This data reuse, or leverage, is also enabled by limiting the scope of enterprise applications' data responsibility, limiting or eliminating the practice of mass duplication and customization of data, and supporting standard levels of quality, history, detail, and availability. Data warehousing has delivered on all of these promises. Therefore data leadership is largely a function of leveraging data efficiently. Data warehousing established that fact and analytics continues to expand on it.

Leverage is a function that requires a consistently managed balance between supply and demand. It also requires standard processes, services, and measures so that people know how to accomplish effective leverage and understand what level of leverage they are providing. As we navigate the data Playbook and its context, we will illustrate ways that its practitioners and sponsors produce and enjoy data leverage.

WHAT IS THE DATA PLAYBOOK? HOW IS IT USED?

We have come to an understanding with our clients that the old paradigm is no longer effective or extensible enough to cover their changing needs. Their expectations have changed; they now expect to get the "how to" along with the "why," "what," and "who" from their consulting partners. All too often, consultants present themselves as the answer to "who," converting solution-oriented consulting into staffing. Worse yet, staffing firms display a thin veneer of expertise that addresses only the minimum "why" and "what," then go straight to staffing to solve the problem without a consistent, documented, or repeatable "how."

The old paradigm says that:

1. Businesses need to accomplish specific goals such as resolving data integrity problems, improving data controls, and delivering new analytics.
2. Consultant businesses accomplish their goals with experienced people, examples, and templates. Consultants then fail to give customers the methods and mentorship (Playbook and deployment) to sustain and improve critical new capabilities.
3. Businesses are required to continue to operate and improve the things consultants showed them.

Our new paradigm insists on a partnership aimed squarely at sustainable capability development, deployment, and improvement with commensurate improvements in key business areas. Developing, deploying, and improving core data capabilities drives measurable gains in regulatory compliance, data risk and exposure, reduced costs, and time to produce enterprise.

The Playbook paradigm is:

1. Businesses know what they need to accomplish and understand the value of a repeatable, scalable, and sustainable approach to long-term success.
2. Consultants must provide the "how" along with expertise and examples of the "why," "what," and "who." As part of the initial "who," consultants must demonstrate a documented way for the business to transition from knowing, to doing, to mentoring.
3. Businesses will select and continue relationships with consulting partners who consistently demonstrate a commitment to expanding business capabilities with shared methods and mentorship.

This paradigm shift is not universal. Many clients continue to engage consultants and staff on an ad hoc or project basis in order to address critical business issues or help them run their business efficiently. Many of these businesses are also engaged in varying levels of technology and operations outsourcing, requiring a different kind of partnership model than most consultants provide. The common thread to the new paradigm is the need to produce sustainable capabilities and results. The world of Big Data, analytics, and virtualized computing is expanding this paradigm, as it underscores the value of data capabilities at the enterprise level.

The data Playbook is a proven way to standardize, deploy, and leverage value through enterprise data management methods. It conveys experience, because it contains a framework for action as well as the specific methods, actions, and actors needed to execute that framework. The framework is simple enough to be communicated quickly and complete enough to bind four core disciplines of governed data quality: governance, stewardship, coordination, and quality.

This Playbook reflects years of experience across hundreds or even thousands of people in ways that foster sustainable success. So we focus on the Playbook construct as a way to provide people who need to do governance and improvement work with proven ways to accomplish that work. We also provide methods to maintain, customize, and apply the Playbook to suit the needs of each organization it serves; this creates a living, growing experience set for users.

The Playbook contains detailed activities that can be assembled into simple or complex work sequences. The execution of these activities in a sequence accomplishes three key outcomes:

1. The ***delivery*** of basic governance and control, quality, and improvement, analytics enhancement, and other facets of data management. Delivery ***is*** value.
2. The improvement of behaviors by ***doing*** competencies and, over time, enterprise capabilities. Doing ***is*** knowing.
3. The realization of ***defined benefits*** by business, customers, partners, or other constituents. Benefits ***ensure*** sponsorship.

WHAT IS THE ROLE OF COMPLIANCE, RISK MANAGEMENT, AND AUDIT?

In short, active engagement, which is the posture in firms and federal agencies where data is recognized as a critical asset and revenue driver. The old days of "defensive" Playbook-based data strategy aimed at meeting the minimum requirements of compliance are ending quickly. Data leaders are now recognizing the ongoing challenges brought on by dynamic regulation and compliance enforcement. Defensive areas, ranging from antimoney laundering, watch list monitoring, and identity theft alerting to capital adequacy and stress testing, are all moving to a proactive, offensive stance. There is a growing sense of urgency about stress testing data itself, and the notion of data risk testing is rooted in the understanding that data has multiple risk dimensions. The simplest way to look at it is to understand the difference between risks TO data and risks FROM data.

Traditional risk and controls frameworks don't completely address this dichotomy. Their goal is to identify risks arising from data, based on controls related to the handling of that data. Fair enough, but "the times they are a changin'." That approach now has two added facets. The first is risks posed from data based on its downstream dependencies and, often unknown, recipients. These risks are something conventional data governance programs attempt to cover but often struggle with due to a lack of engagement with users. Their top-down data governance mandates still fall short of proactively engaging key business, operational, and technical leaders, because they are perceived, and often experienced, as a drag on the company rather than lift. This is where the data leadership paradigm changes organizational willingness to commit resources and change behaviors. Data leadership promises a benefits-based approach. It also offers efficient core data services that produce, manage, and leverage core data assets, while freeing up business partners to focus on the competitive forces and outcomes needed from enterprise data. The second chapter highlights ways chief data officers are organizing themselves to support this approach.

Internal audit, risk management, compliance, and other controls-focused experts are now able to drive sustainable, measured controls into the requirements and design phases of work on all data-handling and delivery systems with much resistance. This streamlined involvement occurs because the DLC sponsors a controls committee from their outset. Such an organizational construct puts controls-based outcomes on the same footing as competitive data delivery needs. This is the embodiment of what top risk management executives refer to as "controls conscious management." The key message from leaders in this area is that there is a permanent requirement for a controls-conscious management but no other effective means of supporting controls across the enterprise. The controls committee gains business support because it focuses resources, actions, and outcome measures on a central group, which concentrates its efforts on shared enterprise data services and assets. Cloud, mobile, and other external computing paradigms increasingly require this level of organizational commitment to support efficiency.

BOOK ORGANIZATION

When using this book, make it as easy and repeatable a process as possible to find and use what you are looking for—even if it means folding pages, highlighting, dog earing, or otherwise marking out what works for you. Of course, our publisher fully supports major Website material as well as electronic publication formats to make this material immediately available anywhere you need it.

Second, we include the real, working material you need to get the job done. We provide plenty of basic "how tos" based on real-world experience and success. This is what distinguishes this book and its value. There are many good books on data programs, data governance strategy, data-quality management, business terms, and metadata management (authored by one of our own) and many other areas now broadly seen as part of data governance. This book is about specific, useful methods and activity sequences that get you going and keep you ahead of the pack.

Finally, we tie the Playbook together with real benefits, measures, and assessment tools so you can establish your value proposition, then exceed it.

We've arranged the book into three sections that support the three key aspects of business data governance listed above: The Basics, The Behaviors, and The Benefits.

ABOUT THE COVER

The cover of this book uses a familiar paradigm, the soccer field and players, to communicate our context. The 11 players on the field have all been given named roles and play positions that align with two requirements. The first is the familiar identification of stewardship and governance activities. The second is a specific mapping to the "three lines of defense," now common in public institutions as a means of engaging the enterprise in coordinated risk management and mitigation. This has been traditionally considered a vestige of financial services regulation but the shape and functions you see here are increasingly commonplace in many industries.

NOW, LET'S GET STARTED...

So if "information about money is becoming almost as valuable as money itself," we can see why a controlled approach to handling data and analytics is so important. Add to that the requirement to attest to the quality of this information, just as we have always had to attest to our actual money and its use, and we see a new level of governance is needed.

CHAPTER

PURPOSE, SCOPE AND AUDIENCE

1

This book describes an approach to making data governance repeatable, reliable, and cost-effective in your organization. Our approach uses a Playbook, a play-by-play description of how to set expectations as well as perform data governance jobs right the first time.

Before we dig deeper into the Playbook, we want to highlight the impact of data issues on organizations, industries, countries, and yourself. While many of the stories were taken from recent headlines and seem like once-in-a-million events, some of the stories describe recurring themes. These stories illustrate the type of data governance issues the Playbook was designed to solve and reflect real problems that can ultimately cost an organization money or its reputation.

SPOTTING THE NEED FOR DATA AND ANALYTICS GOVERNANCE: INDUSTRY EXAMPLES

The examples we cover are a sample; new stories and situations surface every day. Data governance conferences, books, and articles abound with stories from the trenches. Stories describing issues and solutions have been the primary way to describe approaches to data governance because, until now, there have been few best practices that have worked well across multiple organizations. The examples include a few stories around the industry of "you." Often, the best way to understand the impact of something in our professional lives is to understand the impact that it has on us.

The general concept of "data" is simple to understand at a high level. But as soon as someone actually needs to work with data to perform their job, knowing how to use data quickly becomes difficult and requires additional skills many people have not yet acquired. Similarly, while you may think that writing policies for data usage and access should be simple, understanding all the ways that data is used at an organization makes it difficult to write an effective policy.

INDUSTRY: YOU AND YOUR COUNTRY

Target, a major retailer, was hit hard in 2013. It was initially thought that fraudsters made off with the payment data of 40 million customers and the personal information such as phone numbers and email addresses of 70 million customers. Shortly after, the CIO and then CEO were replaced.

Neiman Marcus, a major retailer, was also hit hard. Hackers floated internally unnoticed for eight months. The estimated number of customers exposed was initially 1.1 million. Later that estimate was reduced to 350,000. Malware was directly installed on terminals similar to the intrusion at Target.

Holden Security, based out of Milwaukee, claimed that a Russian hacker group stole 1.2 billion usernames and passwords. While it is believed that the hackers plan to use the information to send out email health-products spam, the full extent of the theft is not yet clear. Spamming our mailboxes may not seem like it has a large impact. If the hackers sell the lists to companies, you may receive email that must be manually deleted. Spam filters are not perfect. If you spend 1–2 s to identify a spam email that passed through the filters and push the delete button, possibly over 600,000 h of time has been wasted across people just like you. That is equivalent to an organization of over 300 people working an entire year doing nothing but deleting email.

Facebook claims over 1 billion active users and is one of the largest social networking sites in the world. It has faced constant criticism over its privacy policies. Several lawsuits and complaints to the Fair Trade Commission (FTC) have highlighted that Facebook's policies allow the routine use of members' images and names in commercial advertising without consent. Facebook has updated their Statement of Rights and Responsibilities and Data Use policies. It was later disclosed that Facebook ran experiments on their members in order to test the impact of user-interface changes to their members' emotions and actions without consent. Facebook noted that recent updates to their data use policy clarified the language in the policy, but they did not actually change the policy that allows them to perform these experiments.

After a lengthy lawsuit in the European Union, Google launched the "right to be forgotten webform" to handle removal requests. European citizens can request that links to information about them be removed from search results. The webform is the first step toward supporting the court ruling. However, Google says the form is used to evaluate the request and the process of how to comply with the ruling and requests will come later. Information such as the needs for public information, timeliness of the information, and other factors will be considered in the request. Other search engines such as Bing or Yahoo must follow suit.

All of these stories highlight issues that affect you directly:

- You have provided a substantial amount of personal and financial information both explicitly or implicitly to many different types of organizations. Most of these organizations have different levels of privacy, data use policies, and different levels of maturity around implementing them.
- Nearly all companies have explicit data policies. You may not be aware of them, you may disagree with them, or they may be hard to understand.
- At least 1 billion people knowingly share a significant amount of detailed information that can be used by fraudsters for identity theft. Or that information can be easily stolen. At the very least, access to this data could cause you pain and suffering.
- The impact on both you and the country can be huge when your customer data is not well managed.

INDUSTRY: MANUFACTURING

An international computer manufacturer operates direct and indirect sales channels. Manufacturers have generally focused on operational quality metrics as the key management model – ie, manage by the numbers. Manufacturing is amenable to metrics-based management because a vast majority of supply chain processes are automated or electronically monitored. The era of Deming and other quality gurus raised the bar not only by lowering costs but also improving product and process quality. Improving quality often also lowers costs, which makes some business managers report that quality is free.

When any organization has a direct sales channel to consumers, they should also become focused on ensuring the customer experience is optimally tuned. The customer experience is often directly tied to product quality and supply chain variability. For example, if a manufacturer delivers a laptop to a customer, it may care about the following types of metrics:

- Shipping target variance
  - The percentage of times that you ship to a customer within a certain time window.
- Shipped product defect rate
  - The rate at which a customer requires or perceives to require parts, service, or system replacement within the initial ownership period, say 60 days.
- Missing or wrong rate
  - The rate at which the customer receives or perceives to have been sent the wrong order or did not receive the order.
- Service delivery on-time percentage and first-time resolution percentage
  - The percentage of service calls where the technician arrived within the contractual or committed hours.
  - The percentage of service calls where the technician resolved the issue on the first visit.

These customer experience metrics reflect what customers have said impact their economic behavior over time. However, similar to all customer experience metrics, creating these metrics, setting targets, and monitoring them requires substantial amounts of integrated data from many different groups. Identifying and defining these metrics may take a substantial amount of time and may involve subcalculations with many nuances.

Here are some examples of the types of issues that may occur when defining these metrics:

- Are the metrics gathered at the individual component level (eg, monitor, computer, printer) or at the customer level? What about smaller peripherals?
- If products have staggered ship orders, how is this evaluted?
- Are all countries included in the calculation? Should South America be included in North America's rollup?
- Which orders should be excluded from the calculation? What if an order is missing key date fields such as order entry date or ship date?
- What should the time window be for shipping target? Promised date or a general level of service commitment such as 5 days? What if the customer asked for a ship and delivery date outside of the 5 days?
- How do you count business days versus nonbusiness days? Do you count holidays? What if there was corporate work during a holiday, such as the end-of-year holiday?
- What defines a ship date? When the factory order entry system provides a specific code? Or should it be the invoiced date?
- Should leased systems be counted?
- Should these metrics be tracked on product exchanges?
- Should you count employee purchases? How do you define an employee?
- If we are using a percentage, should the denominator be a fiscal quarter or a month?
- Who maintains the table for "field incidents" that is used to determine service delivery events?
- What hierarchy should be used for reporting the metrics?

As the metrics need to be sliced and diced, the number of combinations between the various factors such as hierarchies and master data becomes large (Fig. 1.1). Merely trying to establish a common vocabulary, a first step, can become a huge hurtle.

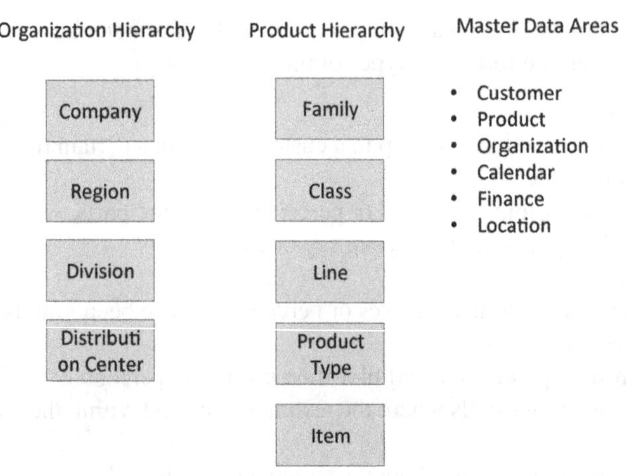

FIGURE 1.1

Key hierarchies and master data involved in customer experience reporting.

Here are some key thoughts to extract from this story:

- Most of these questions need to be resolved by business managers or executives.
- All of these questions require a substantial amount of effort around defining, locating, and determining the data's "readiness" to calculate the metrics.
- In addition to the actual "event" data, there is a substantial amount of related data (eg, country hierarchy, product hierarchy, and lists of valid product codes).

INDUSTRY: FINANCIAL SERVICES

Financial service firms provide many complex services to customers. In addition to standard deposits and loans, financial service organizations engage in global money management and movement activities. By helping create liquidity in the financial marketplace, financial service firms provide service to individuals, companies, countries as well as the marketplace itself.

As drugs, terrorism, and human trafficking have risen to the forefront of global politics, new policies have been directed at squeezing the money supply of these acts. Some estimate that the total amount of "bad" money flowing in the global economy to be close to 1 trillion US dollars annually. If "bad" money were a country it would make the top three in total Gross Domestic Product (GDP).

A money launderer takes money produced from illegal activities and cleans the money so that it can be used to purchase legitimate assets such as a house or car. Today, even clean money is a problem. Some donors send their clean money to bad people. For example, clean money, such as revenue generated from selling cigarettes, can turn dirty if the cigarettes were smuggled into a high-cigarette-tax states to generate higher profits. Sometimes, clean money is directly wired (electronic transfer) to terrorists. The entire money movement process is global, complex, and a source of concern for many countries. Ultimately, money in the hands of "bad" guys comes back to haunt sovereign states.

The Bank Secrecy Act of 1970 as well the USA Patriot Act of 2001 created authority and policies to reduce financial institutions' role in funding terrorist activities. As part of the broad antimoney laundering agenda, multiple US government agencies, working in concert with other countries, enacted laws and imposed regulations to support antimoney laundering detection and prosecution.

Federal enforcement actions against banks have increased. Banks have been hit with Office of the Comptroller (OCC) consent orders, Financial Crimes Enforcement Network (FinCEN), or federal and state regulators for material weaknesses in their Anti-Money Laundering (AML) and Bank Secrecy Act (BSA) or The Currency and Foreign Transactions Reporting Act of 1970 programs. OCC consent orders must be resolved or the bank will be shut down or severely restricted. The list below shows some recent fines as documented on the FinCEN website:

- JPMorgan Chase: $461 million
- TD Bank: $37.5 million
- First Bank of Delaware: $15 million
- TC National Bank: $10 million
- HSBC: $9.1 million (multiple assessments)
- Saddle River Valley Bank: $4.1 million

Recently, regulators have started aggressively pursuing both corporate penalties as well as personal penalties against company officers in order to create an environment of deterrence.

There are specific regulatory requirements to ensure that a bank is not doing business with a money launderer. Financial institutions must perform checks, which are called "controls."

For example, when a bank opens an account, it must perform Customer Due Diligence (CDD) to determine if the account is legit. If the due diligence results are negative, a bank can and should decline to open an account and even close an active account. CDD is part of a broader Know Your Customer (KYC) theme. KYC involves gathering significant amounts of information about a customer and using the information to assess customer risk.

Another example of a control is the set of steps taken before an electronic wire transfer can be sent. The receiver's name, country, and other information must be validated. When a wire is created, the name and destination country are listed on the wire instructions. It should be easy to match the name and destination against a known sanctions list, but some banks use multiple lists internally to represent country codes and these lists are sometimes conflicting. Various international groups such as the International Standards Organization (ISO) have created "master" lists of frequently used country codes. However, the ISO list is not always quickly updated with changes, and it is possible to have country names appear or change and not be reflected in the ISO list. Furthermore, the two- and three-letter codes used to represent different countries can be the same code on different lists but map to different countries on an ISO and a non-ISO list.

Another control is used when assessing commercial banking services. Similar to the due diligence with an individual, a bank wishing to do business with a company must understand who that company is, how it generates money, and assess its AML risk. For example, a company that is a money services business or a "cash" oriented business like a cleaning or massage service will have a higher AML risk score. Validating a company's "industry affiliation" is an important step in the process. Like country names, industry affiliations are kept on standardized lists and nonstandardized lists. Similar to the country name and abbreviation issue, industry affiliation can be misunderstood. FinCEN recently assessed a civil money penalty on Mian, doing business as Tower Package Store, because it determined, with help of the Internal Revenue Services (IRS), that Mian was performing as a money services business. A favorable industry affiliation can sometimes dramatically reduce the risk score in some risk models and create a sense of false security.

In addition to controls, simply defining the terms used in the policies can be difficult. In 2012, the FinCEN was preparing to issue updated guidelines on its policies and per its policy solicited feedback on the changes before finalizing the guidelines. The policy update was fairly explicit, but there were areas that needed further clarity. In their public feedback, the American Banker's Association (ABA) expressed that more definition was needed:

> ...And, within each type of legal entity there are many variations among the states. Therefore, ABA believes and strongly urges FinCEN to create a chart or outline of the many different entities that exist and then indicate the perceived risks for each type of entity and the appropriate steps that should be taken. Otherwise, the expectations are too vague to be workable and may not reflect actual levels of risk. Clearly, with the great spectrum of varying legal entities, one size fits all approach cannot begin to work.

Here are some key thoughts to extract from these stories:

- The financial impact of not performing a function, such as BSA compliance and fraud prevention, can be large and material. Many of these functions are now data driven.
- Changes in policies at an industry level can have a large and sometimes confusing impact on individual companies. Running a healthy communication and consensus process is important so that the intent of the regulation is understood and can be effectively implemented.
- There are substantial amounts of change management issues associated with data including timeliness and correctness.
- A few, critical data elements can make the difference between doing something well, such as following BSA regulations, or putting your organization at serious reputational and financial risk.

INDUSTRY: HEALTHCARE

The healthcare industry is undergoing massive change. The Patient Protection and Affordable Care Act (ACA) changed the risk, reimbursement, and power structure in the industry. Rapid consolidation of physician groups is leading to stronger pricing resistance against insurance companies as physicians fear future reimbursement reductions. Overall, healthcare spending represents roughly one third of total government spending today. Anything that touches healthcare touches a large part of the US economy.

Health information is private information. A broad set of policies has been enacted in the healthcare industry to enhance protection of personal healthcare information (PHI). Title II of the Healthcare Insurance Portability and Accountability Act (HIPAA) established national standards for electronic healthcare transactions and national identifiers for providers, health insurance plans, and employers. It also established civil money penalties for violations of its provisions.

The healthcare industry, often led by the federal government, create initiatives to accelerate value delivery with special emphasis on high-cost chronic diseases. For example, National Institutes of Health (NIH) Department from the U.S. Department of Health and Human Services sponsored the cancer Biomedical Informatics Grid (caBIG) project, now retired. Focused on improving cancer outcomes, the program accelerated investment and capabilities along several fronts. One focus area was on improving access and use of cancer data including extensive amounts of PHI. It has been and continues to be a challenge to share data in healthcare settings due to HIPAA and other policies. Because cancer funding is highly fragmented spread across many constituent states, cancer-related data is created and housed in many different research, government, and commercial locations. To make this data more sharable, the caBIG project worked to make data dictionaries, medical taxonomies, and the ability to run queries across distributed databases as easy as using a spreadsheet. This makes data more accessible and usable to all cancer researchers.

The caBIG program funded projects to establish common vocabularies. Common vocabularies help researchers identify data for their queries. A word describing a condition used in one location needs to mean the same thing in another location. Medicine is still largely implemented and practiced locally with localized standards and practices. Merely identifying data of interest to a particular research query is the first step. There are many cultural and policy impediments to moving and using healthcare data in consolidated facilities. These impediments reduce the ability to run integrated analysis across larger datasets to improve analysis results. Additional caBIG-funded projects created tools to allow a cancer query to execute on a local database and return results to the query requester. The highly fragmented state of healthcare research databases coupled with privacy restrictions has led to greatly reduced access to data for analysis and significantly higher healthcare costs.

Understanding what data is available and its fitness for use is an important step in analyzing data to answer questions. The Center for Medicare Services (CMS) was ordered to provide broader access to the data it collects as part of its mission of administering Medicare. CMS made a dataset available that describes reimbursement dollars and prescription counts for physicians that provide Medicare services.

Once the data was released, many articles were published by experts to explain the data. For example, it was found that some physicians had prescribed more expensive drugs even though proven, lower-cost alternatives were readily available. The data also suggested that some physicians wrote excessive prescriptions counts, high enough that it was nearly impossible to correlate the counts with any form of patient schedule. It was later explained that prescriptions are often attributed to a department head or another physician manager and not the physician providing the actual care.

These datasets were also truncated. Due to HIPAA concerns, physicians who had fewer patients than a threshold were excluded because it is possible to infer from very small datasets actual patient specifics.

The cost of combining data together to answer healthcare queries can be high. As part of the desire to improve clinical analysis, the healthcare industry decided to migrate from a specific set of industry classification codes to a newer set. The industry is in the process of moving to the ICD-10 standard from the current ICD-9 standard. The ICD codes describe diagnosis and procedures performed while delivering healthcare services. The diagnosis codes are the boxes on the form your healthcare physician fills out during a doctor's visit. ICD-10 codes are more descriptive than ICD-9 and allow analysts to perform more fine-grained analysis between the diagnosis, the procedures used to treat the underlying issue, and eventually outcomes. ICD-10 also enhances the ability to analyze patient data by episode of care (longitudinal analysis) versus one-off interactions with the healthcare industry. Even though it may seem like a fairly straightforward process to migrate from ICD-9 to ICD-10, the road has been very difficult. The industry started moving to ICD-10 a decade ago. Fig. 1.2 summarizes how ICD-9 and ICD-10 differ.

In addition to the cost of migrating technical systems being much larger than expected it has also been found that changing diagnosis codes changes reimbursement levels because the reimbursement rules are based on these codes. Changes affecting reimbursement are highly susceptible to political forces and conservative change. As you might expect, there have been multiple delays in implementation deadlines, increased costs as well as extensive and advanced financial analysis and modeling

ICD-9 Format (3-5 digits):

BNN . NN
Category
Category, anatomic site, severity

ICD-10 Format:

ANB . BBB B
Category,
Category, anatomic site, severity
Extension

A = Alphabetic character
B = Either numeric or Alphabetic (Alphanumeric)
N = Numeric

- # ICD-10 Codes = 4-5x # ICD-9 Codes
- 1 ICD-9 Code can map into Many ICD-10 Code

ICD-9 Code	ICD-10 Codes
1550 Malignant neoplasm of liver, primary	C220 Liver cell carcinoma
	C222 Heptablastoma
	C227 Other specified carcinomas of liver
	C228 Malignant neoplasm of liver, priamry, unspecified as to type

- Many ICD-9 Codes can map into Many ICD-10 Codes

ICD-9 Codes	ICD-10 Codes
5362 Persistent Vomiting	K3189 Other diseases of stomach and duodenum
5363 Gastropareisis	
5375 Gastroptosis	
53789 Other specified disorders of stomach and duodenum	
538 Gastrointestinal mucositis	

FIGURE 1.2

ICD-9 versus ICD-10.

around the changes. Healthcare organizations simulate code changes based on their current book of business (it refers to the current customers and transactions they are experiencing) and project the impact to future reimbursement under the new codes. Based on the simulation, they provide feedback to the government. Then the cycle repeats. If reimbursement goes down, negotiations around reimbursement become intertwined with the technical changes, causing further delays and costs.

Here are some key thoughts to extract from these stories:

- Healthcare data is complex and difficult to analyze because of the nature of healthcare issues as well as the set of policies that have been enacted to meet society's privacy needs.
- Changing access to healthcare data could significantly affect healthcare costs.
- The need for innovation in certain data areas, such as providing access to data while still honoring privacy needs, is important to improving outcomes.
- Understanding what data exists where and its appropriateness to answer questions are key ingredients in increasing healthcare value delivery.
- The cost of changing data, such as ICD codes, can be substantial. Even small changes can trigger waves of efforts and anxiety. In general, trying to make large changes all at once can take a long time. Migrating to ICD-10, still in progress, has taken several years.

WHAT THIS BOOK IS ABOUT AND WHY IT IS NEEDED NOW

The industry stories note many data issues, that if addressed, could decrease costs and improve outcomes – the definition of value. Many business issues can be mitigated or eliminated with information-based approaches.

This book describes a detailed approach to executing data governance consistently with the objective of improving business outcomes. Organizations need to execute data governance better than they do today. Regardless of whether your organization uses the data governance term to describe how it manages data, your organization manages your data using some type of process even if that process is not explicit or purposeful. Some organizations may be actively managing their data, and they may be doing so without the benefit of three decades' worth of experience in the information management field. If you have data, you have some form of data governance. An organization has a responsibility to manage that data appropriate to its operations. As consumers, we have the right to ask organizations to manage the data we create.

An organization has many functions such as finance, human resources, sales and marketing, and manufacturing. There are many ways organizations can configure these functions. Most of these functions have common characteristics across companies. For example, the finance department produces financial statements each quarter. Finance departments also have highly variable responsibilities. For example, some finance departments may also own the strategic planning process. Sales and marketing, which has little regulatory motivation to standardize its functions, also shows remarkable similarity between companies. For example, many sales and marketing departments have a sales-lead pipeline process and a marketing events calendar-planning model.

The roles and activities of these functions have been studied and analyzed for decades, which has resulted in a multitude of organizational models, process definitions, and technology components to make these functions more efficient and effective. These functions provide a rich ground to draw from when new functions develop. For example, many companies want to improve their ability to innovate over time. While innovation management may sound like a dichotomy because innovation suggests a free-wheeling activity with little if any process, innovation is being studied and analyzed so it can be managed into a repeatable and reliable process.

Data governance needs to a repeatable and reliable process. Data governance needs to be consistent.

While corporate functions are often reorganized and changed and employees come and go, the jobs that need to be done in an organization remain mostly the same. Organization functions are often organized by the types of jobs that are performed and the need to efficiently perform them. To become repeatable and reliable over time, a process needs explicit details that describe it as well as the flexibility to adapt when needed.

Without specific and descriptive details, it is very difficult to maintain consistency. However, even being specific is not enough. Schools and universities have created specialized classes in finance, accounting, human resources, supply chain, and management that cover the gamut of jobs performed in a company. Training can provide foundational knowledge, but the basic ingredients must then be mixed together in a special, organization-specific way. Many organizations provide specific job aids, corporate functional training, and other supportive efforts so the jobs can be done regardless of the functional configuration or the employees executing them.

For outcomes that are heavily data-driven, organizations need detailed, step-by-step procedures for performing data governance jobs on a daily basis, and they want to adapt those procedures to their organization as it changes.

These needs can be seen by the types of questions we encounter:

- What is the core focus of data governance? It seems to cover everything.
- How do we ensure our data governance can prove its relevance and effectiveness?
- How do we justify ongoing investment beyond initial funding?
- How do we clarify and reduce confusion around the scope, roles, and execution of activities under data governance?

- What should data governance do and not do?
- How do we take it to the next level?
- Data governance seemed to start with a bang, but now it feels like it is languishing and no one shows up to the meetings anymore. Why is that?
- How do we avoid reinventing the wheel every time something around data governance comes up?
- Why do the people we put in data governance jobs keep quitting?

The industry stories demonstrate that data-related issues and their disproportionate impact on an organization are on the rise. Fortunately, at the same time, organizations have increased their data governance efforts. At this point, there is widespread adoption of data governance activities. Unfortunately, many organizations have tried multiple attempts at standing up data governance and have found it difficult to sustain them over time.

This book provides a detailed description of the jobs data governance needs to perform and detailed processes required to accomplish those jobs all collected together in a "playbook." The Playbook captures the tactical steps each player needs to take in order to consistently perform the jobs that need to get done.

A Playbook approach is needed now because many organizations have finally realized that while it is fairly easy to start a data governance program, it is difficult to sustain it. Each organization will have a slightly different approach reflecting its unique characteristics. No single, static Playbook is appropriate for all organizations, and since organizations change over time, the Playbook must also adapt.

This book provides the starting point and adaption process for your organization's Playbook. We cover all the plays, the supporting components, and how to maintain and customize it for your company. Additionally, we provide numerous tactical examples while blending in four decades of information management best practices.

BASIC CONCEPTS

Data is the electronic representation of information required for a company to operate and fulfill its purpose. Some companies are very data intensive, such as banks. Other organizations are less data intensive. Every organization engages in data governance whether explicitly managed and supported or implicitly assumed and unsupported. Some organizations have found that executing data governance is critical while others have found that an ad-hoc approach meets their needs. In all information-intensive organizations, data and the capabilities to manage that data well are a critical part of fulfilling its purpose. Data governance has become a critical capability.

We like to explain data governance by describing the data-related "jobs" that need to be performed. You can consider these jobs to be similar to objectives or goals. Employees perform these jobs following a process. The Playbook describes the process.

There are four core data governance jobs. Sometimes the scope of data governance appears to be large and absorbs many more jobs than those listed below. Lumping more "jobs" into data governance can cause confusion. A broad definition also makes it difficult to organize and execute because a broad definition includes too many noncore issues peripheral to solving the underlying issues.

The four jobs are:

- Locate and catalog data
- Understand data limitations and constraints

- Determine data readiness for use
- Improve and control

That's it!

Some organizations have defined data governance (perhaps with capital letters – Data Governance) to be a broad set of programs, projects, and initiatives with impressive desired outcomes and large funding. Others may define it to include substantial amounts of technical development resources for implementing data management software programs. These are all choices organizations have made for their data governance programs. Implementation models are highly variable. By carefully designing how these four jobs are defined and performed, you can reduce the overall cost footprint of data governance and reduce confusion.

In the next few sections, we describe common organizational areas and capabilities that are often lumped into data governance. We argue that they are separate and distinct but intersect with data governance.

INFORMATION AND DATA MANAGEMENT

Information management generally refers to the following areas:

- Extract, Transform, and Load (ETL)
  - The process of moving data from one resting place to another.
- Data Quality (DQ)
  - A characteristic or state of the data that affects its usefulness for answering questions or solving problems.
- Data controls
  - A set of monitoring points that detect scenario-specific data issues.
  - Controls already exist in companies. For example, requiring approval to purchase office supplies is a financial control. A data control is the capability to detect, prevent, or correct data issues that may affect the data's ability to be used. For example, if data passes through a system prior to being used to create a list of customers, a data control could monitor the number of customers passing through the system to see if it varies too much using a statistical test. If the variation is large, an alert would be generated and the issue resolved.
- Master Data Management (MDM) and Reference Data Management (RDM)
  - The process of managing lists and hierarchies of data.
  - A list could be a list of countries, a list of customers, or the hierarchy of products and product categories your organization sells.
- Data Modeling (DM)
  - A data model is typically a graphic with boxes and lines representing business concepts and their relationships.
  - Data modeling is the process of creating models of your data.
  - The models are often used to communicate with stakeholders or to develop a technical system.
- Data Marts and Warehousing (DM and DW)
  - The process of grouping data together and preparing it to answer business questions.

Information management grew into a strong discipline over two decades ago. There are differences between "information management" and "data management," but the distinction between the two terms is not important for this book and we will use the two terms interchangeably.

There has been rapid convergence to best practices for managing and deploying information management resources and capabilities. However, consistently achieving expected business outcomes in the information management areas has remained elusive. Reasons include:

- Lack of business sponsorship or an "internal customer"
- Lack of talent for and commitment to
  - Planning
  - Resourcing
  - Execution
- Misunderstanding of roles and capabilities
- Poor data quality

The top three issues above are really caused by management deficiencies: starting projects when they should not be started or when they lack adequate support to be successful.

We have seen severe deficiencies in many organizations' capability to define realistic roles for the IT group. Business groups sometimes contribute to this problem by completely delegating oversight and responsibility of information management projects to the IT group. IT groups are often eager to absorb responsibility for creating full solutions. However, business groups do not always need end-to-end solutions as they can cost effectively do part of the work. Sometimes, having IT do less and ensuring responsibility is placed where it is best executed is a better solution. Organizations that experience multiple, successive information management project failures often have IT groups carrying too much scope. Business groups that have their own analytics applications, such as SAS or R, are fully capable of working on the "last mile" of information delivery.

It's better to stick to an "understand the jobs" approach. If we understand the jobs that need to be performed, we know what needs to be done regardless of who does the job. Once the organization's dynamics have been mapped into the "jobs," the assignments for who performs which jobs can be assigned and the Playbook adapted appropriately.

The Playbook provides workstreams across stages and phases that collectively perform the data governance jobs. The Playbook workstreams we cover in this book intersect the following information management areas:

- Data quality: The Playbook provides a specific workstream for working through data-quality issues.
- Data controls: The Playbook has specific provisions to identify needed data controls.
- Master data/Reference data management: The Playbook provides a specific workstream for working master data management issues.
- Data modeling/Data Catalog: The Playbook speaks directly to capturing definitions and locating data that would support conceptual, logical, and physical data models.
- Data marts and warehousing: The Playbook creates repeatable processes that can be owned and executed by any group that wants execution consistency. This will help improve data mart and warehouse development value delivery and success rates over time.

BUSINESS INTELLIGENCE

The term "business intelligence" has been used to refer to the following areas:

- Reporting
- Reporting tools and applications

- Data mining
- Analytics, which is sometimes described differently than data mining
- A general state of knowledge about business operations
- A market research group
- All of the above

The term can be confusing without more context. Business resources often use the term to refer to activity that uses data and math to answer business questions. IT resources often use the term to refer to reporting and reporting applications.

Using any of the above definitions, business intelligence depends on data. The data used in business intelligence is often:

- Aggregated
  - Example: Quarterly summaries across geographies.
- Integrated
  - Example: The sales totals from all products are summed together.
- Cleansed
  - Example: All sales are included with a ship date in the calendar quarter.
- Attestable
  - Example: The head of operations knows that the cost calculation is properly represented in a performance metric.

Business intelligence data is a major beneficiary of data governance activities. Data suitable for aggregation and integration must be cleansed to a certain degree. The field of data cleansing and the concept of cleansing data can be a bit abstract, but we define it as the activity that changes data so it is more suitable for use. Restructuring dates consistently so that sales figures can be aggregated is an example of data cleansing.

Integrating or aggregating data often occurs across functional groups. Data governance can help ensure that each data concept can be conceptually "added" together. Data governance is not a "specific" answer to solve disconnects between groups that do not want to agree to integrate and aggregate their data. If groups do not agree, they do not agree. While the Playbook has processes that can be used across groups, organizational dynamics can still affect the ability to execute the process regardless of who owns the data governance jobs. We provide some insight into how to manage these organizational dynamics in later chapters.

Attestable data is data that has data controls applied to it. Data controls allow the data consumer to attest that the information is correct for their needs. Attestable data requires structured processes and well-defined controls and the Playbook provides activities for creating these controls.

The best way to think about the Playbook and business intelligence is that the Playbook is not business intelligence – the Playbook makes business intelligence better.

MATH, STATISTICS, DATA MINING, ARTIFICIAL INTELLIGENCE, ANALYTICS, AND MORE

Businesses cannot get enough analytics. In the past few years, the claimed use of analytics to solve large-scale, global problems as well as help you decide what to purchase next has dominated media outlets.

Analytics was typically physics- and engineering-oriented rather than business-oriented. Applied and theoretical mathematics were targeted at understanding and explaining various physical phenomena. For example, new mathematical approaches have been developed to understand why Newtonian physics break down at small scale.

As populations grew, more scientists and engineers were available to work on other problems. Mathematics turned its attention to solving business and social issues such as improving health, alleviating traffic, or building timesaving machines such as dishwashers and airplanes. Mathematics and statistics became a potent corporate weapon, but initially only large corporations could afford the talent.

At some point, the use of mathematics went into hyperdrive. Starting with mundane tasks such as reducing the costs of mailings for magazine subscription solicitations (ie, junk mail), the field of statistics morphed into the field of data mining and machine learning. Thousands of analytically oriented employees worked on problems such as how to optimally select ads and optimally place them on websites. Fairly quickly, advertising became the primary focus of the largest companies on Earth.

The widespread availability of talent and infrastructure led to dramatic decreases in the cost of deploying business analytics, and a funny thing happened on the way to profit heaven. The data used in the analytics suddenly became a bottleneck in achieving better analytical outcomes. Data is noisy due to the nature of data collection (eg, web page data entry) and is often conflicting. As data was integrated from significantly larger numbers of disparate sources, data quality reduced the effectiveness of the analytical models.

Large areas of the information management space can trace its growth to the rise of analytics and the rise of systems to create analytical outputs. New industries arose to address the data warehousing space. A plethora of data-quality tools, now integral to the dataflow processing inside a company, became routine.

The rise of data-quality issues and their impact on analytics rapidly created the need to drive agreement across aggregation, integration, cleansing, and attestable data. New issues arose such as whom in an organization should have access to certain data elements? Who gets to make that decision? Although these questions are really business management questions, employees began to believe that data governance should answer these questions.

This book is not about the math behind statistics or data mining, but it does deal with the need for improved data and is specifically designed to make consuming data in analytical applications consistent for analysts. Just like business intelligence, the Playbook makes data mining better.

BIG DATA, NOSQL, DATA SCIENTISTS, CLOUDS AND SOCIAL MEDIA

Big Data may solve all of the world's problems – at least this is what you may have been led to believe from vendors and the press. The success of social media companies such as Google and Facebook, coupled with their openness concerning algorithms and commodity infrastructure software applications, has given rise to the Big Data movement. Originally targeted at search, ad selection, and placement, Big Data technologies are applied to a multitude of industry problems and are starting to see wider use. Along with the rise of Big Data and social media, a new kind of employee, the data scientist, has emerged. A data scientist is able to fuse math and information management together at large scale to arrive at business insight.

With the rise of Big Data, NoSQL databases also took center stage. No longer restricted to a single machine, NoSQL databases promise to span commodity infrastructure on-demand to solve large data management problems. Many believe that NoSQL databases have a flexible schema more suitable to applications that require highly connected data and specific access patterns. With different guarantees than traditional relational database management systems (RDBS), NoSQL databases and related technologies such as graph databases have become a common complement to Big Data.

For example, many NoSQL databases running on clusters offer "eventual consistency." Eventual consistency fits social media interactions well. Most social media users are fine if the time it takes to reflect a new "post" is a few minutes or hours. The same guarantees applied in the business world, say around trading data, might be costly. The use of Big Data for storing specific types of data across large clusters provides cost-effective solutions to web-dominant applications that require enormous scale or to business applications where these guarantees are sufficient.

Big Data technologies became synonymous with cloud computing. Because Big Data technologies often use parallel computation and data management processes, they are applications that inherently assume that single-system limitations will always be present. These technologies assume large clusters. Early Web companies relied on commodity clusters to scale as their businesses scaled upward, ie, scaling horizontally instead of vertically became the norm. Public clouds, and even private clouds to some extent, allowed these companies to take advantage of pay-as-you-go plans as their needs increased. As security and other factors became more significant to some commercial clients, public clouds and private clouds became the basis for deploying Big Data technologies.

The motivation behind Big Data technologies is rooted in a specific set of processing scenarios. Today, these technologies are entering mainstream use and are used in other scenarios such as offloading processing from more expensive, dedicated systems such as datawarehouse appliances. Big Data and NoSQL have shifted the cost and capability landscape and will continue to do so as these technologies mature. Big Data enjoys the most success where the technology fits the need. For example, Big Data is very useful in the life sciences upstream in the discovery process where large datasets generated from assays generate enormous datasets and eventual consistency guarantees are fine.

Interestingly, current parallel extract, transform, and load (ETL) tools already contain the same components that popular Hadoop-based Big Data systems are developing such as parallel filesystems, resource management, and scheduling and parallel algorithms. However, the cost of purchasing and keeping the talent needed to run ETL tools can be large and beyond the reach of many smaller companies. Whether true or not, some businesses feel that the cost curve for newer Big Data technologies has shifted enough to enable these technologies at their organization. While Big Data technology will certainly be misapplied to situations that do not benefit from its value proposition, Big Data will be present in the landscape and data governance needs to take them into account.

Big Data technologies have the capabilities needed to store and process data. While the specific technologies may be different compared to traditional data management technologies, Big Data and traditional technologies are conceptually the same – they are applications that hold, manage, and process data.

Big Data deployments can strain a data governance program because of issues such as:

- Flexible and changing schemas make it a challenge to have up-to-date information on "which" data is "where."
- Big Data is often applied to unstructured data (news stories vs. tabular data). Unstructured data are can make it harder to understand "what's in there" and is more difficult and interconnected than tabular data.

- The number of processing layers in Big Data architectures is often larger than traditional environments. More layers lead to more data to be tracked. For example, Hadoop is both a storage system and a processing system. The creation and retention of large datasets in an analytical processing sequence is normal. Many of these intermediate datasets are large and retained so that the analytical process can be restarted or resumed midcourse.
- The results of Big Data, especially for web applications, are often quickly applied to customer-facing situations. But there is more risk that the data's correctness for a particular situation may actually be lower than datasets that have been processed and curated. While it is true that all datasets typically have unresolved quality issues, Big Data often accelerates business velocity, thereby increasing the risk of unintended customer experiences.
- Datasets may be located in highly disparate locations especially when cloud applications are considered. Similar to the data governance story around healthcare data and distributed datasets, data that is distributed and under the control of third parties is often more difficult to work with and understand.

While it may seem that the integration of Big Data is really just a policy definition exercise, elements of the technology at different cost points makes the data volume and diversity managed under Big Data "bigger." Data may move faster and be more complex. Many organizations already find it difficult to apply data governance to the data they oversee today in traditional technologies. Data governance needs to eventually have 100% coverage over data in the organization. Big Data deployments increase the surface area that must be covered. These issues are not insurmountable. Just as vendor products make using Big Data technologies easier, the data managed under Big Data technologies will be added to the queue of data governance work. When it comes to Big Data, the Playbook applies just as it does to any other data.

MATURITY MODEL

Maturity models help you assess your capabilities across a range of capability areas. By assessing your capabilities, you can better understand your current maturity level and identify a reasonable target level to achieve in the future. The results can be used to communicate expectations for advancement and create a sense of urgency for action.

The maturity levels are often set by an independent body or based on analysis of the industry or function. In addition to serving as a great communication and consensus-driving tool about current capabilities, the categories and levels also help educate an organization on what capabilities need improvement. Most maturity models are descendants of the Carnegie Mellon University's Software Engineering Institute's Capability Maturity Model Integration (CMMI) for application development.

There are multiple maturity models available in the information management space. Many of the information management maturity models such as the Enterprise Data Management Council's Data Management Maturity Model (http://www.edmcouncil.org/dmm) overlap somewhat with the capabilities needed to implement data governance well. CMMI Institute's own Data Management Maturity Model (DMM) is specifically designed to align your data management strategy to business results. These organizations also work together to help improve alignment between the models. We greatly encourage you to use these models to understand the capabilities that may be important to you across the entire data management landscape.

The Playbook is not a capability maturity model. While we find that maturity models are great at communicating and identifying improvement areas, organizations are constrained because they do not have a detailed execution plan for data governance that provides day-to-day guidance. The Playbook describes an execution path represented by a series of specific activities that should be performed to successfully perform the data governance jobs. The areas described in this book cover those that are most commonly addressed by many organizations.

There are variations in how some data governance activities can be performed. You also need to look into your organization's toolbox to find and select tools that help you execute. The selected set of options forms the "toolkit," which could be very simple, such as using spreadsheets and email, or it could be more complex. For example, using advanced business glossary and workflows tools to manage the workload and achieve your complex communication and validation requirements is an advanced approach.

The Playbook contains a basic set of activities needed to accomplish the jobs in a reasonable, cost-effective manner. Essentially it describes how to conduct data governance operations. The Playbook is designed to be customized, and optional activities added by an organization can reflect different maturity levels.

We tend to think about maturity along two distinct dimensions:

- Execution maturity
  - Execution maturity is more aligned with the capability maturity model concept. To execute a process, you must have the capabilities to perform that process. Execution and capabilities are related.
- Service maturity
  - Service maturity is aligned with the concept of coverage. For example, if you execute the Playbook workstreams and are only covering 25% of the data your organization has, then your coverage is low. Coverage is sometimes more important than execution maturity.

Fig. 1.3 shows that maturity along these two dimensions can vary not only company to company but also within a company, department by department. Typically, maturity starts low. Different groups often

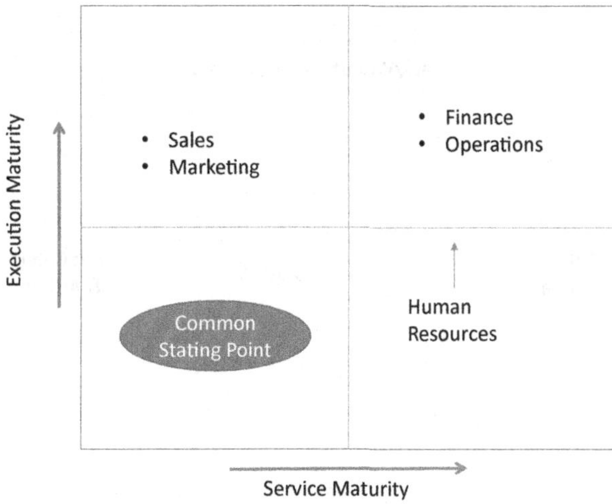

FIGURE 1.3

Execution versus service maturity.

wind up in different parts of the grid over time. For example, as Human Resources become more quantitative, its potential to move has changed allowing it to mature its execution.

These two maturity dimensions are the "breadth" and "depth" of your Playbook. Execution maturity increases if you adopt a Playbook and adapt it to your organization. Service maturity increases when we discuss data governance as an operational process. We address Execution maturity by providing a process to adapt the Playbook to your organization and update it over time. Service maturity increases over time as you repeatedly apply the Playbook to your organization's data. Most maturity model literature calls out consistency of execution as a key outcome of using a maturity model.

THE PLAYBOOK AS AN ORGANIZING PROCESS MODEL

We have provided examples about data issues and their impact on people, organizations, and countries. There are many areas in an organization that need data to operate. While recent decades have created a good set of best practices around data management, gaps still cause organizations to miss their targets.

The Playbook is a set of processes an organization uses to consistently execute the core set of data governance jobs. The Playbook is organized by workstream. Workstreams group together a set of activities. You can think of workstreams as a selected set of data governance jobs that have been grouped together to realize a specific outcome.

Adaptions of the Playbook for your organization may add additional jobs and activities. We have tried to focus on the core data governance jobs, activities, and deliverable outcomes. You may feel that additional activities and outcomes should be added. Feel free to do so. Adapting the Playbook is essential.

Each workstream in the Playbook contains a small set of content as illustrated in Fig. 1.4:

- A set of activities that make up steps in the workstream.
- A set of inputs and outputs for each step.
- A set of roles and responsibilities for each step and what jobs the roles perform in that step.

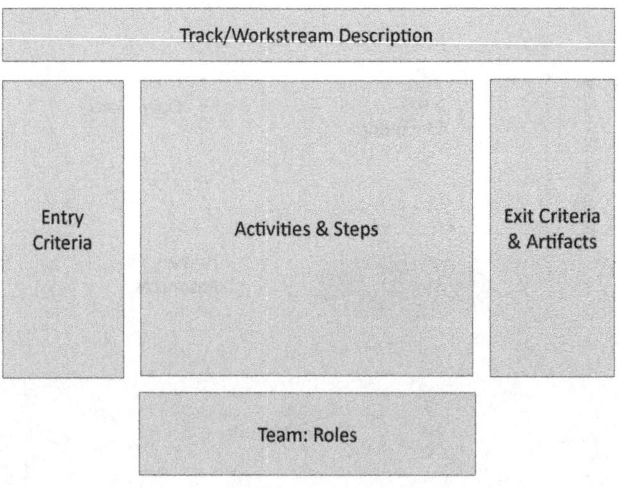

FIGURE 1.4

Playbook general schematic.

You can also consider the Playbook to be a "methodology" or "route map" for performing jobs. However, the words methodologies or route map do not always convey a specific level of detail. We think that the word "playbook" communicates expectations around the level of detail found in the activity descriptions.

This book covers the workstreams we think are tablestakes an organization needs to manage their data well. The workstreams are:

- Data stewardship
  - Managing data on a daily basis.
- Data cataloging
  - Collecting information about your data together.
- Data quality
  - Improving the state of your data so it is ready for use.
- Master/reference data
  - Managing lists and groupings of data used by many different data consumers.

The Playbook is designed to be adapted to your organization. The workstreams we cover in this book are good starting points. We also provide insight on how to customize the Playbook for your organization. You can start using the Playbook as is, but we think that most organizations will find value in customizing the Playbook's language and activity descriptions based on the actual set of functional groups, technologies, and data issues you think are important.

WHAT YOU CAN GET FROM THIS BOOK

The Playbook describes the roles needed to perform each activity. You can think of the role list as a simpler view of a traditional roles and responsibilities matrix. Working with data often involves fluid processes. The adjustments we inherently make in our daily work lives to keep an organization moving are fairly numerous.

The roles we cover in the Playbook include:

- Chief Data Officer
- Business Sponsor
- Business Data Owner
- Data Analyst
- Data-Quality Analyst
- Program Leader (Business or IT)
- Data Steward
- Data Steward Manager
- Subject Matter Expert (SME)

A single individual may play multiple roles or the same role may be played by several people. Because of this fluidity, a detailed roles and responsibilities matrix can be too detailed to use easily by most practitioners and is sometimes difficult to maintain.

If you are playing or will play one of these roles, the Playbook will provide you with a specific set of instructions around what activities and outcomes you are expected to produce. Many labels you can be given to these roles. You may find that other terms for these roles are already used in your organization. You may want to change the labels or expand the list as part of customizing the Playbook. However, the more labels you create, the harder it may be to communicate "who" is doing "what," "when," "why," and "how."

In addition to obtaining daily guidance around activities, you can look at the value of the Playbook based on your organization's role. In the following, we list several types of categories and the value a person in that category can obtain from using the Playbook.

- Business management and executives
  - This category includes line managers and executives including managing directors, senior directors, and directors, vp and svp, and senior analyst- to analyst-level business workers in revenue areas, cross-functional areas including finance, marketing and hr, and operations areas.
  - This category also includes positions for those people tasked with or building governance, quality, or control functions or programs in an organization. In this case, the Playbook provides a specific set of activities that can be immediately deployed and evolved over time.
  - By providing explicit workstreams, activities, and roles, management and executives can rely on concrete guidance for each person and know what activities and outcomes each person should follow and achieve. In other words, the Playbook can establish a concrete action plan that can be managed.
- Data management/information delivery professionals
  - While many of these labels typically describe professionals in the IT group, there are many data management professionals in other groups as well. For example, professionals who live in data preparation groups attached to an analytics function in a line of business or functional group like underwriting/actuarial sciences or claims processing.
  - This book provides explicit guidance on activities that should be performed in a data governance role and what to expect as outputs of the workstreams. If a Playbook has been deployed at a company, data management professionals will know how to adjust their own expectations, project plans, and efforts to be consistent with the Playbook model.
- Enterprise data services
  - An enterprise data services group often lives in the IT group and provides data services as needed for a project. For example, if projects need data quality profiling or data cataloging support using the approved corporate data cataloging application, an enterprise data services group can provide a targeted level of support. Data services groups typically provide services to all projects and programs across both IT and business groups. Data services will require data governance activities to be sustainable.
  - The Playbook helps in two ways. First, the Playbook will help enterprise data services groups identify the sets of services they should offer to support data governance jobs. Second, the Playbook can identify where the data services can play a role in the process. This improves overall value communication and utilization of the services and improves overall viability.
- Project and program management
  - Project or program managers often live in two groups. First, as part of the IT group and second, as part of an operations or a business functional group.
  - Project and program management professionals can view this book as a process description for performing data governance and managing many aspects of the data.

    - A Playbook is not a System/Software Development Lifecycle (SDLC) methodology. Playbooks do intersect and overlap with parts of an SDLC. IT-oriented project and program managers can use the Playbook to tune or instill best practices into their management development process.
- Application development
    - Application development professionals almost always deal with data issues in their applications. Many applications can be viewed from a technology perspective as software programs that manage data in a database using a set of transactions or queries.
    - The Playbook helps application development professionals understand the steps they should follow to access and use the best data. The Playbook also makes application development easier by enabling discipline and support around data areas, which directly reduces their development effort and risk. For example, if the Data Cataloging workstream is performed as described in this book, the outputs from the activities can be directly used as inputs into a developer's analysis and design steps, reducing or removing the need to perform those steps in their project.
- Risk management
    - This category includes many different areas of a company including antimoney laundering, fraud examiners, internal auditors, enterprise risk managers, and external auditors and examiners.
    - Internal risk management professionals can view this book as a set of best practices the organization should follow to reduce risks caused by data that is not ready or suited for a risk management purpose. This book covers the concept of data controls, which like regular corporate controls, are a set of processes and procedures that should be in place to ensure the data used in business processes is of suitable readiness.
    - External auditors and examiners can use this book to establish or enhance audit or examination guides. While the nature of external auditing varies by industry and regulatory area, a Playbook establishes a baseline. Deviations from the Playbook can identify additional areas to investigate.

SUMMARY

We introduced the area of data governance through multiindustry examples and highlighted the different discussion areas that will be covered in the book. We also defined basic terms and concepts. This chapter touched on a variety of topics that often intersect a discussion around data governance including maturity models, Big Data, and operational models. We created a foundation for understanding what a Playbook is and why this approach is needed now. Finally, we identified the benefit of using a Playbook for different audiences.

CHAPTER

EXECUTIVE CALL TO ACTION—HOW CHIEF DATA OFFICERS AND BUSINESS SPONSORS CAN EMPOWER RESULTS

2

EXECUTIVE CALL TO ACTION—WHAT DO WE NEED FROM YOU?

First, develop a clear sense of data's importance to you and your enterprise. Much of this importance stems from the risks and rewards that data presents:

1. Risks—Regulatory, Operational, Market, Client and Reputation, and Cost
2. Rewards—Data and Analytics Opportunities—Regulatory, Cost, and Speed or Competitive Advantages, and Sustainable Performance, Efficiency and Market Improvements

We discussed the value of data delivery and the commensurate value and importance of governing data delivery in the Introduction. The most direct path to proactively engaging data leaders in your firm is to establish a message that clearly balances what you expect in terms of risk reduction and performance and financial and competitive rewards. Second, construct a mandate and viewpoint for the way you want your enterprise to handle its data. Establish an expectation that, as part of the journey toward your risk and rewards targets, you expect the enterprise to permanently improve its data-handling behaviors, practices, and skills with appropriate, efficient controls. Establishing your controls perspective communicates a sense of having a "controls conscious management," which is irreplaceable and critical to the enterprise.

Here are four major drivers behind the movement toward data leadership:

Each driver presents risks and rewards. Rewards are best defined and understood when tied to a committed enterprise strategy and goals in a clearly communicated mandate. For example, a firm commitment to outstanding customer experience or innovative products and services would identify reward areas that bolster those goals. Customer experience goals require tremendous customer insight and a consistently high reputation with customers. The corresponding data reward zones would be comprehensive data gathering, integration, and protection for shared customer experience insight and improvements in experience. These boil down to an emphasis on operational and competitive analytics as well as Big Data integration and exploration. A firm focus on continuous product and service integration would target Internal Reporting and Analysis for deep quality and knowledge testing as well as Operational and Competitive Analytics to define target markets and innovation focus. Increasingly, firms must balance between operational and regulatory issues and the desire to grow and innovate, and this balancing act poses the greatest challenge.

The bottom line for executive messaging and involvement is: articulate your passion for growth, innovation, and excellence. Share, in the same message, your continuing commitment to provide a "controls conscious management team" that supports the efficient use of corporate data and process

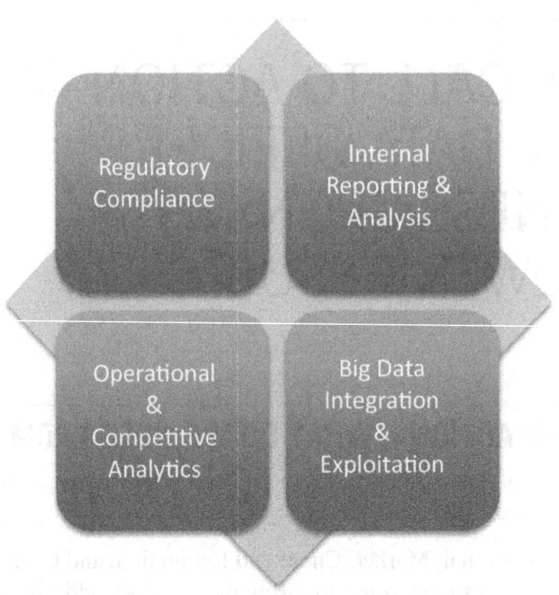

governance as a means of reliably reaching your goals and preserving your reputation. Let your organization know that you are not looking for herculean efforts to keep things running in "business as usual" mode while innovation and transformation efforts are underway. Rather, you actively encourage your leaders and teams to provide regular feedback on the pace at which major improvements can be achieved within a controlled and sustainable environment. The next step is a bit easier. Once you've laid out a vision and some guardrails for the journey, the next step is to help everyone understand how to get the scope of data and related processes right. Defining what is critical and therefore in scope for this work is a way of managing expectations and building confidence. People will see a clear sense of direction, speed, and course as a real enterprise commitment they can support.

So what happens to companies, government agencies, and nonprofits when the management team does not value controls? What about smaller firms or firms where lesser levels of controls insensitivity are prevalent, how do we improve on this for data?

Fair question. Some fail under the weight of the results of a consistent lack of controls. Others face repeatedly stiff fines, penalties, and other financial impacts from years of control ignorance. We've seen a spate of banks and insurance companies recently caught manipulating foreign exchange, interest rate, and related markets, even after a 10-year global recession wrought by uncontrolled speculation and leverage.

The other side of the equation is clearly the benefit story. In firms where controls are not on the agenda, benefits we would ordinarily target become the entire rationale for governance. Escalating the benefits discussion may require tying specific benefits to individual initiatives. Major initiatives that target enterprise, business line, or technology transformations often require multiple cost/benefit mappings. These mappings can provide sponsorship and funding to both "fix the data" needed as part of systems migration and "improve the data handling" to resolve underlying issues and introduce new controls. The table provided previously shows examples of some of the benefits that can be used to acquire sponsorship when control focus is not sufficient.

Governance Benefits	Capability Benefits
Improved transparency in tracking of data and analytics	Improved employee satisfaction due to alignment of required activities, less data cleanup and more business analysis
Defined improvements in controls and integrity of enterprise data	Higher collaboration and improved output due to standardize methods and behaviors
Targeted standardization of data and analytics models	Improved controls awareness and behaviors due to standard focus and approach provided by playbook capabilities
Planned Consolidation and integration of overlapping data and analytic models	Reduced cost and dependency on external vendors and staff due to improved skills and execution
Measurable improvements in enterprise reporting and analytics due to improvements in quality and control	Improved expectations and commitments to quality, reliable and attestable data and analytics outputs
Reduced enterprise risk in audit findings resulting from improved change and quality controls	Improved consistency of reporting quality and timeliness due to shared standards and improved capabilities
Improved time to market for large scale system and business process changes as reflected in data and analytics	Improved employee retention, career options and job mobility due to measured and standardized capabilities
Consistent and measurable enterprise improvements in reporting and analytic quality, timeliness and accuracy	
Consistently improving employee satisfaction, skills and productivity, resulting in more standard-based control and improvement in data, analytics and performance outcomes	

One additional cost/benefit issue can often be used effectively. Mapping out a data flow to depict the controls problems often shows that a multitude of controls are actually in place. The problem is not so much a lack of controls but a lack of controls effectiveness. Perhaps everyone rereconciles data they receive, even though the provider has already reconciled it to an authoritative source. Perhaps there are import filters for inbound files that reject records or entire files, but there is no profiling of these files before the import and no little or no exception handling for the rejected items. The opportunity to provide a management team that does not value controls with a way to actually reduce the number of controls used by simply improving a few key items often gains sponsorship.

SCOPE AND FOCUS AREA DEFINITION

Defining critical data is the subject of much discussion. The truth behind this definition is so simple it's a wonder why it takes up so much time and energy. Think about your data in terms of what it represents, as you normally do when discussing reports, analysis, and projections. What reports and numbers do you use to run your business and make strategic decisions? Operations executives, including operational risk executives, use a run book with all their operational and strategic performance indicators and other dashboard level numbers in order to see trends and issues. What is critical to you as a stakeholder, an officer of the corporation, and a leader? The answer we get once we simplify this exercise is remarkably consistent and clear: "I care most about customers, partners, and associates and am equally responsible for our financial and regulatory reporting requirements. These are the things I lose sleep over and must attest to as an officer and steward." This is a solid, actionable list. The data we need to govern and improve for these responsibilities can be boiled down to three primary areas, as shown.

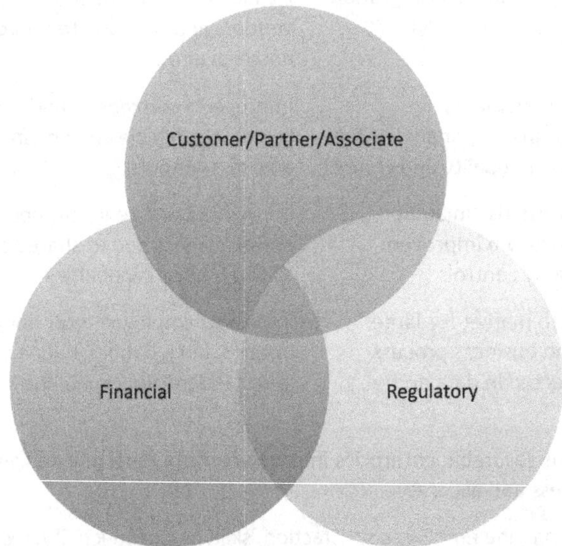

Many other domains of data may be critical to a firm. Examples include intellectual property, such as analytic models and results; clinical and other studies; analysis; and human capital data, including internal and external resource-protected data. The value of this data is most obvious where the quantity, quality, and timeliness of it are most impaired. Gaps in reporting and analysis, as well as material inconsistencies, indicate where valuable information is not being delivered as required.

Master and reference data are increasingly seen as critical data. Early examples included financial, organizational, and human resource hierarchies. These eventually expanded to include product, supply chain, market and customer hierarchies, and valid values. The master data focus is now centered primarily on customers, products, and suppliers. Financial systems now routinely provide integrated master and reference data. Master data refers to the objects of your business that you can master, including customers, accounts, products, and organizational structures or geographic locations. Reference data is generally specified outside your control, and you need to ensure you are using and reconciling to it consistently. Examples include everything from tax identifiers, to currency codes, to diagnostic codes, and so on.

There is value in the simplicity of a message about scoping critical data and related processes to focus primarily on customer, financial, and regulatory areas. Consider your partners and associates as part of the extended financial record, to keep this simple. Then you can communicate this initial focus so that everyone understands what to target for governance, stewardship, quality improvement, and related efforts. Other data subjects will be added over time, but in the beginning, it is most important that everyone understands where we are starting and why.

Critical Data requires some level of "attestation," or commitment, from its producer or owner, usually a business executive. The more formal the attestation required, the more critical data controls, quality, and ownership transparency become to both the producer and consumer. Data that carries an implicit or explicit commitment is called "attestable data" and should carry with it some measures of its integrity, timeliness, completeness, and, as of its effective date, accuracy. Attestation submissions to external constituents, especially regulators, should be logged in the system of authority used to produce them along with their quality and integrity level.

Your contribution as an executive, sponsor, and mentor for your data leaders is a clear and consistent mandate. Your data leaders will then bring this mandate down to more detailed program and project planning. The "why" and "what" answers are what everyone needs from their executive leadership. You have a simple approach to providing the "why"—the four basic drivers mapped to your strategic goals and imperatives. The "what" starts with the identification of which data and related processes are critical, as we covered above.

The key is people seeing that an overall executive mandate and sponsorship is present, along with regular attention to progress and support in order to resolve issues as they occur. We know that sustainable competitive advantage requires sustained executive commitment, oversight, and active support. Improving your data leverage to become a data leader is no different.

Some background and context on data governance as well as stewardship and quality approaches and practices will be useful as you help guide and monitor the actions of your data leaders and teams.

TRADITIONAL APPROACH TO (DATA) GOVERNANCE

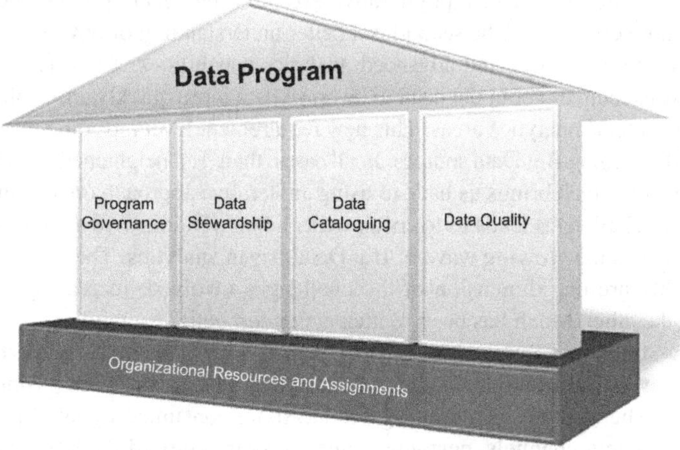

The typical approach to data governance is framed using standard governance approaches. We're all familiar with the pillar model of governance. Each pillar represents a core domain of governance activity, within which specific controls and behaviors limit the use of certain assets, while managing access and change permissions to ensure asset preservation. Data governance and quality programs typically leverage this model, providing activities for overall program governance, data stewardship, data cataloging facilities, and data-quality testing and improvement. All of these are appropriate domains to focus on for data management; however, they do not function discretely, and most organizations have moved beyond using finite projects and programs to institute them.

The traditional four-pillar approach to governance is also very monolithic. The model presumes that each pillar will stand in a permanent manner independent of the others. It also assumes that, once the roof is installed, the pillar will be standing with the necessary strength and size to hold its share. For these and many other reasons, this model is increasingly outdated. It is however, more prevalent than many of us realize, since newer models have yet to be fully deployed. The other challenge is that, in many organizations, these models are not uniformly defined or deployed at the enterprise level. Acquired companies, now run as and pockets of "legacy" systems and stores, each have their own governance model or activities. Many look more similar to this monolith than they do to newer models and approaches. It is wise to review the various models, efforts, and resources in place, rather than assume they are up to date.

However, we know that improving data and its outcomes takes a much less monolithic and much more iterative set of actions. Therefore it's important to be able to support different levels of resources, activities, and timings of outcomes across various parts of the enterprise in a staggered, parallel execution model. Some areas will start sooner and progress more quickly because of a business or regulatory imperative. Other areas may delay their start or extend their duration because they have more business process or application changes that must be made. There is also the overarching set of enterprise activities that must occur, even as these domain areas begin to be executed. Thus it is worth pulling out the organizational governance pillar and understanding that it rightly belongs in the center of the cycle. It's also important to understand that the organizational governance function will mature at its own rate, sometimes letting domain-specific activities that are being conducted lag behind.

A strong movement toward a more sustainable cycle of data management is emerging. This cycle is driven by a growing recognition of the complexity of the corporate data landscape and the regulatory and stakeholder demands it must address. Cyclical data management takes advantage of two trends in business today. The first is the use of agile or rapid iterative execution models to produce faster results and engage key resources more efficiently. The second is a better understanding of how to achieve a sustainable competitive advantage using data and advanced analytics capabilities. There is clearly a growing sense of urgency among executives about the need to leverage data more quickly and with better integrity within operational and strategic analytics areas. This new requirement level has to be met by both legacy operational systems and emerging Big Data sources. In all cases, there is a heightened need for data-quality visibility and improvement, which brings us back to using an iterative approach on a continuous basis.

This expanding set of challenges leads us to speak with clients, vendors, and analysts about the need for an approach that handles the growing wave of Big Data-driven analytics. The new requirements for integrity and attestability are one dimension of the challenges involved; increasing the volume and variety of your data is the other. Much has been written about competitive analytics capabilities. A long period of sustained investment in enterprise resource-planning suites and enterprise performance-management systems has driven a substantial change in the way analytics are used in business. Today, it is safe to say that much of the analytic results being produced are consumed by systems making, decisions about inventory, pricing, channels, customers, and so on in a closed analytic loop. This closed analytic loop raises the bar on data integrity and quality requirements. Analytic engines and algorithms now routinely feed operational systems, including enterprise resource planning and financial management systems, with near real-time updates on pricing, shipping, and customer retention functions. The automation of this process does not allow for human intervention or quality control over the data in use. So the data must be controlled, and, where necessary, improved in quality enough to be attestable and auditable.

We use the term "attestable data" to reflect the commitment corporate officers and executives make when they rely on data and the results of closed analytics loops in their decision-making process. This includes pricing decisions, product decisions, and large-scale acquisition and re-organization decisions. Each of these decisions represents a commitment of resources and reputation. All of them are based on data and analytics flows so must bear the weight of attestability.

The move from "information as an asset" to "trusted data" to "attestable data" is a transition driven by reputational as well as financial risk. "Attestable data" is less apt to vary in meaning across different people than terms like "trust," "golden," or other terms currently in use. Attestation requires an executive commitment under specific terms and conditions that can be held against an executive if their data is subsequently shown to be flawed. The level of commitment is more specific; the attestation is that both the data and the controls around its production are adequate to all regulatory requirements. This is a higher-level commitment reflecting a higher level of scrutiny and control.

Taking a more integrated and sustainable approach still requires addressing all four of the core governance domains. In order to ensure that we address each domain, we must first articulate each domain's challenge so that we know what action is required and can gauge the overall support needed to succeed across domains. Here we see the four domains displayed more in terms of the nature of the challenge than in terms of monolithic success. We recognize that whether you start with a single project, multiple projects, an enterprise program, or a dedicated enterprise function, there is an organizational dynamic that we must have in place to begin.

To stand up any programmatic or functional business capability, you must have executive vision, sponsorship, communication, and ongoing support. In this case, you also require solid guidance from key people in the organization who have a clear understanding of and experience with the data challenges, as well as an understanding of the benefits of resolving those challenges effectively.

It's important to engage what will become your first-line data officers early in the germination of a data program or data function. There is always time to adjust membership, assignments, and responsibilities as people's other responsibilities and your needs dictate. Building a small group of data leaders with whom you socialize your strategy and vision is an essential building block for your success. Part of that socialization will be understanding what roles and responsibilities are going to be important both initially and over time. There is always a difference between building something and running something, so your small group of leaders will need to include folks with strengths in each or both areas. This is also where we see the integrative nature of these four core capability areas.

Your data stewards will be doing the work to uncover data and its issues, catalog and resolve its meaning, and ascertain and improve its quality. Understanding what has to be done in data cataloging and data-quality areas is essential to identifying the right data stewardship function and to assigning responsibilities of that function to the best people possible. Also critical here is the notion of cost-effective data stewardship. This concept flows from cost-effective computing, a discipline John Clark and members of Gavroshe have applied globally for two decades. In the context of data stewardship, it is applied to the selective use of part-time resources under the guidance of full-time officers. We do not ask stewards to be full-time, proxied owners of data and take on the underlying problems that come with it alone. Rather, we provide leadership to data officers, part-time data stewards, and subject matter experts in business and operational areas so they can work together to govern and improve their data.

Getting to cost-effective stewardship requires a balance of training, mentorship, and experience. Traditional training approaches have given way to more effective and repeatable methods. Classroom training is still used, but leaders have moved toward using a "Khan Academy" approach with Learning Management Systems (LMS) and other online means of delivering knowledge and supporting collaboration among the stewardship community. Finally, the use of expert mentors from inside the organization as well as from consultant experts is very prevalent. Using a combination of training, experience, and outcomes is an emerging standard. The belt system popularized by Six Sigma and other enterprise programs allows us to distinguish stewards not just in terms of their job title or position but also in terms of their belt status. An example is shown in the following table. A simple approach like this one communicates the value of learning and achieving.

Belt Level	Requirements
White	Training: Initial onboarding and orientation Experience: General background suitable for stewardship Outcomes: None yet
Green	Training: Formal classroom on online training, completed testing & mentorship Experience: at least one data sprint or other cycle with critical data Outcomes: at least one set of critical data under change & quality control
Brown	Training: Multiple classes and online sessions with testing Experience: Multiple data stewardship cycles and mentorship of green belts Outcomes
Black	Training: Has completed and contributed to training & testing program Experience: Has lead multiple teams and cycles Outcomes: has implemented or improved data services, monitoring and alerting, data problem root cause identification and resolution

Our first order of business in creating a more sustainable or cycling view of this process is to pull the organizational construct out of the pillars and put it at the top of our framework. This format expresses that the organizational construct is an essential, creative element for our program or function and must be created and managed distinctly from the work streams that it mandates. The result is a framework that describes three key aspects of improving data through governance, all of which are driven under a common executive mandate and organizational construct as shown.

DATA LEADERSHIP CYCLE—FRAMING YOUR MANDATE

Beginning with the end in mind is a common proposition when dealing with enterprise issues. As you consider the type of controlling and improving data mandate you want to provide your organization with, it's very useful to consider what your peers are doing across industries and where similar programs and functions have already gleaned substantial benefits. Identifying the benefits and risks you are

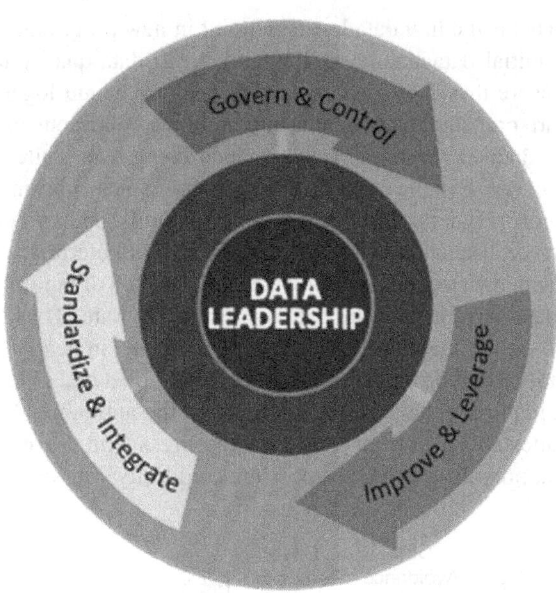

targeting with your program or function is a critical first step; then tying those to each of the three core areas becomes fairly simple.

There's a great deal written and discussed in major conferences about the benefits data programs are delivering in different industries specific to different targets. Some examples include the financial services industry, where capital counterparty and enterprise performance-analytics risk is driving substantial activity to improve the quality and timeliness of data. In health and life sciences we see a growing need to provide both protection and privacy subject to HIPAA and other regulations as well as rapidly growing complexity and diagnostic, machine-based, and connected care domains of data. In manufacturing and supply chain areas, we see the rise of the machine data and its attendant challenges: timeliness, quality, and integrity from multiple purposes across organizations and geographies.

Mapping some of your most challenging data-related initiatives and imperatives against the three core areas often highlights the need to deliver multiple benefits. Anti-Money Laundering (AML), Watch List Monitoring (OFAC), Financial Planning and Analysis (FP&A), and Comprehensive Capital Analysis and Review (CCAR) are all examples of programs required in financial services firms that demand multiple data capabilities and outcomes. Data for your imperatives must be traced, cataloged, and tested for integrity regularly, because the outputs of these programs are regulatory reports and filings requiring executive attestation.

ITAM, or IT Asset Management, Information Security and Privacy (CISO/CPO), and Governance and Regulatory Compliance (GRC) are all ongoing corporate functions with similar data requirements. Legal Entity Identifiers and Relationships (LEI/LER) are emerging requirements for financial services providers enacted to support Counterparty Risk Management (CCR) and will ultimately require coding each transaction with these identifiers.

These are just a few of the growing regulatory requirements being levied in the financial services industry, as regulators establish new guidelines and requirements in the aftermath of the great recession. Leading firms are increasingly tying these programs, functions, and requirements to broader enterprise data services. This is the first data leverage point in new programs. Enterprise data services provide everything from initial data tracing and cataloging to data-quality testing and dashboards. Advanced services can ensure that data sources, quality, and issues are logged with the data so that when reports and filings are prepared, prior to attestation, all the conditions of the data being used are exposed. These enterprise data services are often provided using lean, agile methods and have been shown to save between 2.5× and 4.5× the cost of simply allowing lines of business and individual initiatives to provide these outcomes independently. The expertise, tools, and specialized methods required by these services are far more efficient when housed in a shared or enterprise data service function.

The second leverage point data leaders are using is the integration of multiple programs or functions to share both enterprise data services and the data they each generate. Thus savvy risk management executives have learned to ensure that their GRC systems integrate, in nearly real time, the data feeds from their AML and Identity Theft programs. This process is critical and efficient, since a red-flagged account in Identify Theft requires enhanced due diligence in the antimoney laundering area. The fact that both areas are using attestable data from documented sources with proven controls further streamlines the entire process and provides the highest possible credibility with regulators, as shown.

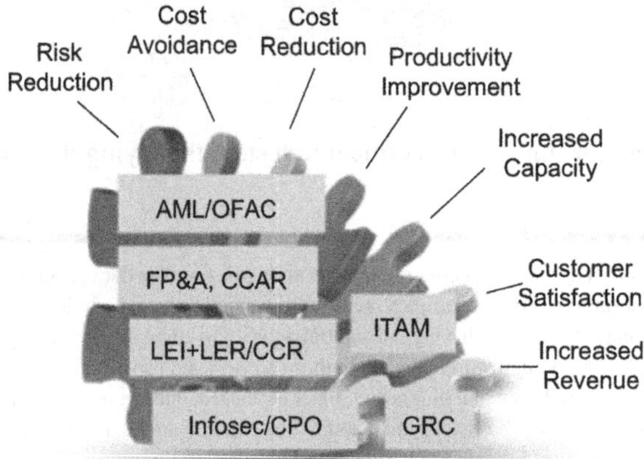

Risk, Cost & Benefits Examples from Financial Services Industry

TAKING A MORE SUSTAINABLE APPROACH

We see Business Data Governance as a function of business data ownership, production, use, and interchange. Similarly, we see other corporate governance functions over cash or marketable securities as ways to control changes in their location, condition, use, or ownership. Our opening quote from Walter Wriston indicates our simple, direct focus on this issue of data as an asset. In fact, that data is almost as valuable as the asset it describes. Thus data about money, income, expense, or risk is of critical value to the enterprise.

We treat "business data governance" as a noun representing a business function, just as one might treat the term "corporate governance." "Governing business data" is the verb and we treat that very expansively. We include the many facets often separated into their separate subtopics like stewardship, quality, cataloging, relationship management, and so on. More on this later—this is just a callout to establish some basic operating assumptions, so we can make sure we are speaking the same language.

Data Leadership also seeks to leverage organizational leadership. We've seen the rise of dedicated data roles and positions including stewards, officers, and scientists, as well as long-term data programs focused on governance, quality, and analytics. Some firms have fully committed to organization functions and to units dedicated to governing and improving data. These groups often spring up in finance, marketing, and other crossfunctional areas of a large business, since these areas are recipients of all upstream data behaviors and problems of the enterprise.

DATA LEADERSHIP ROLES—LEVERAGING MORE THAN THE CDO—THE POWER OF DATA OFFICERS

The Chief Data Officer, or CDO role, has come to the forefront in recent years as the person who is accountable for data outcomes. Recent elevation of the digital experience has resulted in the use of the CDO title to also refer to Chief Digital Officers, so the title can be confusing, and many firms choose to use other titles for this role including "Global Head of Data." All these titles and positions underscore the importance of data and provide for data leadership positions. It is worth noting that different industries are highlighting this role in different ways. Media, creative arts, and retail industries, with heavy content and user-experience domains, tend to reserve the "D" for "Digital" and use "Global Head of Data" titles. Financial services, on the other hand, emphasize the CDO as one of their key positions to deal with regulatory concerns. Whatever the title, the role and sponsorship are clearly understood to be critical to enterprise data management and governance.

Different styles and approaches are emerging in data programs that reflect the mandate and focus of their CDOs. Some basic patterns we now see in financial services, healthcare, and other industries include:

1. Regulatory and Compliance (Controls Focus)—Enterprise financial and regulatory reporting must satisfy a myriad of complex, multiagency regulatory requirements. Meeting those requirements depends on executing a complete, consistently applied, and continuously monitored set of data controls for all source data used in these reports.
2. Data and Reporting Improvement (Data Transformation Focus)—We need to improve our data management capabilities, behaviors, and outcomes in business-unit and enterprise-level reporting. We have clear and compelling evidence that many of our operational challenges and cost bubbles are occurring because of underlying data-handling issues. We are therefore committing ourselves to changing the way we handle our data and produce our reports.
3. Analytic Competitiveness (Analytics Leadership Focus)—Our business and industry is increasingly driven by analytics, both operationally and strategically.
4. Hybrids—Transformational and Analytic Leadership-based efforts can often merge or evolve to address both of these areas. Control-focused efforts are generally relegated to the core controls and quality issues they start with since their mandate and resources are so constrained.

CHIEFS OF DATA, GOVERNANCE AND ANALYTICS

The CDO is very much in vogue now, even as we simultaneously embrace highly commoditized technologies and methods for data management. Cloud-based computing elevates virtualization and hosting to new levels, while further removing day-to-day management of data and analytics platforms. Look no further than

3 Approaches to Data Office & CDO

Different approaches with different focus and proponents

Compliance Focus
- Material Weakness
- Restatements & Penalties
- Closures & Restrictions
- Risk Models & Stress Tests

Supply Side Focus
- Operational Reporting Integrity
- Data & Process Improvement
- Risk and reward based investment
- Enterprise Lean/Six Sigma Agility
- Integration Friendly Architecture

Demand Side Focus
- Strategic Top Down Leadership
- Consolidated Initiatives Portfolio
- Enterprise Data & Analytic Services
- Enterprise Data & Analytic Targets measuring demonstrated capabilities

BANK FOR INTERNATIONAL SETTLEMENTS

Data and Process Governance - Operating Model

Standards & Methods Working Group(s)

Business Catalog & Governance Reporting

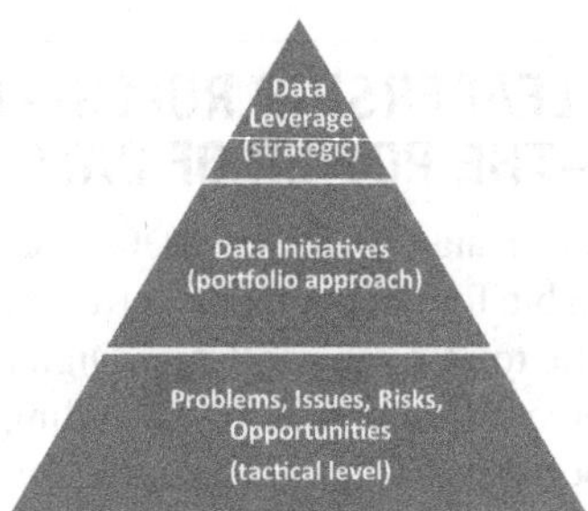

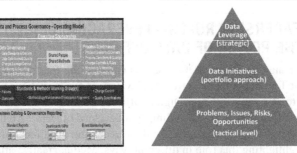

Compliance Proponents
- Systemically Impactful Financial Institutions
- Global Systemically Impactful Banks
- Banks, Investment Firms, Online Banks and Payment Processors
- Small to Mid-sized Banks

Supply Proponents
- Investment Banks
- Asset Managers
- Alternative lenders, emerging and next generation credit syndication models (e.g. blockchain enabled settlement)
- Financial Data Services Providers
- Regulators

Demand/Delivery Focus
- Online Brokerages
- Bank Investment Units
- Custodians/Trustees & Clearing firms
- Top Analytic Competitors (Finance, Energy, Retail, Mfg, Private Equity)
- Banks & Investment Firms with End to End Risk Ownership & Management

Salesforce.com and its effect on entrenched competitors like Oracle, Microsoft, and IBM to see the impact of a new class of cloud-service components that grew from the Customer Relationship Management seedling. Pending merger and strategic alliance conversations are increasingly public, sometimes resulting in brief stock exchange trading halts and always driving uncertainty into cloud-computing service contracts. Data executives watch these market forces and actions with a great deal invested in their outcomes. Executives have a growing voice in the contracting and strategy for use of cloud-based analytics environments.

The wide range of interests and responsibilities that executives have has also driven a growing array of chief titles and positions. The CDO role is well established and new positions, such as the Chief Analytics Officer, Chief Data Governance Officer, and Chief Data Risk Officer, are emerging as hiring priorities. The type of organizational construct needed or available to enable these positions is less clear. Each of these titles is really an offshoot of one of the primary responsibilities of the original crop of CDOs. Some CDOs have made names for themselves as governance leaders, most notably in money center banks, where they used self-assessment and top-down approaches to show progress in basic data governance areas. Others have shown a more holistic and business-benefit-driven set of capabilities, embracing the business directives and requirements while working to satisfy compliance and risk issues. These CDOs work hard to engage and support business partners with realistic data improvement efforts that are both measurable in their outcomes and sustainable over time. The rare CDO is able to address both data and business process, sometimes covering business process areas like counterparty risk management and credit-pricing leadership.

Some newer CDOs have come into their positions with two key assets. The first is a direct reporting line to the Chief Operating Officer (COO), ensuring consistent business engagement, sponsorship, and demand for enterprise data services. The second is a keen understanding of and often decades of experience with data integration, warehousing, reporting, and analytics delivery. These CDOs also understand the need to engage their organization with a new structural approach. They are usually asked or given the opportunity to collect key groups of data modelers and architects: data integration, warehousing, and delivery teams; data stewards and quality experts; and analytics and Big Data experts, which they then form into a coherent team with the CDO. These CDOs usually move quickly to identify a line of "data officers" who lead each of their respective areas, while collaborating as a team with the CDO and his or her constituents across the enterprise. In this emerging best practice model, the CDO establishes the Analytics Officer as the leader who provides the "voice of the decision" for the business. This voice provides transparency and control over the analytic algorithms, models, and integration points across the enterprise, giving business partners a clear picture of their analytic capabilities, options, and outcomes. In some places, there is a Chief Analytics Officer (CAO) who reflects a return to the notion of decision support with the new facet of decision/action/outcome traceability. CAOs will move us beyond closed-loop analytics and machine learning and into organizational learning that binds business intelligence with behavioral intelligence. It is worth noting that the "chief" qualifier may not be the most effective way to establish this role.

DEMAND MANAGEMENT MODEL

Demands are most often clearly expressed at the tactical, project-oriented level. These include demands for data, data resources, data services, or data outcomes that must be compared with available resources in an open-resource management model. These are often called Demand Management Models, or Offices, and this where the allocation of resources is made. Demand management efforts start at this level through listing demands and are often composed of nothing more than disparate projects and issues people are trying to resolve, as shown.

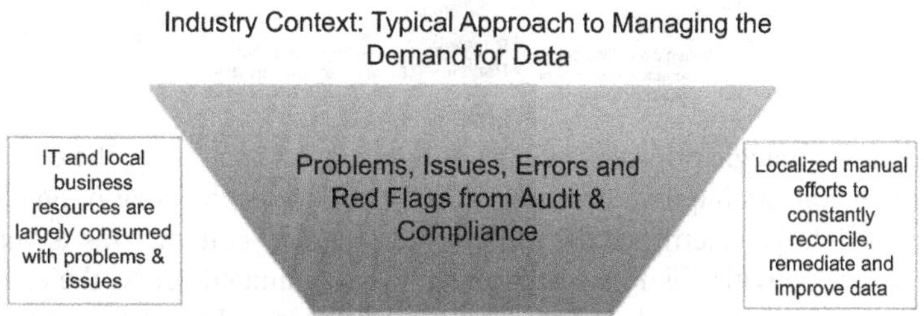

Once these issues are collected and we have a sense of their size, current resource load, project timing, and priority, the current state of data conditions begins to emerge. This is still only a partial, if imposing, picture. The CDO still needs to collect broader management initiatives that often span years and sometimes business areas. Summarizing those initiatives adds another layer to the picture:

These management data initiatives have usually been created, funded, and resourced based on a single line of business or an operational area's needs. The initiatives may be "burning platform" projects, transformation programs, system migration, or virtualization programs, and even cloud migrations or IT outsourcing events. It is important to determine the extent to which an overarching business-driven data strategy and planning model was used to approve and fund these initiatives. It is also critical to

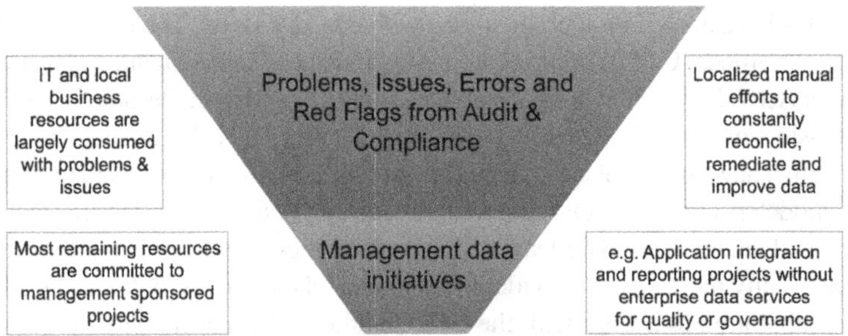

identify the level of shared enterprise Program Management Office (PMO) services in place and that are coordinating the execution of these programs, the use of any existing shared services, and the calibration of resource requirements over time. The PMO can also help identify what level of agility, reflected in the current development and deployment methodologies, these initiatives follow. Finally, the PMO should include any shared or common success metrics and updates.

The last layer of the demand management model is the strategic piece: the enterprise vision-driven actions with data and analytics that are planned or already underway, as shown.

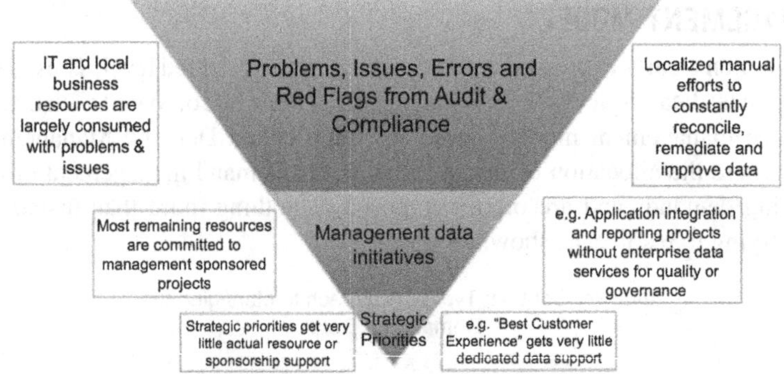

When you add these strategic priorities and actions, a complete picture of the enterprise data landscape emerges, which you can improve over time. The first impression is that of an elephant standing on its head: all the weight is teetering at the top on a very narrow bottom. This is very typical, since most, or even all, of the activities and resources previously committed across the enterprise for data-related issues and needs were not guided, directed, or even evaluated by a data executive. Turning this picture right side up is something an enterprise data executive can do when supported by the top enterprise and business executives. Obtaining and maintaining that support requires a clear, transparent approach that puts business executives' representatives at the table, ensuring prioritization and changes to human, financial, or political capital are made equitably. A more effective, efficient, and sustainable model emerges from this effort over time:

The method behind this reversal and aligning process is detailed in Chapters 3 and 4. In these chapters we focus on the methods used to provide strategic alignment, so you can get the top of this pyramid right. This Demand Management function is a critical component in your data leadership effort and will dovetail with existing portfolio management processes once in place. Providing the strategic mapping

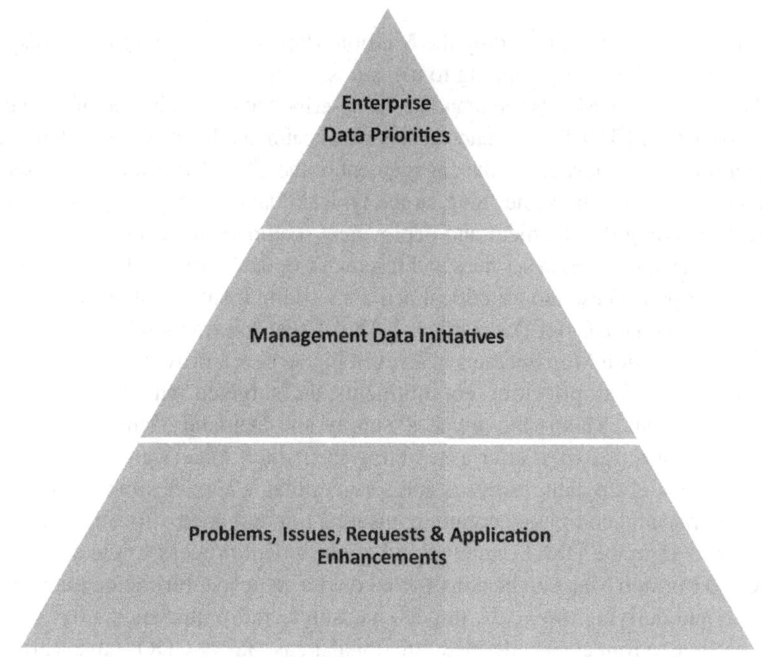
Enterprise Data Priorities
Management Data Initiatives
Problems, Issues, Requests & Application Enhancements

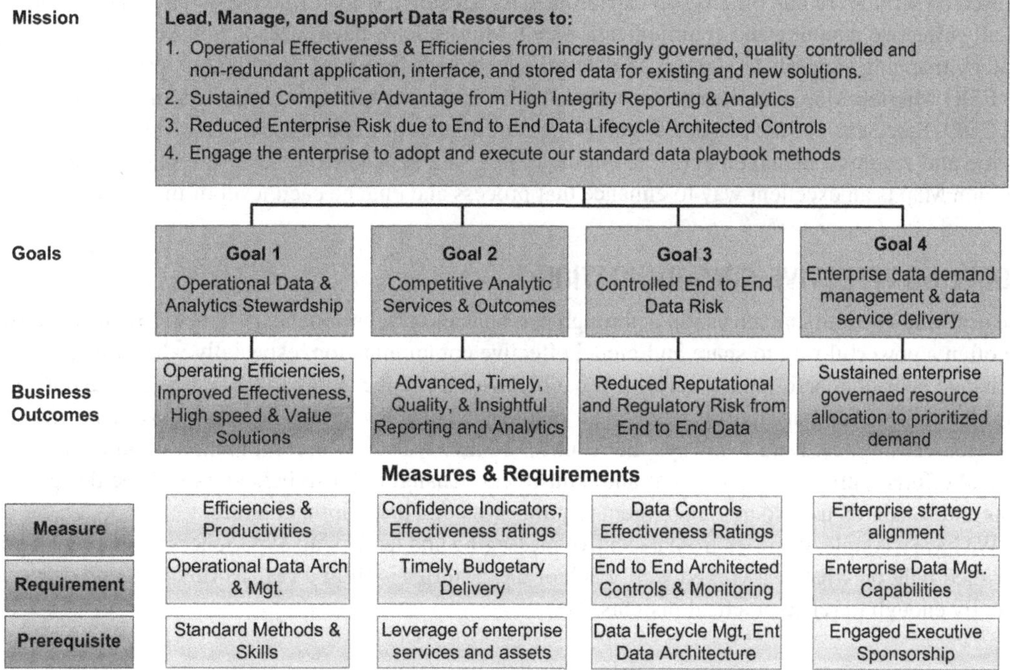
CDO Data Mission Map
Mission
Lead, Manage, and Support Data Resources to:
1. Operational Effectiveness & Efficiencies from increasingly governed, quality controlled and non-redundant application, interface, and stored data for existing and new solutions.
2. Sustained Competitive Advantage from High Integrity Reporting & Analytics
3. Reduced Enterprise Risk due to End to End Data Lifecycle Architected Controls
4. Engage the enterprise to adopt and execute our standard data playbook methods
Goals
Goal 1 Operational Data & Analytics Stewardship
Goal 2 Competitive Analytic Services & Outcomes
Goal 3 Controlled End to End Data Risk
Goal 4 Enterprise data demand management & data service delivery
Business Outcomes
Operating Efficiencies, Improved Effectiveness, High speed & Value Solutions
Advanced, Timely, Quality, & Insightful Reporting and Analytics
Reduced Reputational and Regulatory Risk from End to End Data
Sustained enterprise governaed resource allocation to prioritized demand
Measures & Requirements
Measure
Efficiencies & Productivities
Confidence Indicators, Effectiveness ratings
Data Controls Effectiveness Ratings
Enterprise strategy alignment
Requirement
Operational Data Arch & Mgt.
Timely, Budgetary Delivery
End to End Architected Controls & Monitoring
Enterprise Data Mgt. Capabilities
Prerequisite
Standard Methods & Skills
Leverage of enterprise services and assets
Data Lifecycle Mgt, Ent Data Architecture
Engaged Executive Sponsorship

for the top of the triangle is accomplished by the Mission Map, a simple tool that serves to capture and communicate strategic thinking and mapping to measures of success.

The top level of the Mission Map is the mandate, as described at the beginning of this chapter, worked out by the CDO and COO or CEO. Large financial services, health and life sciences, retail, technology, and even federal agencies now routinely enjoy the engagement of the CEO, CFO, and other executives in strategic data planning. This is not the same thing as the typical "data strategy" approach used in IT. Data strategy is critical to building development and deployment roadmaps for data architecture components. Some data strategies even address data services and resources, or data virtualization approaches, as well as Big Data integration efforts. These are all critical activities and outcomes that are increasingly managed under shared leadership with the Chief Data Officer (CDO), Chief Information Officer (CIO), and others.

However, the CDO Mission Map operates at an even higher level, providing key executives with the ability to direct alignment of all priorities, commitments, and targeted outcomes across the enterprise and over long-term horizons. This is the arena of Supply and Demand Management, or the Demand Management Office. CDOs are able, after assembling their data officers and functions, to identify a demand management model for data resources and services that is at once simple enough to communicate across the enterprise and complete enough to ensure a fair and open allocation of capital. The first order of business is to align the DMO planning and commitment process to the strategic plans of the enterprise. The CDO Mission Map can be constructed on one page, capturing the mandate for the CDO from the enterprise and deriving the goals, targets, measures, and requirements for success from that mandate in each of three to four clearly defined functional areas. Savvy CDOs have learned to start with their programmatic requirements in this Mission Map in order to highlight for their executive sponsors what it will take to provide all of the initiative and service-based delivery support required by the enterprise. The typical Mission Map divides a CDO program into two to three functional areas, generally focused on services or outcome-based capabilities. As a result, a well-formed Mission Map becomes an equally effective planning and communication tool. Many clients have cascaded mission maps the way strategy mapping suggests to support an enterprise strategy Mission Map at the top level, followed by the CDO Mission Map, and then maps completed by each data officer who leads a functional area of the CDO. Since each of these maps contains measures and requirements, they can be used for performance and resource management. Communication is a consistent theme in the data arena, so the Mission Map is an excellent way to enhance that process and engage each level of the organization.

MODELING EFFECTIVE COMMUNICATION

The best way to communicate vision is through personal and professional experience. Executive stories are often a powerful way to share and model effective communication, especially when we are trying to change behaviors across the enterprise. That behavioral change is key to this messaging and leadership: the recognition that, like so many other challenges, data leadership is an organizational change-management journey. Data is always the result of behavior, usually a combination of automated and manual efforts with manual oversight and adjustment. Changing those behaviors and the design patterns and standards used to automate them requires systemic behavioral change.

We have a couple of stories from executive messaging and leadership experiences to share with you that shed light on what has worked well. Each of these stories is from a real-world client and occurred recently enough to relate practical insights.

Large initiative review and alignment

Storyline: A C-level executive cuts through the noise to deliver a simple, three-part test for large, complex programs and then applies it consistently to enterprise class initiatives:

Mary, an IT and Operations Executive in a large asset management firm, started a review of the current portfolio of initiatives upon joining the firm. She knew how critical it was to get a handle on the committed work she inherited and to get a sense of the health of these initiatives as well as the expectations of her sponsors. Many of these were more than a year old, with large, some even very large, spending and investment levels. She had seen this trend before and was always concerned about inheriting an aging portfolio of initiatives that could not be clearly traced back to a solid demand management process or executive sponsorship and business case foundations. Her experience indicated that she had very little time, perhaps only a few months in which to engage her constituents positively. She also wanted to highlight the process they used to consider and review these major commitments. She had learned, many times over, the importance of these initiatives, especially multiyear programs. Past experience made clear the value of large, complex programs and she wanted to share this with her leads and her constituents: "large, complex programs often highlight organizational capability and leadership issues." While the focus on capabilities was immediately obvious, the leadership dimension was less clear. Her approach indicated that her thinking about effective leadership was rooted in the quality of the decisions and commitments made by leaders and thus required clear decision-making and communicating. Therefore she decided to provide an incredibly simple and clearly communicated three-part test for these programs. It was something Mary routinely asked when anyone requested her sponsorship of any major program or initiative. True to her values, Mary also used it to discuss supporting major initiatives demanded by her peers. As a result, the approach to enterprise class initiatives was utterly consistent, and, over time, she began to expect it from everyone who approached her for support.

The three questions/mandates were:

1. Who is the business person "pounding the table" for this project, and why?
2. When have we effectively executed something of similar scope and import? Are we including people and processes that served us well before?
3. Does our execution of this initiative take us further down the path we have set for ourselves, or does it take us off that path in some way?

Mary then reviewed her portfolio of business and technology initiatives to determine which satisfied these criteria and which required some remediation. In each case, she was able to explain her reasoning to the program sponsors and how they could work together to align with the program over time. In each case, there were gaps or hurdles, but the sponsors and leads understood the need to raise the bar on such large and impactful commitments. Some programs were found to be outside the three-part criteria and were merged with others. A couple of very large programs, already well underway, required interventions to put them on track with enterprise direction, design, and development patterns. In less than 6 months, the entire portfolio had been subjected to a simple set of tests where everyone recognized the alignment of the remaining programs with all three mandates. Even more impactful, no new initiatives had been approved or proposed without these three critical criteria. This executive and her team successfully changed key behaviors with corresponding improvements in outcomes.

Similar tests from C-level executives follow this pattern and ask more data, controls, and risk management centric questions, including:

- Will we maintain control and ownership of our data when we do this?
- What visibility do we maintain over the custodianship and handling of our data?
- How has this program engaged internal audit and risk management in its business-case and high-level solution design?
- Does this project leverage our enterprise data services or attempt to provide data cataloging, testing, and controls alone?
- Does this program intend to leverage our standard data change and quality controls or create its own from scratch?

In each case both the correct answer and incorrect answer were fairly obvious. Communicating these to sponsors who routinely evaluate requests for new initiatives from their teams conveys these expectations early enough to stop the noise from rising to executive levels. What questions do you routinely use to ensure the quality of major initiatives, and how do you communicate them as expectations at early stages?

Executive experience: Chief Information Officer, Fortune 100 global manufacturing firm

Context: A CIO was recently installed from outside the firm and recognizes the need to galvanize new thinking, behaviors, and outcomes with data. He had already started an IT Transformation program aimed at unifying key IT services and components with a vision of service excellence for business partnership. Then, he saw the opportunity to add data as a service to this vision.

Storyline: We can improve our results with improved data—but must improve our data habits and behavior first.

"I'm getting to know more about our teams every day, and today is no exception!"

The CIO used this opening to engage a large group of IT leaders, managers, and team members assembled for an announcement about the new data program. The participants were selected because of their teams' involvement in key initiatives that produce, integrate, and rely upon enterprise data. The CIO knew he had a tall order because little attention had been paid to these people and their relationship to enterprise data practices and outcomes. Even worse, enterprise data practices and outcomes had not been addressed, formalized, or even explained by his predecessor. So he used a tactic he knew would resonate with these crossfunctional teams. His IT leadership team had been hard at work formalizing and socializing Enterprise IT Services, so IT would better align with the needs of the business and be recognized for superior performance. His team had developed a solid foundation of critical infrastructure, application, and integration services and was rapidly reforming key teams around these core competency areas. He and his leadership team had already started mapping key data services into this foundation, working to identify key managers and team members who had deep experience addressing data problems from "cradle to grave," while constantly under the gun to deliver new systems and upgrades linked to business capabilities. The progress his leadership team was making in mapping out data services suggested that certain key people would be needed to lead new data services, while many others would need to better understand the role of data services and improve their "data habits" to rapidly support better outcomes.

He then told the leadership team: "You've all been pressed very hard for a very long time to deliver new systems and upgrades that support improved business capabilities. You've delivered these while constantly dealing with difficult data issues at every turn. Some of these deliveries were data centered, requiring massive data integration and delivery. Those have taught us that data deliverables are becoming a critical business requirement as part of enhancing their capabilities. We even have business partners from finance, marketing, and design clamoring to partner with us to deliver rapid, scalable, and sustainable data-driven capabilities. So, the business has learned that data capabilities are as core as any other automation-based capability."

There, now he had the basis for his challenge and sponsorship offer—he was ready to make the ask and offer all in one: "…so now we embark on a shared journey with our business partners to deliver, in tandem, data-driven outcomes using a set of standardized services, skills, and teaming models." He was prepared to support this claim directly. The CIO had engaged a key business partner from marketing who was respected across the organization. She was known for driving efficiencies in the way of marketing-sourced and used data, especially from outside providers, while simultaneously holding the line on some of her group's "shadow IT" desires. As the CIO introduced her, everyone began to realize this was no longer just an IT exercise; it was something unlikely to fade into the background like so many previous data projects. She had prepared her remarks very carefully to fully support her CIO and his commitment to partner with her organization at every turn. She knew she had to engage her IT teams as never before.

So, she started with a simple commitment, first to the business goal and second to her IT team: "I am here to ensure we, as partners in data, will deliver best-in-world data driven outcomes for the enterprise. I am also here to share that commitment with you exclusively. That's right, you're it, I mean IT! You're our IT partners, so we are here to collaboratively build a new way forward to leveraging our data."

She knew she had to continue; she had to tell enough of the story to get some acknowledgment from this critical group of partners.

"We must know more about our customers, markets, competitors, economics, performance, risks, and opportunities," she continued. "We must know much more about these areas with far greater speed, accuracy and completeness. Our speed to market is in all our hands because it is driven or constrained by our speed to delivery! You've all been deeply involved with major programs that enhanced our operational capabilities. In recent years, you've delivered on our emerging analytic needs and have helped us understand the challenges and risks inherent in our enterprise data. It's time to step up our game by a factor of ten; we can't get by doubling our data flows and technology inventory or manual efforts with data every year or so, as we have been. We must make a leap forward together and fast!"

She paused and held her breath for a long minute before seeing signs of recognition and acknowledgment. Her IT partners did understand the critical role of data to the business and the challenges in meeting her requirements. They also seemed to care about helping, as many team leads and members were shaking their heads and nodding assent toward one another. Now for the one-two punch: "I am here to offer you a new level of partnership…IF you will craft and deliver the best data in the world and the services to scale that delivery across the enterprise then…I will commit to our exclusive use of those services as they become available." She went all in based on her trust in her CIO, his organization, as well as her desperate need for competitive data and analysis to help grow the business. She didn't share what everyone already knew, at least to some extent.

Now the CIO needed to expand on his intent. He stepped forward, standing shoulder-to-shoulder with his business partner. He began by explaining his intent so he could showcase her willingness to collaborate: "I asked our key business partner to share her time and her story with us so that we might all begin a sea of change in our thinking about data. I really thought she was going to share the nature of her challenges and maybe ask for some help or offer to engage us once we organized our thinking. She has far exceeded my highest hopes and provided us an opportunity to drive enterprise impact that everyone sees, benefits from, and builds interest in leveraging for themselves. We could not hope for a better first and best client partner!"

He reiterated the challenge, sharpening the request she had started to make of his teams: "What our marketing partner offered is a direct, exclusive partnership. What she requires from us to make that work is a dedication to provide best-in-world data and ongoing services that scale to meet all the needs of her and her peers over time."

Now he knew to stop and let that sink in. He saw his leaders surveying the assembled crowd and felt the pride of a leader with strong teams and partners. He felt certain that this approach to open, dedicated partnership would engage his IT teams and his partner's marketing teams in a sustainable and scalable way. He also recognized that he and his marketing partner would need to demonstrate and reiterate this commitment across the enterprise constantly and over a period of years to change the game permanently. He knew they were committed to doing just that.

This firm went on to globally compete and beat every major competitor for over a decade, surviving the global "great recession" with a solid balance sheet, growing domestic market share and steady margins and financial performance. This firm also held on to its key leadership talent for an extended period, well beyond its peers and competitors. Did data do that? No—they simply treated data the same way they did everything. They treated their data as a "performing asset" that merited measurement and scalable, dedicated services to produce the required returns.

Everyone says executive support is critical for effective business data governance and management. We agree but find that the path to gaining executive support is not always the same, nor is it always direct.

In addition to these executive stories, we have interviewed several midlevel managers to see what their current perspective is on three simple questions:

1. How do you see data governance expanding its scope and value as it matures into a standard practice?
2. How do you see the value of standard, repeatable methods and processes as companies deploy data governance?
3. What is the typical level of adoption for your data playbook or operating model? Are you embedding them into data governance solutions from vendors like Collibra, Adaptive, IBM, and SAS? Are you using e-learning, wiki, or other knowledge-building or -sharing solutions to build enterprise knowledge and practice?

The answers surprised us in some cases and reflected an overall deepening awareness of the enormity of the challenge embodied by data and analytics governance.

Managers from firms with repeated iterations of data programs indicated marginal improvements amid repeated strategy, roadmapping, and planning efforts. There was a general sense that standard methods were important and valuable, but there was little commitment to exposing them through data governance or knowledge coordination tools. Some of these firms are experiencing pockets of data governance advancement based on regulatory or risk management issues they need to resolve. Current examples include antimoney laundering regulations, HIPAA compliance, and information security overhauls. None of these soloed efforts were accepted or sponsored by executives as the enterprise standard or mandated approach. Technology managers with proxied business stewardship rights were handling most of the efforts.

Firms engaged in deploying data governance programs with executive support and specific business goals are fairing better; they are also leveraging either data governance or knowledge coordination solutions to expose and expand standard methods and practices.

Firms that have an executive sponsor, dedicated data officer, and standardized methods, practices and measures are achieving enterprise results with cost-effective resource leverage. They also exhibit a technology-driven commitment to provide enterprise data services that are best-of-class and operate at efficiency levels of three or four times what local technology or business area activities can attain. These are the award winners enjoying consistent data improvements and business impacts.

We reached out to data governance solution vendors to understand how they are helping clients and what challenges clients want help addressing. These vendors were willing to give us even greater insight into how some of their clients are becoming data leaders. We have been fortunate to be engaged by clients to help with each of these and many other solutions in use in data governance programs.

Our dialogue occurred with vendors such as Collibra, Oracle, and GlobalIDs. Stijn (Stan) Christiaens, Collibra cofounder, was quite clear about the level of benefits his clients were experiencing as they adopted and deployed a standard operating model for data governance. We confirmed this with two different clients and found two additional prospective clients engaged in contracting with software vendors, who identified the acquisition of data governance software as their turning point. The specific benefits these clients were targeting were all requirements of a sustainably successful data governance program: identifying, defining, and taking accountability for critical data and providing a common operating model for its control.

Our work with Oracle product management, sales, and engineering teams consistently points to two key benefits their clients expect and generate. The first is the ability to manage complex master and reference data hierarchies for use in analytic and operational systems, which presents an advanced data change control challenge. The second is much more broadly impactful: the sense of confidence that multiple business areas gained from having a clear and simple set of data governance workflows to follow.

Dr. Arka Mukherjee, founder and president of GlobalIDs, shared a set of benefits his clients continue to realize several years after implementation. His approach provides ways to automate massive data discovery and relationship mapping, a critical set of functions for data governance programs to trace their data assets and lineage. Arka says that automating discovery and mapping dramatically accelerates the process of identifying "authoritative sources" of data and consolidating lesser copies to improve attestation and reporting outcomes.

Two basic themes emerge from all of this client and vendor feedback. The first is that there are now multiple capability areas that data governance and quality programs must deliver. Cataloging data, definitions, and stewardship assignments is a critical first step but the addition of data-quality requirements and testing or profiling outcomes is also a requirement. The second is the increasing sense of value large companies are finding in the use of data governance software-based solutions to support a robust and continuing success in their programs.

SUMMING IT UP

Your data leaders, teams, and the entire enterprise need your leadership in three key areas:

1. A clear, crisp, and consistently communicated Data Leadership message with the vision, scope, and targeted outcomes of the journey (implicitly or explicitly including improved data capabilities and behaviors).
2. A Data Leadership Team with a chief where appropriate and officers who are empowered to lead and execute on your vision.
3. A set of measures, methods, and models or templates that demonstrate the commitment to ongoing execution and progress tracking and rewards. In other words, a Data Leadership Playbook.

CHAPTER

ASSESSING CONDITIONS, CONTROLS AND CAPABILITIES

3

Assessment process is built with a policy-driven approach in mind. As any governance or risk-management executive will tell you, the trick to using policy to drive action is applying it in ways that people understand well enough to act upon. We have broken out three areas where an executive mandate produces requirements for action. This mandate is comprised of both mission or business strategy and compliance-based policies. The policies have to articulate priorities, resources, and measures at a level detailed enough to support each of these three areas, where action occurs. The first area is in assessment and planning. This is where we continually assess and monitor our conditions, controls, and capabilities, using gaps to identify required activities from our Playbook and then establishing execution sequences to close this gap. The second area centers around the execution approach, which includes a long-term roadmap and work plans. These plans include Playbook activities that you're going to use in the sequences and an approach to operationalizing governments. Playbook activities are structured to support both gap-fill and operational approaches so many of the activities described in the Playbook are ongoing or continuous in nature. Finally, we have to support the creation of measures and communication forms so that the impacts of our work are understood broadly. This is where measures become critical, since we have to measure our progress to plan for capital and our ongoing operational efficacy. These three areas of assessment and planning, execution, and impact monitoring are all driven by business and compliance policy requirements. Since the Playbook gives us procedures, we can show very close alignment in executing those procedures with what the policy mandates require.

Applying Policy & Procedure to Enterprise Data

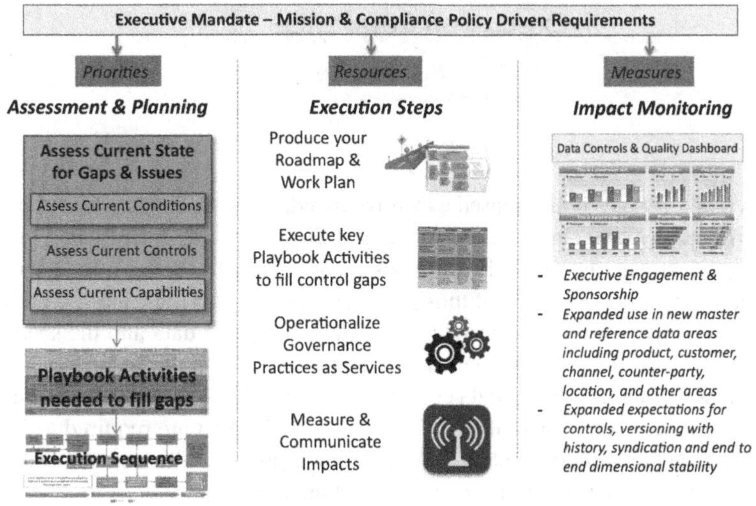

Executive Mandate – Mission & Compliance Policy Driven Requirements

Priorities — ***Assessment & Planning***

Assess Current State for Gaps & Issues
Assess Current Conditions
Assess Current Controls
Assess Current Capabilities
Playbook Activities needed to fill gaps
Execution Sequence

Resources — ***Execution Steps***

Produce your Roadmap & Work Plan
Execute key Playbook Activities to fill control gaps
Operationalize Governance Practices as Services
Measure & Communicate Impacts

Measures — ***Impact Monitoring***

Data Controls & Quality Dashboard

- *Executive Engagement & Sponsorship*
- *Expanded use in new master and reference data areas including product, customer, channel, counter-party, location, and other areas*
- *Expanded expectations for controls, versioning with history, syndication and end to end dimensional stability*

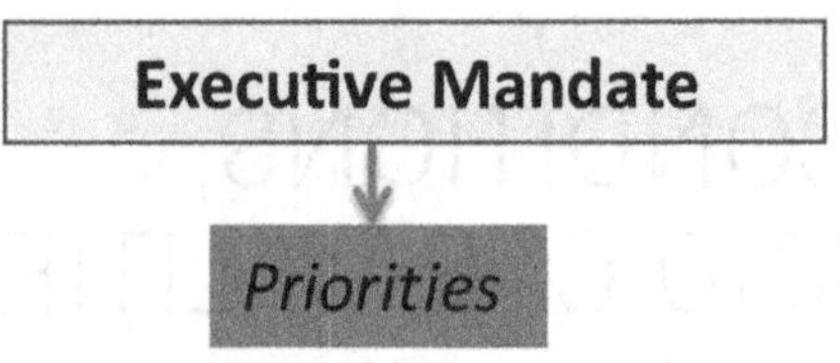

Assessment & Planning

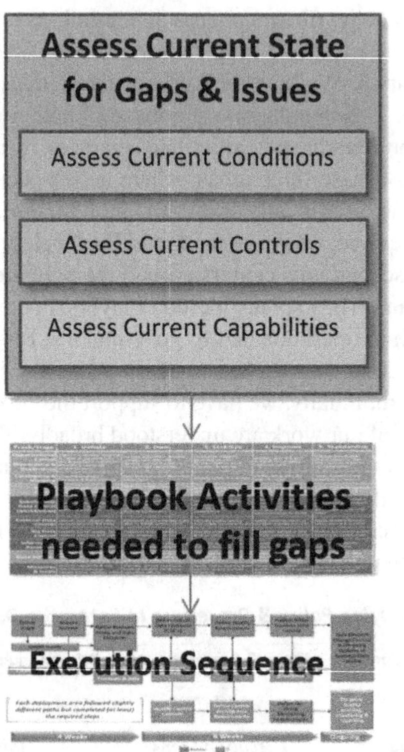

The first area that leverages policy-based executive mandates is assessment and planning, the focus of this chapter. We break down and describe in detail each of the assessment targets in the following two pages. Here we just want to highlight the assessment approach we're using to look at the conditions, controls, and capabilities for each of those subjects and the activities that should be provided for teams to perform. This assessment will provide us with the scope of data and the scope of the people necessary to close the gaps related to issues with data and issues with our teams' capabilities. Adding to a team's experience while improving data conditions and controls is a key construct in the Playbook. The output from the assessment is a series of Playbook activities that are required to fill the identified gaps. Those activities are then sequenced into an execution sequence, which can be added to the overall roadmap you are using for your program or permanent function.

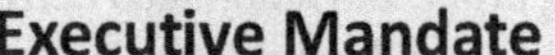

Execution Steps

Produce your Roadmap & Work plan

Execute key Playbook Activities to fill control gaps

Operationalize Governance Practices as Services

Measure & Communicate Impacts

The second area is in the execution of Playbook activities and its operational aspects. When you have a large program or corporate function for data and analytic governance, build out a roadmap that identifies which areas of the business, subjects of data, and terms you want to expand and improve upon. Identifying and expanding your Playbook set of activities to do this is a key step, because it provides standard methods and measures for your execution. This is typically a requirement of solid policies and procedures. Many of the activities are actually operational governance practices and can operate as an ongoing service. Identifying such activities is a compass in the Playbook, and many firms expand this area of the Playbook to describe large, complex global data services established at the request of the business or in partnership with them. Some of these services transition key resources during data administration and work in lines of business over to a global data service. Data services, like any other enterprise service, have service-level agreements and metrics associated with their delivery and outcomes. Data services often save the business time and money around their development and ongoing operational activities. A data service example is the duplication and validation of names and addresses against live and dead name indexes to ensure we reduce the scrap and rework of returned mail. More complex examples come from the Big Data arena, where we see new delivery tracking and emerging drone and automated delivery methods driving the need for much more precise delivery information. Identifying the right measures, and the best way to communicate those measures as they change and over periodic requirements, is the last stage in the execution steps.

Once the measures have been defined, they need to be vetted against the executive mandate to ensure all of the aspects of the policy-driven mandate are being addressed with regular measures and impact monitoring. This very dynamic area requires consistent measures as well as some flexible measures that can change over time. Flexible measures refer to services that change in scale, nature, or scope over time. Standard measures around data quality, availability, and impacts are maintained with baselines. Measures related to execution and resource levels are maintained against baselines over time. Executives can expect to see comparisons of long-term resources allocated after levels are expended and outcomes achieved.

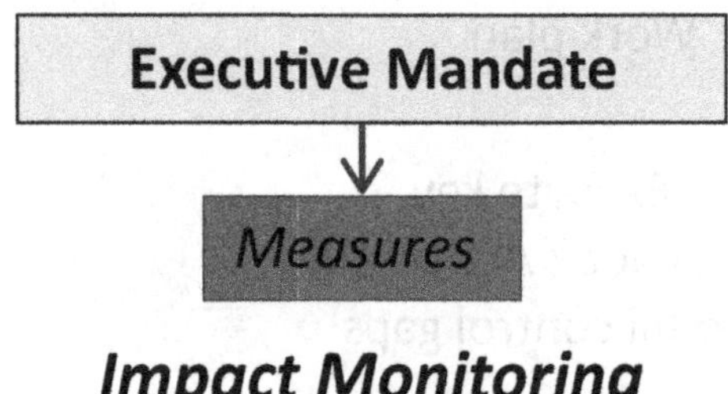

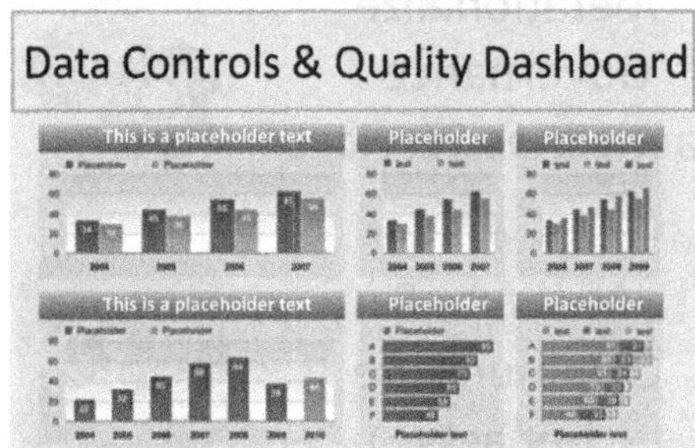

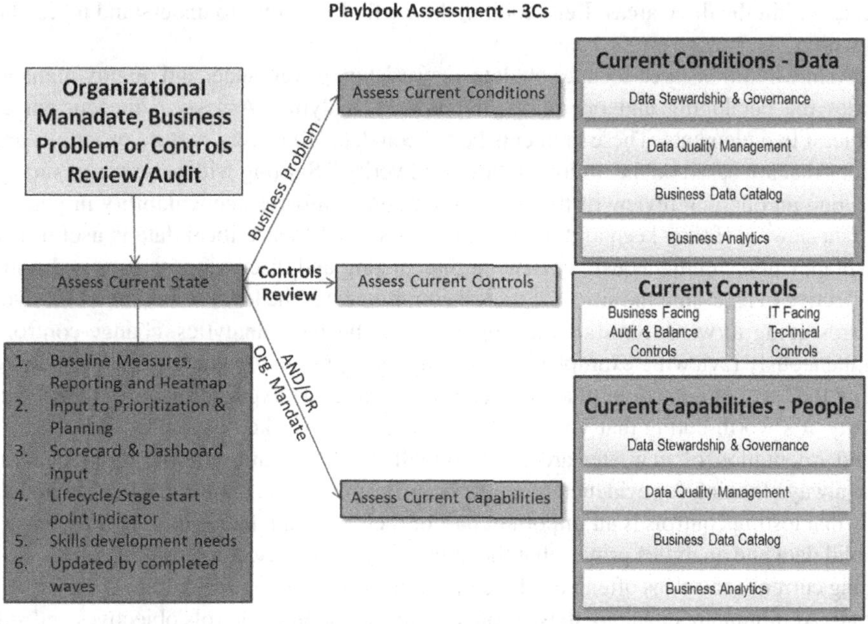

The Playbook assessment process is focused on three key areas, which collectively provide a clear view of the current conditions, controls, and capabilities of the enterprise, with regard to critical data and analytics. Many quality and governance programs focus on the conditions, and to some extent the capabilities, but often lack permanent controls and the measures that prove their efficacy. Balancing conditions, controls, and capabilities, as the Playbook suggests, ensures that our execution and operational support levels are consistently high enough to certify integrity and quality in our critical data and analytics. It's also worth noting that this approach focuses on assessing the current state of these areas, in order to create baseline measures that support ongoing reporting and heat mapping. In addition, the outcomes of the assessment work are inputs for prioritization and planning along with the demand management cycle, which we will address later. In order to make the assessment effective in terms of measuring the gaps, it's important to have baseline measures for each of the three areas in mind before you start. In this way, you ensure that your assessment is a fit-gap assessment that produces a list of gaps from expected values. Many data governance and related data management maturity models and assessment tools have been developed and published in the last 10 years. Each of these has unique value, but we came to the conclusion that the Playbook assessment approach was essential. This is because our emphasis includes a balanced focus on controls, whereas others are not as clear about that critical area. For example, it is important to be able to assess your capabilities with the controls focus in mind. Having strong data stewardship or analytic quality skill sets does not always translate into solid, reliable, and efficient controls in those areas. Thus it's important to look at the controls as well as the capabilities in order to gauge the amount of energy that is being consistently applied to operating solid controls. It is also important to remember that, as capabilities improve, controls efficiency should improve, because it takes less effort from a well-schooled and experienced resource to identify, put in place, and operate an effective control. So we can expect to see improvements across these three areas as they occur within the three areas. Let's look at the each of the areas to understand more about what we assess within.

The Current Conditions area focuses on data stewardship, governance, and quality management. It also includes the cataloging and operation of business analytics. Assessing the current condition requires at least two elements. These elements have been detailed in very mature programs and corporate functions that are based on the notion of "trust and verify." Starting with assessment surveys, while communicating an ongoing review of the work being done, enforces accountability in your stewards. Asking a data steward if they keep and maintain the catalog of their critical data is useful. But asking those questions while simultaneously reviewing that catalog and discussing its gaps and omissions is far more effective in assessing the situation and, it communicates the level of accountability you expect from stewards going forward. Similarly, asking about the business analytics, change-control process, while simultaneously reviewing examples of currently used production analytics, is far more effective in validating the level of control in place and communicating the expectations for controls going forward. Finally, it's worth noting that you will amass a series of worked examples that can be used for training and orientation of new stewards. Additionally, internal and external audit and regulatory experts are always looking for evidence of controls sufficiency in the conditions of data and analytics. They know that testing controls is an important part of their job, and that testing the way those controls result in solid data and analytics proves that the controls are being used consistently.

Assessing current controls is often best done in conjunction with internal audit and risk management professionals. At minimum, engaging these professionals in defining controls objectives and sufficiency tests is far more likely to result in a control's assessment profile that meets their requirements as well as your own. Risk and audit professionals are also continuously monitoring industry and public threats, risks, and best practices. This makes them solid partners in defining controls, based on the risk and exposure we face with data and analytics. Assessing data and analytic controls often requires some segregation of business-based audit and balance controls, from the IT-based technical controls. We are seeking an assessment of control effectiveness and efficiency, so we must test those who operate the controls in order to understand how well the controls themselves are being applied. We are simultaneously testing for whether the controls actually help us monitor, manage, and remediate risk and exposure based on our specific risk profile. We don't need to control or test controls for risks that we do not face or that do not rise to a level that necessitates controls. We do need to ensure that appropriate controls are in place and tested where there is known risk and exposure. Finally, it's worth noting that assessments should be conducted on a periodic basis to create a baseline for the ongoing controls' effectiveness and cost. We should also be collecting anecdotal information about controls that are known to have prevented loss or other risk from being realized.

Due to the way we interact with certain people, it can be difficult to measure people's data and analytics capability without skewing the measures. There are many complications identified with measuring people's behavior and attitudes in business settings. In this case, measuring capabilities is best quantified through their collective experience in executing the Playbook, managing controls, and reporting on status and issues. Our experience indicates that tracking people's outcomes with data and analytics governance is the surest way to determine their overall capability levels and commitment to quality. Here, as in current conditions, we're looking across data stewardship, governance, quality management, and analytics to understand how experienced and effective our people are. People's experience and the effectiveness of their part of our program or corporate function can be combined to determine our capability level in that area. However, we must not become too monolithic in the expression of summary information. Many capability models find it very difficult to provide granular views of differing capability levels or maturity levels across lines of business, geographies, and other business segments. We find it most useful to survey and observe, particularly with newer, less experienced people. Many times we see new people come into a company with a very long resume and list of accomplishments, but these do not always apply directly to the challenges in their new environment. So tracking their activities through survey and observation can identify where they are not aligning with the company's approach. Similarly, when you have somebody who is relatively inexperienced but rapidly adapts to challenges, this sort of assessment approach can highlight those abilities.

Now that we've covered the basic areas to assess and talked about the use of surveying and observation, we can address another input in the assessment process. Status reports compiled by the overall program, which describe the progress of their work across both the organization and the data scope, are a primary input. From quarter-to-quarter and year-to-year, we can expect to see progress in expanding a program or function across the company and addressing commensurately larger bodies of data and analytics. Tracking that progression across the company and its data is a critical part of evaluating the growth of the program's coverage. Many approaches use coverage as their primary measure of program success. We've found that doing so creates a gap between the perceived success rate and actual success rate, because what we identify as covered is often not treated in a consistent manner. We therefore use our assessment survey and observations to confirm that each area of the firm and subject area of data formally addressed by the programmer function is actually completely addressed to the level identified. Trusting in openly verifying with your business partners, who have invested time and energy into doing this well, is the surest way to confirm the coverage leads to success.

	Demand Management	Deployment	Outcome	
1	Problems, Issues, Requests & Application Enhancements	Engage Stakeholders	The first step engages stakeholders in with a quick survey of their major data problems, issues, and requests. This produces a list of prioritized demand by business areas.	Data Demands
2	Management Data Initiatives	Manage Demand Pipeline	The second step follows up with discussions and the capture of broader business and technology initiatives that depend upon or change data across systems. This produces a demand pipeline enabling us to supply our resources and services to the demands of our stakeholders.	Demand Pipeline
3	Enterprise Data Priorities	Weigh Strategic Goals	The third step weighs strategic enterprise goals, including transformation, industry and regulatory based initiatives or challenges. The result is the addition of supporting or enabling data activities and an overall strategic ranking of the pipeline to produce the Deployment Plan.	Deployment Plan
4	Data Road Map or Transition Plan	Manage Deployment Schedules	Deployment Schedules are produced from the Deployment Plan for each major business area so that resource and timing requirements can be detailed with stakeholder partners. Deployments are scoped at this point to the level of an "activity sequence".	Deployment Schedules Activity Sequences

All of the assessment outputs should be considered as evidence of progress and improvements. Where there are clear gaps in the current conditions, controls, and capabilities, we can circle back to the Playbook to identify the required sequence of activities to close the gaps or to bring up our overall levels as needed. Please remember that the Playbook can be customized and extended to address things that are critical or somewhat distinct to your company. But these assessed gaps are only part of our input into the overall roadmap and work plan for Playbook-based activities across the company. Another key input is a demand management function. We address this in other areas of the book, but need to summarize some steps here to show how we add inputs from it into the overall roadmap and work-planning effort.

Solid demand management for data and analytics engages stakeholders to understand their problems, issues, requests and enhancement needs but does not stop there. These various requirements for improvements and services must be vetted against two more levels. The first is management data initiatives, which can broadly address data and analytics needs that multiple groups of the company or key functions of the company have identified as gaps in today's environment. Those gaps often lead to a major project or initiative that addresses a number of the individual problems or issues we collected before. These initiatives also establish broader priorities and improve data and analytics based on what you choose to focus on and how far you go in making improvements. These initiatives are also critical because they have managed to acquire funding and executive sponsorship, and so are already a part of the committed demand pipeline.

The final level we have to include in our analysis of demand is a set of enterprise data and analytics priorities. These typically emerge from the executive team. Some of these will be reflected in the type of management data initiatives that are underway. Additional enterprise priorities will be reflected in strategic dashboards, goals and objectives, and mission maps, which the enterprise uses to drive organizational behavior. It's critical to understand the enterprise data priorities in some sort of ranked order, and these must be tied to desired outcomes, goals, or measures in order to be useful. We typically weigh the strategic goals by associating the initiatives that we reviewed and the request that we have of them. This gives us the ability to prioritize the coverage of initiatives and actions for requests and problems against the enterprise stated goals.

The combination of all of these components enables us to develop and maintain a roadmap or transition plan for data and analytics. It's important that this plan have a communicated sequence, along with the logic behind why things are sequenced the way the plan indicates. Therefore we need to point back to the enterprise data priorities and management data initiatives in order to indicate why we have sequenced our work in the manner the plan suggests. This plan produces deployment schedules, which become a work order for various parts of the organization to engage in Playbook activities. It also drives the supported activities and initiatives for the shared or global data services partners.

This demand management process adds a corporate management and local set of priorities to the assessment outputs, which helps us craft our overall pipeline and sequence a roadmap based on the priorities of the company. It allows us to adjust the prioritization we use from the demand management side against the gaps that the assessment has identified we need to fill. Demand management can also point out emerging areas where additional data and analytics capabilities are needed and may in fact need to be added to the Playbook. Recent examples include the ways companies are mapping Big Data with conventional database and other technologies. We will talk a bit about the data in a future chapter, but the first thing to think about in terms of governing is knowing when it makes sense to invest in the first place. Thus this approach allows us to balance the current assessments gaps and issues with the demand and priorities already in place, so that we address all of our issues in a prioritized way.

ASSESSMENT METHODS

Assessing your conditions, controls, and capabilities is a job best done using multiple methods and based on a number of factors. A key factor to consider is the type of people you're working with as you assess your 3Cs. People working in technical and operational areas have very limited time and may become impatient when asked to take large amounts of that time to answer questions or be observed. Another factor to consider is the way you ask questions or frame surveys. It is important that it's not overly obvious you're looking at these underlying conditions, controls, and capabilities; rather, you are looking at functional areas related to stewardship in governance. The survey below includes questions that are sectioned into four areas. These areas, while they relate to certain aspects of the 3Cs, are clearly written around functional activities and outcomes. We included the survey and observe columns to point out the fact that, while you may ask these questions in writing, through dialogue or perhaps in a facilitated session or meeting, you'll often need to include observations to validate the answers. The key factors in question framing and delivery are really centered around the nature of the people, the work they're doing, and the work environment they do it in. People who work in open, fairly busy, and often fairly noisy environments, operationally or in technology, are less apt to be able to answer questions or fill in surveys quickly. It may be more useful to pull them into short, facilitated sessions, where you ask the questions and get the answers.

Data Playbook Survey – Conditions

Survey Areas & Questions	Survey	Observe
Data Stewardship & Governance – Sponsorship & Resource Engagement (includes IT support)		
1. Do you have formal executive sponsorship?		
2. Do you have informal support at the Director level?		
3. Are Managers permitted or expected to address DSG?		
4. Do you have designated, experienced Data Stewards?		
5. Do you have time/action commitments from Data Stewards?		
6. Do you have designated Data SMEs?		
7. Do you have designated technical analysts or SMEs available?		
8. Do you have technical support for accessing technical meta data?		
9. Do you have production supported meta data services for cataloguing and publishing?		
Data Stewardship & Governance – Data Coverage (Includes Meta Data, Business Model)		
1. Do you have a current data glossary (logical or conceptual level) of business terms and definitions?		
2. Do you have a current data catalog of your physical data elements with definitions & owners?		
3. Have you prioritized your data elements in terms of financial or other criticality?		
4. Do you have a contextual model or listing of your business subject, function or process areas?		
5. Have you profiled or evaluated those subject areas for scope, criticality & resources?		
6. Have you mapped your critical data elements to their respective owners, stewards & subjects?		
7. Have you planned and assigned resources to DSG across subject areas?		
8. Have you mapped data intensive initiatives to subject area coverage?		
9. Do you currently have more than 25% of all listed CDEs under stewardship & change control?		
10. Do you currently have more than 50% of all listed CDEs under stewardship & change control?		
11. Do you currently have more than 75% of all listed CDEs under stewardship & change control?		
Data Quality Awareness and Management		
1. Have you assessed or profiled the quality of your CDEs?		
2. Have you defined your quality needs or requirements for your CDEs?		
3. Do you periodically monitor the quality of your CDEs		
Data Controls and Outcomes		
1. Have you identified your data handling and balancing points in data flows of CDEs?		
2. Have you defined the controls (ABCs) needed for those handling and balancing points?		
3. Do you monitor the control conditions and resolve events or exceptions?		

The key is to keep the period of time you spend asking questions or asking people to complete surveys to a minimum. Ideally, engage them with questions that get you to two levels of detail. We sometimes go through an iterative cycle of asking a subset of our questions in either a facilitated session or sitting with people as they do the work one-on-one. We also use online surveys wherever possible, then follow up one-on-one or in small groups. The reason for the face-to-face or facilitated session, where we have groups that can be drilled down or questioned, is to get context from those groups. We often hear people tell us they are doing certain work related to stewardship, for example, cataloging critical big business data terms and rules. But they don't go further in a private session or small group session with people they trust in order to share how that effort is typically done. Only when a major data problem has been identified through reporting or analysis do they undertake these sessions. These are all really valuable insights, and they reveal that your audience is committed to learning about how to do this work and is interested in finding a better way to move forward.

There is another critical factor in your method of getting questions answered, engaging with your stewards and subject matter experts, and understanding the underlying conditions, controls, and capabilities. This focuses on being able to observe, either directly or indirectly, the artifacts of the work you are asking people about. When we start to survey people or interview them about data controls, we must be careful to understand what they tell us in very specific ways. If, for example, a person tells us that they have detective controls for their financial and other critical data, because they are reviewing the data manually, we know to ask about how they do that annual review. There's nothing wrong with manually reviewing data when you don't have profiling tools, but it's unlikely, unless they're using a fairly sophisticated approach, that manual approaches can produce reliable, consistent results. Direct observation allows us to see the work they do as they do it, which means we can observe things like spreadsheets, Word documents, SharePoint documents, and even advanced stewardship and governance tools like Culebra and Oracle. This will help us understand how effectively they are using the tools they have, the change control they have over what they capture, and their methods for sharing these with other people. Indirect observation, where we request samples of these documents and artifacts as a result of our interview or survey-based questions, is another valuable way to assess the maturity of their capabilities and tools. It also provides insight into their documented controls and their understanding of the conditions of the data. So direct and indirect observation yields far deeper results than surveys and interviews alone can provide.

As you formalize your governance program or function, you'll be engaging stewards and subject matter experts in various meetings and other work sessions. This enables you to continuously gauge their activities, outputs, and challenges. It's important to formalize the way you look at their capabilities and to create meaningful measures that can be communicated simply and engender a sense of equality and fairness in evaluation methods. We'll look at capability measures later in this chapter and call out the fact that engaging people's capability maturity should be as empirical and comparable as possible across people and time. Finally, it's important to treat survey and interview results with care. We often collect more contextual information in the written results or interview notes than the direct questions would indicate. People will often tell us additional information beyond the answer to the question that was posed. For example, the first question in our surveyed sample size is: do you have formal executive sponsorship? We've had people answer this question "yes" or "no," and then explain why they answered as they did and who's involved in some of the history. That kind of information is much more sensitive than the direct answers to the questions themselves. Handling this in a private and confidential manner, and abstracting what we learned in that context, should obviously be treated with critical care as we engage in the process.

Let's take note of several aspects of the survey, since this can drive your interview questions, physical surveys, or online survey process. Our survey focuses on four key areas: Stewardship and Governance from a sponsorship and resource level, Data Coverage, Data Quality Awareness and Management, and finally Data Controls and Outcomes. These categories of questions are functionally oriented and intend to gather insight when asked in a professional manner. Note that this survey contains 26 questions across these four areas. This survey should only be used in an environment where a governance function or program has already been established. Even if it's just a local project, it will have formal leadership and activities occurring. In an environment with a functioning program, these questions would be relatively easy to answer, as they would be understood and answered affirmatively by those responding. We would need to tailor these questions to place them at a level that is appropriate for a firm or a business area that has not yet engaged in formal stewardship and governance. We would also adjust the categories of questions that we select around the experience level we know to be in place or expect to find. Therefore adjusting for all of these factors is something you need to do at the beginning and over time as maturity levels improve.

Now that we've covered various methods to get answers to our questions about the 3Cs, discussed the way you get these answers, and covered the way you engage people, it is time to consider the kinds of answers and how to aggregate them into a coherent picture. Producing a coherent picture of conditions, controls, and capabilities requires a bank of empirical information that is quantifiable as well as anecdotal. The best way to depict a complex system of people, processes, technology, and data, like a governance program, is to blend quantifiable data with qualified data. When looking to take a snapshot of a program or function across the business, we're looking to understand how that area is progressing on its journey toward maturity. We also want to understand the results that come from having solid controls and governance in place. We want to create visualizations based on measures that enable people to see the current conditions and competitors. But we also want to capture some of the anecdotal stories and context. This can be shared at least verbally if not in writing as we share the quantifiable data illustrations. Asking these questions in ways that produce quantifiable answers (eg, on a scale from 1 to 10 how solid and consistent has your executive sponsorship been over the past 6 months?) as well as capturing stories and contextual information is essential. Finally, it's very important to take the pulse of the people you rely upon to do important governance work. Their attitude, level of energy and engagement, and level of frustration and concern, are all things you want to note as you survey and analyze results. We typically gather quotes from people about their overall experience. Often these are offered before we can even ask, but we always get the respondents' permission and make the comments anonymous before sharing them with the group and with executive management.

As you compile your results and start building visualizations, it is valuable and important to share draft versions of your graphical outputs and your storylines with the people from whom you gather the information. You want to engender a sense of trust and belief that this process is sustainable and valuable. Showing people the ways you are aggregating their responses and the expected perception of those responses is a great way to keep the teams willing to participate in this going forward. Be aware that as you move questioning people across the line of business operational area, they'll talk with each other very quickly and some skewing in the way questions are answered can result. When we encounter this behavior, we sometimes change the questions as we move from the subgroup or even person-to-person. Having an array of similar but differently worded questions gives us the right outputs and is useful in undermining skewering bias. The last point you should consider is the control questions themselves. We sometimes find that asking about controls results in very uncomfortable answers. Occasionally we have found that there are little or no controls in place and that this lack of controls is reflective of a broader lack of controls. This can be very disconcerting, especially after a program has been running for some period of time. In these cases it is fair to capture what people share about broader controls, such as corporate governance, financial controls, and so on. However, this should not be shared with anyone except an executive sponsor in a private session and should not be attributed unless respondents are willing to do so.

ASSESSING DATA CONTROLS: AUDIT AND BALANCE CONTROLS

Let's move into more specific assessment areas, assuming that both direct and indirect observation have been used to augment physical, electronic, or direct interview surveys. Understanding and applying a simple framework for data and analytics controls is central to evaluating the level of effectiveness of controls in place.

Audit & Balance Controls Grid – Control Points & Types

	Control Points → (placement locations)	SOURCE (AUDIT)	MOVEMENT (AUDIT)	TARGET (AUDIT & BALANCE)
	Control Point Examples in the Target Architecture for each Control Type	Transaction Processing Systems of Record, External service provider, External data provider...	Data Movement, Integration and Replication Mechanisms (ETL, FTP, ESB.SOA, ...)	Downstream application, ODS, DW, DM, ...
CONTROL TYPES	**Detection** Detect all manner of material variances & deficiencies with data, provide specific output to support analysis, maintain audit trail of issues and quality levels	**SOURCE DETECTION CONTROL** Includes profiling and query based review	**MOVEMENT DETECTION CONTROL** Includes before/after audit totals and comparisons	**TARGET DETECTION CONTROL** Includes both the audit of data and comparative balance analysis of target and source values
	Correction Corrective measures to resolve problems identified in detection controls, maintain audit trail through capture of all original and corrected values as required	**SOURCE CORRECTION CONTROL** Includes data changes based on validation rules, rejection and suspense processing for user correction	**MOVEMENT CORRECTION CONTROL** Includes suspense handling by originator with corrected values, cross-reference look up of valid replacement values, ... based upon the controls specification	**TARGET CORRECTION CONTROL** Reset data types as required to support physical indexing and join select conditions per ***controls specification.***
	Prevention Requires changing causes of data problems and deficiencies at the source with the support of the source provider or preventing downstream propagation based on root cause analysis of detection control generated issues and deficiencies.	**SOURCE PREVENTION CONTROL** Includes application edits, system based entry or acceptance controls	**MOVEMENT PREVENTION CONTROL** Includes rejection & suspense handling to prevent deficient data from downstream propagation	Not applicable

This audit and balance controls grid describes control points and types we've used successfully for a number of years. The original ABC grid was developed by Knightsbridge solutions, a firm where we were all partners for a number of years, and which was known as a leading data integration and analytic delivery leader. The ABC framework helps us point out simple ways of applying three types of controls across three basic levels of control points. We use detection, correction and prevention to describe the different control types that are prevalent, observable and effective in an analytic environment. We understand that detection is the core control type and is the most prevalent, since it is necessary to determine correction and prevention requirements and options. Many firms and lines of business have matured to the point of using detection along with correction in an iterative cycle. This is because prevention-level controls are the most difficult to build and deploy. They often require code, base-level changes to applications, and databases. One example of prevention is the use of validation edits in an application. Validation edits ensure that when new records are added or changes are made to a record, certain fields, such as gender, age, zip code, and other known, valid values, are forced to select from only those valid values. We often see manual processes for the detection of variances from those values and after-the-fact corrections as the de facto standard when improving the base application is too costly or beyond our reach.

Knightsbridge applied this type of thinking to the source, movement, and target population areas of data and analytics. Most of the analytics work we did with data controls was about backtracking control gaps as a result of analytic inaccuracy or inconsistency. Today, we know that analytics are built with many of these controls embedded, since the data integration, particularly with Big Data, is done with analytic streams and applications. Advanced analytics today therefore requires a combination of data and analytic output controls. Put simply, analytics now spans the source, movement, and target levels. Understanding where to place detective, corrective, and preventive controls across source, movement, and target location is the job of data-quality and controls experts. Engaging enterprise risk management, audit, information security, and other experts in the organization of consulting firms is often necessary and is a good practice to ensure control sufficiency. Remember that your internal audit and enterprise risk management professionals will at some point be reviewing data and analytics controls for critical enterprise data including financial data, customer data, and regulatory reporting. The ability to define these control types and locations or placement is critical to assessing your controls efficacy.

CONTROLS REPORTING—ABC CONTROL LEVELS

Below is an example of a control's assessment report we can use to summarize control conditions for an area of your program or function.

CONTROL POINTS	Data Generation or Ingestion	Data Movement & Integration	Data Storage & Delivery
	Source Audit	Movement Audit	Target Audit &Balancing
Detection Controls	• Controls in place • Monitoring in place • Reporting in place • Gaps	• Controls in place • Monitoring in place • Reporting in place • Gaps	• Controls in place • Monitoring in place • Reporting in place • Gaps
Correction Controls	• Controls in place • Monitoring in place • Reporting in place • Gaps	• Controls in place • Monitoring in place • Reporting in place • Gaps	• Controls in place • Monitoring in place • Reporting in place • Gaps
Prevention Controls	• Controls in place • Monitoring in place • Reporting in place • Gaps	• Controls in place • Monitoring in place • Reporting in place • Gaps	
Overall Controls Level			
Audit Trail Level	Complete	Sufficient	Insufficient

This chart summarizes some statistical measures gathered in observations and interviews and applies them in a way that allows us to score them for audit trail and overall control levels. One of our goals with this type of report is to use a format and communication method similar to what enterprise risk management typically uses to measure corporate governance for business and operational controls. Bar and pie charts, radar diagrams, and advanced visualizations are all equally useful and depend on the appetite of the audience. We always try to understand the range of people who will be acting upon these reports. So while we need to be able to summarize a level appropriate to executives and sponsors, we also need to make sure this resonates with the people whom we have interviewed and reviewed conditions with. It's also important to note that these things change over time, so being able to compare one to another over a period of one or two quarters is important. The ability to look at them side-by-side and see the changes and even put directional indicators on the measures is also useful. We have found that putting too much on the slides makes them unreadable, so it's a constant balancing act that you'll sort out as you understand your audience and needs over time. In addition to a report like this, the anecdotal information you've gathered from people, without attribution, is an ardent voiceover you can use when you present these reports. When you have an insufficient area, as this report does, such as data storage and delivery for detection and correction controls, it's important to have a voiceover about whether that area is going to change in the near future, or has other challenges that would explain this state. It's also important to gather anecdotal evidence about the level of executive support your respondents are getting and the number of resources they have in order to fully contextualize the report.

CAPABILITY MEASUREMENT

Earlier we discussed four-capability level determination. We do not determine or assess capability generically or monolithically at the pure program level. We've found that it is simply too aggregated a level for the score to be meaningful or actionable. Instead, we identify the kinds of activities that must be performed and the scope of that performance across data and the business. We use a series of three-dimensional constructs to help visualize a company and its data and show where these capabilities are being exercised and applied in those areas. Assessing people's capability is very valuable and important but also very sensitive, so what we've learned to do is determine with key sponsors what level of experience we require people to have to progress through various designations of capability.

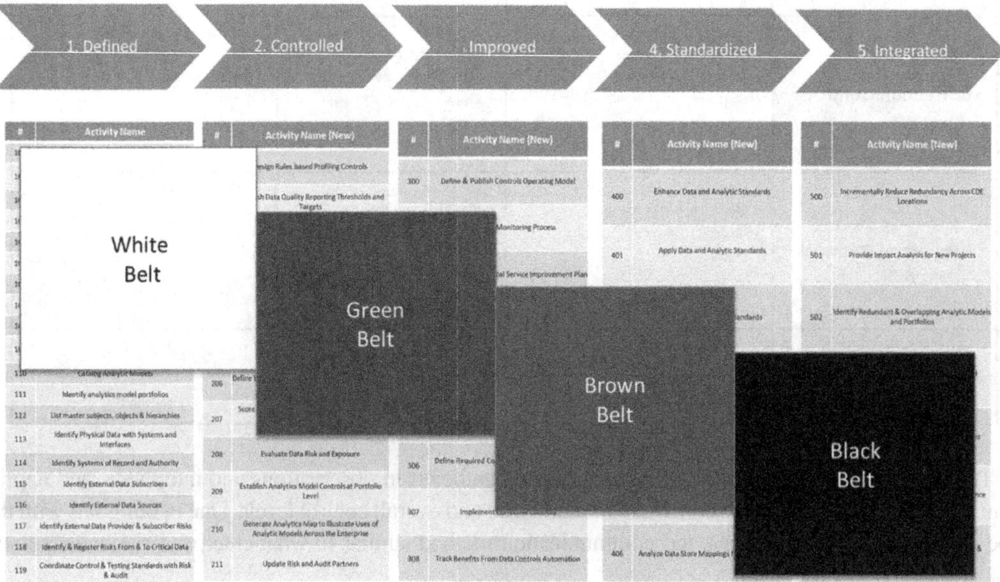

We often use the karate belt analogy, such as white, green, brown, and black belts, to depict or reflect the overall level of experience people have gained over time. Some firms choose to give credit for attending industry conferences and training sessions along with credit for the work that has been performed in the firm. The key is that each belt is reflective of actual work performed following your Playbook approach. As a person moves from white, to green, to brown, they develop mentoring and leadership skills as a result of moving up in the organization and managing the team or teams of people doing data and analytic governance work. These are often people who lead data and analytics delivery and take on governance functions as part of their responsibilities, which is a highly desirable outcome since it ties accountability for the quality and control of data analytics to the person responsible for delivering them in the first place. A black belt is generally reserved for someone who has successfully led multiple successive program iterations or corporate waves of governance across multiple parts of the business. These belts are not grades as we might apply to a student on a report card. They must never be communicated as an indication of the quality of work people are doing. Our approach is to treat people as successful based on their continuing roles and responsibilities. It is the job of their direct report supervisor or manager, as well as indirect report data governance and analytic governance managers, to continuously assess their performance and manage them accordingly. This capability measurement is about the experience gained and assumes ongoing success.

This is an example of different levels of experience and the resulting belts that are awarded based on that experience. Notice that we include things like formal classroom and online training. We also include testing and mentorship activities, but we are very specific about the level of experience and outcomes necessary as part of the test to make it to the new belt.

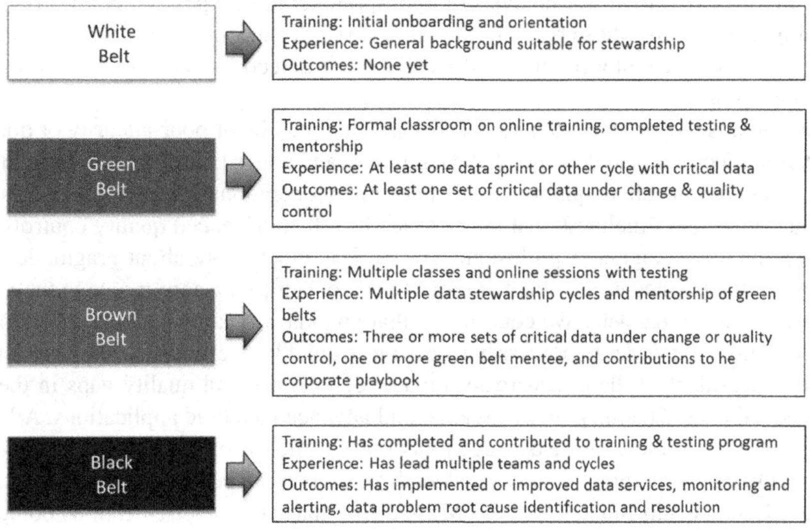

DATA AND ANALYTIC CONDITIONS REPORTING—A RISK AND EXPOSURE APPROACH

We've covered the ways we can communicate controls and capabilities, now let's address data conditions. Many programs benefit from general health statuses of their program's coverage in terms of data, organization, adoption, and so forth. We'll look at those areas in a moment. We've found that a heat map or similar way of looking at data risk and exposure is the best means of expressing a program's coverage. This is another area in which partnering directly with enterprise risk management and internal audit is extremely valuable. This work should be done in conjunction with the professionals, as they will be able to determine the appropriate thresholds and scoring values for enterprise risk and exposure into key areas.

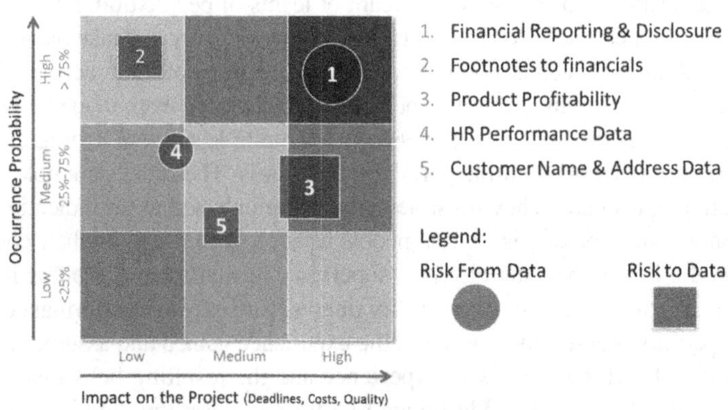

The first area is data at risk, or risks specific to data. Some of these can be visualized as gaps in controls around the production and use of data, which can put data integrity and reliability at immediate risk. Risk to data is a key driver for analysis of appropriate control types and control points and will ultimately mitigate or resolve those risks. Data that is at risk for inconsistency due to a lack of control over the way data is entered, moved, or stored clearly needs detection controls at a minimum and prevention controls optimally.

The second area is risk arising from the use of data that may be of poor integrity or quality for the intended use. It's important to understand that data quality and integrity are often a suitability issue. We can't afford to get absolute about quality levels, since many operational processes and systems require data at a certain level and timeliness that may not lend itself to advanced quality controls and levels. This is never a matter of dogma or philosophy for us; it is much more about pragmatic approaches, which ensure that the businesses are able to produce and consume data appropriate to their needs. This approach always emphasizes detective controls, so that you know what the quality levels are and what risks you may be taking in order to process business more quickly or efficiently. Risk arising from data requires more assessment of the downstream impacts of integrity and quality gaps in the data. This includes embedded data, data integration streams, and advanced analytic applications. A key example that has proven itself over more than a decade in this space is the use of the Data Relationship Management tool from Oracle Corporation by advanced analytic users of Hyperion tools from Oracle Corporation. The Data Relationship Manager, or DRM, is a tool that provides tremendous control over the generation and change of mission-critical financial hierarchies and complex data relationships. Using this tool appropriately creates a preventive control for major financial reporting and analytics, which prevents risks from data arising and driving significant exposures, financial statements, projections, and decision-support outputs.

Together, these two areas of data risk and exposure should be measured and heat mapped with executives on a regular basis and in collaboration with enterprise risk management and internal audit. Getting the measures correct for the proper placement in the heat map and identifying the difference between risk from data and risk to data areas has proven to be a critical value proposition for our clients.

OVERALL REPORTING AND VISUALIZATION

We now cover the assessment and assessment scoring and recording process for all three areas: conditions, controls, and capabilities. What we found in repeated engagements with clients across industries is the need to visualize the firm or the area of the company we are dealing with on a three-dimensional scale. Existing maturity models tend to look very flat and are difficult to see visually as differentiated across different parts of the company or the data and analytics areas you are assessing. There are two ways we've seen this work effectively in a three-dimensional world. The first approach can be disassembled and manipulated for more granular expressions of overall conditions or specific areas of concern. The other approach is to use geographic models for large organizations but that model is more specific to certain industries, such as oil and gas, so we elected to use the cube representation in this book.

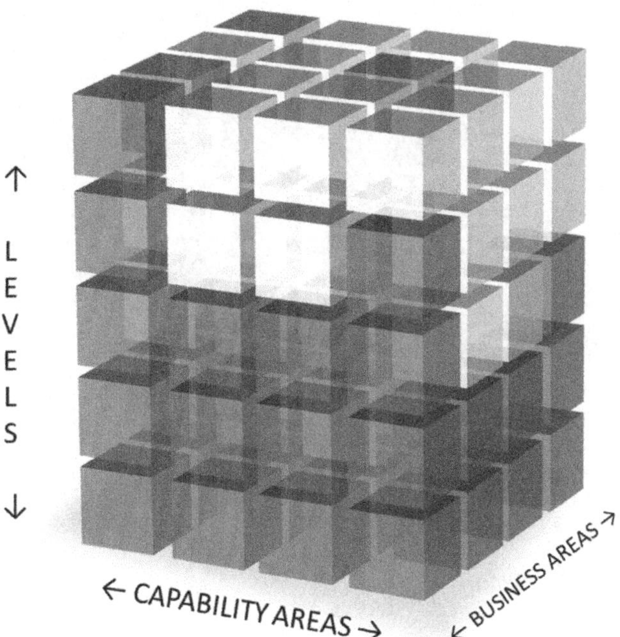

This cube representation allows us to color code subcubes in a way that gives us a very quick visual identification of overall conditions. In this example, you see the capability areas represented across the bottom row, the business areas going back through the data, and the level of maturity achieved from bottom to top. This is a relatively intuitive visual that can be shared all the way up the executive level. Using different colors and coloring from the bottom to the top and across capability areas by business area visually represents the penetration of governance activities into the organization. There is one note of caution on any and all reporting and visualizations we need to point out here. We view any form of assessment we provide management with as potentially critical to their current conditions and therefore very sensitive. We handle that information with great care in terms of our own systems and distribution, as well as the way we present it to clients. We often preview our detailed results with the people from whom we gathered them, while holding the aggregate reporting and visualizations for a very select few sponsors. These sponsors can direct us on how far and wide they want to distribute or share the information. They typically choose to distribute and expose them broadly in order to move behaviors and develop reasonable expectations about what must be accomplished. But where results are highly sensitive and a program or corporate function is just getting underway, executive sponsors often use discretion and control distribution until they feel people will fully understand what it represents. It is essential that people do not take this as a poor score or result on their part, which could negatively impact their careers. Instead, they should be able to contextualize it with regard to the amount of change they feel is needed and the sponsorship they are willing to provide.

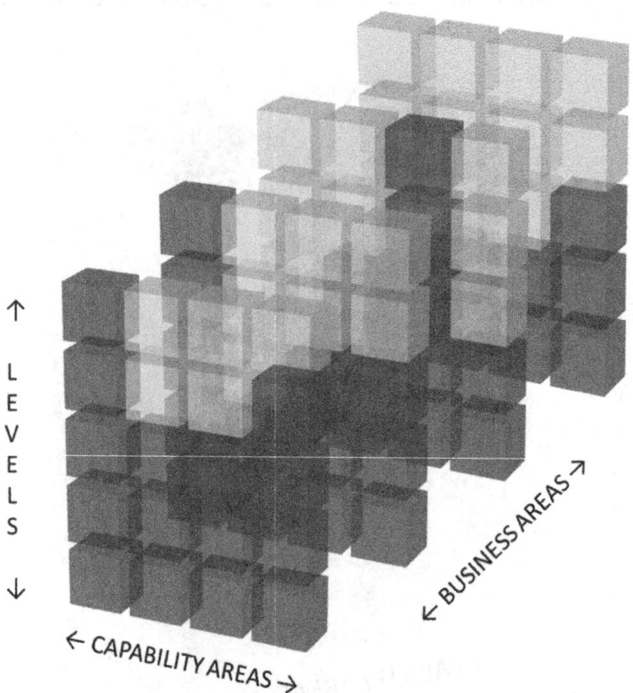

The overall 3-D cube is very useful at the executive and management level. Snapshots of this as conditions change over time are also directly comparable and useful in board, steering committee, governance council, and other group settings. We have found with working groups, lines of business, and other regional or local groups that decomposing the cube into 3-D grids is a more useful way to dive into a granular set of views. These decompositions provide meaningful views of a subset of the business, typically a business area or geography, as you see in this exploded view. Determining the right way to visualize and communicate information is always a challenge; it puts us in the business of providing analytics and visualization. So let's be clear about governing our own data and analytics as part of this process. We should be following our own advice and guidance in terms of using Playbook activities to control the quality and integrity of our data in the analytic outputs we produce for our clients. Put simply, it means that we should treat this as a testable data and analytics. Our work product is our attestation of our assessment and analysis of their conditions. We need to be prepared to provide evidence of our quality-control process, even as we assess our client's quality-control process and outcomes. As a client, if you are consulting and internal resources are engaging in this work, is it certainly fair and reasonable to ask on a regular basis about the controls they apply to their own processes, data, and analytic outputs they are asking you to rely upon.

SUMMARY

This chapter has provided specific examples and an approach, including an assessment framework the controls framework, for understanding current conditions, controls, and capabilities. These examples have been used in many clients and industries over two decades of shared experience. That said, it's equally important that these examples and approaches resonate with you and your needs. So we encourage you to review these in detail, consider how they would work for you, and contemplate what changes may make them even more valuable for you. The key to the Playbook-based approach is that we use standard methods and introduce standard measures to understand and improve our data and analytics.

CHAPTER

DETAILED PLAYBOOK ACTIVITIES

4

PLAYBOOK FRAMEWORK: CAPABILITY ORIENTATION

Capability models are typically used to plan and measure progression toward what are known as maturity levels for specific types of capabilities. Capability maturity models emerged and became highly standardized within the software development and technology development markets. The most well-known of these, the Software Engineering Institute Capabilities Maturity Model, has long been used to evaluate not only software development capabilities but also a broad array of technical and development capabilities. Much has been made of the CMM SEI model being the standard for capability maturity but new models have emerged that differ significantly based on the need they serve.

Our approach differs from models targeting development capabilities in two ways.

- First, we start at a target level of initial achievement, leaving the preceding level (chaos, ad hoc, initial) as Level Zero. We are forward looking, not diagnostic with our progression.
- Second, we use a different maturity sequence, because we need to emphasize governance strengths and prerequisites. We must define the data we will govern and the way we will govern it before we can actually govern (control, improve, standardize) it. We are not trying to support development activities or methodologies.

We applaud the EDM Council for recognizing the need for a more data-oriented view of these capabilities; they have created the first differentiated model for data. Their data management capability maturity model is central to their overall approach and fully supports their combined mandate of governance and development.

COMPARATIVE VIEWS OF INDUSTRY MATURITY MODELS

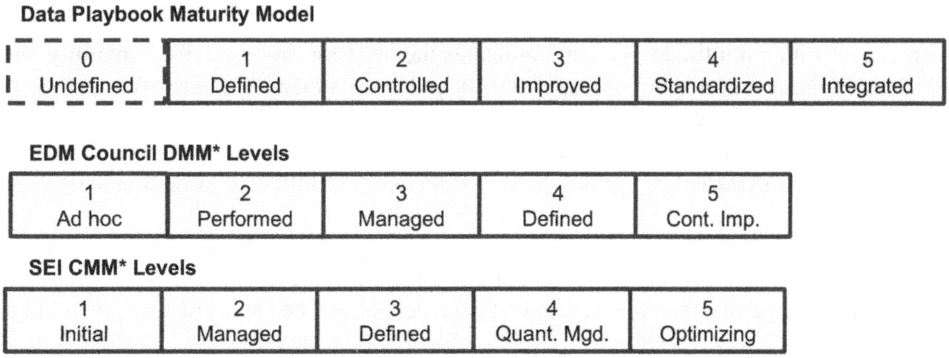

Data Playbook Maturity Model

0	1	2	3	4	5
Undefined	Defined	Controlled	Improved	Standardized	Integrated

EDM Council DMM* Levels

1	2	3	4	5
Ad hoc	Performed	Managed	Defined	Cont. Imp.

SEI CMM* Levels

1	2	3	4	5
Initial	Managed	Defined	Quant. Mgd.	Optimizing

*EDM Council DMM and CMM are copyright or trademark materials of the Enterprise Data Management Council and SEI respectively.

We've taken a specific approach to leveraging the thinking behind capability maturity models. We've done this in order to describe capabilities in a specific way as well as the stages through which people acquiring those capabilities evolve. Our approach to capabilities is to treat them as the combination of ability and capacity. The Playbook provides a way to improve and add to the abilities of key people throughout the organization so that they may manage, improve, and control data and analytics. The Playbook also provides methods for assessing, deploying, and operationalizing key aspects of data and analytics management. Getting work done using standard methods across a defined scope and obtaining key outcomes from that work would be indicative of a capability maturity level being reached. We have found that we need to adjust the capability levels that are described in the typical maturity model so that our framework is unique and specific to the domains of data and analytics. Our focus also highlights the measurement of outcomes as indicators of reaching certain levels of maturity over time, rather than simply measuring activity as a reflection of improving capabilities. Our business goals always drive our technical work, so we measure outcomes from the work to show both business impact and value as well as capability improvements. In this way, capability improvement actually reflects the aggregate of business outcomes and value produced.

We also note very carefully that capability levels are achieved at different levels of speed across an organization. In some organizations, cross-functional or enterprise functions such as finance, marketing, sales, and others excel at certain types of data stewardship and governance because of their specific needs. Organizations value the outcomes of these areas but often leverage those efforts into another line of business, enabling functions of the enterprise. Other firms or organizations choose to start with a top-down approach and establish enterprise governance functions, programs, and resources in order to proceed across the organization and improve capabilities and outcomes. Both approaches yield valuable results, and the selection of an approach is really a reflection of a business's priorities. The key is understanding that we typically do not reach specific capability levels at the same time across the entire business and that this condition does not indicate any loss or inefficiency. Rather, it indicates real-world situations that individual lines of business and cross-functional areas face as they adopt stewardship and governance methods.

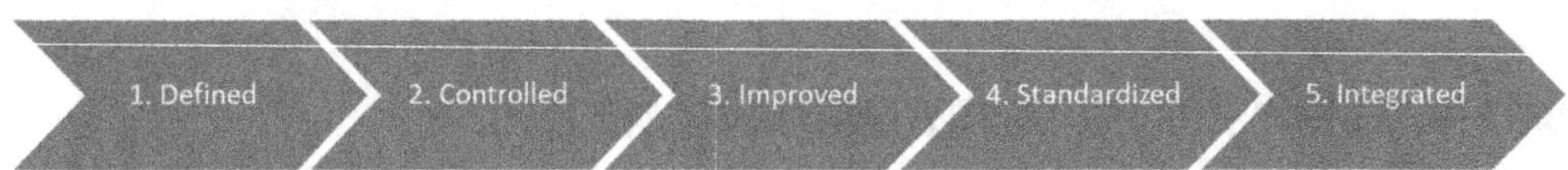

Our experience with a multitude of clients indicates the need for more specific capability levels or stages, whose names evoke a sense of responsibility and commitment. We have also come to recognize the need to start at a Level I, rather than starting with ad hoc, disorganized, or other free, formal activity levels. Level I requires some consistent degree of methods and activities and conveys the sense that, once you start this journey, you should be committed to formal outcomes and improvements.

Additionally, it's important that the name of the phase or level reflects the conditions of the data, analytics, and activities at the end of that level. For example, when we describe a capability level as "defined" then we're suggesting that, for the scope of data, people, and business areas for any particular effort, that the data or analytics are defined. We've also found that, in adopting the mindset that John Zachman established in his framework for enterprise architecture, there are many slices and iterations of work that occur throughout an organization to progress through these capability levels. The discipline that John Zachman provides us is extremely important in this area and encourages an understanding of how to work through many levels of detail, associating our work based on crime, or foundational elements.

Now let's look at the specific capability levels to understand why we named them as we have and what is expected as each level is achieved in any given part of an enterprise.

1. Defined

We start our framework by identifying the minimum foundation required for success in each of the subsequent levels. The essential first step is to define the scope of work and the specific data, analytic components and portfolios of any part of the organization. We presume, in the absence of an assessment demonstrating that this step has already been taken, that the current circumstances are at best ad hoc and at worst utterly absent data and analytic definitions. We also assume there is no defined program or function for doing this work. We expect this capability level to be fully realized in any part of the organization when both the program or functional aspects of the work are clearly defined and supported with specific roles and when some scope of data and analytics has been carefully defined and cataloged.

In the second capability level, we leverage the work we did to define our assets in order to managing them through the establishment of an initial set of controls over these assets. The work done in the first capability level also supports our identification of which assets and activities are critical to the enterprise and therefore merit specific and ongoing control. Finally, because we have engaged stakeholders and execution resources in a coordinated manner, we are able to define and standardize controls specific to our quality requirements.

Moving to an improvement posture requires the previous work to define, prioritize, and establish controls and quality requirements for our critical assets and activities. The consistent engagement of stakeholders and execution resources through our program ensures the ability to apply cost-benefit analysis and business case validation to the improvements we identify in this level. The execution of these improvements and enhancements to the controls we previously established creates sustainable, measurable and valuable impacts business constituents.

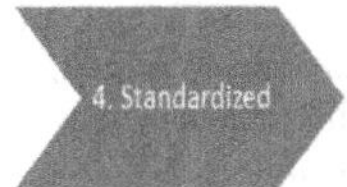

Standardization of our assets and activities is a very challenging and rewarding capability level. Standardization of data, analytic models, and analytic portfolios enables more reliable and rapid change capabilities in the enterprise, while asserting a consistent level of quality and change control. The level of skill required to standardize data and analytics will be built up through the execution of Levels I–III. It is important to note that this sequence must be followed for you to be able to standardize assets and activities for any particular set of data and analytics. Standardization specifically requires that we are applying explicitly documented quality and performance standards to our critical data and analytics activities.

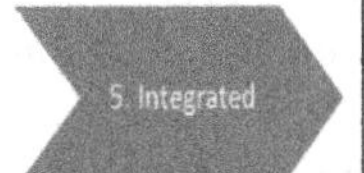

Integration is something all organizations continuously attempt with varying levels of success. Integration and consolidation are not routinely possible or sustainable without completion of the previously described capability levels. It is almost impossible to reliably consolidate or integrate data that has not first been carefully defined and quality tested. The additional requirements imposed through control, improvement, and standardization establish a solid foundation for evaluating the authority level, quality level, veracity, and reliability of data. This enables us to select the "winners" and "losers" in any consolidation effort. On achieving this level of capability, large amounts of redundant or nonauthoritative data and analytic components will be removed, and future redundancy will be largely prevented or control.

PLAYBOOK FRAMEWORK: CAPABILITIES

We've covered the capability-level progression and described what is accomplished and expected as you achieve each level. Now we move on to understanding the capability areas that describe the skills, type of work, and specific activities of the Playbook framework. Capabilities are often treated as work-streams when planning specific projects, sprints, or waves of deployment for the Playbook. It is critical to respect interdependencies across these capability areas when planning the work and assembling the resources in your program. Each of these capabilities is described below and has specific activities associated with it in the Playbook.

Note that there are only four capability areas covered in detail in this book. We have defined and deployed a total of 10 capability areas for clients across industries, including financial services, health-care, and federal government agencies. The scope and length of this book is intended to focus on core capability areas, on which all other capabilities rely or are built.

Govern programs and service

The data playbook framework distinguishes governance from stewardship by applying governance at the top level of a data or analytics program as well as at the enterprise service level, where data or analytic services have been standardized and deployed as a shared set of services. This capability area includes activities related to establishing the charter, scope, organizational structure, operating model and performance measures for your program and the services it provides.

Steward data and analytics

We define the Stewardship capability as the places where data and analytics are expressly defined, controlled, improved and managed with business and technical representation. This is the primary capability in which data and analytics stewards engage with their assets, activities, and stakeholders in a sustained engagement containing specific scope, measures, and outcomes. Stewardship applies the authority of governance established in the previous capability in order to create controls concerning the quality changes of your critical data and analytic assets.

Coordinate data relationship

Data relationship coordination is a capability that has become necessary due to the critical-importance and special-handling requirements for master, reference, and hierarchy data. Managing relationships amongst controlled or valid sets of values within a single domain, such as customer or product, becomes critically important when hundreds of reports, dashboards, and analytic visualizations rely on them. Special activities are often required to manage data relationships of both internally mastered and externally referenceable data, so we have established a separate capability area and specific activities for that purpose.

Manage quality and risk

Our experience in multiple industries, where the quality of data and analytics directly impacts the risks associated with that data, has shown that we need to think more broadly about quality management and include risk in this critical capability. Risk-weighted quality measures, as well as specific measures of risk resulting from quality issues, are becoming commonplace in industries such as government, financial services, and healthcare. This capability addresses both critical functions with specific, proven activities.

The Playbook construct has been used by a variety of practitioners and analysts to describe a dizzying array of activities, technologies, and methods with very little empirical structure or discipline. Our approaches have taken over a decade to build, validate, deploy, and refine to a point where we could publish them for broad consumption. Part of that discipline and experience includes addressing various aspects of Playbook application and relevance to data and analytics. In our focus and discipline world, we see three overall phases of activity that organizations must engage in and complete successfully in order to assert sustainable control over their critical data and analytic assets.

Much has been made of offensive and defensive Playbook strategies that roughly align with the notion of control, the defensive mode, and improvement, the offensive mode. Control over data and analytics is increasingly associated with the three-lines-of-defense model, prevalent in the financial services industry and emerging in the healthcare and digital healthcare marketplace. Improvement is associated with enterprise performance progressions that result from higher-order data and analytic quality.

Consolidation and integration of critical, shared enterprise assets is increasingly important as we continue to expand the universe of data and analytics generated by our business, not all of which fits neatly into the "Big Data" bucket. Even the maturing cloud-computing and storage market cannot completely alleviate the continuously growing cost curve for the high-volume, high-velocity data that includes enterprise performance information and analytics.

These three high-level phases associated with the five capability levels, known as Govern, Improve, and Consolidate, are often helpful in explaining to executive teams and other high-level sponsors what we are trying to accomplish and why our focus is on these areas.

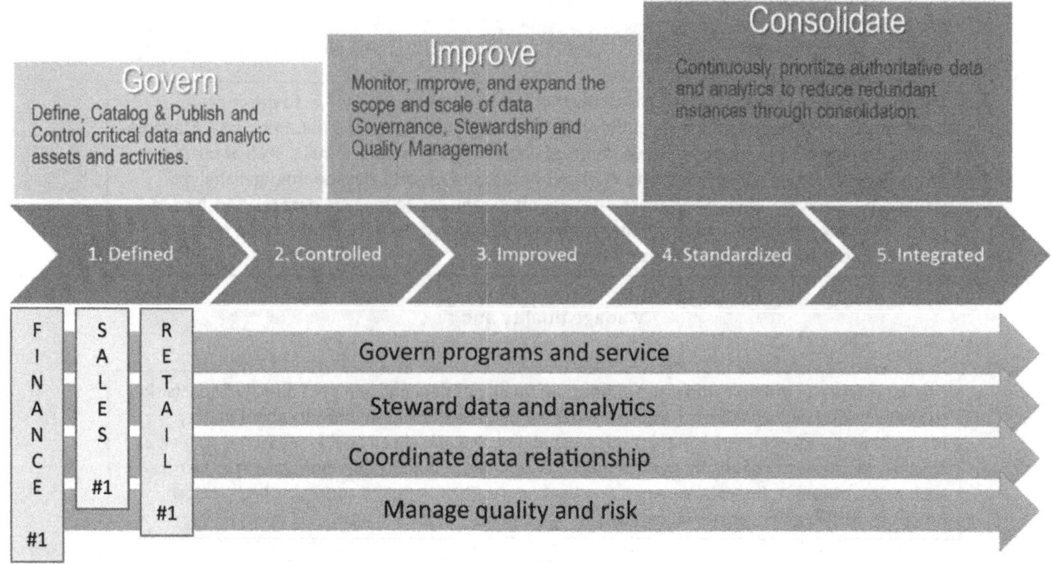

This graphic illustrates the way different parts of an enterprise may progress through the first capability level using projects, sprints, or waves of deployment for one or more capability. Capability areas describe the type of work, outcomes, and skills associated with specific domains of data and analytic management. Work often progresses in ways that require multiple capabilities to be addressed at the same time.

This example shows that work is proceeding into key capability areas; the first is data and analytics stewardship, and the second is risk and quality management. These two capability areas, or perhaps you might think of them as workstreams, are highly interactive and interdependent. It therefore makes sense to structure the Playbook so that deployment activities that combine these capabilities and target Level I outcomes are defined.

The graphic on next page illustrates the number of activities we have defined in each capability level. This view is meant to help us explain both the relative level of effort associated with establishing the foundational capability levels and the embedded notion of recursiveness for many of these activities. Each number in the columns below represents a specific activity within which are activity steps and other information. Completing these activities in any capability level for a given scope of data, analytics or business area, would constitute completion of that capability level for the relevant scope. Many of these activities represent ongoing commitments and so will be iterated over time. The reduced number of activities in the final capability levels is somewhat deceiving since they cannot be accomplished unless the previous capability levels are first achieved.

1. Defined	2. Controlled	3. Improved	4. Standardized	5. Integrated
#	#	#	#	#
100	200	300	400	500
101	201	301	401	501
102	202	302	402	502
103	203	303	403	503
104	204	304	404	504
105	205	305	405	505
106	206	306	406	506
107	207	307		
108	208	308		
109	209			
110	210			
111	211			
112				
113				
114				
115				
116				
117				
118				
119				

Note: the activities listed in each capability-level column are serial within that column. Multiple activities from a single column will typically be executed in a single deployment effort.

PLAYBOOK FRAMEWORK: ACTIVITIES

The core of the data and analytic Playbook is a set of carefully crafted and proven activities with detailed activity steps and other information that supports multiple roles across the organization as they are executed on each capability area and level of the framework. This is a subset of all defined activities in our master Playbook and represents approximately 10% of the total we have defined and deployed to date. The activities we have included in this book form the core foundation for all ongoing work.

This graphic helps us identify the components of an activity so that you can become familiar with the layout and identify the pieces of information you need to use this activity rapidly.

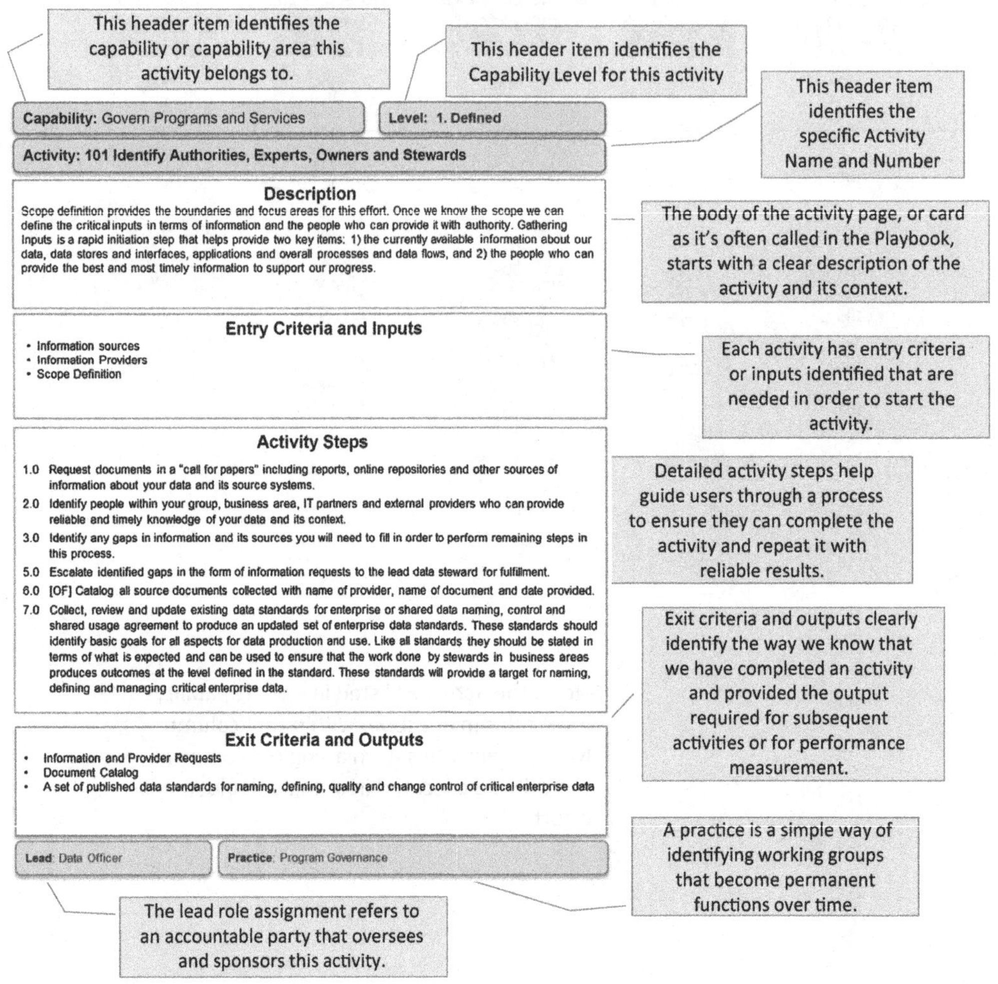

PLAYBOOK FRAMEWORK

The graphic on next page depicts the overall framework, with capability levels across from left to right, and a discrete set of defined activities within each capability. This together comprises the core of the activity areas and their progression through the capability levels. This framework functions as a table of contents for the 50+ pages of detailed activities that follow. The activities are organized by capability level and each new level is prefaced with a table of contents specific to that level. Note that these activities are provided without regard to a specific deployment sequence or strategy. Deployment planning will be addressed in a subsequent chapter and will allow for specialized sequences of activities based on your needs and assessed conditions.

1. Defined		2. Controlled		3. Improved		4. Standardized		5. Integrated	
#	Activity Name	#	Activity Name	#	Activity Name	#	Activity Name	#	Activity Name
100	Define initial scope and sponsorship	200	Design rules based profiling controls	300	Define and publish controls operating model	400	Enhance data and analytic standards	500	Incrementally reduce redundancy across CDE locations
101	Identify authorities, experts, owners and Stewards	201	Establish data quality reporting thresholds and targets	301	Implement monitoring process	401	Apply data and analytic standards	501	Provide impact analysis for new projects
102	Establish governance program operating model	202	Execute rules based data profiling, reporting and alerting	302	Create data or technical service improvement plan	402	Enhance master data standards	502	Identify redundant and overlapping Analytic models and portfolios
103	Identify capability and risk reduction measures	203	Analyze data quality issues for corrective control needs	303	Create analytic testing and improvement plan	403	Execute standards-based master data improvements	503	Apply leading analytic model designs and components
104	Engage or establish data service	204	Identify reporting critical data analytics impacted by data issues	304	Specify data quality improvements for analytics	404	Establish and apply hierarchy standards	504	Identify hierarchy integration opportunities
105	Define and catalog business terms	205	Identify master data control points	305	Identify corrective control candidates	405	Simplify or rationalize data interfaces	505	Define strategic goals for data and analytic performance
106	Define and catalog data elements	206	Define external data quality rules and thresholds for SLAs	306	Define required corrective controls for master data	406	Analyze data store mappings for redundancies	506	Adjust periodic Steward and officer meetings and communications
107	Prioritize and flag critical data elements	207	Score external data providers for quality and risk issues	307	Implement corrective controls				
108	Conduct discovery data profiling	208	Evaluate data risk and exposure	308	Track benefits from data controls automation				
109	Use discovery profiling results to set quality rules and targets	209	Establish analytics model controls at portfolio level						
110	Catalog analytic models	210	Generate analytics map to illustrate uses of analytic models across the enterprise						
111	Identify analytics model portfolios	211	Update risk and audit partners						
112	List master subjects, objects and hierarchies								
113	Identify physical data with systems and interfaces								
114	Identify systems of record and authority								
115	Identify external data subscribers								
116	Identify external data sources								
117	Identify external data provider and subscriber risks								
118	Identify and register risks from and to critical data								
119	Coordinate control and testing Standards with risk and audit								

1. Defined — 2. Controlled — 3. Improved — 4. Standardized — 5. Integrated

#	Activity Name
100	Define initial scope and sponsorship
101	Identify authorities, experts, owners, and stewards
102	Establish governance program operating model
103	Identify capability and risk reduction measures
104	Engage or establish data service
105	Define and catalog business terms
106	Define and catalog data elements
107	Prioritize and flag critical data elements
108	Conduct discovery data profiling
109	Use discovery profiling results to set quality rules and targets
110	Catalog analytic models
111	Identify analytics model portfolios
112	List master subjects, objects, and hierarchies
113	Identify physical data with systems and interfaces
114	Identify systems of record and authority
115	Identify external data subscribers
116	Identify external data sources
117	Identify external data provider and subscriber risks
118	Identify and register risks from and to critical data
119	Coordinate control and testing standards with risk and audit

Capability: Govern Programs and Services

Level: 1. Defined

Activity: 100 Define Initial Scope and Sponsorship

Description

Enterprise data landscapes are often complex, poorly documented, and have inconsistent levels of data ownership, stewardship, and management. This often leads to data-quality problems and inconsistencies that affect business processes and efficiencies. This activity helps define a program's scope to break down the complex problem into manageable efforts that result in tangible change with business value.

Entry Criteria and Inputs

- Do you have data issues such as quality, timeliness, control or gaps or unexpected nulls causing a business impact?
- Do you have current specific impacted parties and potential sponsors?
- Do you have any initiatives that should or could address this issue?
- Do you have named and supported data stewards and data SMEs in the areas affected?
- Collect through a "call for papers," a current initiatives list and a data issues list.

Activity Steps

1.0 List existing, committed, or recently completed initiatives and business problems and/or pain points related to data. Tip: The business sponsor, with knowledge of the company's strategy, objectives and financial goals, highlights key opportunities, business problems, or pain points based on their primary initiatives.

2.0 Map data terms or elements to the highest priority subjects and consider these subjects in terms of:

- 4.1 Importance to their initiatives
- 4.2 Impact on current data issues and problems
- 4.3 Correlation with enterprise initiatives

3.0 Complete the opportunity scoping template (summary on next page) by capturing the answer to key questions and completing the schedule. Provide to business sponsor.

4.0 Identify key stakeholders and impacted parties at the manager, director, and executive levels. Engage to jointly consider:

- 4.1 Importance to their initiatives
- 4.2 Impact on current data issues and problems
- 4.3 Correlation with enterprise initiatives

5.0 Confirm selected scope meets readiness criteria including:

- 5.1 Align with enterprise priority – Product (pricing, cost, master data, etc.)
- 5.2 Align with business area needs and current initiatives
- 5.3 Tie to peer business areas

Capability: Govern Programs and Services

Level: 1. Defined

Activity: 100 Define Initial Scope and Sponsorship

Activity Steps, continued

Optional Steps to Support New Project Initiation

6.0 For each problem, pain point, or opportunity, identify the following (if applicable):

- 6.1 IT systems impact, complexity, conformance, costs
- 6.2 Current state of data governance and stewardship: Is data for this scope of opportunity already covered by finance data governance and stewardship? To what degree?
- 6.3 Current data-quality (poor, good, excellent): This is a subjective assessment or estimate
- 6.4 Alignment and/or dependencies on other initiatives
- 6.5 Estimated level of effort (order of magnitude), resources, and time

7.0 The data officer summarizes the findings in a high-level business case and gets business sponsor agreement on initial scope

8.0 Translate the business cases into impact scoring levels: High (5), Medium (3), and Low (1)

9.0 Identify basic scope for highly rated business cases using scoping questions:

- 9.1 Data/issue type: Operational data, interfaces, reporting, analytics (multiple may apply)
- 9.2 Primary topic or subject focus: eg, pricing data produced in systems of record for a specific product
- 9.3 Data categories(s): structured records/DBMS, semistructured documents, unstructured files
- 9.4 Estimated data elements and instances: critical elements and location specific instances
- 9.5 Expected business areas involved
- 9.6 Expected systems/interfaces involved
- 9.7 Expected stewards/SMEs involved
- 9.8 Other initiatives affecting targeted data
- 9.9 Known issues or problems with target data:
- 9.10 Coverage by current governance

10.0 Obtain sponsorship for high-impact scoring cases with identified scope

Exit Criteria and Outputs

- Officer acceptance of accountability and approval to proceed with analysis
- Initiative cost/benefits or risk reduction request with targeted benefits and measures
- Initial resource requirements including team members and their effort, project duration, and technical service support needs

Lead: Data Officer

Practice: Program Governance

Capability: Govern Programs and Services

Level: 1. Defined

Activity: 101 Identify Authorities, Experts, Owners, and Stewards

Description

Scope definition provides the boundaries and focus areas for this effort. Once we know the scope we can define the critical inputs in terms of information and the people who can provide it with authority. Gathering inputs is a rapid initiation step that helps provide two key items: (1) the currently available information about our data, data stores and interfaces, applications, and overall processes and data flows; and (2) the people who can provide the best and most timely information to support our progress.

Entry Criteria and Inputs

- Information sources
- Information providers
- Scope definition

Activity Steps

1.0 Request documents in a "call for papers" including reports, online repositories, and other sources of information about your data and its source systems.

2.0 Identify people within your group, business area, IT partners, and external providers who can provide reliable and timely knowledge of your data and its context.

3.0 Identify any gaps in information and its sources you will need to fill in order to perform remaining steps in this process.

5.0 Escalate identified gaps in the form of information requests to the lead data steward for fulfillment.

6.0 Catalog all source documents collected with name of provider, name of document, and date provided.

7.0 Collect, review, and update existing data standards for enterprise or shared data naming, control, and shared usage agreement to produce an updated set of enterprise data standards. These standards should identify basic goals for all aspects for data production and use. Like all standards they should be stated in terms of what is expected and can be used to ensure that the work done by stewards in business areas produces outcomes at the level defined in the standard. These standards will provide a target for naming, defining, and managing critical enterprise data.

Exit Criteria and Outputs

- Information and provider requests
- Document catalog
- A set of published data standards for naming, defining, specifying quality and change controls and ownership of critical data

Lead: Data Officer

Practice: Program Governance

Capability: Govern Programs and Services

Level: 1. Defined

Activity: 102 Establish Governance Program Operating Model

Description

Program governance is key to successful execution. Ensure the operating model for the program governance, including key meetings, reviews, and escalation paths, is documented and approved by an executive sponsor and communicated. Producing and following a simple operating model with a set of scheduled activities enables the program to provide its stakeholders with clear responsibilities and expectations about the level of effort required to execute them.

Entry Criteria and Inputs

- Program charter or sponsor scope mandate
- Organization chart and included resources
- Sample governance operating model and communication plan
- Sample escalation plan for alerts and issues with resolution confirmation

Activity Steps

1.0 Define, based on the scope of the area and data to be governed and the priorities of the sponsor, the organizational mandate and resource requirements.

2.0 Define the critical oversight and sponsorship or support functions for members of the governing body (eg, data council) and the specific reporting duties of business or functional area data officers who oversee and direct efforts in their respective areas.

3.0 Define the level of effort, timing of meetings and reports, and overall expectations for both data officers and enterprise data resources, including the chief data officer and other data resources shared across the enterprise.

4.0 Produce a schedule of standing meetings and reviews with stakeholders along with expected reports or summaries from dashboards and the time needed to prepare them by the data officers.

5.0 Identify communication and participation levels for data stewards and SMEs.

6.0 Identify participation options and requirements for enterprise risk, compliance, and audit members.

7.0 Define the program or function organization including: the organization of data steward council, steward and service working groups, and officer-level committees.

Exit Criteria and Outputs

- Data/program governance operating model
- Standing meeting and review schedule and participation
- Escalation paths for issues and alerts
- Data governance policy and principles
- Communications plan

Lead: Executive Sponsor

Practice: Program Governance

Capability: Govern Programs and Services

Level: 1. Defined

Activity: 103 Identify Capability and Risk Reduction Measures

Description

Setting target measures sets expectations and allows for regular monitoring of progress toward goals. Key measures for improvements are needed in two areas. The first is capability improvement, the growth in competencies applied to specific data and process scope. The second is risk reduction, the elimination or reduction of risk *to data* due to poor controls or handling and *from data* as a result of poor understanding of the nature of the data and resulting misuse. Setting meaningful measures and targets over time expresses support for the work required to achieve these goals and communicates their importance.

Entry Criteria and Inputs

- Business, technical, and data-oriented mission maps or strategy statements
- Business policies and standards for data handling and consumption
- Technical standards and guidelines for data
- Industry best practice/leading practice examples and documents
- Enterprise initiative requirements for data handling, quality, and usage

Activity Steps

1.0 Identify measure candidates for:

- 1.1 Capability areas for data such as stewardship, quality, and other services with simple rating-level instructions
- 1.2 Risk measures related to what can happen to undermined data sufficiency or effectiveness including control gaps and weaknesses, unclear lineage or authority, etc.
- 1.3 Risk measures related to downstream impacts that can occur from data including unintended use, poor understanding of data constraints, timeliness, quality, and inappropriate or uncontrolled data replication and misuse or sharing
- 1.3 Risk measures related to analytic models, drivers, and user permissions

2.0 Validate and formalize measures

- 2.1 Attain data and analytics officer approvals
- 2.2 Identify timing and source availability of data to populate these measures
- 2.3 Set initial target levels with data and analytics officers

Exit Criteria and Outputs

- Approved data and analytics risk measures and initial goals
- Simple rollout plan communicating the timing for availability and monitoring of measures
- Identification of data and analytic officers who own those measures and will monitor (approvers)

Lead: Data and Analytics Stewards

Practice: Stewardship

Capability: Govern Programs and Services

Level: 1. Defined

Activity: 104 Engage or Establish Data Services

Description

Data services are needed to support automation for data stewardship, quality management, and other critical capabilities. These services can occur at the local or line of business level or across the line of business and function when a shared or enterprise service group is in place. This activity defines the services and activities they provide. Leading practitioners provide enterprise or global data services through the enterprise data officer or head of data, often a chief data officer. Line of business or functional areas can and do regularly engage their own data officers who can lead this effort in the absence of an enterprise service provider.

Entry Criteria and Inputs

- Data service needs due to initiation or expansion of data stewardship activities
- Data service users and scope of data to be serviced
- Local or enterprise IT support including software or cloud-based software to automate key activities and provide consistent security, change control, and communication services

Activity Steps

1.0 Identify existing or committed shared data services or your approach for them including:

- 1.1 Change-controlled file directories with change communication/subscription for document tracking for source documents and potentially spreadsheet-based terms tracking absent a business glossary tool.
- 1.2 User level change-controlled glossary tool for business terms, definitions, owners and stewards, and other required elements.
- 1.3 Data-quality testing/profiling tools or services allowing stewards to identify data scope and basic business rules (eg, "business boolean" such as date of birth before date of death) with data-quality tools and service providers executing those tests using tools or scripts and providing useful reports on the outcomes, including execution timing/repeat.
- 1.4 Data stewardship reporting including stewardship coverage of data, quality work, and outcomes, etc.
- 1.5 Durable, ongoing data controls execution and outcome tracking for data change and rules-based quality—a data control is an ongoing, monitored test or limit on change activity based on business rules and requirements for a specific set of data.
- 1.6 Check with data stewards to understand the existing and future state of governance technologies

Exit Criteria and Outputs

- A simple plan describing the use of shared services or alternatives for supporting the data stewards
- For newly established data services, provide a training plan
- Updated Communications Plan

Lead: Data Officer

Practice: Data Services

Capability: Steward Data and Analytics

Level: 1. Defined

Activity: 105 Define and catalog business terms

Description

The first activity for effective data stewardship and governance is to capture and catalog the business terms for data in our selected scope. business terms operate at the conceptual or logical levels (eg, Revenue) and are also reflected in different names at the logical level (Investment Revenue) and physical level (eg, Invest_Int_Rev_1). Our goals are: to ensure we understand and can communicate the data in scope for our effort; to capture knowledge sufficient to provide local terms and definitions that can be rationalized at the enterprise level; and to validate our scope and provide a foundation for further work.

Entry Criteria and Inputs

- Subject scope from completed opportunity scoping template
- Business data glossaries or other business meta-data sources
- Business reports, dashboards, regulatory reports, and statements
- Enterprise data catalog or local version (eg, spreadsheet)
- Documents from "call for papers"
- Guidelines for business term definition and name creation

Activity Steps

1.0 Identify business terms

- 1.1 List terms
  - 1.1.1 Harvest terms from application information, process models or workflows, reports, dashboards, business SMEs, and stewards
  - 1.1.2 Capture the term names, definitions and their sources, and stewards
- 1.2 Define business terms
  - 1.2.1 Derive from enterprise data glossary and/or area data models.
  - 1.2.2 Capture from business reports, dashboards, and public output.
  - 1.2.3 Derive from owner/steward/expert knowledge and inputs.
- 1.3 Review and analyze for redundancy, harmonize across units or other coverage:
  - 1.3.1 Terms already covered in the enterprise data catalog.
  - 1.3.2 Synonyms, homonyms, and other redundant elements
- 1.4 Review and validate this list with the business sponsor

HINT: Accelerate initial delivery with a spreadsheet until a business glossary service is ready.

Exit Criteria and Outputs

- Business data catalog "business glossary" published via local or shared data service including:
  - Ongoing change control
  - Published updates
- De-duplicated list of business terms with definitions and owners
- A simple plan for migrating any spreadsheet glossary to an enterprise glossary or data service

Lead: Data Steward

Practice: Data and Analytics Stewards

Capability: Govern Programs and Services

Level: 1. Defined

Activity: 106 Define and Catalog Data elements

Description

Once we have identified and defined the business terms (conceptual level) we can proceed to identifying more detailed (logical) business data elements, these most often occur at the reporting and query level. They are somewhat more qualified than the conceptual terms but are still directly related to them (eg, term = Revenue, element = Investment Revenue). Data elements are used to provide standard definitions and other meta-data (instructions on how to format, populate, or use data) and to start mapping physical data points for controls and quality management.

Entry Criteria and Inputs

- Subject scope from completed opportunity scoping template
- Defined business terms
- Business data glossaries or other business meta-data sources, other application or reporting specifications
- Business reports, dashboards, and statements
- Data definition format/template
- Enterprise data catalog

Activity Steps

1.0 Identify data elements
- 1.1 Derive from business terms.
- 1.2 Derive from enterprise/area data models (subjects, entities/relationships, and hierarchies).
- 1.3 Capture from business applications, reports, dashboards, and public output (financial statements, client statements, regulatory reports).

2.0 Define data elements
- 2.1 Collect or derive from application and reporting documentation, specifications (eg, meta-data or instructions in the form of specifications).
- 2.2 Collect from expected and stewards.
- 2.3 Rationalize and normalize to eliminate redundancy and enforce distinctness.
- 2.4 Capture in template form or directly in the business glossary.

3.0 Review and list business hierarchies these data elements are used in.

Exit Criteria and Outputs

- Business data catalog
- De-duplicated list of data elements with instructional meta-data
- Data ownership assigned and signoff on definitions
- Business data catalog updated, stakeholders informed of the update

Lead: Data Steward

Practice: Steward Data and Analytics

Capability: Steward Data and Analytics

Level: 1. Defined

Activity: 107 Prioritize and Flag Critical Data Elements

Description

Identifying critical data elements is important because it refines our scope of data for advanced data stewardship and control. We don't want to try to "boil the ocean" so we need a way to establish the importance of data and focus our efforts on it for maximum gain and efficiency. We use a simple set of criteria to define criticality for data; generally these criteria include Financial, Customer and Regulatory impact. Partner or supplier and product data is also considered critical in many firms. The key is to criticality assign it carefully using standard criteria; it will expand over time.

Entry Criteria and Inputs

- Business terms and data elements in the business glossary
- Key data officers and subject matter experts (SMEs) from functional and line of business areas
- External facing reports that constitute "commitments and attestations" by the firm
- Data officer and executive support for simple, clear, and consistently applied criticality criteria

Activity Steps

1.0 Establish and validate criteria for critical data based on business conditions and priorities.

1.1 Consider external commitment data (reports, filings, statements, etc.).

1.2 Consider internally relied on data (financial, performance, quality, risk).

1.3 Consider analytic drivers used in models including dimensions and master data elements.

1.4 Consider externally sourced or referenced data including standards and master data.

1.5 Use a "decision tree" to apply the critical data criteria developed to make decisions.

2.0 Review data elements in the business glossary by subject to assign criticality based on criteria.

3.0 Review critical data elements with stewards to ensure they fit the criteria.

4.0 Add a criticality flag or suffix the element name in the business glossary.

5.0 Ensure all stewards and officers are in agreement/alignment and support these designations.

6.0 Add a periodic review of the criticality criteria by officers and stewards not less than annually to consider additional criteria that may be required by regulatory actions, business or market changes, and organizational changes. Also consider large, enterprise program requirements.

Exit Criteria and Outputs

- Documented data criticality criteria
- Flagged or titled critical data elements in the business glossary
- Planned reviews of criticality criteria for needed changes

Lead: Data and Analytics Stewards

Practice: Stewardship

Capability: Steward Data and Analytics

Level: 1. Defined

Activity: 108 Conduct Discovery Data Profiling

Description

When defining business terms or data elements, sometimes sample data needs to be examined to determine the true meaning. Numerous techniques exist, both manual and automated, to perform the evaluation. The goal is to know for certain the proper definition based on the physical characteristics of the data and the data store and to understand the current data coherence (consistency with database requirements for population/required field, data type, and uniqueness).

Entry Criteria and Inputs

- Critical data elements in business glossary
- Technical meta-data sources
- Data-profiling tools
- Data models
- Access to sample data

Activity Steps

1.0 Utilize either a data-profiling tool such as IBM quality stage or create simple SQL queries (eg, Select from X all/* where data = null) to determine the consistency and gaps in basic database schema rules application to data population (required field population, data type mismatch, unique field requirements, etc.).

2.0 Review definitions – Review existing entries in available repositories/documentation. Examples include: business data catalog, data Dictionary, database catalog, report design document, reporting Tool abstraction layer (eg, business Objects Universe, Cognos catalog), Extract, Transform, Load (ETL) meta-data repository.

3.0 Refine definitions and names – Business term definitions and names must be consistent with the data content values and intent. It may be necessary to identify new terms or change term names.

4.0 Evaluate data structure – Review the data store's characteristics, eg, data types, column length, uniqueness, and nulls.

5.0 Examine data values – Determine the range of stored values by constructing a manual query or using an automated data-profiling tool. This will create a frequency distribution of the stored values. Also check for data type compliance, eg, all numerical values in an alphanumeric field.

6.0 Analyze relationships – Review the table-to-table and column-to-column relationships looking for referential integrity in the primary and foreign keys. Known business rules can also be evaluated.

Exit Criteria and Outputs

- Seven data-quality dimensions/rules types
- Data analysis reports and insights into the data
- Ambiguous terms resolved

Lead: Data Steward

Practice: Data and Analytics Stewards

Capability: Steward Data and Analytics

Level: 1. Defined

Activity: 109 Use Discovery Profiling Results to Set Quality Rules and Targets

Description

This activity brings a dose of reality to the enterprise's data, namely, the data officers and stewards define their thresholds for data-quality of the critical data elements (CDEs). Taking economic impact of poor data into account, the owners/stewards specifically define which data elements must be cleansed and what data-quality dimensions will be applied to the data. These specifications will be used by IT to create the data models, ETL, and report design documents.

Entry Criteria and Inputs

- Activity 108 discovery-based profiling
- Business Requirements
- Business assessments of current data-quality issues

Activity Steps

1.0 The data steward will define the data-quality requirements/specifications for each CDE. It's important to understand that all data does not need to be perfect. Using his/her business acumen, the data steward will define data specifications, taking into account the use of the business terms in decision making and regulatory reporting. This is an iterative process that leverages the business data stewardship group and IT data experts. Typical considerations include:

- 1.1 Completeness – Is a correct value (within the range of allowed values) required for this element or are blank/null values allowed?
- 1.2 Allowed Values – A clearly defined range of values that define the norm for this element. Explicit directions for handling out of range data values needs to be part of the specification.
- 1.3 Data Type – Will the data element contain only numeric, alphabetic, or both numeric and alphabetic character values?
- 1.4 Referential Integrity – Are there relationships with other data elements that must be enforced?

2.0 Ensure that the data-quality specifications are entered into the business data catalog.

Exit Criteria and Outputs

- Business data catalog format/template provided by IT
- Seven data-quality dimensions/rules types
- Enterprise profiling process/guidelines
- Data-quality thresholds established
- Business data catalog updated

Lead: Data Steward

Practice: Data and Analytics Stewards

Capability: Steward Data and Analytics | **Level: 1. Defined**

Activity: 110 Catalog Analytic Models

Description

Analytic models exist in spreadsheets, analytic applications, and other document types that are often spread across an organization in shared network drives and other physical locations. Identifying and cataloging these models, including information about their owners, data sources, intended uses, and underlying logic, is a necessary first step in governing analytics models and processing. This activity also provides the foundation for a portfolio approach to managing analytics models and providing a coherent change control function.

Entry Criteria and Inputs

- A "call for papers" should be issued to all analytic model developers and users to ensure a complete listing of models can be created.
- A review of shared directories and files storage locations as well as currently distributed analytics models and reports should be completed to add to and complete the list.

Activity Steps

1.0 Create a list of analytics reports and identify the models used to produce them.

2.0 Create a catalog (file-based with meta-data) to maintain a list of analytic models, producers and contributors, algorithms, and drivers used in each model, and courts and other outputs that rely on these models.

3.0 Establish and initiate use of a versioning or change control method to ensure each model is versioned as changes are made to its design or logic.

4.0 Share the catalog with analytics modelers, developers, and users for completeness and accuracy.

5.0 Publish and maintain the catalog by adding a step to the model creation process (development methodology) that requires catalog addition or update for model updates or additions.

6.0 OPTIONAL: Add a "Category" or "Portfolio Type" field to the catalog to allow the categorization of models based on a portfolio or other grouping process to track their use and lifecycle stage.

7.0 OPTIONAL: Identify common or shared algorithms and other logic designers or developers share across models. Start a catalog of these with primary developers to support reuse and versioning. Include full descriptions of the logic employed and any caveats or constraints for their use.

Exit Criteria and Outputs

- A catalog of analytic models with information about their sources, contents, and uses
- An update method to keep the catalog current based on changes to models it tracks
- An optional way to categorize models for portfolio or lifecycle management
- An optional way to track model logic components such as algorithms over time
- An updated business glossary with terms and definitions from the analytic models

Lead: Analytics Steward | **Practice**: Data and Analytics Stewards

Capability: Steward Data and Analytics

Level: 1. Defined

Activity: 111 Identify Analytic Model Portfolios

Description

Analytic models are generally assembled into libraries or portfolios based on either the local business owners or their topical focus, or both. Managing these portfolios is a form of stewardship since the portfolio provides the cataloging, change control, usage information, and quality or sensitivity indicators that apply to its models. These analytics stewards can also interact with data stewards to improve the incoming data timeliness, content, format, and quality needed to enhance model performance. Model portfolios often share hierarchy structures they can leverage from reference data services or a shared hierarchy environment.

Entry Criteria and Inputs

- Survey or dialog contacts for the business area(s) in scope
- List of models, their storage locations, versions, and owners
- Primary topics covered by the models (descriptive analytics for sales, risk analytics for finance, etc.)

Activity Steps

1.0 Engage with contacts responsible for or knowledgeable about analytic models, owners and data sources to determine the library or portfolio locations and controls.

2.0 Identify versioning or other change control methods in place and retention polices for models including models that retain data values when stored and updated.

3.0 Identify stewards or others who manage the portfolio.

4.0 Identify the level of portfolio management in place, from basic library and change control functions (complete model versioning, model component or section changes, etc.), performance or sensitivity analysis, and ratings for models or the portfolio overall, etc.

5.0 Identify and capture any constraints on intended uses and or users for the portfolio models.

5.0 Add the portfolio mame and owner/steward as attributes of the models already captured in the model catalog.

Exit Criteria and Outputs

- Updated model catalog with portfolio, owner, and stewardship information
- Optional coverage of portfolio quality or sensitivity ratings

Lead: Analytics Steward

Practice: Data and Analytics Stewards

Capability: Coordinate Data Relationships

Level: 1. Defined

Activity: 112 List Master Subjects, Objects, and Hierarchies

Description

Master data is comprised of facts about objects that have a discrete set or range of valid values and structures that are used consistently across an organization, industry, or geography. Examples include all kinds of identifiers such as account number, customer number, and product identifier.

Master data is often highly leveraged or shared across an organization and includes reference data that is produced and maintained by external authorities including zip codes, social security numbers, and calendars. Understanding what critical data is mastered by internal or external authorities and tracking that data enables consistent adoption and enforcement of these as data standards.

Entry Criteria and Inputs

- Data and system dictionaries and data listings that identify controlled domains or fields
- Reports and other outputs that help identify master and reference data columns
- External data service documents identifying reference data and sources

Activity Steps

1.0 Analyze the documents and identify the fields or columns that contain master data.

2.0 Work with users and developers to identify and validate master data types and sources.

3.0 Add to the business glossary the domain, category, or subject for each master data element.

4.0 Identify sources for master and reference data including external providers (reference data).

5.0 Identify objects, such as products, customers, suppliers, etc., that the master data defines.

6.0 Identify hierarchies (supertypes and subtypes or parent and child relationships) in master data areas including organizations. Add these to the business glossary.

Exit Criteria and Outputs

- Master data subject, domain, or category entries in the business glossary for all data elements that are master data members
- Flag or other identifier to hierarchy-based master data in the business glossary

Lead: Data Steward

Practice: Data and Analytics Stewards

Capability: Manage Quality and Risk | **Level: 1. Defined**

Activity: 113 Identify Physical Data with Systems and Interfaces

Description

Stewardship and quality efforts must be applied at the physical data level. Understanding where the data is produced and shared provides the needed context for complete stewardship and control decisions. The data flow or context diagram illustrates the physical systems and services that house and move data. Data movement requires controls, and stores require some level of monitoring for long-term quality. Certain stores are also appropriate places to improve quality through cleansing and other activities. Note: This may be provided by a data-mapping or architecture service.

Entry Criteria and Inputs

- Confirm any available data mapping or architecture service to provide this for you, etc.
- System documentation including data flow and context diagrams showing systems and interfaces
- Architecture models showing systems and interfaces
- Business workflow and process documents showing major systems and interfaces
- Systems scheduling and management documents identifying data movement processes

Activity Steps

1.0 Review systems documents to identify the places where data is produced, stored, moved, and changed.

2.0 Develop a listing of systems and interfaces that produce or handle critical data.

3.0 Use the listing to illustrate data flows and stores using either a left-to-right orientation for landscape viewing or top-down (aka, gravity fed) view for portrait orientation.

4.0 Identify the systems that produce or change data and mark as change locations for controls analysis.

5.0 Identify the interfaces where data is transformed or changes and mark as change locations.

6.0 Publish the illustration and listing to validate with architects, developers, and operational support experts to ensure its accuracy and completeness as the "data context diagram."

7.0 Share with internal audit, risk management, and compliance officers to help identify control points and controls requirements.

Exit Criteria and Outputs

- A systems and interfaces listing with change locations defined
- A data context diagram of these systems and interfaces
- A list of controls tests to be expected for change points and stores
- Addition of physical data mapping to CDEs in business glossary

Lead: Data Steward | **Practice**: Data and Analytics Stewardship

Capability: Manage Quality and Risk

Level: 1. Defined

Activity: 114 Identify Systems of Record and Authority

Description

CDE are likely found in multiple databases throughout the data landscape. To ensure consistent usage and data quality, it's important to identify and communicate the specific database that is authoritative for the specific CDE. This will inform both analytics application developers and information consumers about which databases to use.

Entry Criteria and Inputs

- A systems and interfaces listing with change locations defined
- A data context diagram of these systems and interfaces
- A list of control tests to be expected for change points and stores
- Addition of physical data mapping to CDEs in the business glossary

Activity Steps

1.0 Survey SMEs, system administrators, operations experts, business users, and business or application architects to determine which systems are responsible for creating your CDEs.

2.0 Identify systems that qualify as either SOR, ADS, or other:

- 1.1 **System of record (SOR)** – Any system relied on for operational decision making and reporting and used to capture or transact business events. These are typically optimized for transacting business events in real-time.
- 1.2 **Authoritative data source (ADS)** – Any system integrated from SOR and managed in order to provide business accredited information considered reputable for internal and external stakeholder reporting. These are typically surrogates for SOR that provide optimized reporting and analysis capabilities as well as long-term history retention and summarization.
- 1.3 **Other** – Systems/conduits that may handle, convey, or house data WITHOUT changing the structure, quality, or value of that data.

3.0 Add SOR or ADS values in your business glossary for each CDE based on your analysis.

4.0 Review and adjust your previously identified change points based on the SOR designations identified above. Make sure that any SOR is also designated as a change point for subsequent controls review.

Exit Criteria and Outputs

- Additional of SOR and ADS designations for all systems in the Systems and Interface listing as well as the data context diagram
- Add SOR and ADS designations to physical data columns mapped into the business glossary
- Generate a listing of CDEs grouped by system where the system is an SOR or ADS

Lead: Data Steward or Data Services Lead

Practice: Date Stewardship or Data Services

Capability: Coordinate Data Relationships

Level: 1. Defined

Activity: 115 Identify External Data Subscribers

Description

External data delivery (publication) requires specific handling to ensure service-level or other contractual commitments are met, including timeliness, content quality and range, format integrity, historical retention and retransmission support, and other issues. External data subscribers or recipients often include regulatory and other governmental recipients with high degrees of cost, as well as key supply and customer partners who require high degrees of quality and timeliness.

Capturing the recipients of critical data is a first step in ensuring effective delivery on a sustainable basis. It also provides a single view of all data provisioning and delivery commitments.

Entry Criteria and Inputs

- Current data delivery contracts, scheduling commitments, delivery deadlines, and specifications
- Business area and operations schedules, and responsible parties for delivery
- Service-level commitments for customers, suppliers, regulators, and other governmental recipients
- Trade association and other recipients and agreements
- Information security and privacy information and terms for delivery

Activity Steps

1.0 Engage business, operations, and technical resources to identify key agreement-based and voluntary data provisioning and delivery schedules and terms.

2.0 Identify contract-based delivery specifications and terms. Catalog data delivery commitments and related requirements into the business glossary or other areas for ongoing tracking.

3.0 Capture and catalog quality, timing, format, and other delivery specifications, either in part or by link if supported by your glossary. Remember to enforce version control for linked documents with some level of update notice for changes in the linked documents.

4.0 Engage information security and privacy officers to determine what level of catalog they maintain and what you can extend or leverage for this activity. Agree on who will run the “system of record” for this and proceed accordingly.

Exit Criteria and Outputs

- A catalog of external data delivery commitments and specifications
- A coordinated approach to maintaining this with information security and privacy

Lead: Data Steward

Practice: Data and Analytics Stewards

Capability: Coordinate Data Relationships

Level: 1. Defined

Activity: 116 Identify External Data Sources and Providers

Description

External data sources require a different set of activities and processes for data stewardship, quality management, and change control. These differences occur as a result of the very limited, or often complete lack of control, the firm has over external data providers, formats, timing, and content.
Cataloguing additional information about these sources provides a better understanding of what external data providers deliver, what the firm can do to improve or change that delivery, and what downstream impacts and changes those sources could have to that data based on its lineage and provenance or authority.

Entry Criteria and Inputs

- Lists of external data providers and feeds including formats, timing, and specifications
- Information about the data providers needed to discern their level of authority—contextual information including their type of organization (eg, government, trade group, private firm)
- Key people in the firm who own or operate these external data ingestion points, feeds, or subscriptions

Activity Steps

1.0 Collect documents and online information about the incoming feeds from external sources and catalog with the following information:

1.1 Name of the feed with a unique identifier

1.2 Provider of the feed including organization name, type (government, trade group, private firm, standards group), and primary contact

1.3 Feed specifications (content type and format, frequency and timing, etc., may be in a specification document that is linked and updated based on change notice)

1.4 Name of the internal subscriber and business owner (based on who is charged for this service or is the owner of the point of ingestion)

1.5 Privacy, security, or other sensitive data flags as defined by chief information security officer, contractual limits on the reuse, retention, replication or sharing of this data internally or externally

2.0 Catalog these in your business glossary with unique identifiers that will be used as part of the CDE information to show lineage.

Exit Criteria and Outputs

- Business glossary entries for external data feeds and their properties including providers
- Identifiers or flags for CDEs related to these feeds to identify their external sources
- Privacy or security flags in business glossary for relevant CDEs

Lead: Data Steward

Practice: Data Stewards

Capability: Coordinate Data Relationships | **Level: 1. Defined**

Activity: 117 Identify External Data Provider and Subscriber Risks

Description

The use of external data brings different and additional risks to those presented by internally produced data. These risks can be more difficult to manage, so capturing and tracking them in your business glossary provides the information needed to ensure appropriate controls and outcomes.

External data and its providers brings enhanced or additional risks related to the timeliness, integrity, quality, and authority of the data. Additionally, the lack of internal control over the format and timing of data delivery increases risks to downstream systems and users. Capturing these and related risks can improve the contracting and service-level experience of the firm with its suppliers.

Entry Criteria and Inputs

- Business glossary entries for external data feeds and their properties including providers
- Identifiers or flags for CDEs related to these feeds to identify their external sources
- Privacy or security flags in business glossary for relevant CDEs
- Vendor management support for vendor ratings and risks

Activity Steps

1.0 Review documents and contracts.

2.0 Interview contact points to identify issues with external data feeds and their providers.

3.0 Create a simple listing of issues the firm has encountered with external data and its providers. Add risks or gaps that your interviews provided.

4.0 Review vendor management, information security, and other source logs or dialogs to identify other issues and challenges.

5.0 List the risks based on experience and potential threats to data sufficiency, timeliness, quality and integrity, and supplier viability that you see to internal users of the data.

6.0 Review the list with risk management, compliance, internal audit, and your sources to validate and identify additions to your business area and enterprise risk registers.

7.0 Request a risk framework comparison from risk management to identify any gaps you see from your own work and their approach.

8.0 Include your data officer in this activity and support them with a report that ranks major data risks from external providers along with outstanding issues and suggested actions including data controls.

Exit Criteria and Outputs

- Risk register updates from your working list of issues and risks
- Suggested actions for reducing or eliminating these risks (includes data control improvements)

Lead: Compliance Officer | **Practice**: Enterprise Governance, Risk, and Compliance

Capability: Steward Data and Analytics | **Level: 1. Defined**

Activity: 118 Identify and Register Risks To and From Critical Data

Description

Identifying and managing risks that impact data and problems in data that impact people is a critical to data and risk management. Engaging risk management, audit and compliance experts and methods greatly enhances data capabilities and outcomes. This activity harnesses risk management methods and extends the data's value. We need to understand what risks in the production and handling of data can undermine its integrity so that we can establish effective controls to limit and prevent these risks. We also need to understand how gaps in data-quality and availability or authority impact the data's usefulness in controlling those issues.

Entry Criteria and Inputs

- Current risk registers, audit findings or recommendations, compliance and regulatory issues
- Outstanding requests from users and producers for data improvements
- External data provider issues and service-level agreement (SLA) exceptions from internal users and vendor management
- Market or industry published reports of public and commercial data service issues (eg, government and industry data feed problems with statistics and analytic aggregations)

Activity Steps

1.0 Determine which documents and other sources are most relevant to this activity for ongoing work and monitor regularly.

2.0 Identify CDEs and their systems of record that have some indicated risk to integrity or availability based on document reviews and discussions with data stewards or SMEs who produce that data and use those systems.

3.0 Categorize and measure the risk in terms of the likelihood that an event of the type envisioned by the risk will occur (eg, the risk of a regulatory submission with incorrect data due to late running update processes).

4.0 Identify exposure or materiality level—most risk registers and frameworks seek to establish the range of impacts that can occur when a risk is realized, or to establish the exposure level to weed out immaterial risks (we might lose power but risk is low and exposure is extremely low because of our backup generator).

5.0 Sort your data risk register to highlight high, medium, and low risk level items. With medium or higher exposure, share with risk management and obtain data officer approval to integrate into the enterprise risk register for tracking and reporting.

Exit Criteria and Outputs

- A data risk register aligned with enterprise risk framework or categories and levels
- Risk exposure or materiality levels for all registered risks
- Sharing of the data risk register with risk management
- Approval to publish the data risk register components into the enterprise risk register

Lead: Data Steward | **Practice**: Data and Analytics Stewards

Capability: Manage Quality and Risk

Level: 1. Defined

Activity: 119 Coordinate Control and Testing Standards with Risk and Audit

Description

Managing data risk and exposure requires controls and testing in addition to tracking and measurement. Data controls will be created and managed in the next level of the Playbook, so it is important to start collecting information and collaborating with controls and testing experts in advance of that activity. Risk management, compliance, and internal audit experts all develop and apply controls requirements, frameworks, and specifications along with testing to ensure their efficacy. We collaborate with these experts to ensure our emerging controls are effective.

Entry Criteria and Inputs

- Organizational points of contact in risk management, compliance, and internal audit
- Existing or draft controls frameworks, policies, and guidelines for data or reporting
- Outstanding audit, risk management, or compliance issue or recommendation reports

Activity Steps

1.0 Connect with points of contact in each area and engage in reviews of their current findings, reports, and plans for testing in your area for the current year.

2.0 Engage your contacts to review and understand their controls frameworks, requirements, and expectations based on external regulatory and industry specifications as well as internal mandates.

3.0 Review and identify the key controls standards and likely tests that will be applied to your data and data-handling procedures.

4.0 Draft a plan for the establishment of controls by type for your data production, change, handling, and delivery processes.

5.0 Identify from internal audit, risk management, and compliance sources the types of tests you can expect to be conducted against the change points and stores in your diagram based on your change points identified in Activity 112, Step 7.

Exit Criteria and Outputs

- Points of contact in internal audit, risk management, and compliance for ongoing coordination of data controls and testing regimes
- A list of control types and testing that will be used to validate them
- An expected schedule of testing for data controls you will be deploying and monitoring

Lead: Data Officer

Practice: Data and Analytics Stewards

#	Activity Name (New)
200	Design rules-based profiling controls
201	Establish data-quality reporting thresholds and targets
202	Execute rules-based data profiling, reporting and alerting
203	Analyze data-quality issues for corrective control needs
204	Identify reporting and analytics impacted by data issues
205	Identify master data control points
206	Define external data-quality rules and thresholds for SLAs
207	Score external data providers for quality and risk issues
208	Evaluate data risk and exposure
209	Establish analytics model controls at portfolio level
210	Generate analytics map to illustrate uses of analytic models across the enterprise
211	Update risk and audit partners

Capability: Manage Quality and Risk | **Level: 2. Controlled**

Activity: 200 Design Rules-Based Profiling Controls

Description

Implementing rules-based profiling as an ongoing service provides consistent data-quality controls. Designing these profiling activities as a control requires basic scheduling, monitoring, and resolution activities. Effective controls are the cornerstone of testable business data and can be executed efficiently if designed well. In this activity, focus on business-based control requirements. Examples include testing data as and when it changes and cleansing or correcting when those changes will not impact business use adversely (eg, reconciling and balancing).

Entry Criteria and Inputs

- Business data catalog
- Data-quality thresholds
- Context diagrams and data maps
- Data-quality rules and targets

Activity Steps

1.0 Review data-quality rules and targets.

2.0 Review business glossary for CDEs and identify CDEs requiring regular quality controls.

3.0 Match data-quality targets to CDEs requiring controls.

4.0 Define desired or required schedule to control ongoing execution.

5.0 Identify key stakeholders who will monitor these controls and resolve or escalate/support in resolving issues.

6.0 Define monitoring method, including logging and reporting issue history status and resolution.

Note: Many controls can be operated with minimal logging but some require a detailed history of issues, issue counts, and resolution actions required. It is important to identify what level of monitoring and tracking each control needs, but only as needed for business audit trail. Don't complicate any more than is required.

7.0 Identify and validate escalation plan for issues from controls with data officer.

8.0 Compile or combine monitoring tracking and resolution specifications into a controls plan and share with data services or data officer in their absence.

Exit Criteria and Outputs

- A data controls plan including monitoring tracking and resolution specifications for control execution
- A list of data stewards to assign execution responsibilities for these controls

Lead: Data Service Team | **Practice**: Data Services

Capability: Manage Quality and Risk

Level: 2. Controlled

Activity: 201 Establish Data-Quality Reporting Thresholds and Targets

Description

Data-quality dashboards and reports use thresholds and targets to identify the quality status of data. Absolute measures alone are not enough to support heat mapping of data-quality issues. It's important to recognize current data-quality levels from discovery profiling and set thresholds based on that recognition. We often find data-quality levels well below ideal, desired targets (100%). Setting thresholds at very high levels can show most of the data in a red zone well below the 100% target. This has a chilling effect on business sponsorship, so we adjust our thresholds as we improve.

Entry Criteria and Inputs

- Data-quality rules and targets
- Control points from the context diagrams
- Profiling results from the discovery profiling

Activity Steps

1.0 Review discovery profiling results for CDEs by control point, since each control point will have controls and reporting thresholds associated with it.

2.0 Work with business representatives to establish initial quality thresholds for three levels of dashboard reporting: green = good to use as is, yellow = review and reconcilement or adjustment required, red = intensive manual effort required before use and may not be reliable.

3.0 Capture threshold settings for each level in a document for review and approval by the data officer. Note on the document the timing of these thresholds, which should be quarterly at most.

4.0 Schedule quarterly reviews for data-quality thresholds and suggest raising the thresholds as data-quality improves.

5.0 Communicate data-quality thresholds and intended changes over time via the data officer.

Exit Criteria and Outputs

- Data thresholds listing with effective dates
- A schedule for adjusting data-quality thresholds

Lead: Data Steward

Practice: Data Stewardship

Capability: Manage Quality and Risk

Level: 2. Controlled

Activity: 202 Execute Rules-based Data Profiling, Reporting, and Alerting

Description

In previous activities, the authoritative data stores (eg, system of record, system of Authority) of importance to current requirements have been defined as the locations for CDEs. The data flows and lineages have been documented in the data map and context diagrams. Now we are ready to implement controls at the appropriate control points for our CDEs. Implementing these controls creates an ongoing process with assigned resources that will ensure quality targets are met consistently.

Entry Criteria and Inputs

- Context diagrams and data maps
- A data controls plan including monitoring tracking and resolution specifications for control execution
- A list of data stewards to assign execution responsibilities for these controls

Activity Steps

1.0 Identify, with business inputs as required, locations in the data map and context diagram where data is moved or changed. These are potential control points.

2.0 Identify control points where defined quality targets must be met. Engage data services to implement the control specifications in those locations and publish ongoing results to a data-quality dashboard with details for all noted issues or exceptions.

3.0 Assign data stewards with lead data support for escalation to track data-quality dashboard updates and engage in resolution activities for all observed exceptions.

4.0 Operate the controls as implemented by data services or technical services for each control point and identify overall controls activity reporting needed from data or technical services.

5.0 Review and communicate summaries of controls reports with the data officer and others and needed.

Exit Criteria and Outputs

- Operating controls in required control points for CDEs
- Data-quality control reports and dashboard
- Issue resolution as a result of data steward activity on the controls

Lead: Data Service Team

Practice: Data Services

Capability: Manage Quality and Risk

Level: 2. Controlled

Activity: 203 Analyze Data-Quality Issues for Corrective Control Needs

Description

Data-quality control reports and dashboard outputs provide current and accumulating information about our data-quality issues. Controls placement ensures an end-to-end view of where quality issues are emerging in the data flow. Now we will analyze accumulating quality information to identify systemic sources of quality problems. Our goal is to identify systems and interfaces that require remediation of their output data or internal data integrity controls. These corrective and potentially preventive controls will be defined in subsequent activities.

Entry Criteria and Inputs

- A systems and interfaces listing with change locations defined
- A data context diagram of these systems and interfaces
- Operating controls in required control points for CDEs
- Reporting data-quality control reports and dashboard
- Issue resolution as a result of data steward activity on the controls

Activity Steps

1.0 Analyze reports for repeating data issues, particularly recurring in the same location or control point. List recurring issues by control point or system interface.

2.0 Identify systems and interfaces from this list that technology services is planning to change or upgrade in the near future, and request that data integrity controls are added to their requirements.

3.0 For control points not subject to near term improvement, identify cleansing and data remediation options, including substation, data lookups and, if necessary, default values.

4.0 Identify control points where systematic preventive control option may exist including required fields, required lookups, or required validations within applications or interface/integration logic.

5.0 Compile list of corrective or preventive control options by control point and CDE. Review list with data officer and data or technical services officer.

Exit Criteria and Outputs

- List of corrective or preventive control options by control point and CDE

Lead: Compliance Officer

Practice: Enterprise Governance, Risk, and Compliance

Capability: Manage Quality and Risk

Level: 2. Controlled

Activity: 204 Identify Reporting and Analytics Impacted by Data Issues

Description

Determining and reporting data-quality is a necessary step in data stewardship but not sufficient to provide business value. Business value is realized when the impact of data-quality issues is measured and addressed. Identifying data-quality impacts on reporting and analytics engages the business to reveal business costs related to data-quality and controls issues. In this activity, we will link data-quality controls work with business impact to provide business value.

Entry Criteria and Inputs

- List of corrective or preventive control options by control point and CDE
- Data-quality control reports and dashboard

Activity Steps

1.0 Identify business reports with business users that require manual adjustment or reconcilement by the business in order to reliably use.

2.0 Identify analytic models and outputs (cubes, reports and interfaces to systems) that suffer from data inconsistencies or lack of integrity.

3.0 Compile a list of known report and analytic impacts from data-quality, sort by priority (impact level and CDE).

4.0 Calculate basic counts by report, source, and severity. Ask business users to estimate manual effort, in hours, expended monthly to resolve these issues manually.

5.0 Use business estimates of manual effort required to justify data or technical services assistance in implementing corrective or preventive data controls as required to resolve these.

6.0 Ask data officer to engage business sponsors in business case for controls development and implementation.

Exit Criteria and Outputs

- List of issues impacting reports and analytic models
- The business estimates of manual effort required to resolve
- The business case for corrective and preventive controls

Lead: Data Steward

Practice: Data Stewardship

Capability: Coordinate Data Relationships

Level: 2. Controlled

Activity: 205 Identify Master Data Control Points

Description

Master data requires special handling and has very high-quality requirements. This is due to the fact that it is defined in terms of its valid values and range of values, and, in the case of reference data, its format and contents are informed by external authorities. Data-quality must be measured in terms of strict compliance with valid values and formats. Additionally challenges arise from duplicate sets of master data, such as duplicate customer master files where changes in one are not reflected in another. Consistent, accurate, and timely master data is critical to business operations, reporting, and analysis.

Entry Criteria and Inputs

- List of corrective or preventive control options by control point and CDE
- Context diagrams and data maps

Activity Steps

1.0 Review current control points and CDE lists to identify where master data is produced, moved, and stored.

2.0 Evaluate change controls specific to master data CDEs and review discovery profiling results to identify inconsistent master data values in different places (control points).

3.0 Identify control points requiring additional change control or other methods of synchronizing master data for subjects including product, customer, supplier, and other critical subjects.

4.0 Identify analytic applications and models that rely on critical master data, determine the quality of the master data that are being provided by their source, and survey owners to determine issues they may be having.

5.0 Summarize master data control issues and their impacts on downstream users for prioritized improvement and resolution.

6.0 Ensure that all known issues and control point recommendations are published by the data officer and included in requirements for the master data hub and service changes.

Exit Criteria and Outputs

- Summary of master data control issues

Lead: Data Steward

Practice: Data and Analytics Stewards

Capability: Coordinate Data Relationships | **Level: 2. Controlled**

Activity: 206 Define External Data-Quality Rules and Thresholds for SLAs

Description

External data providers should be subject to contract-based, SLAs. Determining our quality requirements allows us to drive steady improvements in the data we purchase from third-party providers. In some cases, we can also require the provider to share quality measures of their data and even certify it at a certain quality level or for a certain purpose.

Entry Criteria and Inputs

- Context diagrams and data maps
- Data-quality rules and targets

Activity Steps

1.0 Identify data flows from external provides in context diagram and data map.

2.0 Identify data-quality targets and thresholds for externally provided data.

3.0 Define and share with vendor management control-point-specific data-quality measures to be applied for all external data-quality measures.

4.0 Establish detective monitoring and reporting of external data with vendor management oversight. Track exceptions and issues and engage vendor management to form improvements with vendors.

6.0 Produce specific reports tracking issues, durations, and outcomes of data-quality issues with external providers by provider and control point.

7.0 Engage stewards from downstream business areas who rely on external data to estimate the level of effort required to remediate data-quality problems.

Exit Criteria and Outputs

- List of external data providers and your data-quality requirements for them by CDE
- List of data-quality issues, duration and outcome by provider and CDE
- List of estimated data remediation caused by external provider issues

Lead: Data Steward | **Practice**: Data Stewardship

Capability: Coordinate Data Relationships

Level: 2. Controlled

Activity: 207 Score External Data Providers for Quality and Risk Issues

Description

Scoring data providers enables us to see choices for our data sources for similar data. For example, there are multiple providers for name and address data, so we want to constantly score the performance of our selected provider to support options when faced with poor quality or timeliness. These scores also support risk and exposure tracking for critical externally provided data.

Entry Criteria and Inputs

- List of external data providers and your data-quality requirements for them by CDE
- List of data-quality issues, duration, and outcome by provider and CDE
- List of estimated data remediation caused by external provider issues

Activity Steps

1.0 Enhance data maps with specific ingestion point markers for external data.

2.0 Create a simple scoring calculation based on your priorities for quality, timeliness, and integrity of external data. A simple example is to use a scale of 1-10 and weight three variables (timeliness, accuracy, and formatting consistency) in equal proportions.

3.0 Implement the calculation as arules-based profiling control producing its information to the data-quality dashboard.

4.0 Share scores with data officer and risk officers to expose or highlight issues we have with data providers and to identify any required actions to follow.

5.0 Support data officer discussions with vendor management using additional details as needed to support external data provider selection and contracting improvements.

6.0 Use enhanced data map to indicate external dataquality at each ingestion point (red, yellow, green).

Exit Criteria and Outputs

- Consistent, published scores via the dashboard for external data providers
- Data map indicators (red, yellow, green) for external data-quality at each ingestion point
- Ongoing analysis of third-party data provider quality for contracting consideration

Lead: Data Steward

Practice: Data Stewardship

Capability: Manage Quality and Risk

Level: 2. Controlled

Activity: 208 Evaluate Data Risk and Exposure

Description

This activity provides an ongoing model for relating data risk and exposure and for tracking changes in those measures over time. Our model must reflect the elimination or reduction of risk *to data* due to poor controls or handling and *from data* as a result of poor understanding of the nature of the data and resulting misuse. The model will be used to produce risk and exposure ratings over time; we share these with our risk management and business management executives. Communicating the fact that we are measuring risk exposure and targeting improvements over time is essential to improving data outcomes.

Entry Criteria and Inputs

- Approved data and analytics risk measures and initial goals
- External data provider scores

Activity Steps

1.0 Identify the subset of critical data as scope for measurement of risk and exposure, including risks to the data and from the data in its use.

2.0 Identify the data points needed to calculate risk and exposure ratings based on the measures and targets previously identified.

3.0 Build calculations with the input data points to produce the measures and compare them to the targets previously identified.

4.0 Use actual data indicators of risk and exposure including:

- 4.1 Risk: changing or declining data-quality, changes in data timeliness, and uncertain level of authority
- 4.2 Exposure: dependency on identified critical data for financial, regulatory, and other reporting requiring management attestation or reflecting an external commitment by the firm

5.0 Complete the model and test using data as previously described. Validate the model with the data officer.

6.0 Document the data inputs and calculation logic used in the model and maintain with the model as it changes over time.

7.0 Publish the model and work with data or technical services as part of data dashboarding and reporting.

Exit Criteria and Outputs

- A working risk and exposure model for data including: the measures and targets previously identified
- Data risk and exposure reporting and dashboard showing the trend and current risk and exposure ratings

Lead: Compliance Officer

Practice: Enterprise Governance, Risk, and Compliance

Capability: Steward Data and Analytics

Level: 2. Controlled

Activity: 209 Establish Analytics Model Controls at Portfolio Level

Description

Versioning analytic models at the portfolio level enables the use of a consistent set of models and their components, including calculations and data sources on a consistent basis across the enterprise. These portfolio-based models become standard or common for all enterprise users. Local variations can and will occur at the model level outside of the standard portfolios and can be controlled for local use only. Version and change control at the portfolio level ensures shared or enterprise use leverages controlled models. Additional standards for the use of stress and sensitivity testing are often important to apply to shared portfolios of analytic models.

Entry Criteria and Inputs

- Quality and Integrity indicators for model portfolio (stress and sensitivity testing)
- A catalog of analytic models with information about their sources, contents, and uses
- Updated model catalog with portfolio, owner, and stewardship information

Activity Steps

1.0 Identify and define the types of controls that will be applied to shared or enterprise portfolios. These typically include exposure (findable, access, usage, change, deletion, and archive). Note that some models in a portfolio may be hidden subject to certain levels of users.

2.0 Engage portfolio owners to identify either role-based or other schema for applying security and validate the control types you have defined.

3.0 Work with portfolio owners and technical service partners to apply access usage and change controls from your validated list to the portfolios based on the security schema agreed to with the portfolio owners. Note: Use of different schemas across portfolios is not encouraged due to the inherent risk of maintaining a complex security approach.

4.0 Ensure that security exceptions are reported to the portfolio owners on a timely basis as these controls are adopted.

5.0 Establish a periodic review of controls and permissions to ensure adequate control coverage and timely permission updates as people's roles and responsibilities change.

6.0 Periodically review industry publications and advisory sources for leading practices on portfolio model controls and management.

Exit Criteria and Outputs

- List of control types for analytic model portfolios
- Approved security schema
- Ongoing monitoring of control and security exceptions by portfolio owners
- Ongoing monitoring for changes in permissions

Lead: Analytics Steward

Practice: Data and Analytics Stewards

Capability: Steward Data and Analytics

Level: 2. Controlled

Activity: 210 Generate Analytics Map to Illustrate Uses of Analytic Models Across the Enterprise

Description

The analytics map is a corollary to the data map and context diagrams we have already produced. The analytics map is used to communicate the breadth of use of our analytics model portfolios. It is important to provide management with a clear view of the level of adoption of analytics models and engines. It is especially valuable to identify where analytics models and engines are producing results that are automatically consumed by key systems in the enterprise. These closed-loop analytic engines often drive pricing, supply, and other operational decisions. An understanding of their location and importance is critical to good corporate governance and risk control.

Entry Criteria and Inputs

- Physical data map of CDEs in business glossary

Activity Steps

1.0 Acquire from business or enterprise architects a high-level context diagram of business systems grouped by business area. This blueprint or context diagram should be at a level that allows you to locate analytics models and engines and any connections they have to operational and reporting systems.

2.0 Work with portfolio owners and technical services to identify where analytic models and engines are feeding results into operational or reporting systems.

3.0 Identify additional locations where model portfolios are used to produce decisions, projections, and other management inputs (eg, financial planning and analysis).

4.0 Annotate the analytics map to indicate which analytics model portfolios are used in each location. Validate with portfolio owners and technical services and publish with the analytics officer.

Exit Criteria and Outputs

- Analytics map with annotated portfolio locations

Lead: Data Service Team

Practice: Data Services

Capability: Steward Data and Analytics

Level: 2. Controlled

Activity: 211 Update Risk and Audit Partners

Description

As you complete your risk and exposure activities it is worthwhile to reach out to risk enterprise management and internal audit to appraise them of your progress. Enterprise risk management (ERM) will want to update their risk register and identify key milestones you are committing to for future updates. Internal audit (IA) may have questions about the controls you are using, and you may want to learn more about their planned audit schedule for your area. Additionally, ERM and IA are valuable partners in assessing the efficacy of your controls and communicating and validating your progress to management.

Entry Criteria and Inputs

- Audit and enterprise risk-management contact points
- Current audit and enterprise risk management testing schedules

Activity Steps

Note: The following activities apply to both data controls and analytic model and portfolio controls.

1.0 Update your risk register based on your progress in previous control-related activities and share your updates with ERM. Enquire about changes in the ERM risk framework register or review plans to ensure your readiness for their questions and oversight.

2.0 Update IA with the status of your controls as a courtesy and inquire as to the planned testing schedule or audit for your area so that you can be prepared.

3.0 Identify for ERM, IA, and other oversight areas of the firm the ongoing dashboard and report areas then communicate your controls outcomes (eg, data-quality dashboard).

4.0 Enquire from ERM and IA about any additional audit trails, logs, or other documentation they would expect to see related to your controls and outcomes.

Exit Criteria and Outputs

- Ongoing communication with ERM, IA, and other oversight areas
- An updated calendar of likely ERM and IA review or testing activities
- Any additional required audit trail or logging as specified by ERM and IA

Lead: Data and Analytics Officer

Practice: Data and Analytics Stewards

1. Defined → 2. Controlled → **3. Improved** → 4. Standardized → 5. Integrated

#	Activity Name (New)
300	Define and publish controls operating model
301	Implement monitoring process
302	Create data or technical service improvement plan
303	Create analytic testing and improvement plan
304	Specify data-quality improvements for analytics
305	Identify corrective control candidates
306	Define required corrective controls for master data
307	Implement corrective controls
308	Track benefits from data controls automation

Capability: Steward Data and Analytics

Level: 3. Improved

Activity: 300 Define and Publish Controls Operating Model

Description

In the previous capability level we identified and established basic detective controls as well as basic requirements for corrective controls for our critical data and analytic model and portfolios. A comprehensive plan for the operations of these and subsequent controls is the foundation for ongoing improvement. This activity establishes and communicates that plan. This operating model is an expanded version of the data controls plan that also includes analytics model data controls with information about their ongoing operation.

Entry Criteria and Inputs

- List of control types for analytic model portfolios
- A data controls plan including monitoring, tracking, and resolution specifications for control execution
- An updated context diagram and data map

Activity Steps

1.0 Review the data controls plan and analytic portfolio controls specifications. Identify ongoing operations schedules and required actions.

2.0 Construct a simple operating model that describes for each object controls (eg, critical data element, analytic model, model portfolio) that what the schedule and required actions are related to controls execution, results monitoring, and issue resolution.

3.0 Review this plan with data and analytic officers, ensure escalation paths and timing are clearly defined.

4.0 Publish the operating model and hare with internal audit and enterprise risk management partners for comment and test planning.

5.0 Establish an annual review of the plan for improvements and changes.

Exit Criteria and Outputs

- Controls operating model

Lead: Data and Analytics Officers

Practice: Enterprise Governance, Risk, and Compliance

Capability: Steward Data and Analytics

Level: 3. Improved

Activity: 301 Implement Monitoring Process

Description

CDEs and their data-quality Specifications have been published in the business data catalog and Governance placed on them. Stakeholders have been notified of the new accountability to follow the change control process. To ensure the business benefits are being realized and Governance is not being circumvented, a monitoring process needs to be established.

Entry Criteria and Inputs

- Data-quality scorecard
- business data catalog
- Impact analysis tools
- Analytics developers
- DBAs, SMEs
- Change control process

Activity Steps

1.0 The business data steward needs to establish and follow a monitoring process. Specifically, they need to keep informed of:

- 1.1 Proposed changes to CDEs via line of bussiness meeting minutes and CRs
- 1.2 Proposed analytics applications and enhancements that utilize CDEs or attempt to create new, redundant data objects.

2.0 Review updates to the business data catalog

3.0 Review the respective data-quality scorecard (*See 2.1.3 Create a DQ Scorecard*) for changes

- 3.1 Positive Improvements – Communicate the business benefits and recognize progress toward quality goals
- 3.2 Negative Changes – Seek to understand root causes and take corrective action

4.0 Ensure the business impact of the above data-quality changes are linked to business metrics. (*See 2.1.8 Support Quality Impact Metrics*)

Exit Criteria and Outputs

- Change request form
- Change requests reviewed
- Impact analysis conducted
- Positive and negative data-quality changes communicated
- Data-quality remediation action taken as needed

Lead: Data and Analytics Officers

Practice: Data Stewards

Capability: Steward Data and Analytics

Level: 3. Improved

Activity: 302 Create Data or Technical Service Improvement Plan

Description

Controlling and improving critical data and analytics requires increasing levels of shares or standard services. These services are not only cost effective but necessary to expose and address issues we identify across the enterprise. Local efforts and resources cannot scale effectively or efficiently when addressing data and analytic issues that span the enterprise. This activity will capture the needed improvements in either dedicated data services that are shared or, in their absence, data and analytic specific technical services. This improvement plan forms the basis for a business case for our data or technical service partners to expand their resources and scope based on the impacts they have on out work.

Entry Criteria and Inputs

- (Improvement targets/quality targets and goals from lvl2)
- (Measuring business impact)

Activity Steps

1.0 Assemble current information on business impacts from data and model and quality issues. Identify manual effort in business and operations areas related to tracking and resolving these issues.

2.0 Calculate manual effort averted by existing data or technical services in areas including data cataloging, model cataloging, data-quality analysis, model standardization, and issue resolution support.

3.0 Assign an average or loaded cost per hour for the averted manual effort to identify the dollar savings current data or technical services are providing.

4.0 Identify data and analytic controls, you need additional support to address (eg, quality).

5.0 Work with data or technical service pattern to identify the level of efficiency they provide in level of effort for the same service compared to your level of effort. Note: Enterprise data services are typically 2x-4x more efficient than local data efforts.

6.0 Project potential savings rang using the efficiency estimates from your service partners over the next year based on the number of issues you are trying to address and level of effort you are expending today.

7.0 Capture anecdotal and any measured outcomes from current services related to data or model quality improvement and its impacts on business decision outcomes.

Exit Criteria and Outputs

- A summary of service needs and efficiency estimates to be realized by using shared or enterprise service partners
- A list of business impacts and anecdotal examples from existing service success
- Optional: a short list of high-priority target goals for additional service improvement

Lead: Data and Analytics Officers

Practice: Data Stewards

Capability: Manage quality and Risk

Level: **3. Improved**

Activity: 303 Create Analytic Testing and Improvement Plan

Description

Analytic models, engines and outputs all require ongoing testing to ensure their effectiveness for their stated purpose. Establishing a schedule of standard tests and monitoring the outcomes provides two benefits. The first is periodic maintenance and quality control in order to ensure consistently accurate results. The second is an opportunity for continuous or rolling improvements based on a combination of test results and new requirements. Using test results along with new requirements ensures model updates and improvements address known issues as well as new needs. Publishing this schedule confirms your commitment to analytics quality and improvement.

Entry Criteria and Inputs

- (analytics models and portfolios lists from 1 and 2)
- A list of control types and testing that will be used to validate data controls and testing regimes

Activity Steps

1.0 Draft a calendar-based sequence of testing for your analytic models and engines. Define the type of test (sensitivity analysis, stress test, back test) to be applied for each type of model or portfolio and engine.

2.0 Define testing regime including base-test data for use and test steps for each test type.

3.0 Identify template or standard test outcome document to include scores and other measures along with suggested improvements or changes.

4.0 Combine suggested improvements from testing with outstanding improvement requests on a periodic basis as each test cycle completes (eg, quarterly).

5.0 Establish with analytics officer improvement prioritization criteria and include in your improvement plan for use in quarterly improvement reviews.

6.0 Work with analytics officer to determine business impact or value measures for model improvements and include in criteria for prioritization.

7.0 Work with analytic officer to determine business impact measures and criticality levels for analytics engine issues and improvements. Note: Analytic engines often feed operational systems and will be highly prioritized for corrective changes and tuning improvements.

Exit Criteria and Outputs

- A calendar or periodic test plan with detailed list of test types by model and engine type
- A quarterly improvement review checklist including improvement suggestions from testing and user improvement requests
- Criteria-based prioritization of improvement request for analytic models and engines

Lead: Analytics Steward

Practice: Data and Analytics Stewards

Capability: Manage Quality and Risk

Level: 3. Improved

Activity: 304 Specify Data-Quality Improvements for Analytics

Description

Analytic models and engines are extremely sensitive to data-quality issues including timeliness, integrity, accuracy, and completeness. Your work in profiling and analyzing data quality as well as sensitivity to this quality provides a clear view of where data quality must be improved to support analytic precision and reliability. Capturing these improvement requirements establishes clear priorities for corrective and preventive data controls. These priorities will typically rise to the top of the stack because of the direct impact they have on performance analysis and execution.

Entry Criteria and Inputs

- Discovery and rules-based data-profiling results and issues
- Analytics testing results specific to data sensitivity

Activity Steps

1.0 Evaluate test results from analytic models and engines for data-quality sensitivity issues, list these issues, and identify the data sources causing them.

2.0 Evaluate data-quality profiling results (discovery and rules-based) and match up against the data sources you identified in the previous step. Generate a list of CDEs by data source with required improvements or issues.

3.0 Add this list of CDE improvements to your data or technical services que for data control development.

4.0 Stewards monitor and ensure completion of required corrective preventive controls to address the quality issues you have identified.

5.0 Follow up with analytic stewards to ensure subsequent testing of analytic models and engines shows improved results from improved data.

Exit Criteria and Outputs

- List of data-quality improvements required by source and CDE
- Agreed on corrective and preventive controls as implemented by data or technical services

Lead: Data Stewards

Practice: Data Services

Capability: Manage Quality and Risk

Level: 3. Improved

Activity: 305 Identify Corrective Control Candidates

Description

The Monitor and Expand activities should have generated improvement ideas and candidates. Some of these opportunities would be larger in scope than current program charters would permit, or would be generated from business and market changes and would be enterprise-wide in scope and impact. These candidates lend themselves to continuous improvement on a larger scale and are addressed in this activity.

Entry Criteria and Inputs

- Rules-based profiling results
- Data-quality dashboard indicators of long-running data issues by CDE
- List of business issues and concerns with current reporting and analysis

Activity Steps

1.0 The business sponsor and data officer should identify inefficiencies due to data-quality and lack of strong data management that have proven difficult to resolve due to the complexity, scope, and scale.

2.0 Using business analysis techniques, identify 1-10 targets for Improvement. Candidate selection criteria includes:

- 2.1 Poor data-quality resulting in lack of trust, manual correction, and/or manual data gathering for reporting and analysis.
- 2.2 Confusion on which systems, data stores, and reports are authoritative and trusted. Redundant CDEs.
- 2.3 Low business value and/or high operational costs, even if not officially charged back from IT.
- 2.4 High latency in terms of correct data being available when needed for decision making.
- 2.5 Inability or high project costs to add new reports, business processes, or analysis needed for new products/services or to respond to market changes.

3.0 Create business cases for the scenarios. See activities that generate business cases for examples.

4.0 Create a list of high-priority CDEs for corrective controls.

Exit Criteria and Outputs

- Prioritized list of corrective improvement CDEs for immediate action

Lead: Data Service Team

Practice: Data Services

Capability: Coordinate Data Relationships

Level: 3. Improved

Activity: 306 Define Required Corrective Controls for Master Data

Description

Master data corrections are extremely sensitive and therefore have a limited range of associated options. For internally controlled format and values it is essential that we identify business-accredited and change-controlled sources with full stewardship and quality monitoring in place. Externally mandated and provided reference data must be aligned and stewarded to external source values and formats. Care must be taken not to use inappropriate controls such as default values or probabilistic matching algorithms unless specifically endorsed by the data officer and owner.

Entry Criteria and Inputs

- Business data glossary
- Context diagram and data map
- Discovery and rules-based profiling results
- Data-quality dashboard issues and results

Activity Steps

1.0 Identify master data CDEs and their locations in supporting interfaces using the glossary and diagram.

2.0 Specify the type of master data and its original source or sources in these locations.

3.0 Review data-quality profiling results and identify master data CDEs with recurring data-quality issues.

4.0 Separate internally controlled master data CDEs and address with corrective controls based on the type of quality issue faced. Consider cleansing, replacement, or substitution options with the data officer and validate with business owner.

5.0 Address reference data CDEs based on their data-quality issues and recurrence. Identify their primary external sources and analyze the interfaces through which they are fed to determine issues in our handling of this external data.

6.0 Either improve interfaces for external reference data to enforce internal quality or identify better quality sources for that data. Capture outcome as a control requirement.

7.0 List above control requirements or improvements for sponsorship by data officer.

8.0 Include outputs from new controls from data-quality dashboard as implemented.

9.0 Prioritize with data officer and owners corrective control implementation plan.

Exit Criteria and Outputs

- List of control requirements for master data
- List of corrective controls required in data stores and interfaces
- Prioritized corrective control implementation plan

Lead: Data Steward

Practice: Data Stewardship

Capability: Manage Quality and Risk

Level: 3. Improved

Activity: 307 Implement Corrective Controls

Description

Corrective controls can effectively remedy many data-quality issues, especially when changing the root cause of these issues is prohibitively expensive. Using corrective controls is not, however, a panacea. It comes with real cost and impacts. A limiting factor in the use of corrective controls is the need to protect systems-of-record data from change. So we will target downstream authoritative data sources and interfaces that feed them for corrective controls.

Entry Criteria and Inputs

- Prioritized list of corrective improvement CDEs for immediate action
- Prioritized list of control requirements for master data

Activity Steps

1.0 Review the list of corrective control candidates, and map the CDEs to authoritative data stores (ADS). Identify the interfaces that feed these stores with these CDEs.

2.0 Work with technical services partners to determine which ADS and ADS feeding interfaces are undergoing or scheduled for enhancement or retirement.

3.0 For any locations pending retirement, identify the period of time before committed retirement and determine the value of proceeding or eliminating as a corrective control candidate.

4.0 Identify the timing of enhancements planned and the ability to include in their requirements corrective data controls. Engage project sponsors with data officer support to include these controls in their requirements.

5.0 For all other stores and interfaces, identify corrective control types appropriate to the issue and location. These include cleansing of inaccurate values, the addition of additional values not currently being populated, and other data validation approaches.

6.0 Work with data store and interface owners to identify timing and resources for corrective control placement based on analysis above.

7.0 Identify and assist data officer in escalating unfunded controls requirements. Monitor and report on status for all controls candidate to the data officer.

Exit Criteria and Outputs

- List of control points where corrective controls are required
- List of corrective controls requirements to be included in planned enhancements
- List of corrective controls required in data stores and interfaces
- Updates to the data-quality dashboard as controls are implemented

Lead: Data Service Team

Practice: Data Services

Capability: Manage Quality and Risk

Level: 3. Improved

Activity: 308 Track Benefits From Data Controls Automation

Description

A data-quality dashboard (DQ dashboard) is needed to ensure business benefits are being realized. The process of gathering and reporting the data-quality statistics can be a manual or automated process. The data-quality dashboard provides ongoing evidence of data controls automation as well as indications of data-quality conditions and issues. Data stewards, officers, and owners should all have access to and be appraised of data-quality dashboard information. The stakeholders need to know their responsibilities relative to the findings reported by the data-quality dashboard.

Entry Criteria and Inputs

- Data thresholds listing with effective dates
- A schedule for adjusting data-quality thresholds

Activity Steps

1.0 Engage data or technical services partners to develop the data-quality dashboard and an ongoing method for updating its information and displays. Ensure all relevance and effected data users will have read-only access to the dashboard.

2.0 Design DQ dashboard layout and inputs to reflect data-quality measures previously specified.

3.0 Define who will review the metrics and at what frequency.

4.0 Ensure that all stakeholders review and sign off on the DQ dashboard design and requirements.

5.0 Accept the completed system from IT and make sure the stakeholders are trained in the data-quality monitoring process, their responsibilities, and the automated system.

Exit Criteria and Outputs

- Summary of calculated benefits provided to the Data officer on a regular basis
- Benefit calculation review with the data officer to validate logic

Lead: Data Steward

Practice: Data Stewardship

#	Activity Name (New)
400	Enhance data and analytic standards
401	Apply data and analytic standards
402	Enhance master data standards
403	Execute standards-based master data improvements
404	Establish and apply hierarchy standards
405	Simplify or rationalize data interfaces
406	Analyze data store mappings for redundancies

Capability: Steward Data and Analytics

Level: 4. Standardized

Activity: 400 Enhance Data and Analytic Standards

Description

We produced an enterprise set of data standards in Level 1activities that we now need to expand based on our work with data-quality controls, measures, and outcomes. Data standards must evolve to reflect enterprise data needs as well as conditions. Enhancing our data standards will include additional new standards based on our expanded rules of quality and targets. At this juncture we can add analytic standards based on our experience in managing analytic models and portfolios.

Entry Criteria and Inputs

- A set of published data standards for naming, defining, quality, and change control of critical enterprise data

Activity Steps

1.0 Review existing data standards and identify changes and additions from work competed since their inception. Include standards for data-quality measurement and target setting as well as authority levels for systems of record and authoritative data stores.

2.0 Survey analytic stewards for analytic standards inputs including current guidelines or testing criteria for analytic models and portfolios.

3.0 Work with analytic stewards to compile analytic standards for models and portfolios including naming, definition, rules and logic, and portfolio standards.

- 3.1 Review current models and designs to identify potential shared components (eg, designs, rules and logic, output specifications, standardization) for best or leading examples as a foundation for new design.
- 3.2 Identify components and basic design elements from leading examples that can be used to define design standards for existing models within and across portfolios.

4.0 Review updated data and analytic standards with data and analytic officers to gain approval.

5.0 Publish updated standards and include them in regular stewardship reviews to communicate with data and analytics owners and users.

Exit Criteria and Outputs

- Updated enterprise data standards
- Analytic model and portfolio standards
- Formal communication of published standards to data and analytic steward communities
- Examples of model designs and components suitable for use as a template across new and existing models

Lead: Data Steward

Practice: Data Stewards

Capability: Steward Data and Analytics

Level: 4. Standardized

Activity: 401 Apply Data and Analytic Standards

Description

We have enhanced our data standards to reflect all of the work in improving quality and controls and have added standards for data models and portfolios. Now we need to review our data and analytic environments to identify and execute the activities required to bring them up to our new standards. These standards embody our capability maturity goals and tests. The extent to which our data and analytics meet these standards we will achieve our target maturity level.

Entry Criteria and Inputs

- Updated enterprise data standards
- Analytic model and portfolio standards
- Formal communication of published standards to data and analytic steward communities

Activity Steps

1.0 Compare previous data standards with the enhanced version and identify changes and enhancements. Review new analytics standards.

2.0 Work with data officer to prioritize critical data activities and critical data scope for standards-based improvement.

3.0 Work with analytic officer to identify priority-based ordering of analytic models and portfolios for standards-based improvement.

4.0 Based on priorities from data and analytic officers, generate a plan to make the required improvements with other stewards and data owners over time.

5.0 Communicate progress consistently with other officers and stewards, identify issues delays and impacts to the schedule for standards-based improvement.

6.0 Communicate timely completion of standards-based improvements to officers and stakeholders.

7.0 Track improvements in data and analytic quality, as measured by the dashboard, as new standards are achieved over time.

Exit Criteria and Outputs

- List of new and enhanced standards requiring actions and the scope of data or models to be acted on
- Plan for standards-based improvement
- Progress reporting for standards-based improvement against plan
- Tracking of quality improvements through standards elevation

Lead: Data Steward

Practice: Data Stewards

Capability: Coordinate Data Relationships

Level: 4. Standardized

Activity: 402 Enhance Master Data Standards

Description

Master data, including reference data, is subject to higher standards and external authorities. Master data standards are more sensitive and important than broad standards, because master data describes durable objects of a business (eg, customers, products, suppliers). Standards for master data impact a broad array of enterprise users in operations and analytic areas. Additionally, reference data that is governed by external authorities must align with external standards on a consistent basis. Examples include data describing and defining, geography, industry products, and terms and legal entities.

Entry Criteria and Inputs

- Updated enterprise data standards
- Industry reference data standards and sources
- Owners and operators of master data hubs or services

Activity Steps

1.0 Identify standards specific to master data domains (eg, product, customer, supplier, etc.) from master data management (MDM) hub operators and other business sources. Note: Master data standards often reflect requirements for resolution of individual master data values.

2.0 Collect reference data standards and inputs from industry sources and identify ongoing sources and timing for additional updates.

3.0 Identify authoritative master data locations and CDEs for standards-based improvement. Work with MDM hubs to apply standards-based improvements.

4.0 Identify reference data sources (external providers and authorities) and authoritative data stores to establish scope for reference data improvement.

5.0 Develop a plan based on prioritized master and reference data CDEs to apply standards-based improvements.

Exit Criteria and Outputs

- Required standards-based improvement to the master and reference data
- Plan for standard-based improvement of master data

Lead: Data Steward

Practice: Data Stewards

Capability: Coordinate Data Relationships

Level: 4. Standardized

Activity: 403 Execute Standards-Based Master Data Improvements

Description

This activity engages us in bringing our master data up to the new levels defined by our enhanced standards. The value of these improvements is twofold: the first level of value will be seen in the data, and the second level of values will be seen in consistently improved capabilities the standards require us to exhibit. It will take time to improve standards and even more time for these improvements to be reflected in our data-quality dashboards. It is therefore important to engage data and analytic officers as well as master and reference data service providers and hub operators to maintain a sense of momentum and identify interim benefits as they are achieved.

Entry Criteria and Inputs

- Required standards-based improvement to the master and reference data
- Plan for standard-based improvement of master data
- Current data-quality profiling results

Activity Steps

1.0 Identify the most impactful master and reference data areas or domains based on known problems in reporting, analysis or regulatory compliance. For example, difficulties in tracking and reporting accurate geographic or demographic information about our customers indicates a high-impact hotspot for immediate action.

2.0 Engage patterns in these high-impact hotspot areas to define the level of effort and timing of improvements, and establish support with them for permanent enhancements in corrective or preventive controls so that these improvements will be sustained.

3.0 Define and implement ongoing reference data controls to ensure only authoritative values and formats are used. Further enhance data standards to reflect authoritative sourcing requirements.

4.0 Measure changes and impacts to master and reference data users over time based on these changes.

5.0 Communicate the success of the standards-based improvements in the form of permanent controls and the need for continued monitoring of business and external required standards-based improvements in the future.

Exit Criteria and Outputs

- Ongoing tracking of changes and impacts
- Report of standards-based improvements and the controls that were created or updated by these improvements
- Addition to data dashboard of outputs from these controls
- Update to the data stewardship program schedule of reviews to include master and reference data standard changes

Lead: Data Steward

Practice: Data Stewards

Capability: Coordinate Data Relationships

Level: 4. Standardized

Activity: 404 Establish and Apply Hierarchy Standards

Description

Hierarchies represent an additional type of master data that adds to the complexity of embedded relationships and logic. Critical enterprise hierarchies including organizations, financial accounts, and human resource views are used in enterprise, financial, and performance reporting so their structural integrity and controlled change over time is critical to accurate reporting and outcomes. Managing hierarchies to a high enterprise standard, including the consistent use of the same hierarchies for both operational systems and analytic reporting, is critical to the firm's ability to reconcile its past, present, and future views.

Entry Criteria and Inputs

- Business data catalog

Activity Steps

1.0 Review the list of hierarchies and the CDEs that are tracked in them. Identify the master data domain for each hierarchy.

2.0 Outline standards for the generation, change control, structure, and use control of each hierarchy by each domain. Standards may need to be specific to each domain.

3.0 Draft standards with master data service providers and hub owners.

4.0 Identify hierarchy management system of record or authoritative store (hierarchy tools including oracle DRM and others).

5.0 Evaluate Draft standards based on current systems and data owner's ability to apply them.

6.0 Prioritize standards for adoption, and identify improvement actions and controls required by them.

7.0 Collaborate with technical and data services providers to implement hierarchy improvements and controls.

8.0 Ensure data or analytic stewards are assigned to track and manage hierarchy and change control including steward-based changes.

Exit Criteria and Outputs

- List of standards-based improvements and controls for hierarchies
- List of stewards assigned to monitor hierarchy changes and standards improvements.

Lead: Data Steward

Practice: Data Stewards

Capability: Manage Quality and Risk

Level: 3. Improved

Activity: 405 Simplify or Rationalize Data Interfaces

Description

Data landscapes often contain multiple, redundant interfaces that write-many-and-read-once. This is the exact opposite of efficient data utilization. This activity seeks to provide business benefit by reducing the cost of maintaining data interfaces that have overlapping/redundant functionality. This activity can be performed any time after the initial CDEs and authoritative data sources have been established. Events like a new program/project, new business requirements, cost-cutting initiative, and negative impact from poor data-quality can all trigger the need to identify redundant data.

Entry Criteria and Inputs

- Business sponsor backing
- Data analysis

Activity Steps

1.0 Enlist stakeholders in the data interface simplification efforts. Using a crowdsourcing approach, ask folks to identify redundancies that should be investigated as potential cost savings.

2.0 Review the following for simplification candidates:

- 2.1 Interface maintenance effort by application development full-time-equivalents (FTEs). Look for expensive to maintain interfaces, complex calculations, custom-coded instead of an ETL tool, and interfaces to low-value systems/reporting environments.
- 2.2 Data flow diagrams
- 2.3 Batch load windows and job scheduler
- 2.4 ETL meta-data repositories
- 2.5 Code repositories/impact analysis tools

3.0 Review the elimination candidate list generated from the analysis. Assign economic values in terms of the business impact if this interface is removed (should be low $$ impact), estimate the savings from eliminating the interface and its maintenance. Savings opportunities include:

- 3.1 Application development maintenance FTE resources.
- 3.2 Data ownership and data stewardship FTEs. Costs associated with correcting bad data, including regulatory fines as appropriate.
- 3.3 Data load (ETL) costs including interface/ETL maintenance in FTEs. Include a monetized (eg, allocation of IT operations FTEs) value for the amount of effort consumed in the batch load window.

4.0 In addition to the quantifiable benefits gathered above, define intrinsic and soft benefits that will accrue from the interfaces' elimination.

Capability: Manage Quality and Risk

Level: 4. Standardized

Activity: 405 Simplify or Rationalize Data Interfaces

Activity Steps, continued

5.0 Review the economic analysis with the stakeholder groups: data officer, business data stewardship group, data-quality expert and IT data experts. Generate an elimination candidate short list.

6.0 Socialize the elimination candidate list with both the data officer and IT data experts. Ask IT for project cost estimates to eliminate the proposed interfaces.

7.0 Review your business case recommendation with the data officer to gain his/her approval. Inform the business sponsor of the business opportunity via the data interface simplification effort.

8.0 Following the IT demand and governance processes, initiate the project.

Exit Criteria and Outputs

- Business case template
- Data simplification project business case
- IT project request

Lead: Data Steward

Practice: Analytics Steward

Capability: Manage Quality and Risk

Level: 4. Standardized

Activity: 406 Analyze Data Store Mappings for Redundancies

Description

Organic data growth and replication are a natural outcome of an ungoverned or poorly stewarded data resource. Identifying unneeded data store redundancy, in conjunction with governed data replication and growth, results in cost-effective data management. In this activity we identify unneeded, redundant data stores and establish a case for their consolidation and the generation of savings that results.

Entry Criteria and Inputs

- Context diagram and data map
- Rules-based profiling results
- Redundant interface list
- Business glossary

Activity Steps

1.0 Enlist stakeholders in the data store simplification efforts. Using a crowdsourcing approach, ask folks to identify redundancies that should be investigated as potential cost savings.

2.0 Review the following for simplification candidates:

- 2.1 Data-profiling results indicating multiple copies of the same data as defined in the business glossary.
- 2.2 Data map and context diagrams depicting locations and inputs of data stores.
- 2.3 Ongoing data issues reported by stewards from inconsistent reporting and analytic outputs indicating nonauthoritative data is being included in those efforts.

3.0 Generate a consolidation and elimination candidate list based on proven redundancy and identified reporting issues. Note: Consolidation is a viable option when dealing with redundancy since it allows for the combination of overlapping data stores. Consolidation also requires interface consolidation, which must be included in our cost analysis.

4.0 Review the elimination candidate list generated from the analysis. Assign economic values in terms of the business impact if this data store is consolidated or eliminated along with its interfaces (should be low $$ impact). Estimate the savings from consolidating or eliminating the data store along with its interfaces. Savings opportunities include:

- 4.1 Application development maintenance FTE resources.
- 4.2 Data ownership and data stewardship FTEs. Costs associated with correcting bad data, including regulatory fines as appropriate..
- 4.3 Data load (ETL) costs including interface/ETL maintenance in FTEs. Include a monetized (eg, allocation of IT operation's FTEs) value for the amount of effort consumed in the batch load window.
- 4.4 Data-based administration and archival management for redundant data.

Capability: Manage Quality and Risk

Level: 4. Standardized

Activity: 406 Analyze Data Store Mappings for Redundancies

Activity Steps, continued

5.0 In addition to the quantifiable benefits gathered above, define intrinsic and soft benefits that will accrue from the data stores' and interfaces' elimination.

6.0 Review the economic analysis with the stakeholder groups: data officer, business data stewardship group, data-quality expert, and IT data experts. Generate a prioritized elimination and consolidation candidate list.

7.0 Socialize the elimination candidate list with both the data officer and IT data service partners. Ask IT for project cost estimates to eliminate the proposed data stores and interfaces.

8.0 Review your business case recommendation with the data officer to gain his/her approval.

9.0 Following the IT demand and governance processes, initiate the project.

Exit Criteria and Outputs

- Prioritized elimination and consolidation list
- IT project documents

Lead: Data Steward

Practice: Analytics Steward

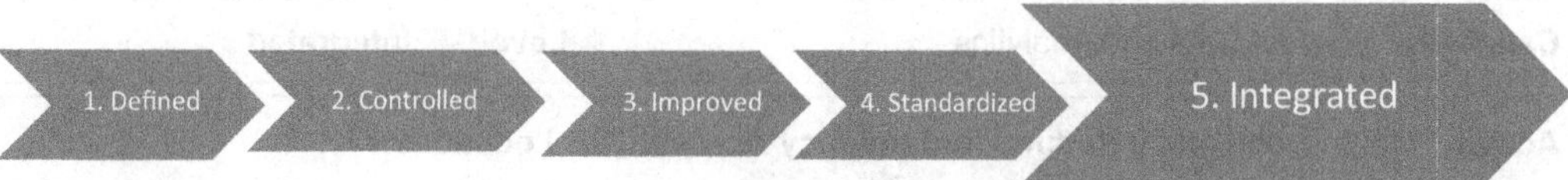

#	Activity Name (New)
500	Incrementally reduce redundancy across CDE locations
501	Provide impact analysis for new projects
502	Identify redundant and overlapping analytic models and portfolios
503	Apply leading analytic model designs and components
504	Identify hierarchy integration opportunities
505	Define strategic goals for data and analytic performance
506	Adjust periodic Steward and officer meetings and communications

Capability: Steward Data and Analytics | **Level:** **5. Integrated**

Activity: 500 Incrementally Reduce Redundancy Across CDE Locations

Description

The previous activities provided a mapping of redundant CDEs by locations, which, when leveraged with the rules-based data-profiling and the data-quality dashboard, guide data consolidation and redundant data elimination. This data integration activity reduces cost, complexity, and confusion due to the use of multiple, overlapping, and often completely redundant instances of critical data in multiple locations. Each CDE instance or location that is consolidated results in elimination of redundant data in data stores, data interfaces, and reports driving more certainty into the use of the remaining authoritative data.

Entry Criteria and Inputs

- Prioritized elimination and consolidation list
- IT project documents
- Business case template
- Data simplification project business case

Activity Steps

1.0 Generate list of redundant CDEs by location. For each location, identify level of authority (system of record or authoritative data store).

2.0 Flag CDEs in the redundancy list based on authority level (SOR, ADS, none).

3.0 Identify for each CDE location which redundant CDEs are nonauthoritative. Add to deletion candidate list.

4.0 Work with technical services to identify downstream interfaces, stores, reports, and users who would be impacted by eliminating the redundant CDE and remapping them to the CDE in the same location.

5.0 Use data-quality profiling and data-quality dashboard to identify differences in the values between the authoritative and the redundant, nonauthoritative CDE.

6.0 Publish an "intent to consolidate notice" with the technical and data service partners, ensuring that all identified downstream users are notified and engaged for acceptance.

7.0 Work through business case and technical design to ensure consolidation is sponsored, approved, and executed correctly.

8.0 Track and report on consolidation costs and benefits including ongoing savings from reduced interface and database administration for consolidated CDEs.

Exit Criteria and Outputs

- Flagged list of redundant CDEs by location
- Published "intent to consolidate notice"
- Report on consolidation costs and benefits

Lead: Data and Analytic Stewards | **Practice**: Data and Analytics Stewards

Capability: Steward Data and Analytics

Level: 5. Integrated

Activity: 501 Provide Impact Analysis for New Projects

Description

This is a business-driven activity to link new initiatives to meet the need for underlying data and process/IT system flexibility and to meet new business requirements. New business models often change the assumptions that went into the current IT systems and require change and adaptation.

Entry Criteria and Inputs

- Business reports
- Financial/client statements
- Business process efficiency feedback

Activity Steps

1.0 The data officer leads discussions with stakeholders to understand business changes and new requirements that break old assumptions and IT system's fit for use. These include:

  1.1 Gaps in process steps or data available to make key decisions.

  1.2 Cost savings opportunities through business process simplification.

  1.3 Low data-quality/low trust in the data source/report that lead to compensating behaviors. (eg, manual data gathering vs. business analysis, poor assumptions from missing or bad data, lack of consistent definitions and measures).

2.0 Generate list of prioritized candidates based on these evaluations.

3.0 Review the candidate list to assign business value, economic impact, and opportunity costs. Create the business case by defining both tangible (hard) and intangible (soft) benefits/costs and use quantifiable measures.

4.0 Review the business case with all of the stakeholders, incorporate feedback, and seek business sponsor approval.

Exit Criteria and Outputs

- Opportunity short list
- Validated business case
- Business sponsor approval
- Project initiated

Lead: Data and Analytics Stewards

Practice: Data and Analytics Stewards

Capability: Steward Data and Analytics

Level: 5. Integrated

Activity: 502 Identify Redundant and Overlapping Analytic Models and Portfolios

Description

Analytic models, and sometimes entire portfolios of these models, are built in business areas with specific analytic requirements and uses. As these areas develop ways to address their analytic needs, they often create models and portfolios that overlap with of their business areas who share similar needs and often data sources. In this activity, we'll work to identify potential overlaps and redundancies and provide stewardship-based communication among these groups to prevent redundant efforts and outcomes in the future.

Entry Criteria and Inputs

- Analytic model and portfolio standards
- Progress reporting for standards-based improvement against plan
- Data consolidation candidates or plans

Activity Steps

1.0 Review catalog of analytic models and portfolios to ensure that there is an analytic steward representing every area with models or a modeling effort in place.

2.0 Engage analytic stewards in dialogue using standard stewardship meetings about their current portfolios and plans for additions in each business area.

3.0 Review the catalog to identify models using similar or identical data sources and business rules or logic to conduct their analysis.

4.0 Generate a simple list of overlaps or redundancies in data sourcing across data models using the same data.

5.0 Share current data consolidation plan with analytic stewards to identify potential changes and impacts from data source and interface consolidation.

6.0 Collaboratively determine where data sourcing can be simplified to support multiple model feeds, ensuring that sourcing data quality, authority, and timing are consistent in each consolidation case.

7.0 Identify where data models are redundant based on both data sourcing and model logic. Coordinate consolidation of redundant models where possible with analytic stewards and officer.

Exit Criteria and Outputs

- Data source consolidation opportunities
- Data model consolidation opportunities
- Prioritized list of consolidation opportunities for steward and officer support

Lead: Analytics Stewards

Practice: Data and Analytics Stewardship

Capability: Manage Quality and Integrity

Level: 5. Integrated

Activity: 503 Apply Leading Analytic Model Designs and Components

Description

This activity seeks to consolidate redundant models or leverage leading model designs and components across similar types of models. Examples include standardizing notation and structure of business rules and logic and the resulting algorithms used in similar models. Standardizing model output including reporting, visualization, and analytic ending feeds to operational applications is another benefit of this activity. This activity differs from and builds on the work done to establish and apply design standards across analytic models in previous activities.

Entry Criteria and Inputs

- Analytic model and portfolio catalog
- Analytic model and portfolio standards
- Examples of model designs and components suitable for use as a template across new and existing models

Activity Steps

1.0 Work with analytic stewards to identify consistently high-performing risk models with little or no history of failure. Use these leading models to review standardizing business logic and algorithm and output formats to identify best-practice components and designs.

2.0 Work with analytic stewards to identify other models with poor performance histories that can benefit from using best-model components.

3.0 Identify opportunities to add best-components to poorly performing models and elevate to a standard at the portfolio level for similar types of models.

4.0 Document best-component design and testing methods including an ongoing maintenance approach and share with model developers to improve current state of model design and operation.

5.0 Review best-practice components to identify consistent methods they apply and rely on, eg, sensitivity analysis methods and back-testing approaches.

Exit Criteria and Outputs

- List of best-practice and performance-based components across models and portfolios
- Specifications for best-component methods and approaches
- List of models suitable for improvement with best-components and plan for improvement

Lead: Analytics Steward

Practice: Data and Analytics Stewardship

Capability: Coordinate Data Relationships

Level: 5. Integrated

Activity: 504 Identify Hierarchy Integration Opportunities

Description

Hierarchies are often developed and maintained by multiple systems in different areas for different purposes. This leads to inconsistencies between the areas using different versions of the same hierarchies, eg, financial statement, organizational unit, market- and product-based hierarchies. In this activity, we review our options to consolidate the authoring and publishing function for shared or enterprise hierarchies. We seek to "write once" and "publish many" of the same hierarchies for operational uses, reporting needs, and analytics. This approach can provide complete consistency across those uses in their results and presentation.

Entry Criteria and Inputs

- Catalog of hierarchies and systems that are currently used to generate them
- Analytics source-systems and interface list

Activity Steps

1.0 Identify all systems used to generate or change hierarchies across the enterprise.

2.0 Engage technical and data service partners in a review of hierarchy modeling, publishing, change control, and history management options. Look for a system and business area that can accommodate hierarchy management for all three types of targets.

3.0 Identify operational and reporting systems requiring internal or specialized hierarchy management. These systems may not be able to integrate hierarchies from a shared system.

4.0 Identify opportunities and high-level cost or effort estimates to consolidate hierarchy management across operational and reporting systems.

5.0 Group systems that can share a common hierarchy management service and identify benefits of consolidating hierarchy management for those systems. Note:/ Substantial benefits are often realized when you are able to share a common hierarchy system or service across operational (EGGL) reporting and analytic systems. This occurs because it forces alignment of the hierarchy dimensions used to record, report, and analyze enterprise performance information.

Exit Criteria and Outputs

- List of hierarchy management system or service consolidation options
- Prioritization of those options based on opportunities to span operational, reporting, and analytic systems

Lead: Data and Analytics Stewards

Practice: Data and Analytics Stewardship

Capability: Govern Programs and Services | **Level: 5. Integrated**

Activity: 505 Define Strategic Goals for Data and Analytic Performance

Description

Data and analytic officers continue to own the goal setting, measurement definition, and strategic roadmapping responsibilities for the data program of function. Leading practices favor permanent organizational functions, but, even within a program design, the officers are the intersection of business demand and data supply. In this activity, officers update the initial goals, measures, and roadmap they used to establish their program or function in the original charter.

Entry Criteria and Inputs

- Original charter with goals, measures, and roadmap
- Current status as reported by stewards
- Current survey or summary of business stakeholder satisfaction, issues, and concerns

Activity Steps

1.0 Review inputs to determine progress toward originally stated goals and milestones in your roadmap.

2.0 Identify roadmap milestones that have been accelerated or are outstanding and determine the cause for these gaps.

3.0 Review business inputs to determine what adjustments are needed to current goals and measures.

4.0 Engage stewards and data/technical services partners to estimate timing and resource requirements for these goals.

5.0 Update and extend roadmap to reflect new goals, timing, and resource requirements.

6.0 Consider strategic enterprise goals and direction including growth acquisitions, dispositions, and changes in markets or products and services. Adjust or enhance strategic goals and roadmap to include planning and requirements milestones for enterprise strategic plans and commitments.

7.0 Publish the updated roadmap, goals, and measures and review with business owners and steward community. Identify updates that may be needed to the dashboard and other reporting systems the stewards use.

Exit Criteria and Outputs

- Revised strategic roadmap with updated goals and measures
- Business owner approvals
- Stewardship community adoption

Lead: Data and Analytic Officers | **Practice**: Program Governance

Capability: Govern Programs and Services

Level: **5. Integrated**

Activity: 506 Adjust Periodic Steward and Officer Meetings and Communications

Description

Data programs and functions mature over time and require periodic adjustment to their operating models. These adjustments can include timing, frequency, and compositions of standing councils, committees, and working groups. They also include changes in our communication process and business engagement model. These changes keep the program of function dynamic and engaged with all its stakeholders.

Entry Criteria and Inputs

- Current schedule of meetings for all levels of the program or function
- Feedback from program or function participants, including stewards, officers, and owners, regarding efficiency and effectiveness of their effort

Activity Steps

1.0 Review feedback provided by all participants specific to timing and duration of meetings at all levels.

2.0 Review feedback for all written, electronic, and verbal communications to identify which are seen as most effective.

3.0 Evaluate overall participation levels and progress to goals in your strategic roadmap.

4.0 Identify adjustments in meetings, communication, and participation including: the organization of data steward council, steward and service working groups, and officer-level committees.

5.0 Review adjustments with officers and stewards and commit to owners. Monitor effects and adjust as needed.

Exit Criteria and Outputs

- Changes to participation, communication, and collaboration
- Communication and monitoring

Lead: Data and Analytics Officers

Practice: Program Governance

CHAPTER

ALIGNING THE LANGUAGE OF BUSINESS: THE BUSINESS GLOSSARY

5

Aligning the terminology used throughout business and technology teams is a critical challenge for the data governance teams in most organizations. This chapter presents solutions for achieving those objectives and answering the following questions:

- Does your data governance team have the processes and resources to accomplish this?
- How many existing term dictionaries or glossaries are in the organization that you can leverage (or resolve)?
- Why are there different definitions for a business term across business units and functions?
- Do you anticipate that your organization will have an informal or formal process for the glossary taxonomy and term definitions?
- Will the creators and contributors to the glossary be limited to the data governance team or can anyone in the organization contribute?
- Will the glossary be used for managing business communications or for managing the alignment of business and technology implementations and metrics?
- How will the organization use the glossary for tactical and operational processes?
- What standards and practices will the data governance team follow to manage the taxonomy and terms?
- What are the expectations for traceability of a business term to physical columns, reports, and metrics?
- What are the activities, tasks, deliverables, and resources roles necessary to manage the data lifecycle for a business glossary?

We want to first bring you back to the graphic of our Playbook framework (Fig. 5.1). The business glossary is developed through the efforts described in the "Define and Catalog Business Terms" activity.

This chapter discusses the activities and objectives of cataloging and mapping business terms and technical data assets, ie, creating a "business glossary." We define a business glossary as a common, consumable business vocabulary for clear communications throughout an enterprise, which is the term generally accepted and used by many software vendors. This chapter discusses the purpose of having a business glossary, as well as the processes for creating and maintaining an efficient one.

WHY DO WE NEED A BUSINESS GLOSSARY?

Why is it so challenging to communicate across an organization? We used to believe that the organizational gaps in communications only existed between technology and business. Certainly that gap still exists, but it also exists between business units, due in part to our individual experiences, education, and

1. Defined

#	Activity Name
100	Define Initial Scope & Sponsorship
101	Identify authorities, experts, owners and stewards
102	Establish Governance Program Operating Model
103	Identify capability & risk reduction measures
104	Engage or Establish Data Service
105	Define & Catalog Business Terms
106	Define & Catalog Data Elements
107	Prioritize & Flag Critical Data Elements
108	Conduct Discovery Data Profiling
109	Use Discovery Profiling Results to Set Quality Rules & Targets
110	Catalog Analytic Models
111	Identify analytics model portfolios
112	List master subjects, objects & hierarchies
113	Identify Physical Data with Systems and Interfaces
114	Identify Systems of Record and Authority
115	Identify External Data Subscribers
116	Identify External Data Sources
117	Identify External Data Provider & Subscriber Risks
118	Identify & Register Risks From & To Critical Data
119	Coordinate Control & Testing Standards with Risk & Audit

2. Controlled

#	Activity Name (New)
200	Design Rules based Profiling Controls
201	Establish Data Quality Reporting Thresholds and Targets
202	Execute Rules based Data Profiling, Reporting & Alerting
203	Analyze Data Quality Issues for Corrective Control Needs
204	Identify Reporting & Analytics Impacted by Data Issues
205	Identify Master Data Control Points
206	Define External Data Quality Rules & Thresholds for SLAs
207	Score External Data Providers for Quality & Risk Issues
208	Evaluate Data Risk and Exposure
209	Establish Analytics Model Controls at Portfolio Level
210	Generate Analytics Map to Illustrate Uses of Analytic Models Across the Enterprise
211	Update Risk and Audit Partners

Improved

#	Activity Name (New)
300	Define & Publish Controls Operating Model
301	Implement Monitoring Process
302	Create Data or Technical Service Improvement Plan
303	Create Analytic Testing & Improvement Plan
304	Specify Data Quality Improvements for Analytics
305	Identify Corrective Control Candidates
306	Define Required Corrective Controls for Master Data
307	Implement Corrective Controls
308	Track Benefits From Data Controls Automation

4. Standardized

#	Activity Name (New)
400	Enhance Data and Analytic Standards
401	Apply Data and Analytic Standards
402	Enhance Master Data Standards
403	Execute Standards-Based Master Data Improvements
404	Establish and Apply Hierarchy Standards
405	Simplify or Rationalize Data Interfaces
406	Analyze Data Store Mappings for Redundancies

5. Integrated

#	Activity Name (New)
500	Incrementally Reduce Redundancy Across CDE Locations
501	Provide Impact Analysis for New Projects
502	Identify Redundant & Overlapping Analytic Models and Portfolios
503	Apply Leading Analytic Model Designs and Components
504	Identify Hierarchy Integration Opportunities
505	Strategic Goals for Data & Analytic Performance
506	Adjust Periodic Steward & Officer Meetings & Communications

FIGURE 5.1

Playbook framework.

FIGURE 5.2

Understanding the context; mole or mole.

cultural factors that provide us our "context of knowledge." We spend years focusing our education and professional life in a given field, such as finance or marketing, and the language and practices of each field of specialization are vastly different. Yet when 10 of us gather in a conference room to discuss the implementation of an application with hundreds of processes that involve 2 or even 70 different teams, we expect that everyone walks into the room with the same understanding of the vocabulary and terminology, has the same vision, and has the same "context" and background. Well, that is just not true. It is not true in smaller nonprofit organizations or in international corporations.

Have you ever been in a meeting and not understood what was being said or even the context of the discussion? Most of us have many times. The discussion may seem trivial so we don't ask questions. This was me for about the first 10 years of my professional life: Make like you understand in the room and then figure it out later. Well, in today's complex enterprise technology applications a lack of clear understanding can have significant impacts. Let's take look at a really farfetched example to make a point (Fig. 5.2).

Let's say this is a land management or farming organization. George is the person questioning what the discussion has to do with a "mole" on someone's face. The actual discussion is about the animal "mole" wreaking havoc on the land. Now if George is the technology Business Intelligence (BI) developer, or the data steward data-quality analyst, he is unlikely to meet his deliverables completely the first time, which may potentially cause project delays that may not be recognized until the phase of integration testing. But the issue is not necessarily George's fault. George did not have the "tribal knowledge" or context to know that the discussion was about an animal and not a skin anemology.

There are literally thousands of examples of language issues that can occur in every line of business. We often present the importance of having a business glossary at conferences. When I speak with a partner we put on a little skit where I talk about the limited amount of "time" we have and my partner, generally Bonnie O'Neil, talks about the vast amount of "thyme" we have. Another play on words, yes, but the language used in organizations has thousands of similarities.

Fortunately we now know we have communication challenges. Even more fortunate is that we now have resources such as data stewards that can establish and manage the vocabulary, definitions, hierarchies, and actual data value sets for us.

Everyone employed in an organization has different professional experiences, yet we must all be integrated into the culture and language of the organization. But how do we know the language of our organization? Historically, we learn the language of our organization one project at a time through what is commonly called "tribal knowledge." But what does that mean for our own individual context?

In most organizations, there is no glossary of terms or the glossary is not up to date. A few years ago we met a team from a large railroad firm that had 26 lists of business terms. Of course, there were 26 from legacy systems, old projects that were not completed, and from lots of mergers and acquisitions. The glossaries were in MS Word, on paper, or stored in Sharepoint. Most had similar terms, and many terms were inconsistent, incomplete, and often conflicting between the two lists. We will talk about how to resolve multiple lists of business terms later in this chapter. But what made us start discussing the challenge of business vocabulary was our work with a media firm. This media firm made billions in sales per year and operated in 14 western US states. While not a multinational firm due to years of merger and acquisition activity, high growth, and recent application consolidation (200+ applications integrated into one new system) the organization had many vocabulary issues. We were engaged to fix the "metadata problems." It took about a week to recognize that the issues did not concern the technical metadata but the business terminology and definitions, mostly of the term "customer" (a yellow page advertiser specifically).

The organization had what we call today a data stewardship committee. They met quarterly over a few years but had not achieved their goal of a single definition of customer. The team was staffed with very knowledgeable, dedicated, and experienced staff members from many business units, all with a great desire to complete their mission but with specific business unit views of the business processes and organizational touch points of a customer. In fact, the committee had been in place long enough to get a nickname, "the donut committee." My guess is that they ate a lot of donuts during meetings, but did not meet their objectives.

They believed they had to resolve their individual business units' definition of customer into one global definition that would apply to all business processes and business units. ***This is an issue many of you may be facing: Creating one definition for a business term that is appropriate for all business uses, which may not be realistic***.

Important Practice—One and only one definition for a business term for all business uses across an organization is often not realistic. It is more effective for communications to create a business term definition specific to the business use and name the term appropriately to align with the definition. Each term name should be specifically derived from the definition (refer to ISO 11179). Thus we may have many types of "customer" defined and named accordingly. In the case of the media firm, it was necessary to define four different types of "customer" to effectively manage the business processes and metrics the organization needed.

WHAT IS A BUSINESS GLOSSARY?

Guess what? There are no industry standards for what constitutes a business glossary. This should not be a surprise, as each vendor defines the glossary to fit the technology implementation they have developed. ***For the purpose of this book, we define a business glossary to be a technology repository that***

can contain many items or objects associated with a business term. This repository must be easily managed, changed, and accessible by everyone in the organization (within certain limitations). The glossary repository may contain business definitions, logical data descriptions, and physical implementation descriptions such as the following:

- Business term names
- Business term definitions
- Business term acronyms and abbreviations
- Related business term names (related but not synonyms)
- Identification (name and contact information) of the individuals responsible for managing the business term
- Related terms (but not synonyms)
- Logical and physical data models associated
- Applications responsible for managing the lifecycle of the associated physical table/column
- Physical table/columns associated with the business term
- Data lifecycle, lineage, and transformations descriptions
- Physical data values for the table/column and the definition of each value
- Business rules and validation rules descriptions
- Data-quality expectations and actual quality metrics associated with the table/column
- Business metrics associated and how to use the metrics
- Security and privacy limitations and use

We have used many different technologies for the actual repository, such as Wikipedia, Microsoft Word, Excel, and many formal database repository products. But the technology you use to store the glossary doesn't need to be formal; we have used spreadsheets, too (this is the basis of our data governance Playbook). The repository can be an Excel spreadsheet or a set of tables in the Playbook. Many of our implementations have used our example of the glossary in our Playbook as an initial repository until a formal database repository could be implemented.

Reader Callout—Focus first on the content of the business glossary and not the technology you will use to store it. A formal data governance technology tool improves the productivity of the team, as well as increasing the usability of the glossary content. However, it is the content that is important. We have used less complex technology, such as Excel, very effectively. Look at what you already have in your organization before you spend time searching and paying for a new complex repository technology. Many people already have the technology they need for a business glossary.

THE GLOSSARY IS A CRITICAL DELIVERABLE OF THE DATA GOVERNANCE TEAM

The business glossary is a critical deliverable from the data governance team. As someone once said, "you can't manage what you can't define." This means the data governance team will need to identify the scope of responsibility and then define the critical data within that scope to manage the organization's data, such as the meaning of "retail customer." For example, the retail customer data governance team should identify the following:

- What is the definition of retail customer?
- How is retail customer data different from any other customer data?

- What is the lifecycle and lineage of the retail customer data?
- What are the security, privacy, and compliance concerns for the retail customer data?
- What are the internal metrics? How and where are the metrics created and maintained?
- What are the associated business rules, data values, and data-quality rules?
- What applications will create, maintain, report, and archive the retail customer data?
- How do we communicate the policies, standards, data, and metrics about the retail customer and our activities to all individuals in the organization?

The business glossary should be the repository used to manage this critical information for the data governance team. We used to try to force this information into a Wikipedia-style dictionary, or into our data modeling tools, but we were not very successful for a multitude of reasons. However, we have successfully used our Excel Playbook format for many organizations, but it may not be suitable for complex organizations. Fortunately over the last decade we have found tools that are functionally better. We discuss business glossary technologies in Chapter 6.

To manage this set of data the data governance team can follow our approach, which includes many of the following objectives:

- Identify and catalog the business terms, data elements, and processes within the scope of responsibility
- Develop a vocabulary and taxonomy for the business terminology within the scope
- Develop the definitions, term names, business rules, etc., for the business terms that will be within the scope
- Develop the best practices and guidelines (iteratively) for using the data to support data governance efforts of
  - Data—How is it defined, where and how is it created, what data models and databases contain this data, how to it should be used, and how not to use it and when
  - Processes—What is the lifecycle of the data, what applications manage the data, what transformations occur, and what is the temporality of data change and use?
  - Controls—What are the internal controls on the data, what are the regulatory controls, what are the regulatory reporting requirements, and how to communicate controls for creation, maintenance, and use
  - Quality—What are the attributes of quality, defining business rules, managing quality expectations, conducting quality analysis, communicating quality results

Of course not all of this business and technical metadata is captured at one time. Much of this information is disbursed across the organization, not captured at all, be captured in many nonintegrated technologies, or be "tribal knowledge." In our work with organizations across many different industries, we have found that it is common for the critical data governance information to be very federated or distributed across many technologies and individuals in the organization. The size of the organization is not necessarily the issue; large international or small nonprofits have the same problem.

We recently worked with a midsized nonprofit and found the challenges to be similar, albeit less in complexity, but just as significant. Different business units have different contexts and thus different definitions, metrics, and uses for the same business term. For example, let's look at the term "constituent." A "constituent" could mean about 10 different things depending on the context and role of the person, and can even mean an organization. In this example, it was made more complex since the two core operational applications had their own context and business rules. Both applications were purchased and managed by outside vendors. Every organization has similar challenges, either through purchased applications or through M&A activities.

On the surface it may seem that those two applications had a common definition of "constituent" since they synchronized constituent profiles three times per day. But that wasn't the case. Application A managed all online (Web-based) profiles and gift donations, while application B managed all offline profiles and gift donations. But the two applications did not synchronize all data of the same type. Since the organization did not want to pay both vendors to maintain the same grain of data and business processes, they considered the definitions the same for both applications. However, application A had 11 million "constituent" profiles and application B had 23 million "constituent" profiles, and only data from a few million had actually been shared between the two applications. Thus many data governance and BI questions had to be asked such as which application is the system of record, which application has the correct business metrics, and which application can be used for financial reporting (neither had all the data)?

This organization had to resolve the business terminology issue through good data governance practices. They found that a "constituent" could be defined in many ways such as:

- Event participant
- Self-donor
- Team captain
- Patient family member
- Patient (having the disease)
- Patient friend
- Individual advocate
- High volume donor
- Event volunteer
- Sponsoring organization
- National donor organization

Furthermore, each definition came with its own unique business definitions, business rules, reporting requirements, financial and compliance concerns, business metrics, data lifecycle management, and business operations activities. And of course, many had unique data-quality and physical data lineage reporting requirements. However, each of those terms was physically implemented as one single identifier in the database of the applications.

The vocabulary/ontology challenge is often made even more complex because of the business and data-quality rules of the business. In this case a team captain can also be an event participant and a self-donor, as well as a high volume donor and a patient friend. Thus one constituent in the database can be recognized as one or as many as five different types of people to count and track. As you can see the business term definitions have a direct impact on the BI metrics, data-quality measures, and what the data governance team may be expected to manage.

The business glossary is a critical data governance deliverable. Our nonprofit example is very typical of the challenges around master data management. Thus it is critical to have all of the various roles associated with each topic uniquely named, defined, and lifecycle managed from a governance standpoint. Then the mappings, data-quality services, and lineage can be related to the business terms as subsequent and ongoing processes.

Architecture Level	Architecture Object	Object Definition Construct
Business Concept	Business Term Name	Business Definition
Logical Data Model	Data Attribute Name	Attribute Definition
Physical Data Model	Physical Column Name	Column Description
Database Table Structure	Data Element Name	Data Element Description
User Report Structure	Report Element Name	Report Element Description

FIGURE 5.3

Business term architecture lineage.

Most development processes can begin with defining our business terms during the initial requirements phase. The objective should be to establish a business-level definition and understanding. The business terms and definitions can then be leveraged during the logical and physical modeling development activities. The business terms and definitions can also be used in the reporting development activities to establish alignment with the business understanding and requirements. Fig. 5.3 shows this flow.

Reader Callout—Identifying the roles and differences in each attribute of master or reference data is critical for the data governance team. A lack of clarity in the business rules across an organization is often the main reason to build a business glossary. Business units and reporting often disagree on metrics due to the lack of recorded and agreed-on business rules, which must be addressed. You must also strive to eliminate synonyms in terms. A "customer" definition may not always be specific enough to manage the roles of "customer," and many terms and definitions are unnecessary for the governance of the business data across the organization. Each business use of data may need to have its own unique definition and name.

IDENTIFYING USERS OF THE BUSINESS GLOSSARY

Business glossary implementations often fail due to a lack of forethought on the potential users of the business glossary. Many early glossary implementations were focused on the technology or even metadata management organization. Some organizations have suggested that the users of a glossary are only part the data management or governance within the organization. But in our opinion everyone in an organization is a potential user of the glossary. Yes, the data governance team may be responsible for approving business terms and definitions, but everyone in the organization that works with data should have access to the business glossary, since everyone in the organization is likely to use data as part of their job, and they need to understand the context of that data, as well as how and how not to use that data.

Many studies over the last decade have found that even highly educated and experienced middle managers and executives have made mistakes simply due to misunderstanding the data presented to them. Thus we are adamant that everyone in the organization is likely to use the glossary in specific cases.

We recommend that the data governance team employ a use-case and user-story approach to identifying the types of uses and users of the glossary. We often start by looking at the business and technical roles within the organization. These roles may include the following:

- Senior leadership team (CEO, CMO, CRO, CFO, chairman)
- Chief data officer

- Data governance team
- Business data analysts in each business unit (they are out there, operational and analytics)
- Research analytics in the research team as well as in each business unit
- Business operational management (marketing, sales, finance, support, operations, HR)
- Executives in decision-making roles in each business unit
- IT analysts
- IT architects
- IT development
- IT QA
- IT project and configuration management
- Compliance, audit, and security

It is easy to say that everyone is a user, but what does that mean in terms of identifying how the glossary should be presented to all users maximize the effectiveness of the glossary across the organization?

Identifying the users and usage of the glossary is critical to the long-term value of the glossary to the organization. It is not a "technology science" exercise. You will not be able to define all of the uses at the beginning of the glossary implementation, but you can define those you know and establish a process to understand the others (see the section, "Glossary Maturity"). Capturing the enterprise knowledge in your glossary is nice, but the desired outcome and economic value is in the effective use of the glossary across the organization. Leverage what tools you already have in your organization such as SharePoint, Wiki, or other collaboration tools. Remember that training is key to long-term success.

CREATING THE BUSINESS GLOSSARY STRUCTURE

The processes of defining business terms, maintaining the data in the business glossary, and determining the roles involved are dependent on the style of data governance implemented. We generally suggest an organization start with an informal governance structure, such as the one in Fig. 5.4.

Each of these categories of processes includes many detailed processes. The creation and update of data may be accomplished by different resource roles. Thus it is appropriate to align the resource roles with the maintenance processes.

INITIAL ATTRIBUTES OF THE GLOSSARY

Data governance teams can be overwhelmed by the number of attributes that can be captured in a business glossary. For example, we consider the following to be the ultimate set of attributes for each business term in a glossary:

1. Term definition
2. Term definition update date
3. Term definition status
4. Term definition status date
5. Term definition deprecated date
6. Term definition updated by user ID

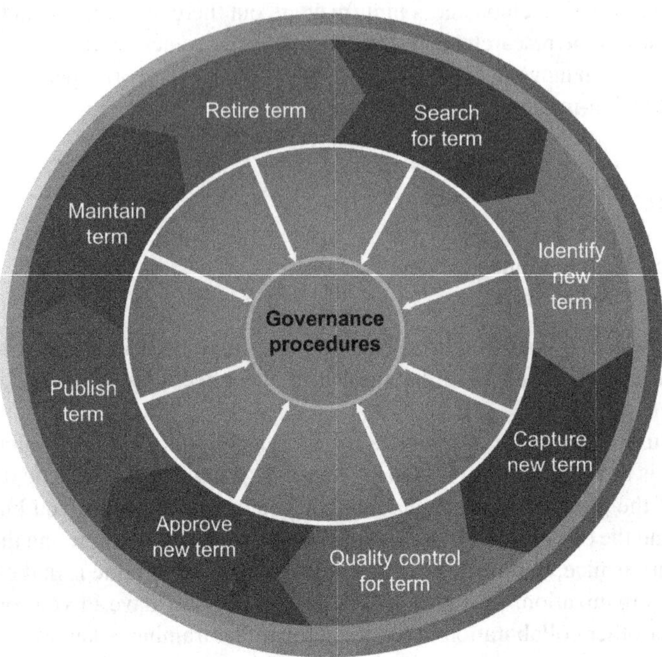

FIGURE 5.4

Business term lifecycle.

7. Term name
8. Term name update date
9. Term name status
10. Term name status date
11. Term name deprecated date
12. Term name updated by user ID
13. Term definition example
14. Term use description (how to and how not to use)
15. Last update date
16. Term category, subcategory name (related to taxonomy or subject area) (1 or many)
17. Term acronym
18. Term abbreviation
19. Related term name (1 or many)
20. Replacement term name
21. Managed by business unit
22. Managed by application
23. Managed by business function
24. Data steward name

25. Data steward contact phone, email, location
26. Data steward alternate contact phone, email, location
27. Term logical business rules
28. Term use restrictions
29. Security and compliance rules and restrictions
30. Mapped IT assets
    a. Physical column name and table name (1 or many)
    b. Database name/scheme name (1 or many)
    c. Report name (1 or many)
    d. Data integration process name (1 or many)
31. Data-quality expectations/profiling
    a. Column name (1 or many)
    b. Business term name
    c. Date profiled
    d. Completeness percentage
    e. Validity percentage
    f. Nonvalid percentage

Does this mean that the data governance team needs to start populating all of the above (about 41 attributes)? Absolutely not.

We believe the glossary team starts and completes the initiate stage by defining the following 10 attributes for each business term. When pressed for time and resources this can be reduced to the six bold attributes. These 10 attributes are the critical data that needs to be cataloged for each business term.

1. **Term definition**
2. **Term name**
3. **Term definition example (can be imbedded in the definition attribute but we recommend against it)**
4. **Term acronym**
5. **Term abbreviation**
6. **Term security and compliance restrictions**
7. Defined by person name (name of the person creating the term definition)
8. Data steward name (assuming there is not just one steward)
9. Data steward contact information (phone, email, location)
10. Term logical business rules (business, referential integrity, and quality)

The description of each attribute will be described in the section on Standards. Additionally, there are about six attributes that can have default values created to eliminate data entry activities. The attributes are:

1. Term definition date (today's date)
2. Term definition status (value of "candidate")
3. Term definition status date (today's date)
4. Term name update date (today's date)
5. Term name status (value of "candidate")
6. Term name status date (today's date)

If there is only one data steward that needs to be identified, then you can use an additional two attributes, the steward name and contact information.

THE STANDARDS OF A BUSINESS GLOSSARY

Reader Callout—Having a "standards document" is important. Every IT organization has a template for a standards document. You should leverage what you have available to create a standard for the content and use of the business glossary. We also recommend that standards be versioned and considered as changeable (not set in stone). It is common for the standards of a business glossary to change as the organization grows, such as additional attributes, physical mappings, or refining the wording of definitions.

Having standards for the business glossary is critical to set expectations for the creation, maintenance, and quality of the content in the glossary. We have found that many organizations struggle to create good business term definitions. Creating a good definition is often a difficult concept for both the technical and business resources. However, creating a good definition is just one of the items the standards document needs to cover.

A business glossary standards document can leverage the industry ISO 11179 standard. While 11179 was originally intended to be a data modeling standard, it does cover how to create good definitions and attribute names based on unique definitions of data objects. While intended for logical data columns, we can apply the concepts to business glossary terms and definitions.

The structure of the business glossary standards should include sections such as:

- Version Management Section
- Approvals Section
- Scope and Objectives of the Standard
- Conformance and Quality Concerns
- Business Term Definitions and Example Standards
- Business Term Naming Standards
- Standards for Abbreviations and Acronyms
- Standards for Glossary Term Completeness
- Standards for Mapping Physical Columns
- Standards for Mapping Reporting Columns
- Standards for Glossary Usage and Reporting
- Standards for the Approval Processes and Workflow
- Standards for Communications of Term Changes (Change Management)
- Standards for Glossary Training
- Standards for Glossary Usage and Access

CREATING BUSINESS TERMS DEFINITIONS AND TERM NAMES

Reader Callout—There are a few areas of discussion in the industry around the creation of business term definitions and names. Some people suggest that one general name is adequate, such as "customer." Then, all of the definitions related to customer are associated with the one term, customer. This creates a dictionary-like glossary where a term may have many definitions and synonyms. We believe this creates ambiguity and makes the context of the term confusing. Remember, the objective is to eliminate ambiguity and provide a specific context for the term in your business vocabulary. General term names and definitions, synonyms, and nonspecific terminology limit the business value of the glossary.

We are often asked, "Which comes first, the business term or the term definition?" This is a great question. I always answer with "it does not matter in this case," because if you have a business term you have to create a unique definition for that term. We often find that when creating the unique definition we have to apply modifiers to the term name, effectively changing the term name. If your objective is to eliminate ambiguity in the organization's vocabulary (and it should be), then the business term name must be derived from the business term definition. It is true that this is often an iterative effort of defining, then naming, then refining the definition, then refining the name. By the way, this is the ISO 11179 standard approach. That is to create the definition of the object and then create or revise the name to be appropriate with the definition. The term name can have the necessary modifiers in it so that the name is unique to the definition.

TERM DEFINITION

Data is used for specific business purposes. Differences in use require different operational manifestations that include some of the requirements and recommendations. For example, different levels of specificity for data definitions are generally required in different contexts such as retail versus commercial. Again, we can follow the principles of ISO 11179. A data definition should:

- State the essential meaning of the concept
- Be precise and unambiguous
- Be concise
- Be able to stand alone (this will be very hard for technology resources to achieve)
- Be expressed without embedding rationale, functional use, or procedural information
- Avoid circular reasoning
- Use the same terminology and consistent logical structure for related definitions
- Be appropriate for the type of item being defined

A good business glossary definition should answer the traditional six operatives: what, how, where, who, when, and why. Capturing all of the six operatives is often difficult, requires detailed functional knowledge of the subject, and time and effort to get the term and its definition. We often want to identify a missing term and add it immediately with just a basic definition, but this is not recommended since definitions like this are not complete and accurate.

Term Definition: A textual description of the business object or term. The definition should meet the standards defined in the standards document including:

- A few descriptive sentences that give the essential business meaning of the concept and how this concept is different from other similar concepts.
- Be concise, precise, and unambiguous
- Define what the concept is **and** what it is not
- Should not be defined exclusively by stating what the concept is not
- Contain only commonly understood abbreviations or spelled out abbreviations
- Be expressed without embedding definitions of other concepts or circular definitions
- Be defined without embedded rationale, functional use, or procedural information
- Data domain or value set must be appropriate for the description of the definition

Broad Term: Many organizations find it valuable to include the concepts "broad term" and "narrow term" in the definitions to establish a relationship between the term and its business vocabulary and taxonomy. A broad term is used to establish the relationship to the highest level of a taxonomy, business structure, or subject area. For example, a teaspoon would have the broad term "utensil–eating utensil." Organizations that have a functional understanding of how to leverage their product or organizational taxonomy find it easier to create broad and narrow terminology.

Narrow Term: Relationship to the lowest level of a taxonomy or business structure or subject area. For example, a teaspoon would have a narrow term of "spoon" (not ladle).

TERM NAME

Term names should be derived from the definition that describes the concept. For example, if the object is defined as "the name of an individual person who only conducts stock trades in the category of institutional products or institutional lines of business products," then the term name could be something like "institutional trader name." Differences in use require different operational manifestations of some requirements and recommendations. For example, different levels of specificity for data definitions are generally required in different contexts.

Business glossary term names should:

- Be stated in the singular (eg, agency not agencies)
- Use qualifiers in a name (if appropriate) to add preciseness (rail station, ferry station)
- State what the concept is, not only what it is not
- Be stated as a descriptive phrase or sentence
- Contain only commonly understood abbreviations in the name
- Be expressed without embedding definitions of other data or underlying concepts

It is common for business term names to be changed once clear definitions has been harmonized across the organization.

BEST PRACTICES

The following recommendations provide an example of the need for varying levels of specificity for different definitions. The practice "state the essential meaning of the concept" is context-dependent, ie, the primary characteristics necessary to convey the essential meaning of a particular definition, which will vary according to the level of generalization or specialization of the data. Primary and essential characteristics for defining concepts such as "airport" in the commercial air transportation industry might be specific, whereas a more general definition may be adequate in a different context. Within a metadata registry, multiple equivalent definitions may be written in different languages or, within a single language, for different audiences such as children, the general public, or subject area specialists. For a discussion of relationships between concepts in different contexts and how characteristics are used to differentiate concepts, see ISO 704, clause 5. Definitions should be written to facilitate understanding by any user and by recipients of shared data.

To facilitate understanding of the requirements for the construction of well-formed business term definitions, explanations and examples are provided below. Each requirement is followed by a short explanation, and examples are given to support the explanations. In all cases, an example is provided to illustrate the explanation. When helpful, a poor, but commonly used example, is given to show how a definition should **NOT** be constructed. To further explain the differences between the good and poor definitions, examples are followed by statements of rationale.

A business term definition should:

1. **Be stated in the singular**
   Explanation—The concept expressed by the data definition should be expressed in the singular. (An exception is made if the concept itself is plural.)
   Example—"Article Number"
   a. Good definition: A number created to identify a unique instance of an article we will publish.
   b. Poor definition: Reference number identifying articles.
   Reason—The poor definition uses the plural word "articles," which is ambiguous, since it could imply that an "article number" refers to more than one article.
2. **State what the concept is, not only what it is not**
   Explanation—When constructing definitions, the concept cannot be defined exclusively by stating what the concept is **not**.
   Example—"Freight Cost Amount"
   a. Good definition: Cost amount incurred by a shipper in moving goods from one place to another.
   b. Poor definition: Costs that are not related to packing, documentation, loading, unloading, and insurance.
   Reason—The poor definition does not specify what is included in the meaning of the data.
3. **Be stated as a descriptive phrase or sentence(s)** (in most languages)
   Explanation—A phrase is necessary (in most languages) to form a precise definition that includes the essential characteristics of the concept. Simply stating one or more synonym(s) is insufficient. Simply restating the words of the name in a different order is also insufficient. If more than a descriptive phrase is needed, use complete, grammatically correct sentences.
   Example—"Agent Name"
   a. Good definition: Name of party authorized to act on behalf of another party.
   b. Poor definition: Representative.
   Reason—"Representative" is a close synonym of the data element name, which is not adequate for a definition.
4. **Contain only commonly understood abbreviations**
   Explanation—Understanding the meaning of an abbreviation, including acronyms, is usually confined to a certain context. In other environments the same abbreviation can cause misinterpretation or confusion. Therefore to avoid ambiguity, full words, not abbreviations, should be used in the definition. Exceptions to this requirement may be made if an abbreviation is commonly understood such as "ie," and "eg," or if an abbreviation is more readily understood than the full form of a complex term and has been adopted as a term in its own right such as "radar" standing for "radio detecting and ranging." All acronyms must be expanded on the first occurrence.
   Example 1—"Tide Height"
   a. Good definition: The vertical distance from mean sea level (MSL) to a specific tide level.
   b. Poor definition: The vertical distance from MSL to a specific tide level.

Reason—The poor definition is unclear because the acronym, MSL, is not commonly understood and some users may need to refer to other sources to determine its meaning. Without the full word, finding the term in a glossary may be difficult or impossible.
Example 2—"Unit of Density Measurement"

a. Good definition: The unit employed in measuring the concentration of matter in terms of mass per unit (m.p.u.) volume (eg, pound per cubic foot; kilogram per cubic meter).
b. Poor definition: The unit employed in measuring the concentration of matter in terms of m.p.u. volume (eg, pound per cubic foot; kilogram per cubic meter).

Reason—m.p.u. is not a common abbreviation, and its meaning may not be understood by some users. The abbreviation should be expanded.

5. **Be expressed without embedding definitions of other data or underlying concepts**
Explanation—As shown in the following example, the definition of a second data element or related concept should not appear in the definition of the primary data element. If the second definition is necessary, it may be attached by a note at the end of the primary definition's main text or as a separate entry in the dictionary. Related definitions can be accessed through relational attributes (eg, cross-reference).
Example 1—"Sample Type Code"
a. Good definition: A code identifying the kind of sample.
b. Poor definition: A code identifying the kind of sample collected. A sample is a small specimen taken for testing. It can be either an actual sample for testing, or a quality-control surrogate sample. A quality-control sample is a surrogate sample taken to verify the results of actual samples.

Reason—The poor definition contains two extraneous definitions embedded in it. They are definitions of "sample" and of "quality control sample."
Example 2—"Issuing Bank Documentary Credit Number"

a. Good definition: Reference number assigned by issuing bank to a documentary credit.
b. Poor definition: Reference number assigned by issuing bank to a documentary credit. A documentary credit is a document in which a bank states that it has issued a documentary credit under which the beneficiary is to obtain payment, acceptance, or negotiation on compliance with certain terms and conditions and against presentation of stipulated documents and such drafts as may be specified.

Reason—The poor definition contains a concept definition, which should be included in a glossary.

BUSINESS TERM DEFINITION RECOMMENDATIONS

A data definition should:

1. **State the essential meaning of the concept**
Explanation—All primary characteristics of the concept should appear in the definition at the relevant level of specificity for the context. The inclusion of nonessential characteristics should be avoided. The level of detail necessary is dependent on the needs of the system user and environment.

Example 1—"Consignment Loading Sequence Number" (Intended context: any form of transportation)

a. Good definition: A number indicating the sequence in which consignments are loaded in a means of transport or piece of transport equipment.

b. Poor definition: A number indicating the sequence in which consignments are loaded in a truck.

Reason—In the intended context, consignments can be transported by various transportation modes, eg, trucks, vessels, or freight trains. Consignments are not limited to trucks for transport.

Example 2—"Invoice Amount"

a. Good definition: Total sum charged on an invoice.

b. Poor definition: The total sum of all chargeable items mentioned on an invoice, taking into account deductions on one hand, such as allowances and discounts, and additions on the other hand, such as charges for insurance, transport, handling, etc.

Reason—The poor definition includes extraneous material.

2. **Be precise and unambiguous**

   Explanation—The exact meaning and interpretation of the defined concept should be apparent from the definition. A definition should be clear enough to allow only one possible interpretation.

   Example—"Shipment Receipt Date"

   a. Good definition: Date on which a shipment is received by the receiving party.

   b. Poor definition: Date on which a specific shipment is delivered.

   Reason—The poor definition does not specify what determines a "delivery." "Delivery" could be understood as either the act of unloading a product at the intended destination or the point at which the intended customer actually obtains the product. It is possible that the intended customer never receives the product that has been unloaded at his site or the customer may receive the product days after it was unloaded at the site.

3. **Be concise**

   Explanation—The definition should be brief and comprehensive. Extraneous qualifying phrases such as "for the purpose of this metadata registry," "terms to be described," should be avoided.

   Example—"Character Set Name"

   a. good definition: The name given to the set of phonetic or ideographic symbols in which data is encoded.

   b. Poor definition: The name given to the set of phonetic or ideographic symbols in which data is encoded, for the purpose of this metadata registry, or, as used elsewhere, the capability of systems hardware and software to process data encoded in one or more scripts.

   Reason—In the poor definition, all the phrases after ."…data is encoded" are extraneous qualifying phrases.

4. **Be able to stand alone**

   Explanation—The meaning of the concept should be apparent from the definition. Additional explanations or references should not be needed to understand the meaning of the definition.

   Example—"School Location City Name"

   a. Good definition: Name of the city where a school is situated.

   b. Poor definition: See "school site."

   Reason—The poor definition does not stand alone; it requires the aid of a second definition (school site) to understand the meaning of the first.

5. **Be expressed without embedding rationale, functional use, domain information, or procedural information**
   Explanation—Although they are often necessary, such statements do not belong in the definition because they contain information extraneous to the definition. If deemed useful, such expressions may be placed in other metadata attributes (see ISO/IEC 11179-3). It is, however, permissible to add examples after the definition.
   a. The rationale for a given definition should not be included as part of the definition (eg, if a data element uses miles instead of kilometers, the reason should not be indicated in the definition).
   b. Functional use such as "this data element should not be used for …" should not be included in the definition.
   c. Remarks about procedural aspects. For example, "This data element is used in conjunction with data element 'xxx'" should not appear in the definition; instead use "Related data reference" and "Type of relationship" as specified in ISO/IEC 11179-3.

   Example—"Data Field Label"

   a. Good definition: Identification of a field in an index, thesaurus, query, database, etc.
   b. Poor definition: Identification of a field in an index, thesaurus, query, database, etc., which is provided for units of information such as abstracts and columns within tables.

   Reason—The poor definition contains remarks about functional use. This information, starting with "which is provided for…," must be excluded from the definition and placed in another attribute, if it is needed.
6. **Avoid circular reasoning**
   Explanation—Two definitions should not be defined in terms of each other. A definition should not use another concept's definition as its definition. This results in a situation where a concept is defined with the aid of another concept that is, in turn, defined with the aid of the given concept.
   Example—Two data elements with poor definitions:
   a. Employee ID Number—Number assigned to an employee.
   b. Employee—Person corresponding to the employee ID number.

   Reason—Each definition refers to the other for its meaning. The meaning is not given in either definition.
7. **Use the same terminology and consistent logical structure for related definitions**
   Explanation—A common terminology and syntax should be used for similar or associated definitions.
   Example—The following example illustrates this idea. Both definitions pertain to related concepts and therefore have the same logical structure and similar terminology.
   a. "Goods Dispatch Date"—Date on which goods were dispatched by a given party.
   b. "Goods Receipt Date"—Date on which goods were received by a given party.

   Reason—Using the same terminology and syntax facilitates understanding. Otherwise, users wonder whether some difference is implied by the use of synonymous terms and variable syntax.
8. **Be appropriate for the type of metadata (business term) being defined**
   Explanation—Different types of metadata, in this case a business term, in a metadata registry (eg, data element concept, data element, conceptual domain, value domain) each play a different role, which should be reflected in the definitions.

Example
Data element concept: "Job Grade Maximum Salary Amount"
Definition: The maximum salary permitted for the associated job grade.
Data element 1″: "European Job Grade Maximum Salary Amount"
Definition: The maximum salary permitted for the associated job grade expressed in Euros.
Data element 2″: "US Job Grade Maximum Salary Amount"
Definition: The maximum salary permitted for the associated job grade expressed in US dollars.
Note: Data element definitions may refer to explicit values domains, since this may be all that distinguishes the two data elements.

CREATING GLOSSARY TAXONOMIES AND HIERARCHIES (ONTOLOGY/ TAXONOMY)

Establishing glossary taxonomies is an important part of organizing your business terms into groups. There are many ways to group your business terms. The groups can be based on legacy glossaries, by data subject area, by industry, by geography, by business unit, by business function, and so on. We generally recommend grouping business terms into an organizational or functional taxonomy. Doing so provides context to the user viewing the business term and its definition. A user can then see "this term is used by operational risk, but the definition does not agree with how we use it. We must contact them and harmonize the term and its definition."

How should taxonomies or categories (the term used for a taxonomy in some technologies) be used for enterprise knowledge? There is no perfect answer to this question. The answer varies based on the focus of the business glossary and may change over time. However, you have to start somewhere. We recommend you begin by creating a taxonomy similar to the functional business area in the scope of the business terms being defined. Also recognize that an individual business term may be used in multiple taxonomies.

For example, let's say we are looking to create business terms to support the antimoney laundering (AML) area and application. The AML application supports the functional business unit of compliance. Fig. 5.5 is an example of how this would look.

Fig. 5.6 is an example of an organization that had many legacy business glossaries. Approving new or old terms and then promoting them into an "Enterprise" taxonomy level aids all users find and understand terminology. Having those glossaries helps those who may not be familiar with the older terms. We added an Enterprise category now to maintain the business terms that will be used moving forward.

Business Glossary Taxomony

Glossary Category	Sub-Category	Business Terms	Comments
Financial Crimes Function	Anti-Money Laundering	Account Customer Contact Address	New Category
		Account Customer Contact Email	
		Account Customer Contact Phone	
		Account Country Code of Citizenship	

FIGURE 5.5

AML category example.

Business Glossary Taxomony			
Glossary Category	Sub-Category	Business Terms	
Enterprise Glossary	Customer Domain	Customer Name	Added Enterprise Level
		Customer Address	Added Customer Domain Level
		Customer Contact Phone	
	Reference Data Geography	Continent	Added Enterprise Reference Data Domains
		Country	
		County	
		City	
		Zip Code	
Financial Crimes Function	Anti-Money Laundering	Account Customer Contact Address	
		Account Customer Contact Email	
		Account Customer Contact Phone	
		Account Country Code of Citizenship	

FIGURE 5.6

New category—enterprise.

Business Glossary Taxomony			
Glossary Category	Sub-Category	Business Terms	Comments
Enterprise Glossary	Industry Taxonomy		Added Industry Taxonomy Level
	FIBO Terms	Derivities	Added FIBO Industry Taxonomy
	MISMO Terms	Mortgage	Added MISMO Industry Taxonomy
	Customer Domain	Customer Name	
		Customer Address	
		Customer Contact Phone	
	Reference Data Geography	Continent	
		Country	
		County	
		City	
		Zip Code	
Financial Crimes Function	Anti-Money Laundering	Account Customer Contact Address	
		Account Customer Contact Email	
		Account Customer Contact Phone	
		Account Country Code of Citizenship	

FIGURE 5.7

Industry model category example.

Organizations that have purchased what is known as industry models will also have business terms that need to be grouped in a Category structure. One way of managing this is by creating a category for the industry terms. Then the organization can group the business terms the governance team has decided to use or put them into another category, as shown in Fig. 5.7.

Hopefully these examples have provided an understanding of how defining categories can be help group business terms in ways that help users find the business terms of interest.

BUSINESS GLOSSARY FOR BIG DATA ANALYTICS

Can the business glossary help organizations that are building Big Data analytics programs? Of course. Many organizations have asked if business terms can be defined before the Big Data has gone through the MapReduce or analytics processes. While some data may need to be analyzed before it can be understood, that's not always the case. Most business terms can be used for Big Data discovery and analytics processes.

From a business standpoint, we often know what data will be of interest to business processes—we just don't know where, when, or how those data are occurring or being used. Big Data can be mined to determine where, when, and how the data of interest is being used in an unstructured world. We define those business terms to help analysts and others determine what the MapReduce processes should be analyzing.

The business terms in the business glossary should be used to guide the Big Data analytics and improve productivity while reducing the cost of the analytics. The MapReduce processing may be set to seek not only occurrences of "customer" but also occurrences of "commercial customer" or "retail customer" to determine the best data for the analytics needed.

Let's look at an example of a product manufacturer that wants to understand how their products are being discussed by people on social media platforms such as Twitter or even on the firm's own "help portal." Some of the business questions we want to know are probably like the following.

- What products and product families are being discussed in a positive or negative tone?
- What types of customers are commenting?
- What is the highest number of complaints?
- What product features are customers having trouble with and what is the number of issues with each?

A good business glossary helps us understand the business ontology as well as the product and customer taxonomies. By parsing the data we can find occurrences of our product names or numbers in the Big Data lake. Analytics can leverage the product names to infer the types and/or classes or products such as retail or commercial types. From the type of product we can infer the type of customer, or maybe even find the critical customer uses that can be leveraged to improve customer retention or revenue opportunities.

CHAPTER

THE BUSINESS DATA GOVERNANCE TOOLKIT

6

Selecting technologies is never an easy task. First, most of us do not do it very often. This is the case for many new data governance teams that have been staffed with resources from the business. Then, most vendors use language and terminology that enhances the description of their products. There is generally no common language to describe the functionality of any class of product. Thus comparing the form, features, and functionality of products is very difficult. One vendor may have functionality bundled in a suite while another may have many individual products. Using a structured approach to making the selection will help to build team synergy and collaboration as well as minimize the "I think we should select A, the demo was great," or "let's select B, it's the cheapest" scenarios.

CHAPTER OVERVIEW

This chapter will discuss alternatives to the extensive toolkit that may be needed by the data governance team. The data governance team in every organization is responsible for the deliverable and management of many standards and processes that may have previously been the responsibility of IT. This is great! However, those standards and processes will require some level (maybe a lot) of technology support to be scalable across the enterprise. Data governance technology provides capabilities that support the activities and processes of data stewardship. These technologies support the creation of data policies, compliance, and security, manage workflow, and provide monitoring and measurement of policy compliance and data usage.

Let's consider the Playbook framework again as shown in Fig. 6.1 and look at the potential workstream tracks.

The Playbook framework implemented in Microsoft Excel is a wonderful tool for managing the business vocabulary, critical data elements, and initial governance implementation. However, Excel is not the only tool the governance team may need to scale to large enterprise capabilities. As you work through the activities across the maturity stages, you will need more than Microsoft Office technology.

Most of the activities in the Define stage require more functionally robust technology support to enable maturity scale improvements. These technical data management tools have traditionally been confusing to business stakeholders, and today we are asking those individuals to sponsor the selection of these tools. Additionally the tools have lacked functionality to support the business governance of data, and technology management professionals have shouldered the burden of educating the business and working hard to fill in the technology gaps. Your IT or procurement group already have a process for selecting technologies, but if you do not have a process defined we recommend you follow one similar to the selection process defined in the next section.

1. Defined

#	Activity Name
100	Define Initial Scope & Sponsorship
101	Identify authorities, experts, owners and stewards
102	Establish Governance Program Operating Model
103	Identify capability & risk reduction measures
104	Engage or Establish Data Service
105	Define & Catalog Business Terms
106	Define & Catalog Data Elements
107	Prioritize & Flag Critical Data Elements
108	Conduct Discovery Data Profiling
109	Use Discovery Profiling Results to Set Quality Rules & Targets
110	Catalog Analytic Models
111	Identify analytics model portfolios
112	List master subjects, objects & hierarchies
113	Identify Physical Data with Systems and Interfaces
114	Identify Systems of Record and Authority
115	Identify External Data Subscribers
116	Identify External Data Sources
117	Identify External Data Provider & Subscriber Risks
118	Identify & Register Risks From & To Critical Data
119	Coordinate Control & Testing Standards with Risk & Audit

2. Controlled

#	Activity Name (New)
200	Design Rules based Profiling Controls
201	Establish Data Quality Reporting Thresholds and Targets
202	Execute Rules based Data Profiling, Reporting & Alerting
203	Analyze Data Quality Issues for Corrective Control Needs
204	Identify Reporting & Analytics impacted by Data Issues
205	Identify Master Data Control Points
206	Define External Data Quality Rules & Thresholds for SLAs
207	Score External Data Providers for Quality & Risk Issues
208	Evaluate Data Risk and Exposure
209	Establish Analytics Model Controls at Portfolio Level
210	Generate Analytics Map to Illustrate Uses of Analytic Models Across the Enterprise
211	Update Risk and Audit Partners

Improved

#	Activity Name (New)
300	Define & Publish Controls Operating Model
301	Implement Monitoring Process
302	Create Data or Technical Service Improvement Plan
303	Create Analytic Testing & Improvement Plan
304	Specify Data Quality Improvements for Analytics
305	Identify Corrective Control Candidates
306	Define Required Corrective Controls for Master Data
307	Implement Corrective Controls
308	Track Benefits From Data Controls Automation

4. Standardized

#	Activity Name (New)
400	Enhance Data and Analytic Standards
401	Apply Data and Analytic Standards
402	Enhance Master Data Standards
403	Execute Standards-Based Master Data Improvements
404	Establish and Apply Hierarchy Standards
405	Simplify or Rationalize Data Interfaces
406	Analyze Data Store Mappings for Redundancies

5. Integrated

#	Activity Name (New)
500	Incrementally Reduce Redundancy Across CDE Locations
501	Provide Impact Analysis for New Projects
502	Identify Redundant & Overlapping Analytic Models and Portfolios
503	Apply Leading Analytic Model Designs and Components
504	Identify Hierarchy Integration Opportunities
505	Strategic Goals for Data & Analytic Performance
506	Adjust Periodic Steward & Officer Meetings & Communications

FIGURE 6.1

Business data governance framework.

DATA GOVERNANCE TECHNOLOGY CONSIDERATIONS

There are a number of significant considerations the data governance team will have to review and consider when selecting technologies. Again, we have worked with large and small organizations that have leveraged the data Playbook and MS Office products for multiple projects before selecting additional technologies. We have also worked with other organizations that have selected technologies fairly early in their life. The approach has to fit the governance processes and staffing models. We recommend the "people and process before technology" approach.

Data governance software capabilities are packaged into a product suite by some vendors, while other vendors market products individually. Thus we recommend that each organization consider the specific capabilities critical to enable the long-term success of their organization. The "industry analyst" top product may not fit the requirements of your organization.

Let's look at some of the potential capabilities to be considered for the data governance organization.

- Organizational Control
  - Organization—The identification, standards, and communications can be achieved with MS Office suite and collaboration tools. Everyone has these tools so the incremental cost for data governance may be zero or may be a cost per team member.
- Costs
  - Cost is generally an important factor to consider, especially for entry-level data governance programs. Many organizations say that cost is never a factor, but we have always found cost to be a significant consideration. No one has too much money.
  - Licensing costs for the data steward roles can be a hidden cost factor. Some vendors will only allow the lifecycle of business glossary capabilities to be managed by specific or named users. That means the license to create and update business terms and all associated data is limited to specific users, and additional users will increase licensing costs. Other vendors have licensing costs based on the size of the production hardware (by CPUs), while other vendors base licensing costs on concurrent users. The different licensing costs options make the evaluation highly complex when comparing vendors.
  - We have often worked with organizations that wanted to allow anyone in the organization to identify and provide an initial definition of business terms. This is done to "seed" the data governance effort, but this approach is cost prohibitive with technologies that license by user.
  - In addition, several data governance tool suite vendors offer their business glossaries at a low price to provide an end-to-end solution bundle.
- Vendor Market Dynamics
  - A longer-term consideration is the ability for the vendor to stay in business and mature the product offerings.
  - Another substantial consideration is if the vendor has partnerships with your existing technology vendors to provide technology integration capabilities. Some vendors do not have open platforms or play well with others.
- Data Governance End-to-End Functionality
  - Some vendors have added data governance capabilities and functionality into existing products that may limit capabilities. How well do the capabilities meet your teams' specific requirements?

    - Ease-of-use considerations cannot be understated. Many governance tools were originally intended to be used by technical resources. Your data governance team may be staffed with resources from business units, thus very knowledgeable but not necessarily highly technical.
    - Data governance requires extensive search capabilities not seen in other types of software. Creating business terms and mapping them to critical data elements (CDEs) is an important means to an end. And the end is providing that information to anyone in the organization that needs to understand "what is this concept, how should I use it, where did it come from, what are the business and technical rules around it, what is the quality of it, where should I source this data from, how can I use it for my purpose," etc. Many vendors have robust search capabilities. Ensure your selected vendor meets the intended requirements of your organization.
    - Workflow and communications capabilities are critical for all data governance teams, small and large, formal or informal.
    - How well does the vendor solution meet your desires and stewardship processes planned to define business terms, define business rules, identify accountability and stewardship roles, define data quality rules, etc.?
    - How well does the solution allow you to manage communications and approvals across the organization around the business terms or data governance activities?
    - How well does the solution provide issue management functionality and escalation capabilities.
    - Integration with data lineage, data quality, reference data, and master data technologies that exist in your architecture. Data governance tools should also provide a mechanism to link a business term to the associated CDEs and reference data. For example, you might want to link a business term called "industry classification" with the list of allowable values for North American Industry Classification System (NAICS) codes from the US Census Bureau.
    - Data governance policy management and its relationship to data governance roles and business terms.
    - Performance and scalability will be a concern as your users grow and data governance capabilities mature.
    - Reporting capabilities must also be considered. How well does the technology integrate with your standard reporting tools? How well does the technology present governance and data-quality metrics? What are the reporting capabilities out of the box?
    - Security of the data in the data governance technology must not be forgotten. What are the capabilities for security, creating user groups, and backup and recovery of content?
- Technical support, education, training, and documentation is critical for all organizations. The data governance team will be staffed with individuals with business and technical backgrounds so training and documentation will be important.
- Administrative functionality and the ease-of-use to administrate the software are also important. Generally, the data governance team will not be staffed with a full-time resource for the sole effort of administration. We have individually been the part-time administrator of software. Our full-time job is data governance not keeping a software product running. Managing users logins and access is not time-consuming, but performing quality checks, running ETL or database scans, doing database backups, and other infrastructure tasks can be a full-time job.

METHOD FOR TECHNOLOGY SELECTION OVERVIEW

Data governance software selection is not an easy process even for those that have selected software for decades. Having a fairly rigorous process is a great enabling tool. We recommend that the data governance team seek out their IT or Procurement organizations to determine if a process for software selection already exist in the corporation. We often find that a formal selection process does not exist or has not been used in many years. Hence we are asked to help implement our approach or a modified version f our approach to select the data governance tools beyond the Data Playbook.

Although many aspects of data governance technologies, such as data modeling, metadata management, and data quality, have been addressed by technologies for three decades, the concepts of data governance management is an emerging market. The capabilities of the technologies are very diverse and inconsistent across the vendors in this market. Some of the leading vendors of data governance tools have evolved the existing functionality from earlier technologies.

We must note that none of the lists of vendors and product names in this chapter are all inclusive. As previously noted, data governance technologies are evolving rapidly. It is critical that any investigation of data governance technologies include analysis of the products on the market at that point in time. It is also possible for potential vendors to change the names of their products and package them differently. Our list of vendors and products in this chapter is only a sample and intended to provide you with a starting point for your analysis.

Vendors can be grouped into the following categories of vendor offerings:

- Data management platform vendors—These are vendors that have assembled broad capabilities from multiple existing products or acquired products. Many of the vendors in this category have been marketing variations of these products for 20+ years. Integration of the separate products into a foundation platform is a work in progress for a few, and some vendors are further along than others. Vendors in this category include such names as IBM, SAP, Oracle, and Informatica, just to name a few.
- Business intelligence platform vendors—Vendors in this category are approaching data governance from the business intelligence market. Some have integrated data governance capabilities into their offerings, such as data quality or master data management. These vendors often have a foundational platform of a repository, collaboration tools, data quality, and reporting/dashboard capabilities. But most have been organically developed and thus the integration functionality may not be optimal. Vendors in this category include SAS Institute and Information Builders, to name a few.
- Metadata repository vendors—Most of the traditional metadata repository vendors now have data governance offerings, especially business glossary functionality. These vendors have added business glossary capabilities to their legacy metadata and data lineage capabilities, as well as collaboration and dashboard functions. Again, the integration of capabilities is a work in progress, depending on the vendor. Vendors in this category include Adaptive, ASG Software, and Data Advantage Group, to name a few.
- Data-quality vendors—There are a few traditional data-quality/cleansing vendors that can be considered as having good data governance capabilities. We have mentioned SAS Institute above, but we also include Trillium and Global IDs in this category.
- Data governance specialist vendors—These vendors are implementing solutions specifically to support data governance and stewardship capabilities. One of the vendors listed in this category is Collibra.

The industry analysts are speculating that the market for data governance software will experience a significant shift in the near future. We anticipate that the market for data governance technologies will increase significantly in the next 5 years. We also anticipate that other categories of software vendors will enter this market to fill gaps in the available solutions. For example, enterprise architecture management vendors and even audit, risk, and compliance vendors may enter this market, but capabilities for security management, audit/compliance, and risk are lacking from most existing data governance technologies.

PROCESS FOR TOOL SELECTION

Hopefully you can see from the above list of categories and vendors that the form, features, and capabilities of data governance software are quite diverse. There is not one vendor that is likely to supply all of the capabilities every data governance team will need. Thus we recommend that every organization consider using a defined process to complete the data governance software selection. The formality of the process will depend on the organization. Some organizations may have a procurement team that requires a very formal RFI/RFP and selection process. Other organizations are very informal and have a few team members make a selection. We recommend you adjust the process steps, functional capabilities desired, and weights to meet the needs of your organization.

First, let's consider the process steps for a software evaluation.

PROCESS STEPS

The steps for a software selection vary greatly by the formality of the organization, the procurement guidelines, and the style of the governance organization. For example, does your procurement guideline call for a formal request for information (RFI) and or a request for proposal (RFP)? If so these steps must be included in your process. Organizations with less formality can start by determining a list of vendors and then selecting a short list of those vendors before contacting the vendors for detailed discussions of capabilities and pricing.

Given the diversity of capabilities of vendor software in this area, we recommend each organization first determine their desired capabilities before doing paper-based research to create a short list of vendors. Now if you are unfamiliar with software capabilities you will need to do some research initially to determine what capabilities you need. One way of determining the capabilities provided by each vendor is to send out an RFI to a selected set of vendors. Thus the first few steps in the process will vary. But the general process should include the following steps:

- Conduct research into the data governance industry expert recommendations and vendor functional capabilities.
- Determine high-level functional categories of your data governance functional requirements.
- Determine the detailed sections, questions and features desired within each section and functional category.
- Prioritize and weight each functional category to total 100 across all categories.
- Prioritize and weight each section within each category to a total 100 within each category.
- Conduct research on paper/Internet sites produced by industry analysts and research organizations to select two to three software products that best match your requirements; this may lead to a single vendor that is a best fit to conduct a POC.

- Prepare a scoring template to score responses for each question in the section and category. It is a best practice to complete the scoring template prior to the distribution of the RFI/RFP to the vendors. This minimizes the scoring template in favor of one vendor's responses. The scoring template should also include examples so the individuals scoring will be more likely to score consistently across vendors.
- Publish the RFI/RFP to gather detailed information from the two to three vendors. This is where your questions have significant value.
- Each member of the evaluation team should independently score each response from the vendors. Scores can be reviewed as a team and resolved.
- Conduct demos with the finalists. Refine individual scores as necessary from the demo.
- Use the scoring to determine final selection. Now is the time to factor in cost estimates.
- Conduct a POC with one vendor to validate your decision.
- Complete the purchase and install.
- Conduct training and implement the resourcing model (RACI).
- Determine a pilot project, if needed.

CATEGORIES AND SECTIONS FOR DG TECHNOLOGY SELECTION

We have discussed the steps for developing the features and capabilities important to your team. These may likely begin as a lot of questions about the technology, which may be similar to the following:

1. Does this vendor have a workflow engine so data stewards can communicate to approve term and CDE mapping changes?
2. Does this vendor have capabilities to customize the attributes in the glossary?
3. How easy is it to learn the user interface for the lifecycle management of the glossary?
4. Can the vendor capture and use our business and quality rules for analysis by their software?
5. What capabilities are available for users to search for business terms and associated definitions?
6. Does the vendor's technology integrate with our existing technologies?
7. Who will be licensed to create and manage business terms in the glossary?
8. What are the initial costs, maintenance cost, and the licensing models? How will my cost be impacted if I add hardware capacity?
9. Is there a cloud solution and what are the associated costs?
10. Does this vendor have partners that can mentor us in the process and technology?
11. How long has this technology been in the market and how many customer references do they have?
12. What is the completeness and depth of the vendor's overall solution?
13. What security options are available in the vendor's solution?
14. What backup, recovery, and archiving solutions are "out of the box," and what can we customize to meet our needs?
15. What audit trail and versioning functionality is in the vendor's solution?
16. What are the system's administration requirements in the vendor's solution, and what are the skills required?
17. What is the number of resources generally required to administrate the solution?

All of these questions, and about a 100 more, can be organized into sections of like questions. Then those sections can be organized into categories based upon relevance. For example, from the above questions:

- Questions 1 to 5 can be in the "Data Governance Functionality" category
- Question 6 can be in the "Integration with Existing Technology" category
- Questions 7 to 10 can be in the "Solution Overview, Costs and Licensing" category
- Questions 11 and 12 can be in the "Company Profile and Product Strategy" category
- Questions 13 to 17 can be in the "Nonfunctional requirements" category

Just as an example we can list the evaluation categories as:

1. Company profile
2. Solution overview, cost, and licensing
3. Integration with existing technology
4. Data governance functional requirements
5. Nonfunctional requirements

Your evaluation criteria may be more detailed but we hope the following example will at least provide you with some guidelines. Our example is structured by category (major area like the five categories noted above, ie, company profile) and then multiple sections within each category.

The following is a simple example of the detailed questions we have asked for the company profile category:

Company Profile (Category)
Market Dynamics (Section)

1. Parent company name
2. Number of years in business
3. Number of employees worldwide, total in the United States
4. Number of developers supporting metadata product being recommended
5. Company website URL
6. Market share (% of metadata market, and percentage of firms' revenue from this market)
   6a. Change in metadata market share last 1, 2, and 3 years
7. Describe the installed base of your product
   7a. Top 5 or 10 customers by database size, company size, company revenue, or other criteria
8. Largest Installation (number of users)
9. Software maturity—how long has current version been in production?
10. Number of clients/installation in production of version of software proposed
11. Provide three customer references that may be contacted regarding quality of software, upgrades, proper sizing, implementation, and training. Provide their company name, contact's name, address, phone, modules installed, and installation date.
12. Comment about the tools with respect to other data governance tools available in the market today

Company Profile (Category)
Company and Product Futures (Section)

1. Describe the company's vision and strategy for the next 5 years.
2. Describe the vision and strategy for the next 5 years for the product.
3. Describe the vision and strategy for implementation of data governance standards.

Company Profile (Category)
Partnerships (Section)

1. Describe the strategic partnerships you have with (and the latest version of the partners hardware, operating systems, or software supported):
   - **1a.** Adaptive
   - **1b.** ASG Software
   - **1c.** Collibra
   - **1d.** Global IDs
   - **1e.** IBM
   - **1f.** Informatica
   - **1g.** Information Builders
   - **1h.** Oracle
   - **1i.** SAP
   - **1j.** SAS Institute
   - **1k.** Trillium Software

Other sections in the company profile category can include the following.

Section: Market Dynamics

Refers to position and longevity of the company.

Section: Product Support

Refers to company vision and strategy alignment with our vision.

Section: Strategic Partnerships

Refers to strategic partnerships with the other vendors in our technology architecture.

The following can be the sections in the category of costs and licensing:

Costs and Licensing (Category)

Solution Overview (Section)

Refers to the vendor's solution in general, the product capital costs and licensing costs for all usages

Proposed Solution Summary (Section)

Refers to solution summary and description of how well it meets our requirements

Product Costs (Section)

Refers to global product costs and maintenance license

Licensing/Support (Section)

Refers to product licensing structure and costs

Installation and Consulting Fees (Section)

Refers to product installation and consulting fee costs

The following can be sections in the category of support, education, training, and documentation:

Support, Education, Training, and Documentation (Category)

Refers to the proposed solution product support, training, and documentation

Support, Education, Training, and Documentation (Category)
Product Support (Section)

Refers to global phone, Internet support, 24 × 7 support, social media postings, and help

Support, Education, Training and Documentation (Category)
Education and Training (Section)

Refers to the types of and extent of the product training available, classroom, online, blogs, and videos

Support, Education, Training, and Documentation (Category)
Documentation (Section)

Refers to product documentation format and completeness

Continued

Integration with Existing Technologies (Category)

Refers to the integration of this technology with our existing or desired technologies. This technology should integrate well with our reference architecture and technology roadmap.

Integration with Existing Technologies (Category)
Data/Process Modeling Integration (Section)

Refers to ability to import or export with modeling tools

Integration with Existing Technologies (Category)
Data Discovery/Quality Integration (Section)

Refers to ability to integrated with data discovery, profiling, and data-quality tools

Integration with Existing Technologies (Category)
Workflow—Business Process Integration (Section)

Refers to the ability to integrate the vendor solution with existing technologies

Integration with Existing Technologies (Category)
Data Integration (Section)

Refers to ability to integrate with existing data integration technologies

Integration with Existing Technologies (Category)
Messaging/Service-Oriented Integration (Section)

Refers to ability to provide capabilities to provide SOA services and integration to existing SOA technology

Integration with Existing Technologies (Category)
Reporting and Presentation (Section)

Refers to the ability to provide reporting and integrate with existing technologies

Integration with Existing Technologies (Category)
Hardware Platform (Section)

Refers to the ability to execute on existing hardware platforms

The next category of your evaluation can be the detailed data governance functionality.

Data Governance Functionality (Category)
Business Terms and Mapping Functions (Section)

How well does this tool provide the business term capture, rules, and status management functionality to meet our requirements?

Data Governance Functionality (Category)
Ease of Use (Section)

Ease of use appropriate for business and governance personnel.

Data governance functionality (Category)
Section: Workflow and Communications Capability (Section)

Capability to manage governance approval and or change management communications across the organization?

Data Governance Functionality (Category)
Scheduling (Section)

Does the technology provide basic scheduling functions to import, transfer, and manage data and processes?

Data Governance Functionality (Category)
Customization (Section)

Does the tool provide the customization capabilities for meta model, imports, exports, and reporting? How well are the customization functions documented and available?

Data Governance Functionality (Category)
Security, Privacy, and Compliance (Section)

Does the tool provide capabilities to manage governance of data security, privacy, and compliance to support the governance processes and standards?

Data governance functionality (Category)
Data Linage and Impact Analysis (Section)

Does the tool provide the data linage and impact analysis functions that meet our requirements?

The final category of the evaluation may be around the administration capabilities and requirements.

Tool Administration (Category)
Administration (Section)

Does the tool seem easy to administer, will it require multiple FTE to maintain, and are critical administration functions missing?

Tool Administration (Category)
Security (Section)

Does the tool meet critical security requirements (ie, supports various types of users, security hierarchy, granting privileges)?

Tool Administration (Category)
Change/Object Management (Version Control) (Section)

Whether the tool provides its own change management function and how well it integrates within the company's present processes and procedures

Tool Administration (Category)
Section: Backup and Disaster Recovery

Does the tool have capabilities for backing up the development environment and the production repository as well as capabilities for recovering/restoring from a "disaster"?

Tool Administration (Category)
Section: Schedule Processing

Does the tool have capabilities for scheduling that can meet our requirements?

Tool Administration (Category)
Section: Auditing

Does the product have the capability to generate an audit trail of all data changes? What will our audit team need from the technology?

PROCESS FOR EVALUATION SCORING

We recommend the development of an evaluation-scoring sheet prior to the collection of responses from vendors. Having the scoring sheet done before looking at vendor responses or demos helps remove the concern that the scoring was tainted in favor of a specific vendor solution. The evaluation-scoring sheet should allow for a mathematical score for each vendor. The objective is to minimize subjective evaluations done by individuals on the team that in the end cannot be supported by facts.

We use an Excel spreadsheet for this purpose. First, the evaluation team must decide on the weighted priorities of the categories of capabilities. Each category should be given a weight or priority "out of 100," which often requires a few iterations by the team. Each individual will have different opinions on the weight that is appropriate for each category. Consensus of the evaluation team is critical. Everyone may not be in complete agreement but look for a majority.

We often see the category weights as the following:

- Company Profile and Product Strategy 10%
- Solution Cost and Licensing 20%

- Support, Training, and Documentation 10%
- Integration with Existing Technology 20%
- Data Governance Capability 35%
- Tool Administration 5%
- Total Weight of All Categories 100

The next step is to weigh the sections in each category. Each section should be given a weight or priority "out of 100." However, now we are looking at the relative priority of the sections within the category. As noted above, each individual on the evaluation team will have different opinions on the weight that is appropriate for that section, but a team consensus is critical and may require discussion and iterations. Consensus does not mean you have 100% agreement—just enough majorities to move forward. However, all members of the team must be able to voice their desires and have the team resolve those to an acceptable level.

The following is an example of the categories, category weights, sections, and section weights we have seen organizations use.

General Categories	Section Total Value	Weight
Company Profile and Product Strategy Refers to the perceived financial stability of the tool vendor, its place in governance industry, its future strategies, and our experience with that company.	10	
Market Dynamics Refers to the position and longevity of the company. Has this vendor been recommended by industry analysts or have they won awards?		40%
Product Support Refers to company vision and strategy alignment with our vision. Does this vendor seem like a longer-term partner?		40%
Strategic Partnerships Refers to strategic partnerships with the other vendors in your technology architecture		20%
Solution Overview/Costs and Licensing Refers to the vendor's solution in general, the product capital costs, and licensing costs for all usages	20%	
Proposed Solution Summary Refers to solution summary and description of how well it meets our requirements		30%
Product Costs Refers to global product costs and maintenance license		40%
Licensing/Support Refers to product licensing structure and costs		20%
Installation and Consulting Fees Refers to product installation and consulting fee costs		10%
Support-Training-Documentation Refers to the proposed solution product support, training, and documentation	10	

General Categories	Section Total Value	Weight
Product Support Refers to global phone, Internet support, 24 × 7 support, social media postings, and help		50%
Training Refers to types of and extent of the product training available, classroom, online, blogs, and videos		30%
Documentation Refers to product documentation format and completeness		20%
Integration with Existing Technologies Refers to the integration of this technology with our existing or desired technologies. This technology should integrate well with our reference architecture and technology roadmap.	20	
Data/Process Modeling Integration Refers to ability to import or export with modeling tools		5%
Data Discovery/Quality Integration Refers to ability to integrated with data discovery, profiling and data quality tools		15%
Workflow—Business Process Integration Refers to the ability to integrate the vendor solution with existing technologies		20%
Data Integration Refers to ability to integrate with existing data integration technologies or platforms		15%
Messaging/Service-Oriented integration Refers to the ability to provide capabilities to provide SOA services and integration with existing SOA technology		15%
Reporting and Presentation Refers to the ability to provide reporting and to integrate with existing technologies		15%
Hardware Platform Refers to the ability to execute on existing hardware platforms		15%
Data Governance Functionality	35	
Business Terms and Mapping Functions How well does this tool provide the business term capture, rules, and status management functionality to meet our requirements?		20%
Ease of Use Ease of use appropriate for business and governance personnel		15%
Workflow and Communications Capability Capability to manage governance change communications across the organization?		20%
Scheduling Does the technology provide basic scheduling functions to import, transfer, and manage data and processes?		5%

Continued

General Categories	Section Total Value	Weight
Customization Does the tool provide the customization capabilities for meta model, imports, exports, and reporting? How well are the customization functions documented and available?		5%
Security, Privacy and Compliance Does the tool provide capabilities to manage governance of data security, privacy, and compliance to support the governance processes and standards?		20%
Data Linage and Impact Analysis Does the tool provide the data linage and impact analysis functions to meet our requirements?		15%
Tool Administration	5	
Administration Does the tool seem easy to administer, will it require multiple FTE to maintain, and are critical administration functions missing?		20%
Security Tool meets critical security requirements (ie, supports various types of users, security hierarchy, granting privileges)		10%
Change/Object Management (Version Control) Whether the tool provides its own change management function and how well it integrates within the company's present processes and procedures		20%
Backup and Disaster Recovery Does the tool have capabilities for backing up the development environment and the production repository as well as capabilities for recovering/restoring from a "disaster"?		10%
Schedule Processing Does the tool have capabilities for scheduling that can meet our requirements?		10%
Auditing Does the product have the capability to generate an audit trail of all data changes?		5%

Every organization has different objectives and priorities for selecting data governance software. Our categories, sections, and weights are based on the requirements of the organizations we have worked with. Some organizations are very cost sensitive and will put additional weight on the Cost category. Other organizations want to put more weight on the Data Governance Functionality category. Your priorities may be different so use this only as a guide. Make the necessary changes. Just remember that all category weights will equal 100 and all section weights within each category will equal 100. If you increase the weight in one area you must reduce the weight somewhere else.

Next, we add a score column to our worksheet. This score column is meant to capture the absolute (raw) score that will be entered by an evaluator. We always recommend that the team agree on the values that will be used to evaluate the vendors. We have found that it is easier for everyone scoring to keep the values in the range of 0–5. We then put these values in as a note in the cells so it is easy for each evaluator to remember. We will show examples of the score values later.

Then add a column to contain the weighted score of the section for that vendor. The weighted score is a calculation of the raw score entered multiplied by the section weight (as a percentage of 100).

Here is an example of scoring for the Company Profile category.

General Categories	Category Total Value	Section Weight	#1 Raw Score	#1 Net Score	#2 Raw Score	#2 Net Score	#3 Raw Score	#3 Net Score
Company Profile Refers to the perceived financial stability of the tool vendor, its place in the governance industry, its future strategies, and our experience with that company	10							
Market Dynamics Refers to position and longivity of the company		40%	3	1.2	4	1.6	4	1.6
Product Support Refers to company vision and strategy alignment with vision for data governance		40%	3	1.2	4	1.6	5	2
Strategic Partnerships Refer to strategic partnerships with the other vendors in the data governance industry		20%	4	0.8	4	0.8	5	1
	Total			3.2		4		4.6

Form the above we can see that the raw score for vendor #1 was a 3 and that equals a net score of 1.2 (3 times the weight of 40%). By evaluating each vendor for each question we get a more informed score since the score is factored by our weights or priorities. In the above example vendor #1 scored a 3.2, vendor #2 a 4.0, and vendor #3 a 4.6.

Each team member conducting an evaluation can complete the scoring sheet independently. We then suggest that large differences in the individual scores be discussed to determine what each person considered in their scoring. Discrepancies are expected, but large discrepancies should be discussed. If one person scores a zero and another five, then we have a difference in view that needs to be resolved, while discrepancies of two points are usually not large enough to warrant discussion.

After each individual has completed a score sheet, the next step is to consolidate the individual scores from the team. This provides to a total score for each vendor that can be used to make the product selection.

WHAT HAPPENS AFTER SCORING (WE ARE DONE, RIGHT?)

Completing the scoring of vendors does not mean we are done. The amount of effort the team still needs to put forth will vary by organization and your sponsor expectations. We have worked with firms that have one executive that can approve the purchase of the team's recommendation. Thus the procurement process can be done in a few weeks. But we have also worked with larger international firms that require the recommendation to be approved by many technology teams, which often takes 3 months or longer for the procurement process to be completed.

The team may need to create presentations to communicate which vendor was selected and how we conducted the selection. We generally create two to three presentations to address the communications needed for both the business and IT management and executives. Then we still have to complete negotiations with the vendor. You may want to conduct a proof-of-concept (POC) with the vendor to ensure your selection will be successful. We generally recommend the POC concept, since it allows for the team to work through the governance processes and the technology in a controlled environment before rolling it out to the full enterprise.

Hopefully we don't have to tell you that the scoring of vendors and even the selection of the software vendor is just one step in a long journey to governance success. The software selection process is an activity we are often asked to help organizations with. It is a complex process if you have not completed it many times, and it is a process that most organizations want to complete very rapidly. We are often asked how long will the process take.

The truth is, data governance software selection can take months when a formal procurement process needs to be followed. It is appropriate to follow a very formal process for larger organizations that will be committing high six figures or even seven figures to data governance software. And we have worked with smaller organizations that could only allocate less than $100,000. In that case we were able to rapidly get to a decision, negotiate a price, and execute a purchase order in just a few weeks. However, in the end it is critical to select software that maximizes the efficiency of the governance processes you will use, as well as the productivity of the resources you can allocate to the governance team. Software is like the third leg of a stool, with the first two legs comprising the people and processes your organization has.

TECHNOLOGY LEADERS TO CONSIDER TODAY

We always have to be cautious about identifying vendors in a book. Not because those vendors do not have great products today. The issue is the duration of time between the writing of the book and when you read the content. For example, we anticipate it will be 7 to 8 months before the first publication of this book is available to any reader. That is enough time for specific vendors to release new versions of their software, which will increase their position in the market. It is also enough time for a new vendor to bring new and disruptive technology into this market. But we would be remiss if we did not give you a list of those vendors that have effective technology in the governance space today (early 2016). Note that this list is only representative of what we consider to be the leading vendors at this time. It is not a comprehensive list as there are some newer vendors we know of that are not listed below.

Again, when you start your research into the vendors in this industry you should contact leading industry analysts such as Gartner, Forrester, IDC, and others.

The follow are data governance software vendors and their product names to consider for your program. We present these in alphabetical order:

1. Adaptive
   a. Business Glossary Manager
   b. Metadata Manager
   c. Enterprise Architecture Manager
   d. IT Portfolio Manager

2. ASG Software Solutions
   a. ASG-Rochade Server
   b. ASG-metaGlossary
3. Collibra
   a. Data Governance Center
   b. Stewardship Management
   c. Reference Data Manager
   d. Data Sharing Agreements
   e. Issue Management
   f. Data Catalog
   g. Collibra Connect
4. Global IDs
   a. Metadata Governance Suite
   b. Enterprise Data Governance Suite
   c. Enterprise Information
   d. Management Suite
   e. LEI Integration Suite
5. IBM
   a. InfoSphere Information Server
   b. InfoSphere Guardium
   c. InfoSphere Optim
6. Informatica
   a. Metadata Manager and Business Glossary
   b. Data Quality
   c. Data Masking
7. Information Builders
   a. iWay Data Quality Suite
   b. iWay Data Profiler
   c. iWay Data Steward Portal
8. Oracle
   a. Data Relationship Governance
   b. Oracle Enterprise Data Quality
   c. Oracle Enterprise Metadata Management
   e. Oracle Data Integrator
   f. Oracle Relationship Manager
9. SAP
   a. Data Services Enterprise
   b. Information Lifecycle Management
   c. SAP Access Control
10. SAS Institute
    a. SAS Data Governance
    b. SAS Data Quality Advanced
    c. SAS Data Management Advanced

11. Trillium Software
    a. Trillium Software Director
    b. Trillium Software Series
    c. Trillium Software System
    d. Trillium Data Quality

In summary, the selection of data governance technology is a complex activity for many organizations that are not experienced in technology selections. You should always follow a structured process in line with your firm's procurement policies. We recommend a formal evaluation process that follows the guidelines we have discussed here. It takes the objectivity out and ultimately leads to a more transparent process for the selection.

CHAPTER

PLAYBOOK DEPLOYMENT 7

WHAT DO WE MEAN BY DEPLOYMENT?

This chapter focuses on getting the work done—real execution. Deployment is about deploying the Playbook methods, practices, and approaches needed to accomplish multiple goals. The first goal is always the improvement of enterprise or shared data. The second, which is tightly linked to the first, is the development and expansion of capabilities related to improving and governing data. The third goal is the overall course of progress that can be made across the scope of enterprise data. As we avoid the methods and build capabilities, more and more of the critical enterprise data is governed and improved in measurable ways.

We use different models of deployment based on what we have learned in assessment and what we understand to work best in our organization. Let's think about organizational fit and approach first. Some companies are very project and program focused. That is, they accomplish things through defined initiatives that generally follow a waterfall or agile methodology. If your organization is driven in an initiative manner or by initiative investments, mapping deployment models to that initiative is a simple thing. If, on the other hand, your organization is focused on more progressive, long-term efforts to improve and change systems, behaviors, and processes, a different deployment method is indicated.

The two primary models we use for deployment of the Playbook focus on initiative and functional, organizational models. Most of today's practitioners, consultants, and data governance-related positions focus almost exclusively on initiative-based work. They often use a fairly heavy organizational model to address the creation of a program or functional office and the resources applied against these initiatives. What you get in that approach is a combination of governance-program resources, organization models, and approaches layered with initiative-based sets of activities and outcomes. Our approach emphasizes as lean and simple an organizational structure as possible, since business benefits needed to justify organizational investments flow only after the work is done. Getting to the point of doing the work and proving the value in the outcomes is our primary goal. The additional benefit of taking an execution-oriented approach is that the initial experiences and outcomes help to refine the nature of the governance organization and the approach that will work best in that organization.

In our approach, we focus on using a combination of functional, cycle-based deployment activities and sprint, or initiative-based, activity sequences. These two deployment models, Cycle and Sprint, can occur in parallel, allowing for the gradual progression of cycle-based activities while initiatives sprint toward outcomes that establish value.

One of the key insights gathered from the most successful organizations we work with is the need to treat the overall data and analytics governance discipline as a function of the enterprise. Consultants and companies often treat these in terms of a program and seek to stand up a long-running program to address data and analytic needs. We've learned that data and analytic governance and improvement is a permanent function that business areas need to improve their performance and reduce their data and analytics operating costs.

Sponsoring these functional activities as a permanent part of a business area or cross-business shared service establishes a more realistic expectation of this work's permanent nature and the ongoing value we expect to flow from it. The rejoinder from successful, permanent governance functions is often "as long as we have data we will provide governance." This type of permanent commitment and thinking is a much more aligned approach to handling critical business assets, as well as program and project methods, alone. The permanent, functional approach and commitment also supports initiative streams, which are often focused in multiple directions and use different underlying themes to produce the required results. For example, one of the first things we do in initiative planning, where we use sprints or other agile methods, is to identify whether the initiative in question is defensive or offensive in nature.

Playbooks are often discussed using defense and offense analogies. We have been very clear and specific about the "three lines of defense" model for defensive Playbook initiatives and deployment. We are also very clear about what constitutes an offensive set of Playbook activities and what the business focus needs to be to produce offensive results. In the offensive world, we are thinking about scoring additional revenue, cost reductions, market share improvements, and other forms of measurable growth in the overall performance of the enterprise. In the defensive space, we are focused more on three lines of defense, which identify, reduce, or remediate risks to the safety and soundness of the business. These distinctions between all offensive and defensive actions are critical to make at the initiative level. However, they can also be supported equally well at the functional level. This explains the need to have some functional focus while still supporting different kinds of initiatives over time.

When we talk about offensive and defensive deployment approaches, we are addressing both the corrective activities to use and the appropriate way to scope individual initiatives, prioritizing them from a governance perspective. Our assessment results have helped us keep, map, and prioritize areas that are suffering from weak or absent controls for defensive initiatives and identify areas poised to benefit the most from offensive Playbook sequences. The mix of defensive and offensive initiatives required over any period of time informs us about the related resource requirements and functional governance support needed to make these areas successful. The overall balance of initiatives work informs the governance structure and resource provisioning process. This information allows the governing structure and operating model to adapt to the data and analytics requirements the organization has for governance and improvement.

The graphic above visually depicts the lines of defense and offense we described earlier. The "three lines of defense" maps directly to industry standard approaches, leveraging business, risk management, and audit professionals in the definition tracking and resolution of enterprise risk. This model is well-established and heavily relied upon, particularly in financial services and other heavily regulated industries.

In addition to the three lines of defense, we've identified all offensive lines that are focused on providing enterprise performance improvements related to revenue, profitability, market share, and other key performance indicators. Initiatives are focused on either defensive or offensive goals, and multiple initiatives can be operating simultaneously against both sets of goals. The positions identified in the graphic illustrate the fact that each position can be played by separate people. In some cases, the same person or role may be focused on multiple positions. When we have a single role such as internal auditor or risk officer asked to play in multiple positions, we are probably seeing multiple initiatives.

The center of the field holds the core governance-operating model. At the heart of this model is the notion that we are building a set of data and analytic leadership capabilities into the firm. These

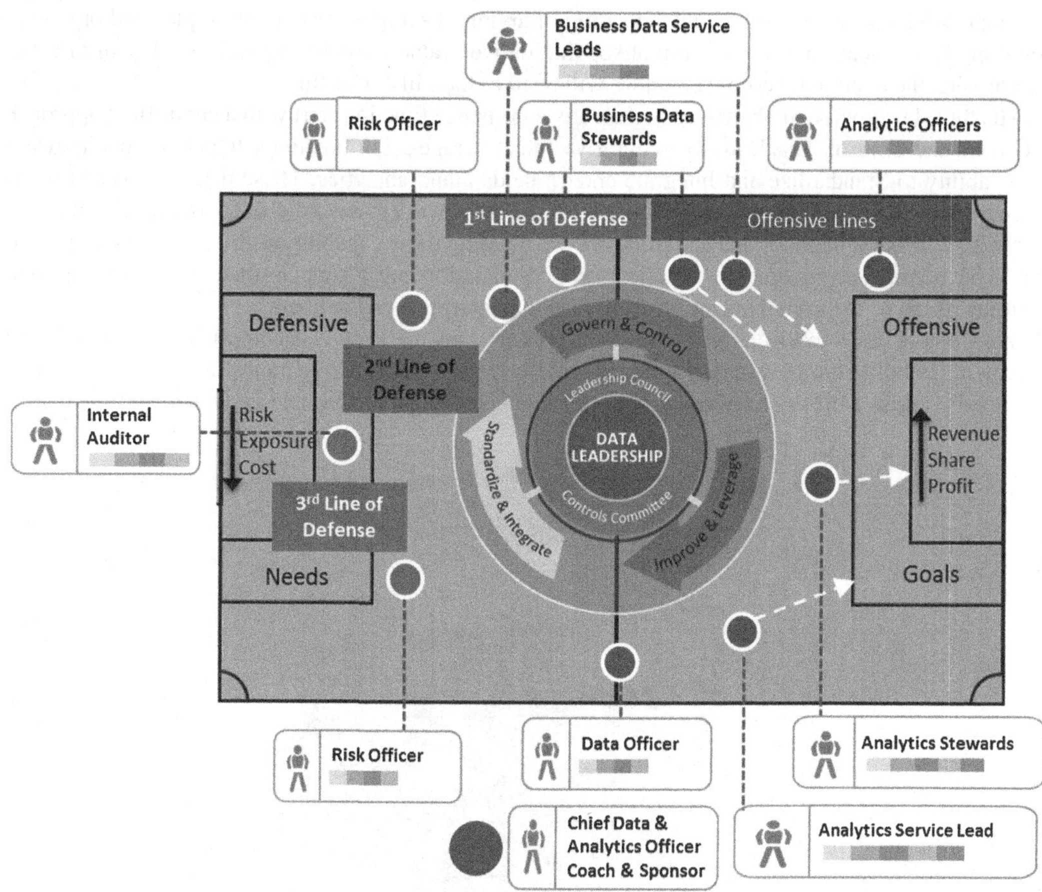

capabilities are intended to balance application- and process-oriented capabilities that are already strongly in place in most firms. Data disciplines and capabilities are still comparatively new process management and application technologies.

From its earliest inception, information technology provided both process and data automation through its execution in the mainframe and distributed computing environments. Applications and application suites met almost all data and reporting needs, until data warehousing and operational data stores emerged less than 30 years ago. These information technology constructs, combined with analytics-specific data structures and applications, formed the basis for a data discipline and emerging data-capability requirements. Some data and analytic capabilities are still relatively immature, and we are all working to better define, develop, and deploy them for enterprise benefit.

The core of the graphic focuses on the functional or permanent governance capabilities, resources, and operating model required to achieve data and analytic leadership. It is in the core that we find the governing committees and standing groups that many people focus on so heavily from the beginning.

Our approach suggests that some understanding of an initial set of governing principles and organizational models is necessary, but the initiatives that deliver value must be engaged quickly in order to inform what the overall governing structure will need to look like over time.

The three key goals and objectives of the core governance function start with a controlling approach in Govern and Control. This leads to an Improve and Leverage set of functions, which ultimately result in the ability to Standardize and Integrate enterprise data and analytics. These three functional focus areas are embedded in the Playbook methodology and framework to ensure that, as we progress through deploying Playbook methods and activities, we are building these capabilities throughout the organization. The permanent governance function and organization must support this capability buildout, maturing ahead of the initiative work used to develop enterprise capabilities.

We are now ready to visualize the different progressions that can be accomplished throughout the enterprise for both core governance functions and initiative-based deployments. Since this visualization requires a three-dimensional construct, we use a cube visual model help explain these concepts.

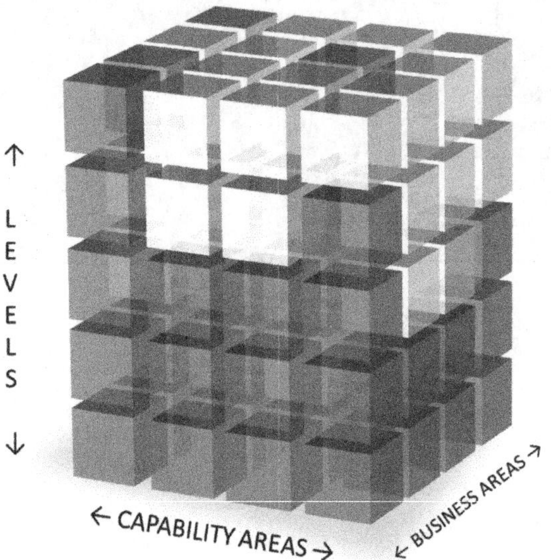

The three dimensions of the cube help us understand the volume of work and progress that is needed across the company. We use the face of the cube to describe the capability areas from left to right and levels ascending from the bottom to the top. These levels are achieved over time and indicate a level of maturity for each of the capability areas listed at the base of the cube. The depth dimension reflects the fact that lines of business, geographies, and other organizational constructs have to be addressed over time. This underscores the notion of volume: the range of people and organizational units that are ultimately touched by and engaged in data Playbook work. This 3-D cube also allows us to visualize different ways of progressing across capabilities and through levels within any one part of the organization.

The intersection of a capability level and a capability area is where we find detailed activities that must be performed. So at Level I for the capability area Govern Programs and Services, the Playbook will provide a number of skilled activities that must be performed to complete that level. Deployment is about sequencing the activities based on our assessment of capability areas and levels that provide for the necessary business benefits or risk reduction. The plan is also about developing a sequence of organizational units or business areas, across which we do this work. Deployment requires thinking across all three dimensions, in order to specify meaningful sequences of activities and engage the appropriate people to produce the required results.

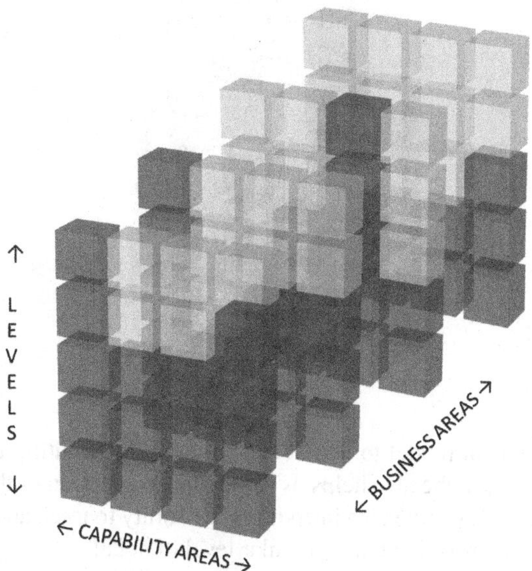

Deconstructing or exploding the cube makes it possible to visualize different sequencing scenarios quickly. It becomes easier to imagine different business areas or organizational units progressing at different paces based on their risks or business benefit requirements. It also breaks down the typically monolithic view that maturity models impose on our work. While an aggregate or enterprise view of maturity is useful, it is so highly abstracted that it obfuscates the real progress being made in key areas of the organization. Average or overall levels often mask critical gaps and insufficiencies in our progress. These abstracted views are also difficult if not impossible to reconcile with our data and analytics dashboard, which identifies specific areas suffering from gaps in governance, controls and quality. We therefore need to use this exploded view to gain a realistic understanding of our progress and to visualize the best sequence options for planning future work.

The exploded view also allows corporate governance leaders and distributed stewardship leaders to engage in business area planning independently and then combine their plans to produce an aggregate view and resource requirement. Engaging the lead stewards for each area in this type of planning enforces a commitment that can be communicated to their sponsorship, while providing central governance with a coherent view of how each unit intends to progress. Marking that progress against the projection is easy and provides compelling proof of progress. Finally, our ability to measure outcomes in each area and align them with the progression the area is making supports the overall data and analytics governance function for the enterprise.

This approach to planning and reporting on overall enterprise progress is critical to maintaining executive sponsorship and communicating our overall progress. We break this prospective down further to get to a level of detailed activities we will sequence in order to achieve these maturity levels across the organization. The construct for activity-level sequencing is a simpler, 2-D view showing capability areas and levels that then deconstruct into specific activity sets by capability level and area. We call this a capability progression view as shown below.

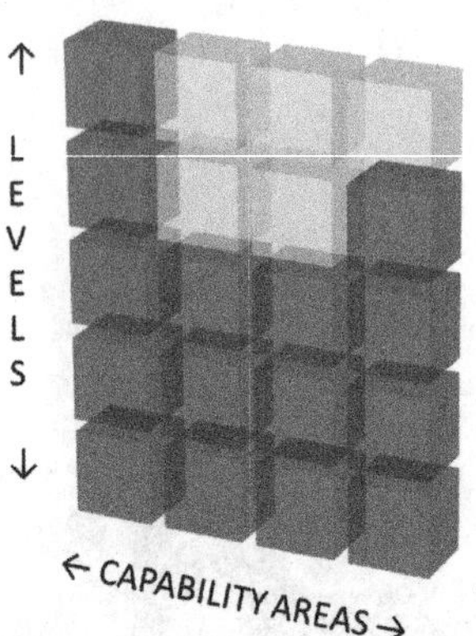

We use the cube deployment model to depict our progress in executing Playbook activities across capability areas and levels. The cube also helps us depict the progression of these activities across lines of business or business areas. The cube also introduces the ability to track and display both governance progression and capability improvement at a granular level of detail.

There are some standard units of measure that can be applied when doing these cube models and assessing our progress against each of these capability levels. The first unit of measure, activity level detail, is described in the sequence graphic. But activities alone do not convey a false sense of scope. It is often helpful to explain that we scope our initiative level work using a standard quantity of critical data. Typically, we can handle between 30 and 50 critical data elements in a short, rapid data sprint that moves us from Level I through Level II. To get some perspective on how many data elements you may be facing in any single business area, let's look at some examples from real-world work. The first is from an end-to-end finance data analysis for a Fortune 50 financial institution. In this case, the institution engaged in a level 1 data sprint aimed at cataloging and analyzing its financial critical data. The outcome resulted in two key assets. The first was a simple chain of custody diagram that indicated the flow of critical data through finance.

Key systems and controls were highlighted in the chain of custody diagram such that it looked a bit like a dataflow diagram but operated at a higher level with some details about control points and control types. The second asset was a working glossary of terms that were derived from financial statements, disclosures, and management reports. These terms were mapped back to the physical data the chain of custody illustrated. The result was a group of about 350 data elements or terms that were clearly defined at the logical level and mapped to over 3500 physical instances in the chain of custody. This gave us the scope of 350 critical data elements we needed to move through Level II governance and toward Level III, in order to map to the required testing and quality controls. This approach of combining top-down, logical business terms with bottom-up, physical data and system flows proved valuable and rapid enough that within four additional, short-term data sprints we had reached Level II for all 350 critical data elements.

Later in this chapter, we will detail different sequences and give estimates of duration and effort required to accomplish the sequences of activities as you move through maturity levels with defined blocks of data.

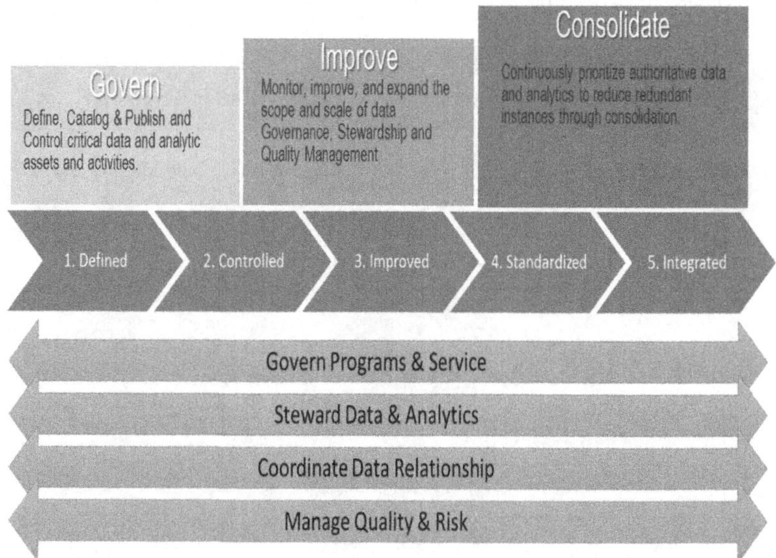

In this view, we see the five maturity levels depicted as chevrons and the four core capability areas depicted as end-to-end arrows underneath them. The stair steps above the chevrons refer to the overall progression that is accomplished and referenced in the core of our cover graphic model.

We have seen a lack of coherent target benefits and outcomes provided in initial data governance programs as well as product and consulting marketing approaches. Getting it "right from the start" was a hallmark of our experience as partners at Knightsbridge Solutions. Knightsbridge used this term in its marketing, selling and delivery to ensure we communicated the expected, long-term outcomes with our clients from day one. Today, we are very careful not to talk in generic terms about the value of governance or the need to treat data as an asset. We've all learned that more specific goals, objectives, and measurable outcomes are needed in order to secure permanent, long-term sponsorship from our executives.

The three stair steps communicate what is achieved as we move through the five maturity levels and allow us to target what level is most appropriate to the needs of the enterprise and the level of sponsorship we currently seek more precisely.

Let's briefly review the five maturity levels and four core maturity areas we defined and supported with detailed activities in Chapter 4. Our model does not start with chaos or uncontrolled environments. "Defined" is the initial level our activities target and the minimum level that must be achieved to move forward in any progression. So while the entry point for these activities may be uncontrolled and undefined, we chose to begin our maturity progression with an initial level that is meaningful and foundational to the rest of the work we must do.

The remaining maturity levels build on a defined state through controls, improvements, standardization, and integration. Each of these levels is clear and distinct enough to support equally clear and distinct activities. As we reviewed in Chapter 4, these activities are also clear and specific about the capability area we are addressing. This distinction is critical, since we do not expect overall capability progression against multiple or undefined capability areas. We also know from years of experience that different clients require different capability area progressions at different times.

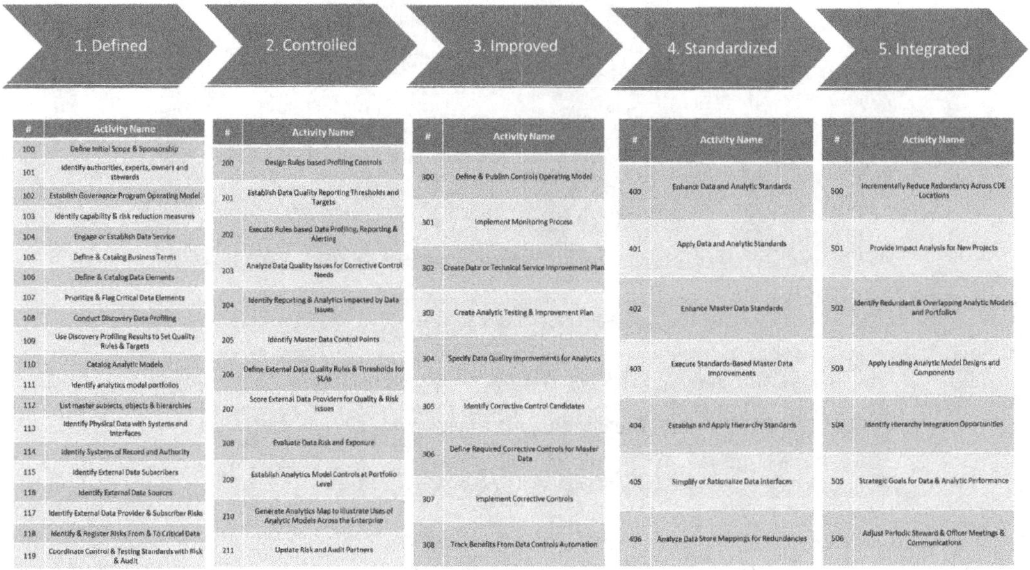

1. Defined

#	Activity Name
100	Define Initial Scope & Sponsorship
101	Identify authorities, experts, owners and stewards
102	Establish Governance Program Operating Model
103	Identify capability & risk reduction measures
104	Engage or Establish Data Service
105	Define & Catalog Business Terms
106	Define & Catalog Data Elements
107	Prioritize & Flag Critical Data Elements
108	Conduct Discovery Data Profiling
109	Use Discovery Profiling Results to Set Quality Rules & Targets
110	Catalog Analytic Models
111	Identify analytics model portfolios
112	List master subjects, objects & hierarchies
113	Identify Physical Data with Systems and Interfaces
114	Identify Systems of Record and Authority
115	Identify External Data Subscribers
116	Identify External Data Sources
117	Identify External Data Provider & Subscriber Risks
118	Identify & Register Risks From & To Critical Data
119	Coordinate Control & Testing Standards with Risk & Audit

2. Controlled

#	Activity Name
200	Design Rules based Profiling Controls
201	Establish Data Quality Reporting Thresholds and Targets
202	Execute Rules based Data Profiling, Reporting & Alerting
203	Analyze Data Quality Issues for Corrective Control Needs
204	Identify Reporting & Analytics impacted by Data Issues
205	Identify Master Data Control Points
206	Define External Data Quality Rules & Thresholds for SLAs
207	Score External Data Providers for Quality & Risk Issues
208	Evaluate Data Risk and Exposure
209	Establish Analytics Model Controls at Portfolio Level
210	Generate Analytics Map to Illustrate Uses of Analytic Models Across the Enterprise
211	Update Risk and Audit Partners

3. Improved

#	Activity Name
300	Define & Publish Controls Operating Model
301	Implement Monitoring Process
302	Create Data or Technical Service Improvement Plan
303	Create Analytic Testing & Improvement Plan
304	Specify Data Quality Improvements for Analytics
305	Identify Corrective Control Candidates
306	Define Required Corrective Controls for Master Data
307	Implement Corrective Controls
308	Track Benefits From Data Controls Automation

4. Standardized

#	Activity Name
400	Enhance Data and Analytic Standards
401	Apply Data and Analytic Standards
402	Enhance Master Data Standards
403	Execute Standards-Based Master Data Improvements
404	Establish and Apply Hierarchy Standards
405	Simplify or Rationalize Data Interfaces
406	Analyze Data Store Mappings for Redundancies

5. Integrated

#	Activity Name
500	Incrementally Reduce Redundancy Across CDE Locations
501	Provide Impact Analysis for New Projects
502	Identify Redundant & Overlapping Analytic Models and Portfolios
503	Apply Leading Analytic Model Designs and Components
504	Identify Hierarchy Integration Opportunities
505	Strategic Goals for Data & Analytic Performance
506	Adjust Periodic Steward & Officer Meetings & Communications

The four core capability areas we have defined in this book start with establishing your permanent governance function so that the detailed activities for your governance are included at the start. Then we progress to Stewardship activities and advance into Data Relationship Management and finally Quality and Risk Controls. Each of these areas has distinct activities that can be sequenced into both defensive and offensive sequences of activities. It's worth noting that, as your experience probably indicates, capability areas must often be addressed simultaneously, particularly at the outset of a new governance function or overhaul of previous attempts.

Both the governance program and stewardship capability areas must be executed together to deliver results. We covered the details of the Playbook model in Chapter 4, so this summary is provided to explain the relationship of the Playbook maturity progression to our cube deployment model.

Several things become apparent when looking at the sequence slide. The first thing you notice is that each capability level has a distinct set of activities associated with it. We know from our assessment work that these activities provide both the checklist and guidance on what needs to be completed to establish progress in each capability area within a particular part of the organization and its scope of data. Providing a clear sense of how much progress each part of the organization has made is one of the challenges of reporting to management and executive teams. It's important to be distinct about progressing the level of governance, controls, and improvement for a certain set of data. We need to communicate the pace of improvement resulting from the overall level of work being completed.

The second thing you notice is that certain capability levels have more activities or appear denser than others. This has to do with the level of intensity required to get through the first two to three levels of capability. There are simply more activities to be performed in early stages of capability maturity than in later ones. Some of these are necessary on a single iteration basis, and others are needed repeatedly. As in so many areas of our life and work, our future work stands on the shoulders of what we produced before. So it's fair to say that the initial foundation is packed very tightly, which allows it to support a very broad base of data analytics for governance and improvement over time.

We've also learned from many client experiences that there are additional activities to be defined for later maturity levels. Very few programs or functions have reached the later levels across the enterprise. There is also the changing nature of Big Data and analytics that emerges only as this very young field matures.

Another thing we notice in the sequence graphic is the lack of lock-step progression indicated by this layout. There are many ways to sequence activities and there are dependencies from one level to the next or even across capability areas, which we often treat as workstreams. These are called out in the Playbook in a detailed level, but overall there is great flexibility in the way you combine activities to produce results.

MAPPING YOUR DEPLOYMENT PRIORITIES

Getting to the point at which you know what you want to accomplish and are ready to produce your sequence is a four-step process. This chapter focuses on the last of these four steps: defining and managing your deployment sequences. The first three steps are addressed in general here and more specifically in our assessment chapter.

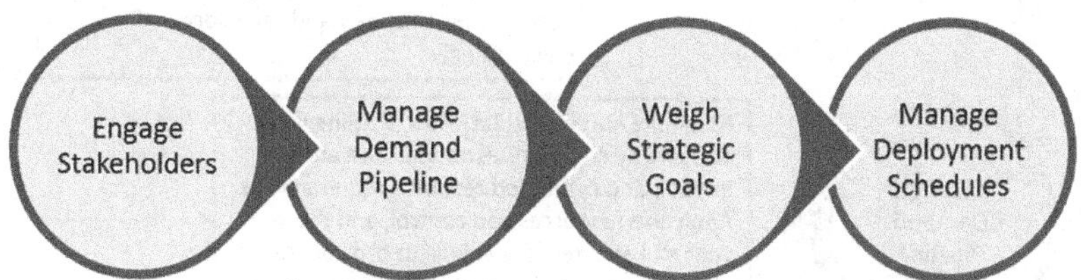

A demand pipeline approach provides a window into your assembly process. Using strategic weighting allows all your constituents to see the application of enterprise priorities to their demands. Once you have this ranked demand list, you can start sorting across the top priority items to determine your scope areas and required activities.

Deployment schedules provide an overall program plan. This schedule operates much like an audit plan that typically shows the annual rotation of internal or external auditors through a business by line of business and geography. The deployment schedule shows all the business areas and their respective data scope. This allows you to interact with your constituents and sponsorship to fully validate your course of action for the year. It is important that this schedule allows for some gaps in order to adjust to new priorities or events in the business and to support the ongoing recruiting, training, and career development of your teams.

THE OVERALL PROCESS OF DEPLOYMENT PLANNING

Generating deployment sequences from this point is a matter of identifying critical activities and their sequences in multiple executions areas. These areas each have a data scope specific to the priorities you are addressing. A finance area such as antimoney laundering (AML) might include data about certain types of financial transactions and counter-parties. At the same time, you might be looking at another area whose data scope includes counterparty risk. Both areas may need the same types of activities from the Playbook, so you assemble the activity sequence and then determine the need to stagger the two areas' execution based on overall resource availability. This last point is important, because resource availability and overall business activities in each of these areas must be taken into account. You may have the right resources to commence with each area at once, but the business, in this case finance group, may be engaged in year-end close or audits and have limited time and access for your teams.

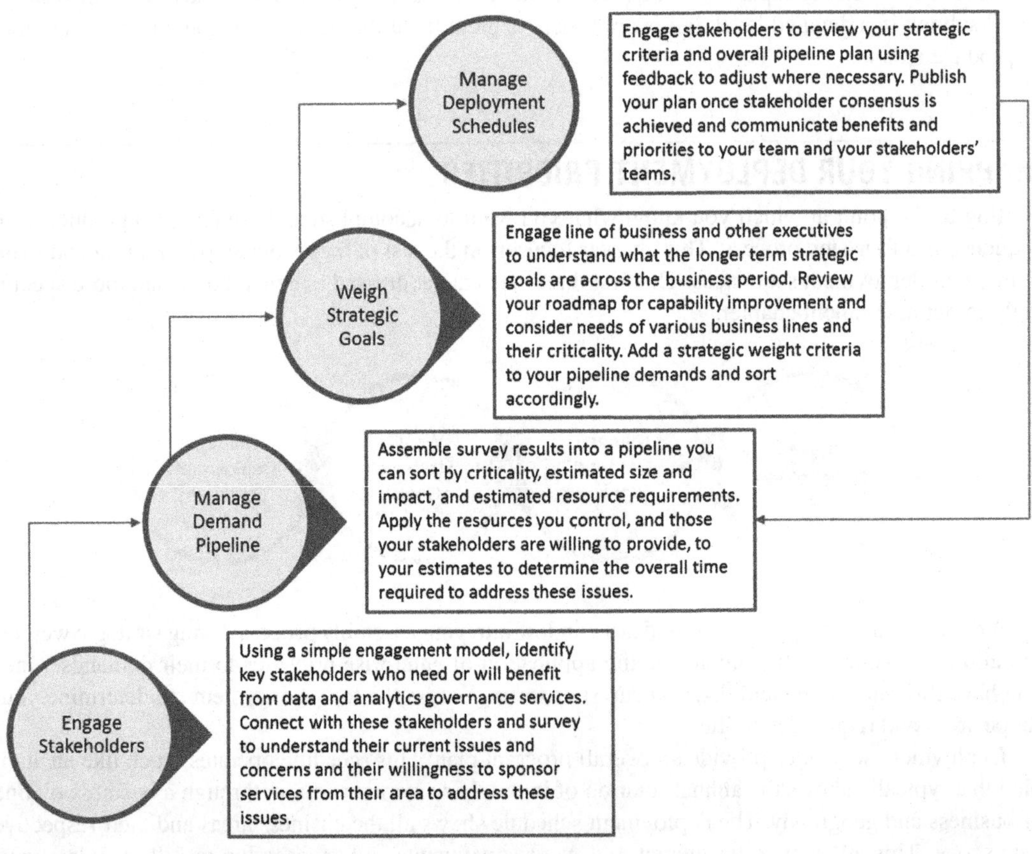

Manage Deployment Schedules
Engage stakeholders to review your strategic criteria and overall pipeline plan using feedback to adjust where necessary. Publish your plan once stakeholder consensus is achieved and communicate benefits and priorities to your team and your stakeholders' teams.
Weigh Strategic Goals
Engage line of business and other executives to understand what the longer term strategic goals are across the business period. Review your roadmap for capability improvement and consider needs of various business lines and their criticality. Add a strategic weight criteria to your pipeline demands and sort accordingly.
Manage Demand Pipeline
Assemble survey results into a pipeline you can sort by criticality, estimated size and impact, and estimated resource requirements. Apply the resources you control, and those your stakeholders are willing to provide, to your estimates to determine the overall time required to address these issues.
Engage Stakeholders
Using a simple engagement model, identify key stakeholders who need or will benefit from data and analytics governance services. Connect with these stakeholders and survey to understand their current issues and concerns and their willingness to sponsor services from their area to address these issues.

Now that a valid deployment schedule is in place, you can focus on the different deployment pattern choices available to arrive at detailed project and resource plans.

DEPLOYMENT PATTERNS

DATA CYCLE

There are many approaches people use to implement data and analytic governance. We've boiled down two distinct approaches that we've used to good effect with many customers across industry and government. These simple approaches each apply to distinct situations. While many variations and alternatives exist, it is very helpful to a program or permanent business function engaged in governance to establish two consistently used tracks. Each track must satisfy the requirements of either an organizational or project-based approach. Each of these approaches leverages the same Playbook activities and resources but allows for different ways of executing and leveraging resources over time. The continuous cycle braces an expansive set of maturity levels. The goal is to produce a sustained set of controlled and improved data that can adjust to changes in business process, reporting, systems, and operational approaches over time. So the continuous cycle pattern is intended to address the breadth of the Playbook, including improvement and often standardization and integration.

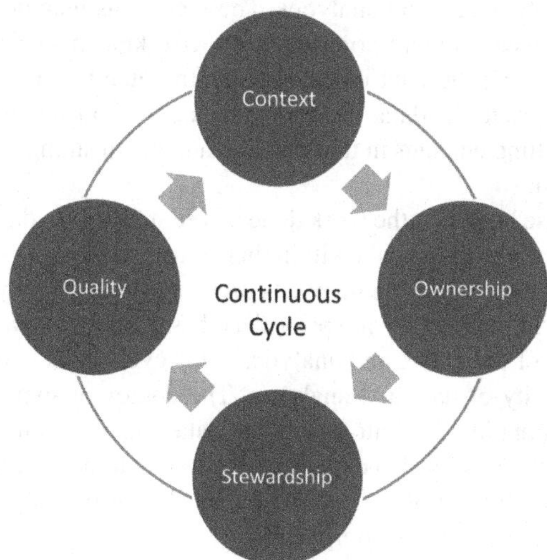

- Ongoing maintenance and publication of data catalog/business glossary with parttime data stewardship
- Automated, ongoing profiling of data using database and business rules tests to determine quality and identify issues
- End-to-end traceability of data quality issues for root cause resolution

The first of these is a cycle approach used when we're deploying in an organizational or functional area. This cycle engages people in the area within your scope through a continuous approach. This is the permanent organizational function we have discussed previously. This approach requires a continuous cycle, because we are placing data stewards, analytic stewards, and others in a position of ongoing responsibility for their data and the changes that occur within that responsibility. So this continuous cycle provides an initial governance standard and an ongoing change control function. Improving the maturity and outcomes of any governance capability across an organization requires some continuous cycle to provide sustained change control and other governance features. Thus consider, even within the scope of project-based governance activities, the need to follow your project with the continuous cycle approach.

The first stage in the cycle is the development of context. This establishes the scope of data, processes, organization and resources, and intended level of maturity to be reached over time by cycle iterations. Level I of the Playbook, or the "Defined" level of maturity, includes a number of activities that establish context for both the scope of activities, and the current condition of the data. The second phase in the cycle refers to establishing ownership and controls over the defined data or analytic constructs. The goal in this phase is to identify and assign responsibilities to owners of key data and analytics constructs. These owners, and the stewards they engage within their business or operational areas, are responsible for both change control and improvement of the data and analytics.

The stewardship phase engages the stewards, with owner support and approvals, and establishes the ongoing work to control changes and improve quality. The first responsibility of the stewards is to provide controls around the defined data and analytics. These controls include change controls and basic data quality discovery and measurement controls, otherwise known as detective controls. Stewards become responsible for knowing the data in their scope, the quality and issues of that data, and the process for controlling changes to the data. We are not trying to control regular flows of value changes in data; rather we are controlling changes in the structure and the meaning of the data through a consistent data stewardship pattern.

The "Improvement" phase builds on the work done by the stewards to date, because they have established the quality level and issues in the data within their scope. Improving quality for data and analytics also requires stewards to understand the demands users have and the ways users consume their data and analytics. Some quality improvements are prioritized based on the impacts the quality impairments are having on critical users of their data and analytics. This cycle closes with updates to context as a result of improving the quality of data and analytics. The context is expanded by both outcomes of quality improvement, including insights into additional data sources or analytic models needed to satisfy business requirements. Context is also expanded due to incoming changes in business process and data. As the context changes, the rest of the cycle is engaged. These changes drive additional data and analytics, requiring the other stages to be completed.

DATA SPRINTS

The other approach commonly required to implement data analytics governance is a project-oriented approach we call data sprints. These projects require a much more agile, rapid execution rate and typically have a limited scope of required governance. Our experience indicates that data-intensive projects such as system transitions, transformations, and reporting analytics programs often need a level of governance that provides definition and control with only limited improvement. Sprints are very compressed, so we use a segmentation approach to limit the scope of data any one sprint addresses. The key is to complete sprinting for weeks, sometimes even less. The word complete refers to reaching a level of maturity for the data in scope. Typically, this level is Controlled, not just Defined. It is important that projects produce controlled data outcomes and so simply defining the data scope and the individuals responsible for it is not typically enough to satisfy the program requirements. Moving to a level of control over your data and analytics as part of your project or program ensures you deliver an outcome that can be sustained. At this point, it's worth reiterating the need to follow successful projects and programs with continuous cycles of governance and improvement.

Sprints can be very aligned with agile methods and can use a variety of their tools, including daily scrum calls, scrum master, and other hallmarks of agile methodology. While these agile methods are not required for data sprints, they have proven highly effective in managing multiple, parallel Playbook activities across resources and within a short period of time. Daily scrum, or hogwash calls, are the single most important tool we found in assuring two key aspects of the sprint are successfully applied. The first is providing an opportunity for all team members to share major issues they face, which operates as a communication tool and a way of getting help or escalating issues. The second and equally as important facet is the ability to engage your sponsor or senior executive in these calls so the entire team feels the support, engagement, and sense of urgency executive sponsors bring to the table. These calls should be tightly run and take between 5 and 15 min to complete. We do not discuss details of an issue or options for resolution on the call. We log the issue and understand the timing and criticality of it, then assign it to the program manager or scrum master for later follow-up to make sure we understand the root cause and can assign actions to resolve it. Every issue raised is addressed the same day by the scrum master with appropriate team members. These methods have proven invaluable to executing sprints in 30 days or less on a consistent basis.

The other key driver to success in fast, short sprints is segmenting or scoping the data you will address. We think in terms of multiple, parallel sprint executions and so we tend to segment data based on the subject of the data. The key team members will be on the sprint to get that data to a level of definition and control within 4 weeks. It's also important that you provide your data and analytic services partners with sufficient capacity to institute data-quality profiling on a discovery level in order to ensure you can actually apply controls into a second sprint event. This preserves the integrity of the execution and highlights gaps in business or other resource availability. A sprint lives and dies on the sense of urgency and the daily heartbeat of scrum or team calls and issue resolution.

We have found that between 30 and 50 data elements are appropriate to address in the scope of a single sprint. Similarly, we have found that three to five analytic models, depending on complexity, are an appropriate scope for a 30-day sprint. Exceptions abound however; we have seen upward of 20 analytic models get cataloged and have basic controls applied in a 4-week sprint. On the other extreme we have seen as few as 12 data elements fully addressed to Control level in a 4-week sprint. The differences in these ranges are often a combination of the complexity of the data or analytic models we are addressing and the information availability and turnaround time we get from key resources. We often have to distinguish effort from duration in the sprints.

- One-time cataloging, mapping, and analysis of data
- Project documentation (excel)
- Validated migration of catalogued data to the target system or store

The sprint diagram is a reflection of the way we often have to communicate the groupings of activities for our constituents and participants to understand. We use the Playbook and a sequence of activities to create a project plan with assignments and estimated durations and effort levels. But this high-level view is helpful with sponsors and with people whose resources we need to leverage. It's also a convenient way to communicate some of the parallel execution features and dependencies of the data sprint.

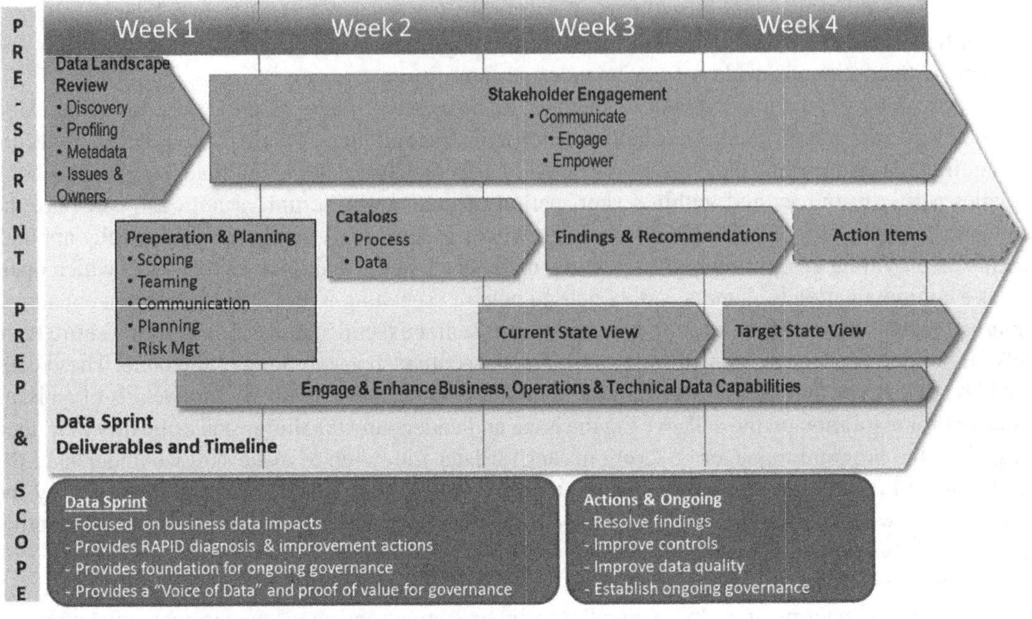

COMMUNICATING DATA SPRINTS

Data sprints can be difficult to explain to people who have not been through a project-oriented implementation of governance. Reactions to an initial discussion range from pushback all the way to an insistence that a continuous cycle approach is used in parallel but not as part of the project itself. We have developed some basic communication language to explain what the key hallmarks of a sprint are and when it is best used. The following is an excerpt from communication we've used successfully with several clients.

1. What is a data sprint?—A rapid, agile, and repeatable process using standard methods from the data management Playbook to assess, address, and establish controls over data and data-related processes, people, and technology.
2. How does it work?—As a planned series of activities conducted jointly by a scrum master and sprint leader and resources from internal business, operations, and technical areas as required by its scope and targeted outcomes.
3. When is this needed?—Nagging data issues are costing more than it will take to resolve—you need a proven, repeatable process that engages the right people quickly and inexpensively. It is especially needed when:
   a. Controls or risk issues are clearly data-induced and require resolution, eg, AML, risk management, financial and client reporting errors, protracted financial and performance reporting issues, etc.
   b. Reporting and analytics requirements are increasingly going unmet because of a lack of quality, authority or source documentation, and lineage.

   c. There is no clear process to engage technical and business stakeholders and to identify or resolve data issues; constant, redundant efforts, data stores, and interfaces are used to plug gaps and replace suspicious data.
   d. There is no clear connection between operational challenges and the sources of the issues, or between reporting inconsistencies and sources.
   e. Data governance has become an imperative, but it is not clear where or how to start without a massive program; you need to start small, win big, and iterate.
4. Key Features and Benefits
   a. Fast, proven, repeatable process that can be taught across internal teams, which reduces external consulting cost
   b. Establishes root causes and best alternatives to resolve nagging, costly, and risky data issues across processes and systems
   c. Provides a solid foundation for ongoing data governance and quality monitoring
   d. Is iterative and parallel; many sprints become relay races covering critical business, operational, and technology areas
5. Proven accelerators (execution and value realization) include:
   a. Standard deliverables and templates transferred to client teams
   b. Real scoping practices (this is the biggest stumbling block for data improvement and governance)
   c. Data landscape review—quick context for planning and engagement

DATA RISK AND EXPOSURE

Maturity models have been in common use for decades and can be very helpful in understanding where there are gaps between our current execution level and our desired or required level. It's important to think about capabilities as the embodiment, or instantiation of skills, methods, and execution. Thinking about capabilities as a general construct relating to how smart or capable you are is not helpful in a business context, unless it is tied to a consistent execution level that measures to the capability model.

We have learned over the past 25 years that even the use of execution-oriented capability models is not enough business justification for major investment. Major industries, including financial services, healthcare, technology, professional services, and even government and regulatory bodies, have all shown the need to apply risk-adjusted approaches to data and analytics governance. Our approach to this is very simple and stems from our experience in internal audit, regulatory, and compliance work.

As an auditor, I was taught two key constructs of audit and control. The first was that there was "no substitute for controls conscious management." This refers to the fact that implementing, maintaining, and testing controls requires executive support, based on the certain knowledge that the lack of controls will, very quickly, result in losses and damages. Therefore controls-conscious management is a critical component of the well-run organization. Seems simple enough, but we all know of companies with significant gaps in controls consciousness and commitment.

The second thing I was taught by the same internal auditor of a national bank, Mark DeLong, was that measuring risk alone is insufficient. Risk is required but not sufficient, because the likelihood of a problem occurring alone does not allow us to evaluate the impacts it could have. We have to measure both the risk of a thing happening, and the exposure we suffer when it does happen. So risk and exposure are the two levers we have to pull together to understand how likely the problem is to occur and how much it will impact us when it does. High risk of recurrence of things like cash and marketable securities losses due to poor physical controls is critical. Extremely high loss of paperclips is probably not such a critical issue. So measuring both the likelihood of a problem and the cost of it are critical to prioritizing the controls we put in place or improve to reduce risk. Mark taught me the balance between controls, risk, and exposure. Our entire Playbook rests on this construct and suggests the need to use risk and exposure ratings to prioritize our controls work with data and analytics. The third thing Mark taught me is that "risks don't age well," so our ability to identify, monitor, and control for risks is critical. DeLong is now Senior Vice President of Risk Management at Freddie Mac.

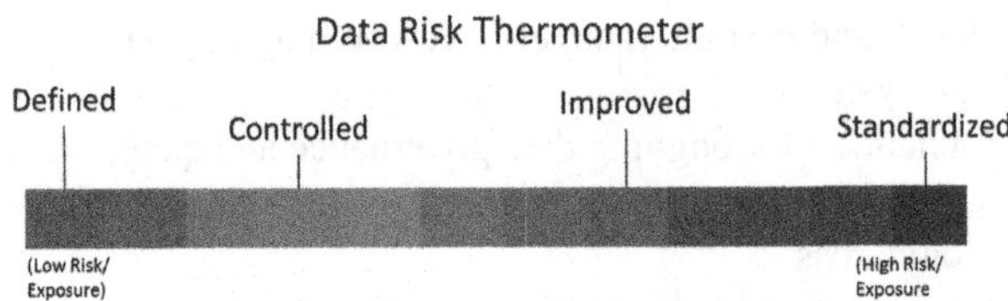

This Risk Thermometer graphic addresses the typical range of thinking people have about risk. It suggests that, as the risk of the thing occurring increases, we would increase the level of maturity we need for it. This is a very unidimensional approach and is necessary but not entirely sufficient for prioritizing our controls work. We have to move to a 2-D model to compare risk and exposure. After all, the risk of losing a lot of paperclips is probably not sufficient to justify a business case for paperclip governance, since the costs outweigh the benefits.

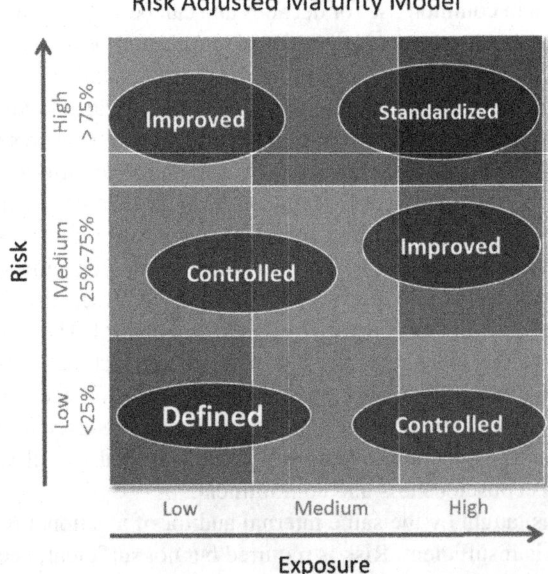

So we moved from the thermometer image to a 2-D approach that allows us to compare risk and exposure on their own axes. This risk-adjusted maturity model is actually risk and exposure weighted. This gives us the ability to determine the materiality, or overall importance and value, of a challenge we face with data or analytics. By scoring each problem or challenge for both risk and exposure, we're able to place it on the grid and understand its relative importance and priority. We're also able to identify the target level of maturity needed for controls, based on the severity of risk and exposure to any problem or challenge. While the placement of these maturity levels can vary, the overall notion is that, as risk and exposure increase, the value of higher-order controls such as improvement or corrective controls and standardization or the introduction of preventive controls is merited by business impact. So this matrix gives us a simple, visual way to understand the relationship of risk and exposure and the required levels of maturity as risk and exposure rise together.

Let's use some examples that have been cleansed from various business settings. This table uses five discrete challenges that were identified to various detective controls approaches. In some cases, these were a result of a business need that created a project, while others came from detective controls over the review of reports and analytics that identified material variances. In each case, these have been vetted and scored as well as assessed for current maturity.

ID	Date	Name	Current Maturity Level	Risk Score	Exposure Score	Required Maturity Level
1	May	Financial Reporting & Disclosure	1	High	High	4
2	July	Footnotes to Financials	0	Low	Medium	2
3	August	Product Profitability	1	Medium	Medium	3
4	October	HR Performance Data	1	Low	Medium	2
5	November	Customer Name & Address Data	1	High	Medium	3

This table gives us the ability to prioritize based on a combination of risk and exposure, to establish our risk and exposure grid, and to set the target level of maturity we need to reach with our controls for each challenge. It is often helpful to use the grid as a scatter graph or plot of the density and set of risk and exposure challenges we're facing. In the graph below you can see that we actually have a broad array of both risk and exposure in our challenges. We have seen high exposure issues brought down

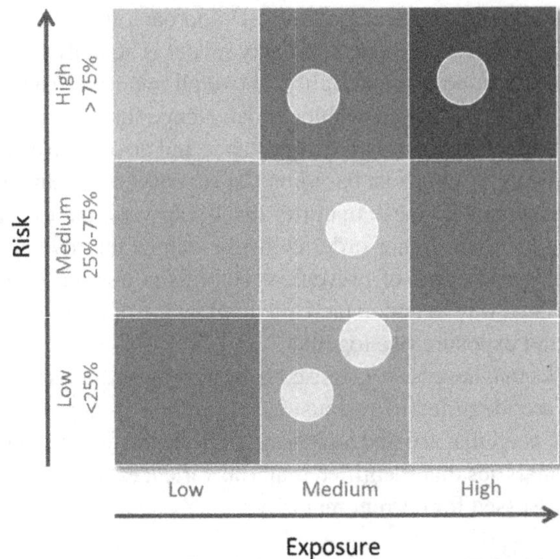

across the board in organizations that engage in a programmatic approach to steadily maturing high sensitivity or impact areas. Many first-generation data governance programs and current attempts to govern analytics are lowering risk but not the high exposure areas first. This seems counterintuitive, especially when you consider the fact that the controls improvements made in high exposure areas often result in building overall knowledge, competency, and execution experience in the organization. This knowledge will help address the other areas you need to resolve.

DEPLOYMENT SCOPING AND PLANNING

Now that we've addressed some of the ways to figure out which areas are most important to address and what deployment pattern options you have, we can move on to scoping and planning efforts. It is important to remember that we're using our maturity levels to group the kinds of activities we must perform in order to reach a certain level of control. This is the overall Playbook content structured as a maturity model, with each activity grouped by level of maturity. We use this in order to select the activities we group for both sprints and continuous cycle of deployment patterns.

In the cycle approach, these activities are bundled based on the descriptions we gave you of the continuous cycle. It's important to note again that in continuous cycle patterns we generally target a higher level of maturity to reach and sustain: typically at least Improvement and generally Standardization. Note that integration requires a distinct business case around consolidating duplicate or overlapping data and analytic platforms or content. In contrast, sprints typically address a narrower range of activities and limit themselves to reaching the maturity level within a short period of time and for a limited scope of data.

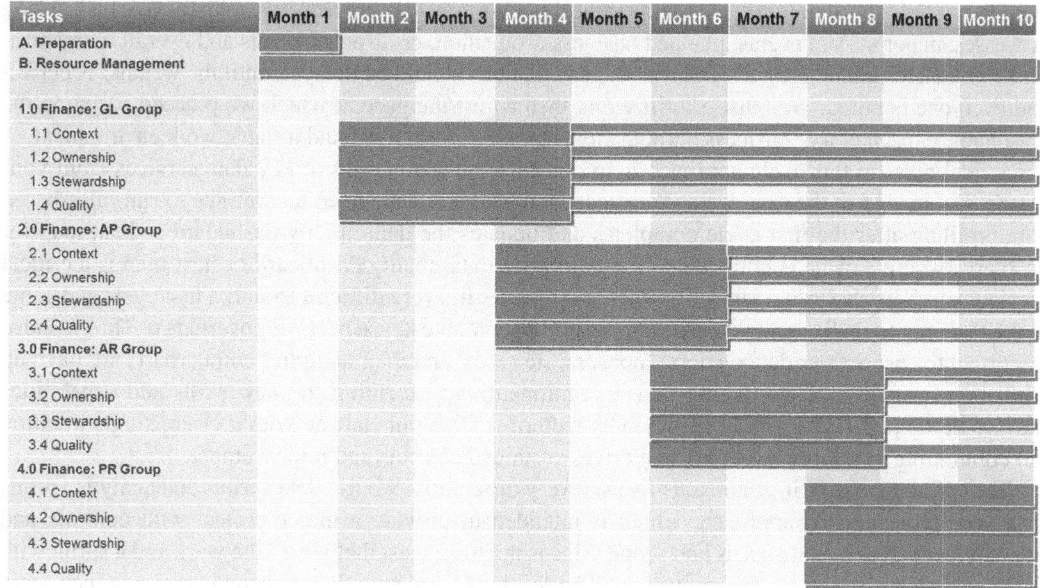

The project plan example above provides a visual representation of the way cycles can be planned and executed. The important thing to recognize is that cycles continue past their initiation. Any cycle initiation is typically about 3 months in duration, during which time you rotate through one cycle in one area of the business. That means engaging all the roles and executing on the Playbook activities based on a description of the cycle approach. There is another critical aspect of the cycle that is indicated in the project plan view: the tale that runs continuously from the initial cycle. We know that the cycle is continuous and that while there is a heavier amount of work to do the first time you execute the cycle, there is continuing work around change control, context updates, and improvements as business conditions, processes, and data change. It's also important to note that the cycle can be focused only on data governance, or on analytics governance or, in some cases, both.

In the cycle project plan, you are trying to depict the relative scale of activity and effort in the initial cycle as opposed to the ongoing iterations. Business and operation folks generally ask how big the overall work effort will be, particularly on an ongoing basis. Much has been written around business cases for data and analytics governance and business impacts and outcomes. The truth is that we consistently find that once a standard set of methods, such as the ones the Playbook provides, are adopted and people's skills and experience allow them to execute quickly, the amount of time per day, week, or month that a data or analytic steward spends on governance is a half to a quarter of the work they were spending to manually handle data or analytic issues.

Some other takeaways from this visualization relate to the amount of parallel execution your program can support. Remember, there are more shared or managed service resources needed to orient, train, and mentor business data and analytics stewards in this work. There are always questions and requests for help in the first iteration of these cycles. So it's important to think about the scheduling of cycles across business areas based on the business areas' annual calendar of activities and your resource capabilities to support multiple first iteration cycles at the same time. We're often very sensitive to fiscal year and closing processes, major system events, planned business acquisition, or disposal events and overall reorganization and transformation efforts. That is not to say that this should be delayed until the weather is perfect and everyone is bored. We must prioritize and then adjust the pace at which we proceed based on the reasonable expectation of business participation, resource availability, and a stable work environment.

A final note on this cycle approach is to consider the availability of key data services from your partners at the end of the first cycle. A critical example here is the need to continue to run rules-based data profiling after the first cycle completes and updates the data-quality dashboard or heat map for each area where a cycle is completed. The enterprise data-quality dashboard or heat map is a critical service that short-share data service groups can provide. It's very difficult to start a first cycle and come to the end only to realize that you are not prepared to continue key aspects of governance. Thus it's also important to ensure your data owners, sponsors, stewards, and their analytics counterparts are lined up with the expectation of continuing their commitment and executing the new skills and capabilities they've developed. The cycle of deployment pattern is all about starting with a clean, single iteration but committing to a sustained effort that drives sustained controls and improvement.

The sprint approach, in contrast, is focused very differently. We use data sprints and analytic sprints in a very project-based approach, which is intended to provide a major project with controls and improvements based on its needs and scope. This is not to suggest that we do the work and a sprint with the expectation that no ongoing controls will be left in place. Quite the opposite is true, we seek to tie project areas that execute a sprint back into an organizational cycle that will result in a set of controls that are executed wherever possible. Not all projects need to result in ongoing governance. Many projects around sunsetting or consolidating systems, disposing of certain business assets or lines, and even certain reorganization or transformation projects will end without the need for permanent governance. It should be noted that, in the case of transformation programs, a cycle or multiple cycles are required in order to instantiate data and analytic controls and governance as part of the transformation itself.

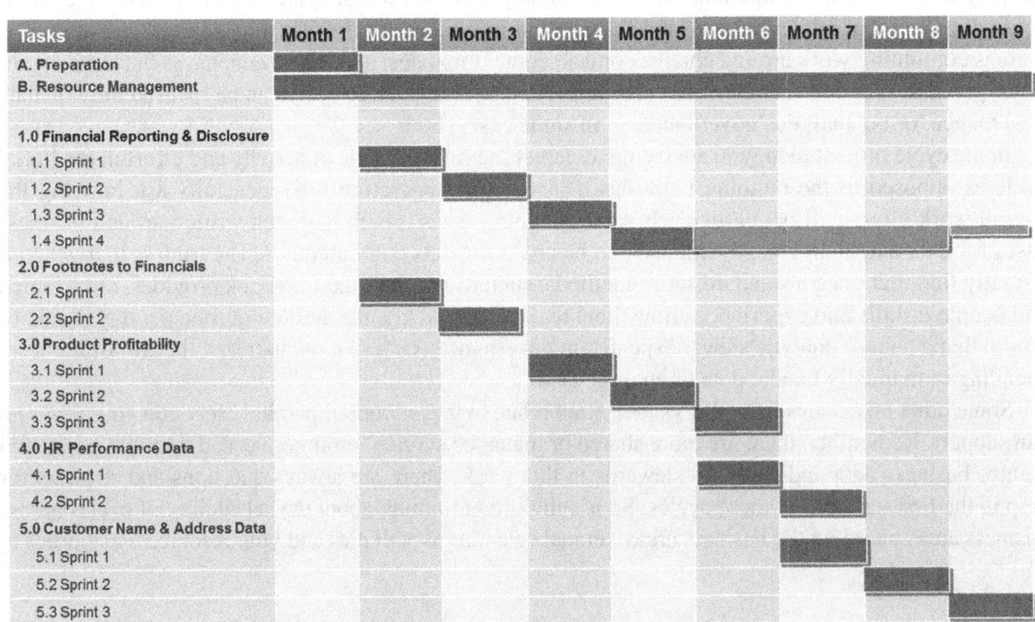

Just as with the cycle pattern, the sprint pattern can accommodate a certain amount of parallel activity. The constraints here are similar to those in the cycle, because supporting projects doing sprints requires the same enterprise or shared services capacity that cycle iterations required. Projects and the sprints we used to support them are often more intensive, because they're very short. Therefore the time allowed to help the team in a project understand the key activities they need to perform as part of governance is very limited. So in sprints, we use a simpler approach, and we limit the number of activities based on the need to get to a "controlled" level of maturity.

There is a risk with the data sprint or analytic sprint approach to addressing all your data or analytic issues in project form. It's important to balance in your overall planning and roadmap activities a set of cycle patterns as well as sprint patterns. We've seen some of the best results occur when sprints were followed by cycles. This can be difficult because sprints are typically a project to construct and not subject to the broader scope of an organization or business unit cycle. Sprints are often very tightly scoped to as few as 30 to 50 data elements and must be completed in 30 days or less. To the best extent possible, it is very useful to make sure you plan your project-based sprints in a way that bundles them with business areas to create an initial critical mass for a follow-on cycle.

We depicted an example of where a cycle follows a sprint in the project plan. It is possible to use a shortened initial cycle when a sprint has covered enough scope to the level of "controlled" maturity. Typically, project-based prints cover too narrow a scope of data to shorten the first cycle duration; often a series of sprints leads into a cycle with the ongoing sustainment tail at the end. This is probably the best way to think about using a sprint in the project to drive to a more permanent governance function in the area that is home to the project.

CONCLUSION

We started this section of the deployment chapter by describing the fact that many different deployment patterns exist and are appropriate or valid depending on your needs and the skills of your organization. We highlighted two approaches that have worked well with our clients in a number of settings. We know it's important to be able to support both project-oriented needs with sprints as well as ongoing committed governance functions with the cycle deployment pattern. We have also learned that where we start in a project with the sprint should be followed, whenever possible, with a cycle that sustains the governance we have started to put in place in the project. Each of these deployment patterns leverages the same standard activities, milestones, tools, and services called out in the Playbook. This means that you can reliably plan and execute either sprints or cycles because the underlying activities are standardized and can be consistently applied given a disciplined scope.

We encourage you to use your own terms to describe the deployment patterns here or variations you find more suitable for your organization, but be sure to do so in a way that is consistent. This consistency helps people understand when they should select a deployment pattern, based on their scope, timing, and required outcomes. Encourage people to consider cycle or permanent governance approaches at the tag end of their project-related efforts. In truth, there are very few sprints; most races are relay races that require ongoing cycle-based governance.

CHAPTER

DATA GOVERNANCE AS AN OPERATIONS PROCESS

8

In previous chapters, we saw what a repeatable, deployable process is, how to gain support for it, details on how to use it, and how to measure its success and progress. Following these steps keeps you proactively improving these capabilities. To execute data governance well, data governance needs an operations model and an operations process. The same discipline used to manage other operations processes can be applied to data governance. This chapter provides examples of operations processes common at many organizations, breaks them down into a few core components, and applies this thinking to data governance and the Playbook. This chapter also covers how a Playbook process can be managed as an operations process and how it can be integrated into the rest of the company. Some of these topics apply to both large and small companies and some topics to large, complex organizations. Dozens of ideas and approaches based on direct experience are included to help you put the Playbook to use.

OPERATIONS

Organizations will always have data. Most organizations would agree that information-based approaches to decision making is an important and a permanent part of the operating landscape. In order to manage data efficiently, an organization needs to think about data governance as an ongoing operational process instead of a one-time project. Operational processes are common inside organizations. Operational processes manage critical parts of an organization's value chain.

It is common to see companies create data governance programs that appear more like a project, executed just once. These projects are often technology focused. Perhaps the rationale is that once an application has been installed, data governance processes are no longer needed because the data governance jobs are being performed by the application.

As an organization adapts to its marketplace, its strategy, products, and operations change. These elements are in constant flux. The data used to manage and run a company is always changing. Data governance needs to be constantly operating to address these changes. Viewed with an operational lens, data governance is an operations management process that is designed to perform a set of data governance jobs.

A key benefit of the Playbook is that it exposes the daily process of data governance. Each individual can see what steps they should perform, in what order, and what inputs and outputs are needed to get the job done. Specifying this level of detail is common at organizations. Organizations have documented operations processes such as customer service, finance, and sales and marketing. To customize the Playbook and to find what works at your company, you should inspect other operational processes and see how they work. These proven operational processes are "proof points" that can help you sell a Playbook approach in your organization.

It is useful to review a few common operational processes in order to show how the language and approach used in other corporate operations processes mirror those needed to make a Playbook-based model successful.

REPORT CREATION

Report creation is a common need across business groups. Report creation, however, may not be the first large-scale operational process that comes to mind when you think about enterprise-wide, corporate processes. Report-creation processes are designed to create, enhance, and manage analytical reports. A report can contain financial information, customer information, or other operational data. A report is a set of tables and graphs that use data to describe events or situations.

Many companies have two paths in their report-creation process. The first path is for reports that can be created by a department without any assistance from other groups. The second path is for reports that must be created by other groups due to another group's access to resources or capabilities such as databases, reporting tools, or business knowledge.

Creating a new report involves the following steps:

- Formulating the request and sending the request to be fulfilled
- Evaluating and validating whether it is appropriate for the receiving party to fulfill the request
- Understanding what business concepts need to be expressed in the report
- Identifying and locating the data sufficient to create the report
- Reviewing the data and determining if it is appropriate to be used in the report
- Accessing the data and creating the tables and graphs appropriate to the requesting party's needs

These steps are usually poorly documented. For example, Sam, down the hallway, may be the go-to person for certain types of reports. You could walk down the hall and make your request to Sam directly. Sam would listen to your request and evaluate if he could help you and then, perhaps, help you create the report.

But if you are new to the company, have never made a request before, do not know who can help you, or perhaps Sam turned you down, you would need to file a request into a request management system. The request management system would queue your request with others. The request would be routed to a reporting group for evaluation. Eventually, someone would discuss your needs with you and a report would be created. The report might be delivered in a corporate portal where you log in and run the report by specifying a time period or other parameters.

There are a few critical parts to the report-generation process. The key parts are:

- Hopefully, a well-defined and documented process to get what you want—a report. The documentation may have been available on the corporate portal or described in a document a colleague emails you.
- A set of applications that support you submitting your request as well a set of applications that deliver the result back to you. The applications for different parts of the process may be different.
- A manager reviews the request and ensures that someone is assigned to fulfill the request. Over time, the manager may gather statistics and information about the total number of reports, the time it takes to create a report, and perform demand analysis to determine if the reporting group should improve their report turnaround commitment or increase costs by hiring more report analysts.
- An organization, formal or informal was created, whether it was Sam or a reporting group, to create the reports. They have been given special training and applications to support their report writing efforts.

Three elements—process, organization, and technology—were needed to allow the report-generation process to work. There were specific elements of these three areas that made a difference:

- Process
  - There was a defined process.
  - The process was published and request forms were available to make the request process transparent, easier, and repeatable.
  - Demand metrics enabled proactive management and hopefully allows a group to improve the process and service-level commitments over time.
- Organization
  - A group with the proper training carried out report-generation tasks.
  - The reporting group was actively managed.
- Technology
  - Specialized applications such as the request management system, the reporting application, and the corporate portal allowed the reporting group to be efficient in their requests.

These three characteristics are needed with the right mix to make the report-generation process a well-managed operations process.

SERVICE CENTER

Most companies that sell standardized products and services at a large-scale have a service center. Whether a company sells to consumers or other companies, a service center often takes phone calls, emails, chat requests, and Twitter communications and addresses customer needs expressed in the communications. A service representation (Rep) can have a demanding job if an organization's customers are prone to emotional outbursts due to the intensity or nature of the relationship they have with the organization.

If you think about wireless providers or healthcare insurance companies, you realize that the scale and nature of service work can be large and complicated. It is not uncommon for service centers to experience 20–40% attrition per year. To mitigate the effects of high turnover, a company continuously runs training programs. Service managers want new Reps to exhibit the same productivity as high-tenure Reps so that a customer's needs are efficiently and effectively resolved on the first call. There are other customer experience metrics that can be used to measure success and are specific to the products and customers.

Service centers typically have the following characteristics:

- Process
  - Processes are often specified at a detailed level to support both training and reference needs. The process descriptions are often explicit and constructed as a "route map"—the paths followed for each service request is fully elaborated. Flexibility in the process is usually documented in the route map so that Reps know what latitude they have before they need to escalate an issue upward for resolution. The route maps contain process steps specific to the technologies used in the service center. There are typically multiple types of service requests covered in the process descriptions.
  - Multiple types of metrics are gathered including those that are related to the process eg, number of calls handled, and the business outcomes eg, number of issues resolved on the first call.

  - Feedback and tune-up support processes are always in effect to keep Reps informed about trends and other operational matters. For example, weekly or daily huddles and review meetings, discussions on trending issues, and sharing of solutions or insights are built into the schedule and strictly followed.
- Organization
  - The design of service organizations varies widely. Larger companies have service operations that span the globe in order to manage costs downward or serve clients in different time zones. Most medium-sized organizations have multilocation service center models. Service groups often have large manager-to-representative resource ratios. Managers move up through the ranks of the service organization.
  - The organization itself is typically placed under the Chief Operations Officer (COO) and is considered an operations process. It runs a full stack of senior, mid-, and junior managers as well as individual contributors. In many cases, Reps are grouped together based on their skill or knowledge area to service a specific customer segment, which is called tiered service. Service representatives are trained across multiple types of service requests so that resources can be focused on hotspots as they develop. The organization performs concentrated training to develop expertise for complex service types.
  - Service organizations often have dedicated individuals who focus on creating operations reports and support ad-hoc operations questions from managers.
- Technology
  - Service center technology has evolved quickly over past decade. The applications and technology employed at service centers are focused on two objectives: improving the customer experience and productivity. It is widely recognized that without automation support it is impossible to efficiently handle service requests. Some service center technologies target self-service scenarios where customers can resolve their issues without Rep involvement.
  - Applications used by service representatives are highly customized to the service request types. Service organizations try to minimize the number of applications that are needed to serve requests because more applications on the desktop usually lead to longer calls and a diminished customer experience. Applications are often integrated into a "cockpit" that Reps use to resolve issues on the first call as quickly and efficiently as possible.

Service operations are intense—a good organization has passionate customers with import problems to resolve. To serve customers, organizations integrate process, organization, and technology cohesively.

FINANCE AND ACCOUNTING

Similar to the report-creation area, finance and accounting operations are often centralized. Larger organizations tend to have a centralized finance function with smaller satellite groups directly embedded in each business unit or major geographical unit. If a company is public, financial operations must be scaled to meet regulatory and industry reporting requirements.

The finance group is involved in several core areas including preparing and publishing financial statements, managing accounts payable and receivables (suppliers and customers), securing financing, and potentially, financial budgeting and planning. The finance group is often the "owner" of financial-related data such as the chart of accounts.

Similar to the way you can think about report generation, the finance group runs a disciplined operations processes. We can describe them using the same three categories as above:

- Process
  - There are many well-defined processes and documentation that describe detailed calculation methods.
  - Many aspects of the finance processes are specified by industry groups or the government. The processes may be elaborate and include specific operations and business metrics.
- Organization
  - The organization is mostly comprised of dedicated individuals.
  - Within business units, there are often "finance people" who are not part of the finance group but serve the financial management needs of that group, eg, budgeting and planning or facilitating accounts receivables and accounts payable.
  - These individuals hold these responsibilities part-time but are financially savvy. They act as proxies for the finance group for a specific set of scenarios.
- Technology
  - Organizations tend to spend significant sums on enterprise resource planning (ERP) systems. Many ERP systems support financial operations explicitly, eg, the general ledger or subledger, as well as budgeting and planning. These applications are implemented by IT but "owned" by finance. Multiple users in the business units use these applications, with the rules and processes defined by finance, to conduct their business.

Finance groups are often some of the first groups to appreciate the importance of data governance. Financial data is critical to managing toward good business outcomes, and financial statements require personal attestation by senior management. Within the finance group, a few dedicated and well-known individuals are considered data gurus. The gurus understand what issues exist with the data and its readiness for use. Data gurus perform the key data governance jobs discussed in Chapter 1.

DATA GOVERNANCE OPERATIONAL MODEL

To create an operations process you need to thoughtfully design three core areas: process, organization, and technology. For data governance and the Playbook, these areas are:

- Process: The day-to-day approach to conducting the core data governance jobs listed in Chapter 1. This includes the improvement process used to refine the Playbook.
  - The Playbook provides a detailed description of the operations processes.
- Organization: The types and locations of human resources that are part of executing the data governance process. The organization also needs to include the oversight and management elements. Most organizations have found that since the data governance jobs and processes cut across functional groups, many data governance resources are part-time.
  - The Playbook calls out the roles used in the process. Each role may be filled by one or more human resources in the organization. Taken together, the Playbook roles define the data governance organization.

- Technology: These are the applications and other tools the data governance organization uses to run the processes efficiently and effectively.
  - The Playbook may describe specific technology actions to take, eg, send an email or post a request to a specific portal folder. We refer to this level of detail as a "desk-level procedure." The Playbook is often one level higher. It is up to you to decide how much detail to provide in the Playbook. The level of detail you provide is based on how prescriptive you need to be for the specific resources that will be fulfilling the roles. In some cases, this level of detail is absolutely essential to helping the organization execute. For others, slightly less detail may be appropriate.

Designing these areas for a data governance operations process can be as challenging as it is to create processes spanning multiple profit and loss centers or managerial boundaries. We use the term "operational model" to mean the specific choices you make in these three areas when designing your data governance program. For example, you may choose to minimize, at least initially, the amount of application support you provide data governance human resources. This may be the "model" you use to launch the data governance operations process. The model could later change as the process matures. Once you cast data governance as an operations process, all operations processes require a guide. The Playbook is the essential guide.

In addition to the core data governance process, organization, and technology areas, you will also need to ensure that the operational process is improved and tracked over time. Nearly all operational processes of significant scale are tracked through metrics. Some operational processes have extensive measures that are identified and reported through a scorecard. Many operational applications have built-in support to collect data for calculating the measures.

Operational metrics will provide information to you on how well the process is meeting its operational targets. Operational metrics may or may not include financial outcome metrics. The decision to use information-based approaches to competing in the marketplace is a business strategy choice. Operations, such as data governance, are the cost of doing business. While data governance may be a critical dependency in growing topline revenue, data governance is often categorized like infrastructure, computers, and people. They are necessary costs. Organizations engage in data governance regardless of whether they have a formal program or manage these costs explicitly.

Designing your operational model requires tradeoffs. We recommend that the Playbook focus on the process and leave application-level details to other training material.

For example, the Playbook describes steps to "obtain approval" for various artifacts such as a business glossary entry or a critical data element (CDE). Depending on the artifact, approval could be obtained in different ways each having different levels of application support. Supporting data governance by implementing technology-enabled "workflows" is a popular topic now in the data governance community. Technology-supported workflows reduce the cost of running data governance processes, enforces accountability, and supports distributed consensus building. Workflows can be implemented using technologies such as email and spreadsheets, Microsoft Sharepoint workflow, and application tools such as Oracle's DRM/DRG or Collibra. In many cases, different workflow processes may be active for different data governance artifacts at the same time. Describing all of the different technology specific workflows in the Playbook may make the Playbook hard to read and use.

Linking the Playbook to a description of a technology-specific approval approach is useful. We encourage you to create an ecosystem of process notes and desk-level procedures that are readily accessible. When designing your operating model, you should realize that the way you communicate the process, the way you organize it, and the way you employ technology may determine the success in deploying the Playbook.

PLANNING AND ACQUIRING THE BUDGET

Supporting data governance seems to always be a challenge. Starting a data governance operations process requires specifying the operating model. Creating a data governance capability can be perceived as creating new layers and groups within the organization and senior management should be rightfully concerned about any effort that may add cost and complexity. These concerns coupled with the abstractness of describing what data governance does and why something different is needed make planning and acquiring the budget more difficult.

We can break the budget conversation into two parts: Ramping and Ongoing. Ramping refers to the initial budget planning and requests, while Ongoing refers to the ongoing budget cycle. Budgeting may be complex at your company if certain technology items are allocated to different groups, eg, if applications used in data governance process are budgeted under the data governance budget or the IT group.

RAMPING

Budgeting during the ramping phase is often more complex than the Ongoing phase because new operational processes are being created and deployed. More educational and justification efforts are required in this phase. Ramping occurs in multiple iterations. The end of Ramping and the transition to Ongoing is marked by a slowdown in the organization's human resources growth and new funding. There are no hard and fast rules for when the Ramping phase ends and the Ongoing begins. Even if data governance was sparked from a crisis, budgeting for the Ramping phase still involves the same analysis and planning because crisis funding is short-term and data governance is designed to be an ongoing operations process.

At the start of the Ramping phase, we see the budget requests focused and learned. Budget items typically include:

- Requests for two or three human resources
- Requests for IT support for creating collaboration sites or shared drives
- Requests for external consulting help to create the operations model
- Requests for external consulting help to create a roadmap to implement the operations model

Requests for data governance applications usually occur in subsequent iterations. Each iteration in the Ramping phase should be incremental and linked to value. Value linkage is much easier to describe on paper than it is to create in practice. Generally, once the basic request has been made, a data governance group wants to show early wins in order to justify further budget in subsequent rounds. Wins can be focused by identifying and resolving pain points. Requests can also be made that align with new project spend whether on the business or IT side. Choosing which pain points or new projects to align to is a bit of an art. Many organizations find it useful to use external consultants to help find a set of issues to address first.

Pitching the Playbook model at the start of the Ramping phase is the most effective approach. The Playbook is a formal specification of how you want to conduct the data governance jobs. Knowing how you want start and evolve the model over time is an important part of convincing managers that you have a proven path to achieve results. The benefits of introducing a Playbook early in the Ramping budgeting phase include:

- Increasing credibility that you can manage the effort. Senior managers may have heard stories from other organizations that suggest supporting data governance is risk. Having a process that is well documented and proven at other organizations helps manage these perceptions.
- Understanding how the work should be performed enhances your communication as to what the people working data governance would be doing. Data governance often seems like an abstract concept to many managers. They may ask, "what do people do when they govern the data?" Being specific about day-to-day responsibilities and activities helps make data governance concrete and actionable.
- Allowing you to engage data stewards early in the process and help train them on the data governance jobs.

A Playbook helps you acquire budget and support in the Ramping phase because a Playbook is concrete and real—key criteria that approvers will evaluate in your proposal.

ONGOING

The ongoing budget process does not need to revisit the motivation for having a data governance-operating model but often does need to justify incremental investments designed to improve the model. Many organizations already have some semblance of a data governance process so we often find that justifying improvements, such as implementing a Playbook, is more common than the Ramping phase.

The following types of requests are common once a data governance program is up and running:

- Implementing new applications to improve data-quality monitoring or expanding their use.
- Implementing new data controls for gap areas.
- Creating training and certification material for data stewards.
- Expanding either the core team or the virtual data steward team to accommodate growth in the demand for performing data governance jobs.
- Creating and deploying a Playbook-based approach because the current process is confusing or not well understood or known. This includes updates to the Playbook to reflect real-world lessons specific to the organization.

Funding requests contain information specific to the nature of the change. A Playbook approach and deploying a Playbook model helps support the case regardless of the request. Data governance managers often use language like the following:

- "We" have already implemented data governance and found that our data stewards need specific instructions on what is expected of them. The Playbook provides detailed instructions stewards can follow.
- "We" need to match investments in new technology with investments in process in order to effectively use the new technology. The Playbook ensures a process is in place to use the new technology.

- "We" need a reference model for performing the data governance jobs so we can test and certify that the data stewards have the skills and knowledge to perform their job. The Playbook provides a benchmark set of processes that can be tested.
- "We" anticipate more work in the future and need to scale our productivity. The Playbook helps create consistent processes with known outcomes, which helps us scale.
- "We" have a process in place today, but it does not cover all of the areas our data governance jobs need to cover. A Playbook will provide us the coverage we need.

The Playbook allows you to more clearly show the incremental impact of your proposal on the organization. By making the data governance jobs more transparent, data governance becomes easier to communicate and deploy.

ADDRESSING CONCERNS

When asking for budget, there are usually multiple people who have questions you need to answer before the budget is approved. We have included common questions below and starting points for your response. The questions are arranged in the order that we often see them asked. The questions address the general data governance story as well as the story needed to justify the Playbook model. You will see that the Playbook acts as glue between the broader data governance questions.

- Why do we need this?
  - The answer to this question needs to avoid hyperbole and be specific. Vague concepts such as the "right thing to do" are too high-level and ineffective for obtaining support. There are many right things to do in an organization, all competing for support. Vague concepts such as "data is an asset" are too vague for a manager to act on. Data is an asset but so are many other things in an organization.
  - When answering this question, you are creating the narrative that describes the "call to action." A call to action is a phrase frequently used in organizations that helps focus people's attention on something they can do to obtain a better business result.
  - Use material from recent events that may have led to the need for data governance, eg, a data breach, the lack of numbers consistency on different senior management reports, or frustration for not being able to calculate a specific business metric such as "net flows." These negative events and the risk of repeating them may be a basis for the call to action.
  - While it always desirable to tie a call to action to large-scale revenue or margin improvements, it is hard to make a direct connection between business benefits and data governance that is credible to approvers. You have to pitch a "sellable story." Data is essential to achieving business results. However, an organization is already performing data governance to some degree simply because applications and analysts exist. You are really pitching an incremental benefits story. Multiple competing programs usually claim central importance in any benefits story. Data governance and the Playbook should be part of the business benefits story but it is not usually the headline.
  - We have found that a call to action based on reducing risk through "attestable" data is specific and resonates with approvers. Attestable data should be combined with a storyline that focuses on reducing risks. A good retort to the question of "why do we need this" is really something like: "we need to reduce the risk of bad business outcomes by implementing data governance

using a Playbook-based model that senior managers can trust to manage data that they use in their daily work."

- Can I capitalize data governance?
  - Eventually the issue of capitalization comes up when new or incremental investments are being analyzed. When casting data governance and the Playbook as an operations process, you are typically positioning it as an expense item. Obviously, different aspects of developing the operations model may be capitalized based on your organization's rules. You will need to check with your finance group.
  - Creating a Playbook to run the operations process is generally a development effort and is often capitalizable. Ongoing execution of the Playbook is generally considered an expense.
- We have been fine all along, why do I need this now?
  - This is a more difficult questions to answer. The person asking the question is right to a certain degree. Data governance jobs are already being performed. Business units have delivered results and continue to do so. The IT group installs large applications to manage the data better including transaction and analytical systems. Responding to this question requires recognizing that without data governance and a Playbook, the approach has been mostly unmanaged or at the very least uncoordinated.
  - Use recent failures or frustrations around the data as a source of material to draw on to answer this question. If critical business issues do not motivate action now, you may not be able to create enough support to make a Playbook-based data governance a reality at your organization. If an emergency is not sufficient to motivate change it is unlikely that an appeal to "manage better" will work.
  - Aside from a short-term, acute pain point, the best way to answer this question is to create a network of support between business groups. Identify individuals in management positions who would support your efforts and adhere to a Playbook-based approach for data governance. Most managers want to have operational processes they can rely on and not worry about. The Playbook offers this benefit. Using a network of supporters is a standard corporate way to obtain approval. Obtaining this support may be as easy as working with other senior managers to define the need and convince them that the proposed approach will work and not be intrusive or shift control from them to another group. It may be as hard as a multimonth- or multiyear-long effort to convince them of the benefits of taking action sooner rather than later. Upcoming projects of significant complexity could also be a motivating event to establish the Playbook now versus later.
  - Large upcoming projects provide opportunity to discuss how a Playbook approach reduces the risk of implementing the system. This approach to risk reduction coupled with a near-term large IT and business spend appears to work well. We estimate that approximately 50% of the efforts for establishing a Playbook-based approach to data governance originates from this scenario.
- Is this the most cost-effective approach?
  - The Playbook-based approach provides a very strong basis of response to this question. By its very nature, the Playbook is designed to create a common approach and operating model to performing data governance jobs. We do not recommend a large dedicated group for performing data governance jobs, preferring instead a virtual organization or colocation of dedicated resources in a crossfunctional "data" focused group. The Playbook approach enables a

decentralized model if you choose it. By providing a common set of processes, it reduces the variability of outcomes. Managers who run operations understand the need for these elements in any process-based solution. By relying on their understanding of operations processes and by linking data governance and the Playbook to a best practice model of implementing an operations process, it can be fairly straightforward to convince managers that the Playbook model is the most cost-effective approach because it uses a model that has already proven itself in the organization.

You will need to customize your responses to what works in your organization. Many pitches for data governance lack specifics and an operations lens. Lacking specifics, these pitches generally do not work because they did not present information and create a sense of urgency or a call to action the management team would want to respond to. You need to make it easy for approvers to say yes to your proposal. Your best approach to obtaining a rapid approval is to use a familiar framing of the problem using realistic expectations and concrete outcomes. If the answer is still no, then you need to respect that decision and possible regroup when the concerns can be better addressed.

ITERATIONS

The Playbook can be rolled out in iterations. There are multiple ways to iterate on the contents of the Playbook. For example, adding workstreams, refining activities, or updating example artifacts are quite common. We have also found that subsequent rollouts enhance noncontent aspects of the Playbook including:

- Improving training: New employees and data stewards can receive electronic-based training versus presentation or in-person/recorded-based training.
- Improving coverage: New workstreams or activities are added or refined. For example, the Playbook can be expanded to cover activities associated with de-commissioning applications such as older data warehouses.
- Improving approach: One popular extension is to add processes for data sprints. Data sprints allow rapid jumps in data governance maturity. Data sprints can also support urgent projects or address critical data issues that require a fast response.
- Improving communication: It is not uncommon to start data governance operating models small and simple and then expand the model over time. This includes expanding communication. For example, meetups, newsletters, posters, spotlights, and other forms of contextual information are often created as a program matures. Communication around changes in the Playbook should also be communicated.
- Refining the set of operational metrics associated with the Playbook workstreams and activities. While operations metrics are a much broader theme than the Playbook, each set of activities in the Playbook should be directly linked to improving a metric. For example, the percentage of CDEs under the Playbook process could be measured and tracked. The percentage of CDEs with matching data controls is another popular metric. Metric expansion in subsequent rollouts is also very common.
- Formalize resourcing: Once a Playbook has been instituted, some organizations may wish to formalize the roles. By working with the human resources groups, the roles can be documented

and enacted in the organization. Different levels of roles can be created, eg, junior versus senior data stewards roles may reflect the ability of an employee to cross more than one data domain. Pay scales and other traditional aspects of organization roles and levels can also be created and implemented.

EXTENDING THE REACH

An operations process like data governance intersects different groups within an organization because the same data is often used in multiple groups. If multiple groups need common data governance offers a process to efficiently and effectively share the data. The Playbook is an approach to ensuring the data is understood and ready for use.

The data governance operations process varies from company to company. In some companies it is highly distributed and in others there may be a more of a shared, centralized group. Obviously, the operations process is only successful if it is used. You need to find entry points in other corporate processes where data governance is appropriate and should be engaged. There are many entry points into the data governance processes as demonstrated in the Playbook.

Part of the effort of deploying the Playbook and creating a data governance capability is finding the intersection with the other corporate processes and altering those processes to engage the Playbook at the right time and for the right reasons. Like other operations processes, data governance crosses many areas in an organization. Unlike other operations processes, data governance relies on other groups performing the jobs or ensuring the jobs are performed at the right time in a highly consistent manner.

There are several areas and scenarios where data governance should intersect. In the sections below, we provide ideas on how to engage data governance and the Playbook to improve outcomes.

CONTINUOUS PERFORMANCE IMPROVEMENT

In Chapter 1, we covered the core data governance jobs that must be performed. For reference, they are:

- Identify and locate data
- Identify and document constraints and issues
- Determine data's readiness for use
- Control and Improve

Within these core jobs, the concept of improving data is central. Data governance should ensure data is improved over time. "Improving" could mean the data is more available to more people in different groups if access has been a key issue. "Improving" could also mean that the quality of the data is improving. For example, date fields are filled out appropriately or that lists of customers or dollar value totals match in different database locations.

In spirit, continuous performance projects (CPI) have the same objective. Many organizations have CPI groups dedicated to improving processes across the organization. They tackle cross-group and complex situations and the solutions require process changes, technology changes, and sometimes but less frequently, organizational changes. Our experience in leading CPI projects suggests that many issues can be solved by rectifying data issues. We see many CPI organizations working on improvements to the underlying data in addition to the process and technologies. Given the presence of data and technology elements to process issues, does CPI overlap with the data governance operations process? How can we reconcile the overlap? Does the CPI group model offer a better approach to performing data governance?

The key to identifying how these two areas can work together in your company is to recognize and understand the data governance-operating model you have implemented. If your operating model states that all data-related improvements must go through a specific data governance group and the two groups have not agreed to this scope, there will be conflict.

In contrast, if we take a "jobs-centric" approach to data governance and have a Playbook model that describes how to get the jobs done through a process that has been approved by the organization, there is significantly less potential conflict. We mentioned earlier that data governance is already performed at your organization regardless of whether you have a data governance program or not and whether or not you have a Playbook. The data governance jobs may be performed poorly across the organization in an inconsistent way. If one of the jobs of the data governance group is to bring consistency to the execution of the data governance jobs, then we can focus on outcomes and results versus issues around who does the work. A Playbook is instrumental in this approach because you can share the Playbook with the CPI group, indicate that you are supporting their efforts, and request that they factor in the Playbook approach into their remediation plans. The Playbook shows a path for consistently performing data governance across the organization. The Playbook is not meant to be an approach used by only a single group.

When CPI groups target a process, there is typically several types of analysis that are performed. Process mapping, statistics gathering, efficiency analysis, and a variety of other well-known artifacts are used to analyze the process and identify opportunities. We have found it useful to annotate data governance opportunities directly on the process graphics. While it is possible that the CPI team has been trained on the Playbook, if they have not, your data governance operating model may need to include services that can perform opportunity identification and annotate the process graphics. Once the opportunities are identified, the overall CPI improvement plan can be traced back to the opportunities to ensure the appropriate Playbook activities are performed at the right step. Example annotations are shown in Fig. 8.1.

The CPI group may defer implementation of their recommendations to another group and make themselves available on an advisory basis to the implementation team. In this model, the Playbook is another element of the implementation plan. Workstreams and activities should be called out explicitly in the CPI implementation plan. Integrating data governance into other parts of the organization also becomes critical. The appearance of the Playbook in the CPI implementation plan should be familiar and expected.

AUDIT AND COMPLIANCE

The audit and compliance function sets guidelines for and monitors risk areas. For example, banks have extensive audit and compliance capabilities because the financial service industry is partially self-regulated. Additional layers of oversight are provided in the form of audit committees, external audit and attestation consultants, and government oversight and rulemaking groups.

The internal audit function creates audit guides and performs audits on other parts of the organization. While not all audit checkpoints are data focused, audit groups should have data-focused checkpoints and checklists associated with different functions. For example, internal audits should ensure that data controls have been identified and are employed by the compliance group.

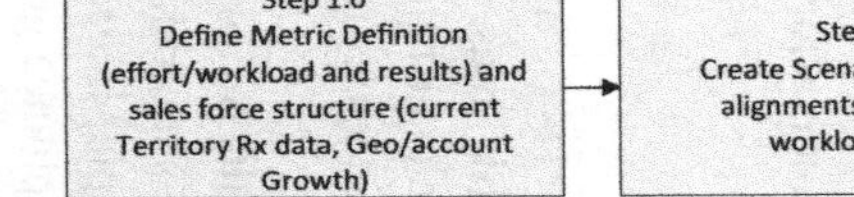

Business Process Steps
Step 1.0
Define Metric Definition (effort/workload and results) and sales force structure (current Territory Rx data, Geo/account Growth)
Step 2.0
Create Scenarios based on alignments and related workloads/size.
Step 3.0
Optimize workload across Territories and Look at balance of Calls/Details and workload
Step 4.0
Finalize new Territory Alignment
Step 5.0
Rollout data to Sales Operations and IT
Example Issues
• Market definition seems to be an older one, further investigation reveals that the market definition has been replaced by an older market definition from IMS. Data needs to be processed again.
• Scenarios are created based on business rules around physician counts, calls to be made. Call data seems to be missing two months of data (calls and details) for some of the geography and does not seem to be consistent.
• Call data is refreshed again, and the step repeated.
• There are missing data for some the geographies that seems odd. The account data seems to be not merged right
• Regional manager demands that the data be processed again, so the whole project now gets delayed by 3 weeks and the steps are repeated.
• District managers impacted by new alignment do not agree with the workload (Total #TRx, #NRx as well as the # of the physicians) that they pull out o a report that IT ran for them directly.
• Market share and growth numbers do not look right for the new alignment.
• IT does not reflect the right alignment and sales operations rolls out the new territory. Sales Reps are not calling on doctors according to the new alignment.
Playbook/Data Governance Opportunities:
• Check master data quality via data controls report (Market definition, Territory, Calls, Rx, etc.)
• Verify right hierarchies and their definitions.
• Verify Control report on effort and result for scenario.
• Recheck scenario data
• Understand sourcing for IMS data usage so that all context/master data used in reports and alignment are the same (understand fit for use).
• Check definitions and calculations for final alignment
• Recheck alignment data sent to sales operation and IT. Validate in data control reports.
• Verify Alignment
Verify Rollout date
• Verify control totals to ensure right alignment between Territory & Market Hierarchies

FIGURE 8.1

Business process with annotated data governance opportunities.

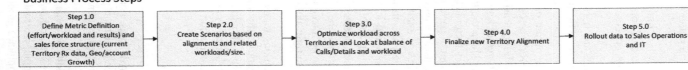

Compliance groups such as the Antimoney Laundering/Bank Secrecy Act (AML/BSA) and fraud groups should employ a Playbook. External auditors and regulators in the AML/BSA area have started looking at data management practices as part of the portfolio of areas they examine and expect regulated entities to have addressed. Initially, you might think the Playbook and the audit and compliance groups are unrelated. However, the first chapter of this book described various fines that have been levied against banks. Many of the processes needed to reduce the risk of fines are entirely data driven.

As part of the data management landscape, the Playbook acts as an attestable process guide that establishes consistent standards across the organization. Bringing the Playbook into the audit function is harder than bringing the Playbook to the compliance function. Compliance is typically very data intensive and the Playbook helps establish processes so that the data is attestable. Attestable data through methods employed in the Playbook allows compliance to manage risk downward. It may be more difficult to engage the audit groups because many audit groups have a fairly wide purview and lack professionals with an understanding and appreciation of how underlying data impacts higher-level risk management functions. This is changing as audit professionals realize that data has become an important area of risk. It is important to work with the audit groups to bring data governance checklists and checkpoints into their audit framework. If the Playbook has truly been accepted by the organization as the consistent approach to managing data, the audit function should reflect this decision directly in their audit guides and processes.

"METRICS" PROJECTS

Almost without exception, when the topic of data governance arises in conversations, "metrics" are discussed. At first, it seems reasonable to comingle the two. Metrics are calculated using data. Metrics supports a data-driven management approach. The data used to calculate metrics needs to be well-defined and the data sourced from attestable sources. This usually leads to the conclusion that all metric projects belong in the sphere of data governance or that data governance is mostly concerned about metrics. At some point, senior managers believe the concept of metrics and data governance are one and the same. This is further reinforced because the subject matter experts (SMEs) involved in the creation of metrics often play roles called out in the Playbook.

While associating data governance and metrics management together may increase the visibility of data governance, "metrics" is not a core data governance job. Nor is "metrics" an optimal lens for viewing data governance. At some point, data governance needs to support metrics projects. Most metrics projects are incremental projects because a set of management metrics already exists and the project is focused on refining or complementing the current set of metrics. Metrics may already be employed to manage the company and more metrics are desired to provide additional insight. This type of project is a very common exercise in the operations world.

As part of our management consulting work, we have helped clients define metrics management processes that help senior management and organizations create a metrics-driven management style. The process of enabling this management style was "performance management through metrics." These projects should not have a data governance label. The metrics-management process involves steps that are clearly related and overlapped with data governance. When performance management and data governance mingle, data governance processes often become heavily distorted and difficult to understand. The tendency toward comingling the concepts of performance management through metrics and data governance people will tend to see data governance as narrowly applied to metrics and miss the substance required for comprehensive data governance. We find this a common problem in organizations. Once the comingling has occurred, it is difficult to disentangle the two concerns.

In Fig. 8.2, we showcase a general metrics management process. The types of questions that must be answered upfront mostly mirror the jobs that need to be performed in the list of data governance jobs.

A metrics project is a great way to showcase the importance the Playbook. The Playbook is designed to create durable data governance artifacts that accelerate the use of attestable data in an organization. Metrics development invariably involves analysis around what data is available and its readiness for use.

We have included a few ideas on how to integrate the Playbook into a metrics project. You will need to discover the best model that works at your organization.

- Identify the Playbook process steps in the metrics project that significantly overlap with the metrics methodology and standardize the language between the two efforts.
- Place links and documentation in the metrics project that references the Playbook.
- Appoint a liaison to the metrics project from the data governance team to ensure that knowledge in one area, data governance and the Playbook, is used in the metrics project.
- Provide team training sessions to ensure that teams working on metrics projects have an appropriate understanding of the Playbook approach.
- Enhance the Playbook to include a "metrics" workstream. While the workstream will be a combination of activities already covered in other workstreams, a dedicated "metrics" workstream will make the activities more clear and accessible to the metrics project team. A metrics workstream can draw clear boundaries around the data governance jobs and the overall performance management process.

There is not a dominant approach that works more frequently than others. Many metrics projects suffer from an overzealous technology focus. For example, we have seen metrics projects overly focus on newer visualization tools and drilldown widgets at the expense of discussions of which metrics are

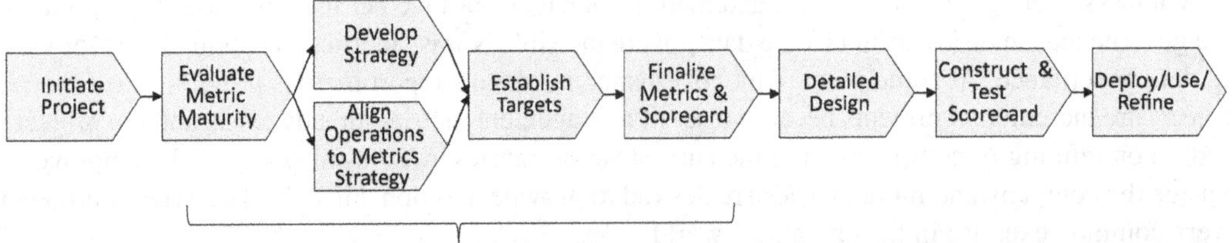

FIGURE 8.2

General metrics management process.

most important for managing the business. Understanding whether data is of high enough quality to use in calculating a metric sometimes seemed to be distant concern.

IT PROJECTS (EG, PROJECT-LEVEL DATA GOVERNANCE)

The Playbook is designed to describe how data governance jobs can be performed in different contexts. For example, there is a master data workstream. Many master data efforts are formulated as IT projects focused on a single domain. It seems natural to ask how the Playbook intersects with projects that have similar objectives or how the Playbook intersects with IT projects in general.

Data governance as an operations process using the Playbook is designed to run continuously. Projects are short-lived and focus on delivering a set of discrete capabilities. It may seem that the Playbook and IT projects are at odds, with different timelines and objectives. The Playbook describes data governance jobs and provides prescriptions on how to perform them regardless of who performs the work. The Playbook can be used directly as a methodology for the data governance activities in an IT project.

IT projects are generally broken into a few core phases of work. The specific language and steps vary by organization. As a broad brushstroke the phases are:

- Initiate: Secure funding, build a team, and align stakeholders.
- Business Requirements: Develop a description of what the project should deliver.
- Design: Design the solution.
- Development: Develop the solution. Create programming code, training material, and other artifacts needed for test, deployment, and use.
- Test: Validate that the system performs as expected.
- Deploy: Ready the production system for use by business users. Engage users through training and other means to ensure they know how to use the system.

Other methodologies such as "agile" are also popular. With agile, unlike the traditional waterfall method described above, there are many incremental, smaller deliveries of functionality. Conceptually, each agile iteration looks much like the steps just described, although the steps have different labels and have slightly different objectives. For the purposes of this section, we treat the methodologies as the same since we are concerned about the data aspects of any systems development lifecycle (SDLC).

Within a few specific SDLC phases, such as Initiate, Business Requirements, and Design, there must be activities that evaluate whether the needed data sources are of sufficient quality. Evaluating whether the data is appropriate and ready to be used are core data governance jobs described by the Playbook. Hence, the SDLC phases overlap within the Playbook.

Since the Playbook was designed to be used by anyone performing data governance jobs, you have a few choices on how you want to integrate the Playbook into the SDLC:

- Modify the existing SDLC so that it points out and uses the Playbook steps as appropriate.
- Modify the existing SDLC so that there are data governance checkpoints between phases as appropriate.
- Integrate the same approach and steps that the Playbook contains into the SDLC so that it is fully integrated.

- Identify the outputs of the Playbook and ensure the SDLC creates the same outputs. We can think of this as the "invariant" approach because the outputs are invariant to the method used to create them.
- Use the direct outputs from the Playbook to lower the implementation risk of the SDLC.

A mixture of these approaches is typically used. The best way to describe how it can work together is to use an example.

Consider a project that is designed to create AML/BSA capability focused on creating a comprehensive view of the customer as part of its transaction monitoring function. All financial transactions from all products a company provides must be integrated together and monitored for suspicious activities such as account-to-account transfers or large account transfers to foreign countries. At the same time, the sales and marketing group needs to create a 360degree view of the customer to help with cross-sell efforts. They are implementing a new data warehouse to create the 360degree view. Both projects are running simultaneously. Both are designed with multiple phases and both significant commitments to various internal and external stakeholders.

Both projects will also need to identify critical data elements required to power their algorithms and processing. For example, name, address, and date of birth are data elements critical to both efforts. AML/BSA will use these data elements to perform Office of Foreign Asset Control (OFAC, a part of the Treasury Department) checks, while sales and marketing will use these elements to segment the data and create special offers. However, the needs for data quality differ between projects. The AML/BSA project needs a complete view of all customers and the information needs to be highly recent. The sales and marketing group only needs the data to mostly cover the customer base and if the data is slightly out of date it's not usually a problem as long as it is eventually corrected.

The Playbook contains the master data management workstream that is designed to support the data governance process for master data. A customer list is master data. It is possible that previous Playbook-based work created some working artifacts including:

- Critical data element lists and definitions
- Data control reports indicating data-quality levels in existing systems
- Business rule and other documentation that describes the state of data in different systems
- Metadata describing how the data is stored in existing systems
- A curated list of pain points that itemize data-quality issues that may be important to the project.

Many of these artifacts can be used as inputs into SDLC activities. Playbook artifacts may help improve estimation and planning in the Initiate phase and decrease the workload in the Business Requirements and Design phases. For example, a business requirements document (BRD) may state desired data-quality levels or cover business rules that need to be applied to the data. Since the Playbook artifacts may describe some, but maybe not all, of the rules and quality levels that exist, the project team would have material that accelerates their analysis efforts.

Ideally, the outputs of the project should be fed back into the artifact base so that future efforts can leverage the information. The Playbook specifies artifacts that should be created and if the SDLC has been infused with the Playbook approach, the project's outputs should be roughly consistent and usable. For example, additional metadata captured as part of the project should be fed back into the metadata repository. It is also important to realize that the critical data elements used for one business process may not be the same as the critical data elements used in another. This is true in the above example involving AML/BSA and the sales and marketing groups. This example highlights that if the metadata is captured and tagged, it needs to have the right context so that future projects understand why a critical data element is critical in one context but not another or how a definition may heavy with the point of view of one business unit or another.

Using the artifacts from the Playbook directly in a project is one approach to integrating the Playbook into IT projects. As described above, feeding outputs from the project back into the artifacts created and maintained from the Playbook suggests that a better approach is to use the Playbook processes directly in the IT project by cross-training the teams and ensuring the SDLC has been modified to produce consistent artifacts.

In the example above, it would be ideal if the business analysts on both projects had been trained on the Playbook and used the same process for some of their steps. If they shared their results, it might be apparent that a single comprehensive 360degree view of the customer could be created that satisfies the requirements of both projects.

Integrating with the SDLC process at an organization can be difficult. Changing the SDLC methodology may seem fairly straightforward, but any changes must be reviewed, approved, and communicated. New artifacts and templates must be created. While many organizations pride themselves on having an SDLC, it is hard to enforce consistent use by both internal and external development teams. In this case, it may take you a while to have the SDLC updated to link to the Playbook. We have seen it take 1 to 2 years for these types of changes to be institutionalized so you need to be ready to champion these changes over an extended amount of time.

As part of integrated the SDLC and Playbook, you need to remain flexible about what the process labels are or who performs the jobs. As long as the data governance jobs are being performed in a manner consistent with the Playbook, data governance professionals should be fine with this approach. If the Playbook cannot be embedded directly in the SDLC, the Playbook provides a strong reference model to work from when making SDLC changes.

ENTERPRISE ARCHITECTURE

Enterprise architecture is a broad topic, and we think most companies now realize the importance of architecture as a foundation for success. A good architecture is rarely noticed but a bad architecture can restrict flexibility and numb the business.

It may seem obvious that enterprise architecture is important to data governance. However, rarely is data governance represented in enterprise architecture discussions or approvals. The technical architecture choice and the set of applications you select to interact with business users greatly affect the availability and quality of data. Using a data governance lens, selecting an architecture is actually choosing the best applications to manage your organization's data and ensure it is available to others—important variations on the core data governance jobs. If the data governance-operating model is newly implemented, its data governance is probably not integrated into enterprise architecture.

There are a few key areas where data governance and enterprise architecture need to collaborate:

- Data sourcing
- Tracking data quality explicitly
- Creating control points to support data monitoring
- Data modeling/data architecture that supports data lineage processing

- Master and reference data management
- Business rule application for business rules that address data-quality issues
- Third-party contracting and data transparency

Integrating data governance processes into architecture will require changing established architecture process. If enterprise architecture processes are not mature at your organization, you may find that data governance needs to fit into ad-hoc and potentially poorly understand and executed architecture processes. The specific way you integrate data governance with architecture processes will vary:

- Ensure that data governance checklists are provided to the architecture group.
- Change the architecture approval process to ensure that sign-off by a data governance leader is required.
- Ensure that there is a designated liaison to the architecture group.
- Provide architect training on data governance objectives and approaches.
- Change the organizational structure for the data governance group and colocate the data governance and architecture resources into one overall group. This approach has other ramifications and issues but it is an often-encountered model in many companies. We generally recommend against this approach because it can greatly impact the effectiveness of the core data governance jobs.

You may need to implement all of these approaches over time. Many companies start with the easier process of assigning a data governance liaison to the architecture group then seeking to influence the approval and architecture development process through checklists and approval changes. The Playbook does not dictate an answer to data-sourcing questions, but it does provide insight into what context a selected architecture must operate in to be consistent with data governance and the operations process.

LABELING FOR SUCCESS

The Playbook prescribes an approach to implementing the core data governance jobs. Part of those jobs is to measure and track data quality, which is typically performed through the use of data controls. Data controls measure various aspects of data quality including sophisticated measures related to completeness, eg, does this source of information have all the customers. Controls can also measure whether different systems are in balance—whether they have the same total dollars or units of products and services.

If you implement the Playbook as described in this book, you will produce data-quality measures. These measures can be used to annotate reports and other analytical outputs to allow the users of the reports to understand what level of quality of the data used to create the report. It may seem odd to place quality indicators on a report and it is certainly not standard practice, but by using quality indicators, you can increase awareness of the quality of the report and how it ties into the data. These types of quality indicators are used by analysts in their calculations. When an analyst creates a prediction, say the forecasted value of inventory, a prediction is always associated with a "quality range" of the prediction, which is called the variance. When the variance is large, the real-world outcome may vary widely from the predicted value.

Fig. 8.3 shows some example data-quality indicators. The graphic on the left is a business data control that shows the value of average electronic transfers in each system that performs these types of transactions. The graphic on the right shows a summary of data-quality indicators such as validity and

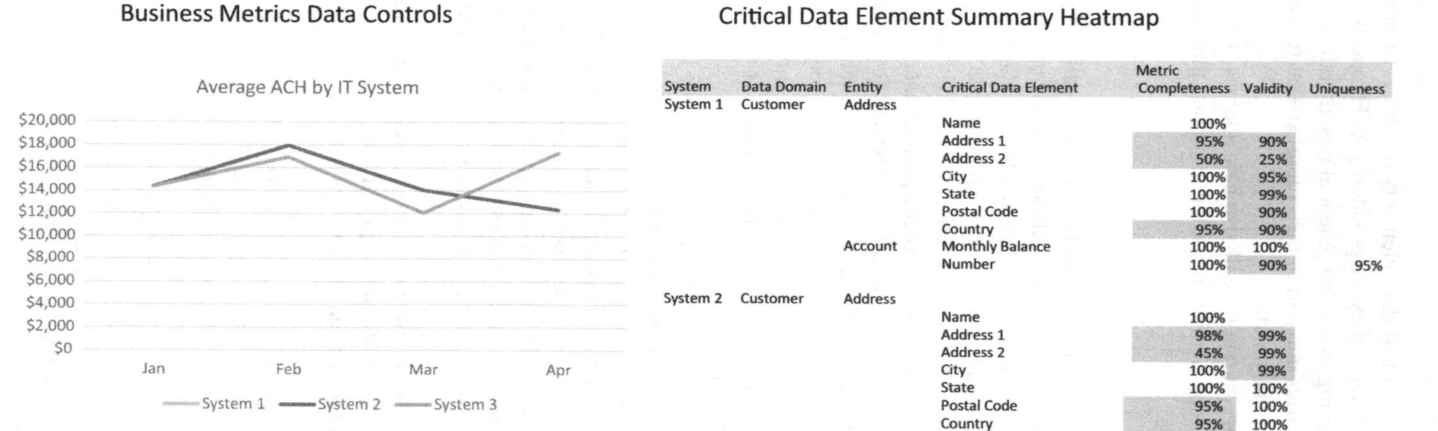

System	Data Domain	Entity	Critical Data Element	Metric Completeness	Validity	Uniqueness
System 1	Customer	Address				
			Name	100%		
			Address 1	95%	90%	
			Address 2	50%	25%	
			City	100%	95%	
			State	100%	99%	
			Postal Code	100%	90%	
			Country	95%	90%	
		Account	Monthly Balance	100%	100%	
			Number	100%	90%	95%
System 2	Customer	Address				
			Name	100%		
			Address 1	98%	99%	
			Address 2	45%	99%	
			City	100%	99%	
			State	100%	100%	
			Postal Code	95%	100%	
			Country	95%	100%	

FIGURE 8.3

Data-quality indicator examples.

completeness for an organization's critical data elements (CDEs). An analyst looking at these data controls reports might be concerned that if they are producing ACH reports by postal code, that perhaps there needs to be additional processing to resolve potential postal code assignment errors. An analyst could also post the data-quality metrics into part of their report so that report consumers can determine their own level of trust in the tables and charts.

These types of quality indicators on reports will also help address "one version of the truth" issues that arise when managers see different numbers on different reports that relate to the same event.

CASHING THE CHECK

Data governance is focused in improving the data and as a result, ideally, improving business outcomes. It is difficult to draw a clear line between improving data and improving corporate financial performance because data cuts across different groups and processes muddy the water. When asking for justification based on issues found from using the Playbook, the financial justification may not always be clear. Eventually, financial justification may come down to one critical issue: Who gets to cash the check?

In a perfect world, if you take an action for improving performance, you should be rewarded. If you spend the money (the cost) you should be able to count the benefit (cashing the benefits check). However, if your contribution is part of a larger effort, somehow the benefit needs to be divided among the contributors to the improvement. Since data governance is often tied up in different projects or runs outside of a project, its contribution to an improvement are not always clear. Data governance and Playbook activities appear to be the cost of doing business, which is a poor position to advocate from when you need to ask for financial support.

Earlier we mentioned working with the CPI group. The CPI group typically claims the entire benefit because their plan will cover not only the costs of implementation but also the last mile benefit that will be seen. A benefit is a not always a financial measure. It may be an improvement in cycle time or other performance metric relevant to the organization or customer base. The CPI group often gets to cash the check. The CPI group can also run into issues depending on how they funded their "costs." Sometimes CPI groups double count benefits to justify their funding and because they have a "benefits" target. In nearly all cases, however, the beneficiary of the process improvement is a business group and not the CPI group. It's not wrong to perform "accounting" this way because it improves corporate communication around issues and solutions.

In general, any group that works to improve the organization has the same issue. It is not just a data governance problem. How can we deal with these types of issues?

There are a few approaches that have been proven to work:

- Partner up with other groups like the CPI group and work with them to perform the data governance job under the Playbook model. If your operating model calls for you executing the data governance jobs efficiently, you most likely need other groups to incur the costs of the activities and improvement efforts. This approach is often built into the model.
- Always keep a separate set of accounting tables that show what benefits data governance has provided. You cannot count the entire benefit but you can show a consistent contribution to benefits over time using benefits cases that are approved on their own. This approach essentially communicates that data governance is a cost of doing business and you are embracing that role.
- Where there are gaps in the benefits calculations from other groups, provide your own. For example, a data governance group often does annual scans of business "pain points" and on occasions has

the opportunity to independently fund or obtain funding to perform an improvement project. In this case, you count the benefit.

- Aggregate smaller improvement efforts into a large one to obtain economies of scale in the benefits case. Of course, as the effort becomes larger, the management team may realize that the ownership for solving the issues lies outside the data governance organization. The balance may change with each request and depends on the nature of the request.

We are not claiming that data governance should be positioned as the owner of other processes and functions in the organization. By not using the data governance label as a broad description of a large set of related and unrelated activities, we can keep the approach to the benefits conversation much simpler and more integrated into a "benefits case approach" already established within the company. We are also not recommending, either way, that data governance carry the burden of executing projects itself unless that is in the chosen operating model. Executing improvement projects often leads to the perception that the data governance group is performing another group's job and leads to intergroup tension.

The ability to command independent funding may be highly dependent on the nature of the operating model and its position in the organization. For example, a data governance group is often associated with a large data warehouse or other analytics project and in this case, the improvement efforts can be built into the overall funding of the analytics program and line-itemed directly. This allows the improvement project to count the entire benefit without contention with other benefits stories that may be vying for attention.

The question of who gets to "cash the check" is a difficult issue and leads us to the next section on dealing with corporate politics.

CORPORATE POLITICS

Data governance as an operations process cuts across corporate business units, groups, and profit and loss centers. Invariably, different priorities and coordination and collaboration issues arise. While the word "politics" is often a euphemism, politics is really the process of working out differences. At times, politics may be petty and personal. There is a reason for these behaviors when different people work through their differences.

Many data governance jobs are performed under a virtual organization model where resources are allocated out of different corporate groups. Group differences can severely impact the ability to perform data governance. Ideally, a good manager should anticipate these differences and seek to resolve them using the same corporate governance processes used to resolve other corporate differences. The lack of a disciplined implementation of data governance operations makes managing political situations more difficult. In addition, key aspects around human resource management to support data governance are often not implemented. These issues are particularly pronounced in larger organizations where more "fault" lines are present in the organizational structure. But issues can still occur in small organizations, so it is important to recognize that the political atmosphere needs to always be part of the management mix.

Corporate politics can overwhelm a process. If you are unable to garner or command sufficient management authority to resolve the issues, you will need to recognize that it may be impossible to continue with the data governance process in its current form. The approach may need to be changed. Creating the proper authority and responsibility structure is important to help manage this type of "crisis" when it occurs. While some in your organization may consider this a failure of data governance, it is really a failure in the approach. Many operational processes experience evolution and revolution over the course of their existence and data governance is no different.

We list some common political situations in the next sections and highlight ideas on how to manage through and around the issues. In most cases, the political issues reflect a poorly designed operating model or a model that has become outdated. Data governance jobs will always be performed. It is really a question of how well and how efficiently they will be managed.

IT WANTS TO OWN DATA GOVERNANCE

It is not uncommon and is perfectly appropriate for a project to be managed by the IT department if it has a large IT component to it. Projects that touch or transform applications that house corporate data typically are managed by IT. To many, the word "data" present in the label "data governance" implies a technology concept. IT also owns and operates large and complex operational processes. Since we have identified that data governance really should be viewed as an operations management process, similar reasoning may lead some people to conclude that data governance should be owned by IT. Should it? There is no right or wrong answer as to who should own the data governance operational process. We have seen it owned equally as much by business groups as well as IT groups, or more confusingly, split between groups.

IT wanting to own data governance is not a problem per se. The deluge of political drama often associated with this situation is caused by some very common underlying reasons that are not unique to IT. We have found that there are two major scenarios where the drama ensues:

- The IT group wants to own data governance but other groups do not trust IT with the process
- Other groups are officially in charge of the data governance process but IT wants to own it.

These scenarios make IT look like the bad guy. They are not. We could even swap "IT" and "other group" in the above scenarios and the statements would still be true. Groups heavily dependent on other resources typically want to manage and control those resources in order to maximize their chance of success. An IT group is no different. Since application implementation projects are so heavily dependent on data, it is natural for IT to want to own the data governance process.

Most of the scenarios that fall into this class of politics can really be summarized as follows:

- One group wants to own data governance because data is essential to their operations but they do not trust any other group to align with their priorities and needs.

Although not spoken out loud, the basic idea is that one group does not trust the other group. Low trust is much more a reflection of the company's culture and management's team skills than it is an issue about data governance. When these types of trust issues are present they are present or are manifested in many ways. For example, companies with products that target dramatically different customer segments or companies that have grown a portfolio through acquisition often show trust fractures. Companies with managers who lack the ability to work with the "corporate team" but are promoted and asked to lead groups often show trust fractures. Corporate cultures that promote "hero models" and "cowboys" will show trust fractures.

When an organization cannot decide on who should own data governance or there are ongoing passive aggressive behaviors or outright verbal wars about data governance ownership, you have only a few choices to try and resolve the conflict. None of the approaches are sure proof and in general we have recommended to clients that they delay starting or continuing data governance when these issues are present. Waiting until a better path is clear to a more civil forum may be the better answer in some situations.

Approaches include:

- Escalating issues up through your chain of command by focusing on the issues that remain unresolved due to the lack of data governance ownership. You should not focus on ownership issues but more on outcomes and business impacts to motivate a timely discussion about ownership. Working up through the management chain can be challenging and take a long time.
- Give the group a chance to execute the data governance jobs. Maybe the group will do a good job. Perhaps the data governance jobs are already being performed well enough to avoid a crisis.
- Use a Playbook as an example of how you would like to see the processes documented and promulgated in the organization. Lobby for the owning group to use something like a Playbook. Start with a small process and progressively increase Playbook coverage. While this method may take awhile, taking baby steps with improving trust through small and demonstrated wins has been shown to be a very effective approach.
- Wait it out. While not a great strategy, if you stay constructively engaged in performing the data governance jobs as best as you can, you may need to wait until the internal value system changes or new leadership brings the issues to the forefront. The owning group may eventually stumble mightily if they are truly doing a poor job. The opportunity for change could come around again.

Sometimes the IT group may skip using a Playbook and run a data governance program that is effectively devoid of business unit involvement. This is unfortunate. The IT group might alienate business groups to the point that the business groups declines to participate, or worse, participates without good faith. At this point, the data governance jobs may be performed, albeit at a fairly low level of real business impact.

When trust is low, the data governance program may split. Different parts of the organization may use two different Playbooks. While less than ideal, it does show that each group recognized the value of the Playbook model.

BUSINESS GROUPS ARE TOO BUSY

In contrast to the last section where the IT group wants to own data governance but there may not be agreement that this is the best approach, it is much more common to find that the business groups declare they are too busy to own data governance and want IT to run the program. There are many reasons for this, some of which reflect deeper, more fundamental issues including:

- The business group may not understand what data governance is.
- The business group may not have a plan to implement data governance and do not know where to start.
- The business group believes the overall data governance program is cross-business group and hence, is something they cannot lead because it would distract them from their business group objectives.

- The business group has been part of data governance programs before and the program did not have positive outcomes or result in positive feelings. They want to avoid a repeat.
- The business group lacks a management talent bench and is concerned that it could not manage an operations process that spans groups.
- The business group is running thin, and indeed, are too busy and issues are not painful enough to motivate change.

Under most of these scenarios, a Playbook approach allows business groups to adopt and own data governance at a much lower cost, higher success rate, and with less management distraction. Some approaches to enabling a business group to own data governance include:

- Present and discuss a Playbook style approach. Because the roles, activities, and objectives of the data governance jobs are transparent and documented, business groups can decide how to proceed based on relevant information versus guessing.
- Ask the business group to pilot a Playbook process for their group alone and based on the experience decide how to proceed.
- Work with the business to customize the Playbook to a process that fits in with their current processes so they can see that the Playbook makes their processes more efficient. Start with something small, such as cataloging critical data elements or metadata capture and build from there.

LACK OF SENIOR MANAGEMENT BUY-IN

As with any operations management process, the presence or lack of senior management support is critical. In any organization, the lack of senior management support will most often diminish or eliminate any hopes for formalizing a process. With that in mind, a key perspective we have exposed in this book is that regardless of a managed process, the data governance jobs are still being performed at your company. The lack of senior management support usually just means that the jobs are performed inconsistently and repeated over and over again as employees cycle in and out of their day jobs and roles.

There are no surefire ways to obtain senior management buy-in. Many employees think that a grass-roots effort to obtain data governance sponsorship will work. Sometimes it does. Usually it does not. The most common change in senior management receptivity is an externally triggered event that brings laser focus to the issues that data governance seeks to address.

There are two elements you need to create in order to get senior management buy-in. First, you need to create a sense of urgency and second, you need to create a call to action. Neither of these is easy to engineer at the grass-roots level. While many people think a "great" business case will provide a fertile bed, it often does not. Since the Playbook processes span multiple groups and involve what essentially amounts to a matrix organization, the span of control may exceed that of the senior managers you solicit. Unless the case for change is especially strong, a senior manager may resist reaching out across boundaries to support data governance.

There are some approaches to obtaining senior management buy-in that may work for you:

- Find a large project you know has critical dependencies on data that has been questioned or is known to have problems. Pitch data governance and the Playbook to be attached to that project. This is sometimes called "piggybacking" or "attaching."

- Plot the span of control of a single senior manager and focus all data governance and Playbook attention on that senior manager's area. If the senior manager has projects in their portfolio that are larger than others, those may be good candidates. Even if it is a small effort compared to other corporate initiatives, you can at least demonstrate that you are trying to help the senior manager's efforts and this may be enough to garner support.
- Focus only on the data governance jobs and skip the data governance language altogether. The name "Playbook" is fairly neutral and common in corporate settings. Since the Playbook is designed to describe a consistent approach to performing the data governance jobs, just focus on the data governance jobs while using the Playbook as a model for describing how the jobs should be done. If bringing in the larger concepts of data governance will not generate support, just focus on the jobs that are important.
- Bring in external colleagues or consultants who can describe what other companies are doing in the data governance space. While it may seem like poor business practices, many companies track what their competitors are doing and often, rather blindly, match what they are doing. You do not want to pitch data governance as a blind exercise because others are doing it. Data governance is often uniquely carried out in most companies. However, using the approach of bringing external points of view inward could spur the right behaviors internally regardless of the external motivation.
- Find a senior manager who has the span of control and interest in setting up data governance. It is quite possible that the managers you work for are not interested in data governance themselves but others may be. If you believe you have the latitude, you may want to solicit other senior managers to implement something like the Playbook especially if a Playbook model will make your nondata-governance job easier. Soliciting other managers for help may or may not be part of your corporate culture so you need to evaluate whether this approach is an option.
- Create a sales deck and a case for change. This approach usually does not work unless senior management is already receptive to the ideas. Grass-roots efforts can work, but not often. You will need to assemble a sales deck that states the reasons why you need to proceed and the benefits of doing so. You may not be able to quantify the benefits or at least quantify them credibly; you still need to perform some directional quantification. You will also need to find a "pitch" person who can make the pitch. You may think that if you put together the pitch deck that you should be the one making the pitch. Making the pitch is a sales job and you may not have natural sales abilities. Finding someone aligned with your cause, at the right level of the organization, that can make the pitch may be a better alternative for you.

You may not be able to garner senior management buy-in. If so, the corporate response is clear: data governance as a managed operations process is not a priority. Accept this response and focus on the data governance jobs that can be done and be helpful to others who are executing similarly.

EVERYONE WANTS TO DO IT THEIR WAY

The Playbook is designed to drive consistent behaviors across the organization. When people want to perform data governance jobs their way, it is a direct assault against efficiency and effectiveness. But sometimes people want to do things their way. Let's look at a common scenario.

Shelly, a business analyst, produces a monthly report that tallies product sales across regions. She produces a report each week that summaries sales for the week, the previous weeks, year to date, and a multiyear trend line. The report shows both unit counts as well as revenue by region. The day before this week's report is due, she is informed that a new product was rolled out with a sales partner and she needs to incorporate the new product. She scrambles to find a contact at the partner company and after several calls asks for information on what is being sold and for the recent sales data from someone that seems to know something about what she is talking about. She receives a PDF description of the product and a spreadsheet with 20 columns of information, most of which is obvious but some of which is not. She works with her contact to document the remaining columns. She deletes the columns that are not useful to her, fixes some formatting issues on additional columns, identifies some default values that need to be used, identifies how the product fits into the product hierarchy at the company, confirms with the sales manager where they want to play the product in the hierarchy, and then adjusts her reporting process with the new numbers. She repeats the process going forward each week. Eventually it's a routine part of her process.

It is clear that Shelly has just performed nearly all of the key data governance jobs. Unfortunately, her knowledge and due diligence will not benefit anyone else in the organization that needs partner data. Shelly is following the process that is efficient for her and it may be the case that she does not want to change. You may already have tried to discuss the Playbook and solicit her buy-in. She may have refused to participate since she does not feel she is a data steward or may feel she does not have time to do things a different way or may just not want to.

You have a few options on how to deal with this situation:

- Establish a Playbook process in another area and revisit this particular data area after other successes have been demonstrated.
- Establish a Playbook process that spans across groups but touches on the data domains Shelly uses. Over time, if the Playbook model is a better approach and benefits the organization, Shelly will naturally follow the process that her peers follow. Surprisingly, this approach works quite well because peer pressure is a strong motivator for behavior changes.
- Use a peer group to discuss best practices and show how other groups may handle similar situations differently and with better outcomes.
- Speak to Shelly's manager and solicit their help in establishing a process.

The last option can be helpful if Shelly responds well to her boss's involvement but the approach could also backfire on you and she may have resentment based on the perception that you are making her job harder. You will want to gauge what might work on a per-issue basis. No single approach will work in all situations.

DATA STEWARDS HAVE NO IDEA WHAT TO DO AND DON'T CARE

We have seen this situation many times. It usually results from a centralized data governance group that has been created top-down in the organization. The data governance group believes in the "golden clipboard" approach and does not understand what data governance is or how to staff and create a new operations process in an organization.

The data steward was probably identified by a manager who was forced to "name" someone as a data steward but probably did not spend the time to understand what the job meant. The data steward's manager probably did not inform the employee of the new role. The data governance group may have shot the data steward an email welcoming to data stewardship, sent them a thick deck, and told them that their job was to read it and follow the process described in the document. The new data steward probably skipped the deck, read the email, dismissed it, and then continued to focus on their day job. Later, when they get a call for help with a data steward task, they tell their boss they do not have time, do not understand the data, and can barely use a spreadsheet. Err, no help.

There are several issues and flawed approaches bundled into this scenario. The result is the same. You have a data steward who is not going to help and will never play a Playbook role. You have a few choices on how to deal with this situation. They are similar to the options in the previous section where we dealt with Shelly, who wanted to do everything her way.

- If the manager supports the data governance effort but the data steward is just difficult to work with, ask the manager for help in identifying a more qualified data steward. You could continue to escalate upwards but we have found that this has limited success rates.
- Establish metrics by data domain. Track the metrics to show how results are improved, either business results or operational Playbook results, when the Playbook is followed. We had one client track "involvement" through metrics and find that the defect rates related to data-quality issues decreased in domains that used the Playbook. This was used as evidence to find a new resource or more strongly state the case to the management team that the Playbook model needs to be followed even by reticent data stewards.
- Establish a Playbook process among their peers and use that to drive learning and behaviors into alignment.
- Ensure other data stewards in the same data domain are appointed and follow the Playbook. At the very least, some work should be performed consistent with the Playbook.
- If the Playbook roles have been formalized in HR, you can use performance reviews or influence performance reviews to drive behaviors in the right direction.
- Move the data steward role to a fulltime role with multiple domains of responsibility. It is possible that by driving more work into the role, there is enough justification to make this a fulltime role in the organization. With this type of demand, you can reresource the role.

If a resource has been assigned to be a data steward and the resource is not a fit, you need a new data steward. You can use various direct and indirect approaches. While the Playbook can be used to bring clarity and transparency to the issues, you will need to engage standard management practices at some point to make a change.

THE WRONG PEOPLE RUN DATA GOVERNANCE

Like any operational process, the data governance operational process needs individuals aligned with the skills needed to launch and sustain it. Since data governance is a more subtle and complex operational process than other corporate operations, the talent requirements are narrower. Other operational processes benefit from full-time resources, centralized management, and application support. Data governance operations are often more decentralized, have immature or nonexistent application support, and employ a highly matrixed oversight group. We still see organizations staff data governance processes with individuals who lack the required skills or cultural values. We list a few examples below:

- A sales-oriented leader who lacks operations management discipline.
- A senior manager lacking a collaborative mentality and significant knowledge about business objectives.

- A technology team supporting data governance operations lacking the ability to see how the complexity of the supporting applications forces data governance stewards into spreadsheet and email-based collaboration.
- An IT leader who wants to own data governance regardless of the business-led data governance program already established.
- A newly formed data governance leader that ignores what has worked in the different business groups and wants to implement an entirely different model.
- Data stewards and others who have been assigned to focus on detailed data issues but are not data savvy.
- A business leader who does not communicate plans, approaches, and objectives well, or does not enjoy the respect of the other groups data governance must collaborate with.

There are many more examples of where individuals were deployed whose skills and personalities were not aligned with the needs of the data governance operational model.

The ability to resolve alignment issues is based on a variety of factors. The factors that influence your ability to resolve these types of political issues is based on the culture and maturity in areas such as:

- Hierarchical control and structure
- Business results oriented versus corporate rules conformance oriented
- Maturity and sophistication of data governance operations processes
- Organizational structure in the data governance operational model
- Your specific ability to influence others that are inside and outside your group and above or below your role or level

There are no magic tricks to resolve people issues. Approaches that work in other groups and similar situations may also work in the data governance area. The approach you take is based on the position you hold (as mentioned above). A few approaches that have been demonstrated to work include those listed below and are often tactics used by middle managers who have individuals in data governance leadership positions that are misaligned.

- Focus on metrics and outputs
  - You can demonstrate that person is misaligned with the operational needs by setting up or motivating a management model based on metrics. The metrics can identify specific areas where the misalignment leads to suboptimal results.
  - The Playbook helps discipline-collecting metrics by standardizing the processes used to perform the data governance jobs. Once the jobs are consistently performed, the metrics become a more accurate description of performance and provide greater line of sight into issues and required changes.
- Motivate a reevaluation of the operational model
  - If the resources do not appear to have alignment with the needs of the operational model, it is possible that the operational model is not configured optimally. It is also possible that if the model changes, the change process could motivate a change in resources that leads to better long-term results.

    - You can motivate a reevaluation of the operating model through a number of actions including ensuring the original operating model has a yearly review step that evaluates performance or suggesting continuously reevaluating the operating model at a leadership meeting while ensuring your motivations are focused on continuous improvement versus targeted at a specific individual.
- Focus on the process
    - Even though a data governance leader may not have the skills or cultural values for leading data governance, they have the job. Focusing on the data governance processes and waiting until an opportune time for change helps ensure the data governance operating model is not blamed along with the misaligned resources if a negative atmosphere develops.
- Frank talk
    - The frank-talk model is where you sit down with the individual that is misaligned and discuss your concerns around misalignment using a nonthreatening, outcomes-focused style. This model rarely works if the misalignment is above you organizationally. If the issues are above your organizational position, you may want to seek guidance from another leader, mentor, or confidant. You could also convince a peer of the misaligned individual to speak to them and broach the subject.
    - Most of these methods do not work unless the organization's culture has a frank-talk value system already established.
- Wait it out
    - Organizations may take awhile to make changes but changes may come. Unfortunately, the waiting-it-out approach often leads to passive aggressive behavior, which is bad for the organization.
    - Obviously, the Playbook does not help you with this strategy, but the Playbook, with an emphasis on promoting a consistent process, can make the daily data governance operational work repeatable and familiar until a change occurs. A consistent process helps reduce the stress of an unfortunate situation.

CUSTOMIZING AND MAINTAINING THE PLAYBOOK

The Playbook is designed to be customized to an organization's environment. Without customization, the Playbook's process may not apply to an organization or be aligned with their priorities or capabilities. Once customized, the Playbook should be updated to reflect changes in the operating environment. If an explicit periodic maintenance cycle is not applied to the Playbook over time, the Playbook becomes less aligned with an organization's needs.

Customization of the Playbook should target the level of maturity you want to implement in the organization and gradually over time introduce updates and further customization as your organization demonstrates the ability to execute it. A Playbook that is customized based on an ideal maturity target that is not based on reality will quickly earn the Playbook a spot on the bookshelf. The Playbook described in this book targets a reasonable level of maturity that is not out of reach of most organizations while at the same time is not as sophisticated as may be needed for a large, complex organization.

TYPES OF CUSTOMIZATIONS

There are a few major areas of customization.

- Workstreams: The Playbook as described in this book has four core workstreams that roughly align with those we have found in many organizations. You may discover additional workstreams.
- Activities: The activities are the steps conducted by a specific role or roles. Activities need to be concrete and specific to the organization. We often see customizations around the approval steps. It is not helpful to merely describe an activity like "approve elements" because such an activity description is fairly vague. Instead, the activity should be specific such as "data steward provides first-level approval." Other activity customizations typically occur around publishing content for others to consume and review actions.
- Roles: The roles can be customized by both the label as well as the activities assigned to the roles. We find that the role labels are customized for most organizations and that the activities for those labels are often divided up and assigned to other roles, though in total, the range of activities across all of the roles remains fairly constant.
- Artifact Updates: The Playbook allows you to specify artifacts for activities and workstreams. The artifacts are often highly organizationally specific and reflect various business and systems development processes and artifacts that exist. Artifacts are often called templates. Some organizations allow different versions of templates to exist depending on the workstream. Most times, the artifacts are tightly aligned with existing artifacts that are needed in other processes so when data governance produces outputs, they can be easily reused in other parts of the organization. The artifacts are sometimes implemented in applications, eg, CDE capture.
- Extensions: The Playbook is often customized based on the specific operating environment found in an organization. Although we suggest that most technology-specific activity descriptions be placed into more specific job-aids versus the Playbook there are no hard and fast rules.
  - An organization may create a data-quality dashboard where data controls post their results for consumption by various data stewards. The Playbook may be updated with some activities as well as enhanced descriptions that describe where in the process to create a new data-quality metric as well as the approval process.
  - Extensions of workstreams and activities may apply to a specific data domain. Although this might seem strange at first, the worksteams in the Playbook described in this book covers master data management as well as general information management. Master data management usually focuses on specific domains with unique requirements. You can develop further extensions for specific types of master data, eg, customer versus product, based on the maturity and capabilities of these domain areas within the organization.
- By Line of Business: The Playbook is designed to be an operations model across an organization, although this is not always possible. We have seen organizations where the finance group has one Playbook model and the IT group another Playbook. While not ideal, it is more important to have "a" Playbook versus "the" Playbook. It may not be possible to merge the workstreams over time. A more reasonable target is to make both uses a common set of activity descriptions and roles.

Regardless of the customization type, the customization should be approved through a process that is transparent and allows input from multiple groups before implementing the customization. Customizations will also require change management activities. We describe these areas below.

CUSTOMIZATION AND MAINTENANCE PROCESS

Much like the operational processes described at the start of this chapter, the process for customization and maintenance is very similar. You should discuss process management with the other groups that share the need for disciplined operations. You will find ideas and approaches that work in your organization.

An important aspect of any change process is deciding who should be allowed to provide input into the changes and who needs to approve them. Your operating model should cover these aspects of operations process management. While it may seem obvious that anyone should be able to provide input, we have found that most people are able to tell you what is wrong with the current process and are more than happy to provide you an endless stream of pain points and issues. The same people are not always great at describing what the new process should be.

A good way to the "who" aspect of change management is to appoint a working group within the operating model to gather the input from various stakeholders and generate concentrated and integrated recommendations. This process is optimal for both the customization and maintenance changes described above.

Many organizations use external consultants to help them perform the customization and maintenance tasks, and we think this is a good approach. External consultants can bring you insights learned from multiple organizations and infuse the Playbook with content on what has been demonstrated to work at organizations similar to yours. External consultants with a dedicated focus may also be able to deliver changes faster than using an internal team.

Some organizations have corporate social networks that gather feedback form a wide audience. If a channel exists for the Playbook, there may be useful ideas in the "feedback" stream you can tap into for inspiration. We have not found corporate social networks at large corporations to be robust in Playbook areas. However, it appears to be a growing phenomenon that could be more useful in the future.

The customization process should be kept simple:

- Interview and solicit feedback from participants and stakeholders as to what worked well and did not work well over the review period.
- Review statistics and other metrics to understand where performance was demonstrated and where performance was lacking. For example, if the number of data-quality issues in a "queue" remained the same, then there may be issues with the resource levels, the Playbook process, or other factors that need to be uncovered.
- Identify Playbook improvement opportunities by reviewing the process with individuals who played various roles throughout the review period. Annotate the activities that were performed well and those that were skipped or deemed to not add much value. We have found that annotating activities and highlighting opportunities directly on the Playbook graphics is an effective way to communicate opportunities.
- Bundle recommended changes together into a cohesive set. Identify the changes to workstreams, activities, artifacts, inputs/outputs, and roles.
- Through an established review process, review the proposed changes.
- Once approval is obtained on the final set of changes, update the existing Playbook material, republish the content, and push out new training or communications appropriate to the level of change.

Similar to other process improvement efforts, it is important to try and link the proposed changes back to metrics that reflect the issues. It is difficult to collect these metrics in the first few iterations of the Playbook. We have found that establishing a clean set of metrics, creating a baseline, and showing where improvements are needed can take up to a year.

UPDATE FREQUENCY

The Playbook should be updated when changes in the process are warranted and the change management processes can be executed in a timely fashion. There are no fixed answers as to how often the Playbook should be updated. We have seen organizations update it yearly as well as every 2–3 years. Smaller adjustments tend to occur more frequently than larger ones. A good initial update frequency plan is:

- Workstreams: Revisit 2–3 years after the initial customization and every 2–3 years thereafter.
- Activities: Revisit every 6 months but target updates annually.
- Roles: Revisit yearly.

Role changes are typically associated with larger system development or organizational changes, so yearly reviews and changes align with these events.

The update frequency is really bounded more by change management communications than other factors. Updated too frequently, the Playbook may seem unstable and every change may cause fatigue in participants. Changing the Playbook infrequently risks making the Playbook irrelevant or causes confusion across Playbook participants, which leads to an erosion of confidence in the Playbook. You should communicate the changes through standard corporate channels such as email and collaboration websites. Foamcore posters and other visual reminders about the changes are also useful but probably less used compared to electronic communication.

Updates to the training should also be made at the same time. For small changes, the training updates can focus only on the changed content while larger changes, such as adding a workstream, would warrant recreating the training module.

UPDATE DEPLOYMENT

Once the Playbook has been customized or updated, the Playbook needs to be deployed. The word "deployed" is used to recognize that rolling out a Playbook involves more than just sending an office presentation document to those identified for the Playbook roles. There needs to be a multipronged approach. The Playbook is designed to become an official part of the "way" an organization operates. Just like many other operational processes discussed above, training, communication, and certification play an important role. Some organizations may create official organization roles recognized and managed by human resources. These job descriptions may also need to be updated.

Major updates to the Playbook may require larger deployment efforts. You will need to match the level of effort to the level of change. Deployment is covered in the next chapter.

CHAPTER

GOVERNING BIG DATA AND ANALYTICS

9

BIG DATA

We begin this chapter very much with the end in mind. The majority of work we've seen published related to governing Big Data analytics is an extension of approaches used in the structured data world. Given the recent Big Data phenomenon and some significant differences between the data approaches, technologies, sources, and challenges, it seems more useful to step back and consider the scope of governance options available, which is exactly what we've chosen to do here. Thus we think the end you may want to keep in mind for Big Data analytics is different from the one used for a structure or legacy data environment. Data governance and controls have been maturing alongside traditional application and data management systems for decades. There was not, in our experience, a moment when anyone questioned whether or not structured data systems, applications, stores, and delivery services would be required. In fact, the opposite was true—governance and controls were introduced as it became clear that the size and scope of the systems required them. In the current Big Data environment, that presumption has still not been entirely proven.

Most firms, governments, and nonprofits considering Big Data initiatives and investments have the opportunity to openly question the terms under which they are going to make those investments. Their business and other functions are already operating and effectively automated with traditional computer systems and data management, including some controls and governance. But the opportunities surrounding Big Data are so new that we must analyze and understand the terms under which we would engage in those options. So we've come to the considered conclusion that Big Data and analytic governance is first and foremost a function of making an informed investment decision. We really believe that governance over Big Data is lateral; we must first choose to engage in investing and controlling Big Data as opposed to adding governance and controls to existing structure data environments.

This choice highlights the need for the demand management and rationalization approaches we discussed in the previous chapter. It also highlights the value of a broader, business-case approach to Big Data. The data-centric business cases often rest on the foundation of structured data-delivery systems and add value layers. These are based on analytic, forecasting, and behavioral change-oriented systems. We're all familiar with the use of Big Data techniques and technologies in the online world to suit consumer preference, purchasing, and crowd-level marketing and communications. Thus business-case analysis has to include the potential benefits that come from these kinds of outcomes.

We also think that, because Big Data is a relatively new phenomenon, it is important to use current, worked examples and cases to highlight where governance and controls are needed or are most useful. In our experience with Big Data programs, federal government and commercial firms seeking to ingest very high volumes and diversities of data do not always have a well-defined purpose. Often these programs are focused on collecting data and storing it in a way so that it can be provisioned dynamically for multiple, undefined uses. The work we have done in intelligence, as well as civilian and federal sectors, is fairly commonplace. We were surprised by how common this approach is in the commercial space. So we'll use a series of scenarios to discover the kinds of Big Data sources, streams, storage options, and business outcomes that can result. Before we engage in scenario-based reviews, it may be useful to consider three real-world examples unfolding today.

It's important to note in these three real-world examples that, in each case, there was a conscious decision to engage Big Data methods and technologies. That is the first real moment of governance over Big Data. Choosing to engage in Big Data methods and outcomes is the initial governance entry point for Big Data and should not be dismissed or assumed in any governance model. This becomes increasingly important as more of the projects we consider in the Big Data world entail extending existing systems or replacing them. In the opportunities that are substantially similar to those we've used to build traditional systems, we should be able to leverage business-case thinking around cost-benefit analysis. In fact, in a direct comparison to traditional system development approaches, many of the initial business cases that have launched successful Big Data efforts showed that data can provide tremendous savings in cost and time.

EXAMPLE 1—PREVENTING LITIGATION: AN EARLY WARNING SYSTEM TO GET BIG VALUE OUT OF BIG DATA, BY WILLIAM "BILL" INMON AND NELSON E. BRESTOFF

This book captures the legal and technical ramifications of joining the Big Data world, or at least one of the domains within the structured data world. For decades, Bill Inmon has led the development of architectures, solution approaches, technologies, and business outcomes for the largest global consumers and producers of information technology. He is best known for his work in data warehousing and data integration, and he has continued that work into the Big Data world by showing how complex, textual data can be disambiguated and selectively mapped into the structured data world. Bill has shown that it is critical to associate objects in the Big Data world with master data objects that are well defined in the structural world. Examples include customers, suppliers, counterparties, products, and so on. In his work on preventing litigation, he has extended this paradigm to show that it is possible to scan through thousands, hundreds of thousands, or even millions of documents related to contractual obligations and structured in unknown or highly varied ways. The ability to scan these documents electronically and provision the text in a way that allows for disambiguation and integration with other data is a game changer for litigation, due diligence, and the legal and business proceedings that often follow. It also establishes a new watermark for the movement toward more intelligent systems, which replaces heavy manual effort loads with rapid, reliable analysis and integration of critical data.

In litigation prevention, Bill and his partner prove that the use of a textual disambiguation engine allows for the pooling of information from hundreds of thousands of contracts. This is done in order to relate it to the key counterparties, time periods, and conditions they have embedded in these long, complex documents. Now questions can be answered quickly about what potential liabilities, responsibilities, or other issues are associated with each counterparty to the firm, for what period of time, and, potentially, with what dollar limitations and impact. This work was previously done, to a limited extent and at best, by manual effort and labor from law firms and individual firms. As a result, it could take months or years to complete. Bill's software and architecture proves that this is another area where Big Data methods that connect Big Data content with structured data concepts are viable and can take orders of magnitude in cost and time out of the equation.

The other aspect of this solution is the decision frame he provides for using a Big Data approach. He frames the governance decision concerning Big Data investment around a business problem that has specific, quantifiable, financial, and legal impacts. So if a pharmaceutical industry participant needs to gauge their legal exposure over a particular drug or other product, they would engage in this investment to quickly scope an analysis of all legal documents and commitments related to that drug. There are many other aspects to Bill's technology, and we've chosen to highlight it because it was one of the first in this space and holds several key patents around its capabilities. Bill's approach also applies controls to the data store it produces, ensuring appropriate change-control and stewardship capabilities. This approach provides end-to-end Big Data governance, starting with the investment decision and completing the cycle with change and quality controls over the data it generates. All of the content that is produced and integrated is then subject to change controls in a typical stewardship approach consistent with the Playbook.

EXAMPLE 2—DIGITAL HEALTHCARE (TELEHEALTH 2.0)

We have identified Big Data investment options and benefits with the president and CEO of a leading Telehealth and digital healthcare firm. The CEO and his team had already started to leverage Big Data methods and technologies to support enhanced, care-delivery options for a large system of community members. While many of the benefits and business case details are highly proprietary and sensitive, we have permission to share a couple of key aspects of the CEO's approach and success. The firm has always espoused the need to enhance medical care delivery at every step of the process. They work very closely with care providers and recipients to ensure the value-added mapping of services and their quality-assurance process extends beyond the initial service delivery. Its desire to extend to every area of care provision was an early distinction for this leading digital healthcare firm. According to the CEO, governing Big Data means making intelligent investments in Big Data partners, methods, and technologies, which are all focused on specific improvements in care quality and patient outcomes. The firm has always been focused on care efficacy across digital channels of delivery.

A key aspect of the firm's success is its ability to ensure that quality-assurance metrics are embedded in the scheduling selection, engagement, and follow-through aspects of care delivery. Many of these metrics require gathering data from Big Data sources, such as the Web, mobile platforms, and cellular phone platforms. These metrics must be tracked, baselined, and analyzed on a recurring basis, which requires large analytic capabilities in advanced, cloud-driven architectures. So the CEO's team thoughtfully engaged a multitude of partnerships, such as with Microsoft for Azure Cloud, to ensure they have an end-to-end, secure environment through which to provide and analyze care efficacy. Their Big Data investment decisions have necessitated additional strategic partnerships and investments to scale out the initial Big Data collection and analysis required by their business. That thinking and execution is what enables this CEO to leapfrog over his competition, in terms of the membership base size he can support, the level of effective care he can provide, and his ability to diversify types of care more rapidly than any other market participant.

EXAMPLE 3—CHIEF DATA OFFICER INTEGRATES BIG DATA FOR FINANCIAL SERVICE FIRM

In a recent industry interview, Derek Strauss, a chief data officer at a major financial service firm, discussed his team's insights into leveraging Big Data. The team leverages data from Web, mobile, and other platforms about its customers' preferences and investment options to provide affinity-based suggestions for customer consideration. His firm and its clients clearly see the value in this approach. His clients receive options and insights tailored to their status and interests. His firm is able to maintain a very close relationship with its clients by providing these valuable insights in a controlled and timely manner. In this case, Derek was able to identify the business case to integrate Big Data into their customer environment, with the appropriate controls and investment that entails.

This investment approach extends the data governance controls Derek had already put in place using his "Seven Streams of Data Resource Management" approach. Along with existing Playbook methods, a final Data Playbook was then constructed using the Seven Streams approach and methods to support his team's work. We encourage you to review some of the basis for that work in the publications Derek and his partners Bill Inmon and Genia Neuschloss published, such as *DW 2.0: The Architecture for the Next Generation of Data Warehousing*.

Derek also noted that they had engaged the college and university community to crowdsource data-science skills and insights. The crowdsourcing approach has become integrated in the Big Data movement and repeatedly proves to have high value, where it is targeted appropriately. Once again, deciding to engage and invest in this under whatever terms that investment makes sense is basic governance. Derek's choice proved to be highly valuable: it gave him access to some of the freshest thinking in research and analysis areas, as well as allowed him to tap into a potential recruiting source for the firm. His willingness to partner with these learning institutions and the data science skills they brought to the table allowed him to sidestep the high initial investment required to build a pool of dedicated data scientists, while ensuring a consistent refresh of thinking and methods. This is a clear example of leadership governance as a focus, as opposed to passive or control governance. Leadership governance moves beyond current models to ensure the investment in the Big Data approach, in this case data science, is done in ways that scale and refresh themselves sustainably.

In the interview, Derek also noted that he had worked with his teams to improve their foundational work for data stewardship, governance, and quality as they engaged in these other areas. Derek is very clear that Big Data layers are built on top of traditional data skills and systems, and he emphasizes the value of strengthening those foundations. His ability to engage his executive sponsors on a regular basis and show the value of improving his foundation while building additional layers of value is what makes it possible for him to sustain his firm's competitive data advantage.

Each of these examples demonstrates the need to engage in Big Data as a formal governance decision and to do so from the beginning. They also identify the different types of benefits that can be obtained and the discipline required to see them through. Note that, in each case, the discussion begins with the business challenge or opportunity and then proceeds to consider Big Data methods and technologies, as the option to traditional systems development approaches.

PERSONAL BIG DATA

There is, of course, a personal dimension to Big Data governance—ie, the choice to opt in or opt out of having the Big Data you generate tracked by others. This is becoming a very complex area but starts with a simple pretext: the digital footprint we leave behind when we engage in certain digital activities is not subject to collection and analysis by others. In the European Union, this became especially important, as a court decided that a search engine like Google has to comply with a citizen's "right to be forgotten." Essentially, under certain circumstances, search engines have to remove the links to a person's personal information. This legal framework attempts to force digital footprint trackers to eliminate personally identifiable information from their vast collections. There continues to be some testing around abstracting people's identity but keeping their digital footprint. In the meantime, we have some choice over what level of digital footprint tracking and analysis we support. There is also the initial governance decision we choose to make when considering Big Data devices and activities. This can include the use of fitness-tracking, wearable devices, location tracking for our smartphones, and even biometric sensors within wireless communications. In each case, we are choosing to generate a larger digital footprint that is at least captured on a smartphone or computer and potentially shared with commercial interest. From a personal perspective, governing our Big Data footprint is a function of understanding what choices we have before we engage in generating more Big Data.

As we move toward understanding scenario-based approaches to Big Data governance and application, we should consider the way Big Data and analytics is delivered and operated within scenarios. The managed analytics services, or MAS space, is rapidly emerging as a next-generation approach to delivering on the promise of Big Data without the large, fixed investments or lengthy time periods normally required to achieve results. There are many providers in this space serving different industries and market segments. One example, Elevondata, has proven that a fully managed, service-based approach can be cost-effective and rapidly produce business results for small, medium, and even global clients. This end-to-end managed service starts with full data provisioning and requirements analysis with business-case scenarios, which allow for flexible target benefits. The creation of the Big Data architectural constructs, applications, services, delivery mechanisms, and consumption tools is all part of the managed-service process. The limited, initial investment allows for a rapid business-case decision to be made, and the short ramp-up time means that initial discovery and analysis results are delivered in weeks or months, opposed to the months or years offered in the traditional systems-development approach. Elevondata has delivered enough of these managed-service solutions to show the ongoing benefit of a managed-service operator, who leverages cloud- and distributed-computing architectures to provide search capabilities without large fixed investments. It is important to keep this kind of managed-service approach in mind as we look at our scenarios, since we may need to partner with managed-service providers in order to establish and operate governance controls for Big Data.

GOVERNING BIG DATA IN LARGE AND SMALL WAYS

The standard approach to Big Data in the data governance community suggests that we take the same basic steps for governing Big Data that we do for structured data. We've already discussed the fact that there is a larger step we get to take in Big Data, that we haven't traditionally had the choice to make in structured and traditional data. That choice is to engage in using Big Data and its data methods and technologies. That is the major decision point when considering Big Data approaches so it is important to formalize the decision and its supporting business case. There is some truth to the approach that applies traditional data governance methods to Big Data. But those take place only after a business case-based decision has been made to engage in Big Data.

Once that decision is made, traditional data governance methods, as explained in the Playbook, are applicable to portions of Big Data structures. In each of the following scenarios, the presumption is that the metadata tags connected to Big Data objects, which are stored in file-oriented locations (eg, Hadoop filesystem), must be governed and standardized just as with traditional structured data. The range of values available to describe metadata tags for Big Data objects, such as media type, subject, provider, contributor, etc., should all be standardized and required fields for any Big Data object we choose to capture, store, and analyze. Governing Big Data objects in a file-store environment has special challenges and conditions. The first challenge is to recognize that these filestores are predicated on the notion of redundancy. In a Hadoop filesystem, mass redundancy is expected, due to the nature of the Big Data collection process and the lack of transformation or normalization steps in its collection. This is the biggest single disparity between Big Data stores, such as data lakes, and traditional data warehouses.

The key concept here is the need to govern or control Big Data objects or files at the metadata level. Standardizing metadata tags and available values, as well as required minimum metadata, ensures vast quantities of Big Data files can be searched, filtered, and analyzed based on the unique properties of those files. Simple metadata, such as the source, time of collection, type of file format, and object it represents, are examples of basic, minimum, required metadata. In large ways, we govern Big Data principally on how we decide to invest and leverage Big Data solutions. In small ways, we govern through our control of the minimum required metadata, our identification of uniquely Big Data files and objects, and our comparison and analysis of them in vast storage arrays or clouds.

SCENARIO 1—HOSPITAL WORKFLOW MODEL

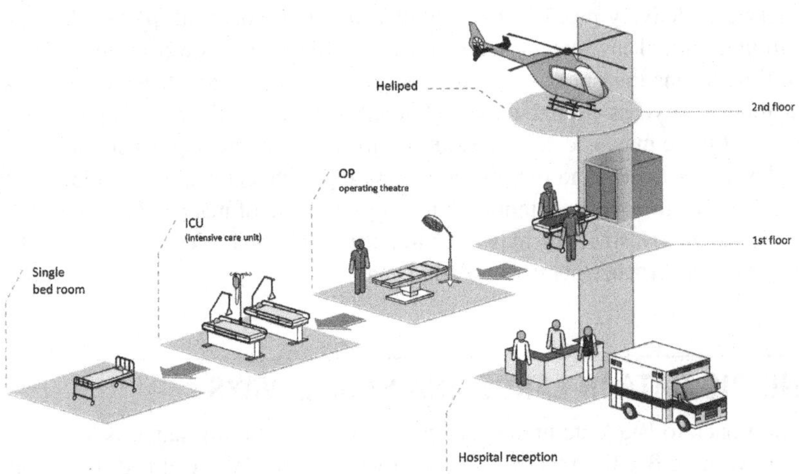

This graphic is a simple depiction of a hospital workflow. At each stage in the workflow, we can visualize the kind of Big Data footprint additions that occur and begin to think about the kinds of questions the hospital, patients, and providers want to be able to answer for any given interaction. This workflow shows two different admission channels: the helicopter pad on the roof and the ambulance portal in the main floor. Each of these clearly carries different components of the digital signature or footprint, such as patient arrival information and condition upon arrival. Visualize if you will a patient on a gurney in either a helicopter or an ambulance. The patient would have some type of sensors connected to them, such as a heart monitor or blood-pressure gauge. These sensors would be streaming information on the patient's condition to both their local caregivers in the mobile platform as well as their hospital-based caregivers. Then also imagine that the admission process provides information about the patient and their history, ideally, via electronic medical record access rather than manual intake procedures and imports. Big data collection about the patient's condition and route would provide the ability to add their status and condition at intake and admission rather than after, as has been the common practice. This information would provide a wealth of knowledge about the kinds of conditions under which most patients are admitted to the ER and could be broken down into time of day, day of week, day of year, age, demographic, method of conveyance, source of referral, decision to route to this hospital, and so forth. It's important to use scenarios to couple the types of Big Data that can be provisioned with the kinds of questions that would provide business value for any investment in Big Data.

Extending the scenario above, we can see where the patient proceeds through to a surgical theater, then beyond into intensive care, and finally a patient room. In each of the settings, we can imagine additions to the patient digital footprint, including doctors notes and videos from the surgery itself, nursing and physician care notes from the intensive care unit, and patient inputs about their pain levels, preferred medication options, and other conditions. Finally, in the patient room as well as in the ICU, we see the introduction of video and other capture tools to help healthcare providers monitor patient conditions remotely. All of these data inputs add to the Big Data collection or digital footprint that can support both the individual patient as well as some aggregated analysis for care improvement and cost controls. Over the past decade, much has been written and proven about the value of checklist-based surgical and intensive care in hospitals. Regimented use of checklists has dramatically reduced postop infections in intensive care and has improved overall levels of patient recovery in many facilities. Big data collection of the type we are describing would further prove the value of those checklists, as well as their contents and use. Similarly, from a cost-control perspective, tracking supplies using data-collection methods such as Radio Frequency ID (RFID) tags and Bluetooth connections would provide insight into cost-containment options. While this is a very simple hospital workflow example, it provides dozens of instances of Big Data collection points and types, as well as business questions that can be answered by them.

SCENARIO 2—PERSONALIZED ONLINE SALES AND DELIVERY

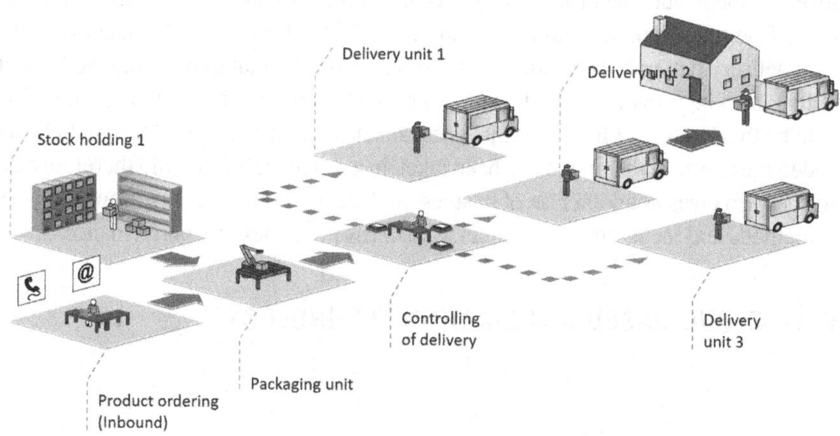

This scenario allows us to think about typical, logistical issues for personal delivery and to add current and emerging trends to such issues, which enables us to see how Big Data is helpful in making key decisions. Let's call this company "Nile" and use it to explain its Personal Best delivery service. The cornerstone concept of personal best is the rapid, reliable delivery of even the smallest orders on a personal level. In this workflow, we can see how orders are pulled together, routed, and delivered to customers. The data that is generated from each step of this process helps with every aspect of performance management, from just-in-time inventory, to intelligent pricing for products and shipping, and to least-cost, most-effective routing algorithms for delivery. The information that is generated from sensors in the product and the delivery vehicle would drive the tuning of these algorithms and the improvement of service over time.

This Big Data approach would also provide the basis for comparing traditional delivery vehicles and channels, such as trucks, to emerging options like drones. Comparing land-based to air-based delivery would begin with cost and effectiveness issues, but it would almost certainly have to add risk and control issues that do not typically arise from land-based delivery. So we can imagine that, if we were to engage a trial of drone-based delivery in certain areas, we would want to understand what factors determined the best locales for the trial and what additional information or Big Data we need to provision from the drone delivery.

Our land-based vehicles produce GPS data, which is sent via cellular connection to the data lake in a hosted cloud. This data is used for both real-time tracking of all delivery vehicles and their contents, as well as long-term, least-cost, most-effective route algorithm tuning. The GPS data is then compared with time of day, weather condition, driver experience, and other factors to improve delivery algorithms. In a pilot with drone-delivery vehicles, additional information, including weather conditions, wind speed and direction, altitude flown, route taken, and obstacle-avoidance patterns required for delivery, are also added to the algorithm. This is but one example of where a business-process change leads to additional Big Data components and analysis.

Imagine this delivery service also comparing public delivery methods, such as the US Postal Service, and drop-and-ship locations, such as local packaging and delivery stores, as options. Each of these options carries with it additional Big Data sources and analysis requirements. When constructing a pilot program to consider trying new methods and processes, such as drones or dropship locations, it is clear that planning for additional Big Data sources and analysis is a critical component. What is less obvious is the fact that the types of Big Data to be provisioned and analyzed may drive additional Big Data governance over minimum-governed metadata. The drone example is instructive, because, in that case, we could expect to see video inputs from the drone to help understand the effects of weather, obstacle avoidance, and the efficiency of its delivery patterns. The addition of this new video format may require additional metadata requirements that must be provided with the video files. One example of additional, minimum-governed metadata might be the duration of the video that is encapsulated in the file. Another might be the relationship of that video file to others that may have been taken in a sequence and should therefore be considered together. This scenario gives us another set of business and technical challenges to consider when employing Big Data methods and technologies to enhance business processes and performance.

SCENARIO 3—CLOUD-BASED INFORMATION TECHNOLOGY

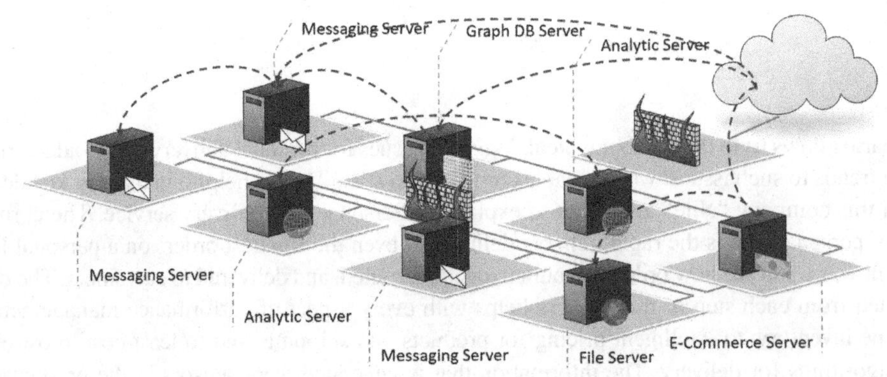

This scenario provides a fairly simple view of managing cloud-based, technology assets. We know that cloud computing is supported by data centers, server farms, and other constructs, which are fully virtualized by cloud delivery mechanisms. If we take the perspective of the cloud-service provider, who needs to track the status of their technology assets in terms of performance, utilization, capacity, and security, we need to identify the types of information those servers and their environment can provide. This is a commercial or industrial version of the "Internet of Things" approach that is so prevalent in the retail market. We see Internet of Things coming to life in cars, appliances, and even retail settings. In this example, we're looking at what are typically referred to as instrumented servers, which track their conditions and report to the Internet. One of the key benefits of cloud computing is the elastic computing capacity, or the ability to provide surge levels of computing capacity on-demand from a pool of shared resources.

Elastic computing, and related dynamic capacity models, requires constant monitoring of overall capacity utilization, as well as the ability to dynamically employ additional capacity that may be available but not in production. So we have an example where Big Data is both inbound, as a means of monitoring status and conditions, and outbound, as a means of changing the capacity and performance of the cloud-computing environment. In traditional operational applications, this is referred to as closed-loop analytics. In those settings we employ an analytics engine that is able to change things like pricing or availability commitments for orders based on volumes, time of day, and other factors in the operational environment. In this model, changes to online capacity and tracking of its use, for billing purposes as well as for performance management, require constant bidirectional Big Data movement and analytics. This is another environment where, in a way, physical sensors are often employed to track the physical conditions of the data center, including temperature and power fluctuation. Video sources may also be included, in order to confirm or deny the presence of fire, water, or other physical hazards. All of these inputs are critical to precisely managing the performance of the data center in the cloud it supports. This example provides a more industrial view of how the Internet of Things and additional Big Data sources are combined to provide real-time updates and changes in the way facilities and technology are managed.

BIG DATA AND ANALYTIC DELIVERY EXAMPLE—ANALYTICS.USA.GOV

The last component of governing Big Data and analytics is to look at the way they are delivered and consumed. It's only through this lens that we understand the impact change control, data integrity, and even visualization approaches have on the realization of the data value. This example is from the federal government site that provides real-time statistics updates on a variety of aspects of a government and its citizen services. It's a valuable example, because it highlights a number of choices the Big Data delivery team has to make, as well as the underlying value of governance in the quality and integrity of the information provided.

We've started our discussion of Big Data governance by reminding ourselves that we have options when it comes to choosing to use it, when we use it, and on what terms we use it. Those same options have to be considered when it comes time for the visualization and exploitation of Big Data, or basic delivery and consumption. The prevailing practice for Big Data projects is to include, from the outset, sample visualizations based on use cases or larger storyboards. These establish the purpose of the Big Data initiative, who its primary audience is, and what kinds of questions it's intended to answer. Marrying the answers to those questions up to appropriate and impactful visualizations is a key aspect of Big Data analytics.

This example demonstrates two different ways that delivering on Big Data analytics can fail. If we learned that the data on this website is deeply flawed and unreliable, our belief in the entire site and its promise would be diminished to the point of not using that service. Similarly, if the data is of high integrity and timeliness but the visualization selected is too complex or undermines the actual understanding needed from the data, we will be unable to rely on the site for decision support and other uses. The Playbook approach to governing data controls and analytics is equally important in this area. The Playbook talks about how to govern analytic models, and it's important to understand that those include the visualization and consumption models, not just the internal algorithms and data structures. Best practice in delivering Big Data analytics now includes embedding feedback capabilities into the delivery mechanism, whether in a website or an application. This allows users to easily provide feedback where they see difficulties in the usability of the interface or perceive gaps in the data viability. This example helps us understand how the combination of data controls and visualization alignment with user needs drives value from all the underlying work that has been done to capture the data and deliver it in this format.

Governing analytic models, including computational and presentation formats, is a critical function in the Playbook. Consider minimum required metadata for analytic presentations. We need to be able to identify the type of visualization being used as well as other heuristic factors in order to gauge the effectiveness of the presentation report's intended audience. We also need to track metadata related to the feedback we receive so that we can assemble a meaningful picture of user satisfaction over time. These are just two simple examples of using metadata-based governance for Big Data analytics and visualization.

CONCLUSION

This chapter focused on two aspects of governing Big Data and analytics. The first is the decision to employ Big Data and analytics, which is the simplest form of governance—deciding where and when to invest in your information technology. The second aspect of governing Big Data and analytics is the adjustments we make for the way the data operates. While many of the methods and approaches we use for traditional or structured data are still important to employ here, they have to be applied in different ways, alluding to the different forms the data takes and the redundancy with which it is stored.

CHAPTER

RAPID PLAYBOOK DEPLOYMENT

10

Organizations need to rapidly deploy and use the Playbook. This chapter describes catalysts for rapidly deploying a Playbook and creating a path to sustainable use while minimizing risk of negative outcomes. Catalysts create a sense of urgency for change. We cover these catalysts and connect the catalysts to the Playbook value proposition. A prioritization model helps identify business areas where Playbook-based activities can be expanded. The final step is to intelligently scope the initial deployment.

A SENSE OF URGENCY

When people have a sense of urgency, they tend to take action, innovate, and change the status quo. A crisis can create a sense of urgency. A strong leader can create a sense of urgency. An exciting market opportunity can create a sense of urgency. A sense of urgency creates organizational focus, motivates alignment to a common cause across disparate points of view, and helps people prioritize their time. A sense of urgency is a good thing.

Creating a sense of urgency in the data governance space is hard. Few data governance programs are started because the organization thought it was a "good idea." Perceptions of risk, managers exhausted from mistakes repeatedly made, or a business crisis are the usual catalysts.

Many data management professionals may be disheartened to find that data governance programs are not started because there was a fantastic ROI story. Since data governance plays a supporting role in business functions, the core data governance jobs are rarely linked directly to topline revenue or margin improvements. Instead, data governance is usually cast as a necessary function to reduce the risk of missing financial targets or to reduce business outcome risk.

Many data governance jobs are performed without the benefit of a formal data governance program and many business programs have some element of the data governance jobs built in to their implementation approach. Under these circumstances, casting the Playbook as an incremental cost may make it difficult for business managers to justify. They may consider it incremental investments with unclear marginal returns for activities that look different than their current plans. Carving out data governance jobs separately from the business program can be a nonstarter. Viewing the Playbook as alternative but better way to conduct the same activities without incremental cost is a key viewpoint to communicate.

A data management professional can rest assured that data governance jobs are being performed. They should provide guidance and suggestions on how the jobs can be performed consistently within the business program—a key outcome of using a Playbook. Most programs have some flavor data governance jobs already baked into their program charters. Organizations often find that these jobs are executed inconsistently and without ongoing, durable value. This inconsistency motivates a Playbook-based model.

The situation is not black or white. Very few companies run only a single program at a time so the need for consistency across programs and projects is important. While a single program may not motivate the need for a more formal data governance program to be established, there are many other situations where managers develop a heightened sense of risk and this in turn motivates a sense of urgency. In addition to a single program view, a systemic risk point of view may also create a sense of urgency.

In the next sections, we provide common catalysts that create a sense of urgency and help you prioritize a Playbook-based data governance program. Since it is common to already have a data governance program in place, we also describe how to find the sense of urgency and launch a Playbook model on top of an existing program. You will notice throughout the different scenarios that there are consistent themes of attestability, risk reduction, consistency, and efficiency.

CHANGE AS A SOURCE OF URGENCY

Change, of any type, can create a sense of urgency. These examples are the start of a checklist you use to scan your organization and identify the best opportunity. No two organizations are the same and the state of their data are always different. You will need to assess each example to judge whether it reflects your organization and whether it is the right vehicle for rapidly launching a Playbook-based data governance model. Increasingly common, "some" data governance is put in place as part of a technical application implementation or as part of a transformation where many existing information management IT assets are colocated. These are great starting points but circumstances may vary.

Integrated sales and revenue reporting

Both large and small organizations need to produce sales and revenue reports. We have worked with smaller companies that are a result of several mergers and acquisitions as well as larger organizations with significant numbers of operating companies around the world. There has always been a need for integrated sales and revenue reporting.

When multiple groups contribute to revenue, their products and organizational structures often vary. For companies that sell essential almost identical products in international locations, multiple business groups contribute to revenue. The quality of sales and revenue reports is directly related to the ability to properly group and tally product-related sales data. Products are usually slightly different, but they may belong to the same category. Different groups may use different geographic models for their territories compared to the geographic groupings headquarters wants to use. It common to have senior managers question the quality of a sales report either because of the way products are classified, how geographies are related, or what "systems" were used to obtain the data.

Data governance jobs are designed to help improve the quality of the data used in these situations. A sense of urgency for deploying a Playbook is created in this scenario under the following conditions:

- Over time, the quality issues around products, categories, and geography data has not been resolved.
- New acquisitions or frequent corporate structure changes require new and different current and point-in-time sales and revenue reporting.

- A new product was launched and the sales and revenue data seem very inconsistent with pre-launch data.
- Senior management expresses frustration at not knowing whether the business groups are using the same word to mean the same thing and the reports are harder to interpret without assistance from a data guru.

Issues in the sales and revenue reports are almost always a great area to find a sense of urgency because sales and marketing groups are often profit centers and "own a number." Senior executives who own P&L have exceptional focus on removing noise and complexity from their organization and operational processes.

Transformation program

A transformation program, with a capital "T" is an organization-wide program designed to catapult a company to a new level of competitiveness. Transformation programs are either business-side or IT-side, but usually not both at once. The transformation may involve reorganizations, new business unit lines, new senior management teams, selloffs, spinouts, workforce realignments, or capital infusions.

While not all transformations are officially labeled transformations, a transformation program often follows a negative event, such as financial performance or the loss of a major customer. Transformations also happen organically, with a little "t." A senior leader recognizes the need for change and reorganizes a few groups to be more efficient, effective, or innovative. Transformation programs may also play out over multiple years as a new CEO systematically works through each part of the organization. What is common, regardless of the model, is that there is a tremendous amount of change that never seems to stop.

A sense of urgency for deploying a Playbook is created in this scenario under the following conditions:

- If there is substantial movement of resources, a consistent process used despite "who" is performing the process can help provide consistent execution.
- As new resources become acclimatized to new data as part of someone's new job, they need to understand and attest to their outputs. As jobs change, you want to ensure the inputs and outputs are consistent.
- When new processes are desired to help improve efficiency, the Playbook provides an efficient approach to improving the jobs, especially if the employee headcount is being reduced due to realignment.
- If the transformation has colocated information management assets and simplified oversight of analytical activities in the company, data governance using a Playbook helps coordinate and improve usage of these assets.

ERP application implementation

Enterprise resource planning projects are large and complex. For large companies wanting to consolidate ERP instances, the cost and complexity of multiple ERP instances can be overwhelming. For growing companies, upgrading to a new ERP application may require significant changes to business process.

Whether ERP consolidation or ERP upgrading, the data within an ERP application is the most sensitive financial, human resources, or manufacturing data in the company. However, many ERP systems rely on external data sources. During a consolidation or upgrade, a significant amount of data is moved to the new environment in a single batch event. It is also quite common to run multiple systems in parallel for long periods of time—often called run-out periods.

A sense of urgency for deploying a Playbook is created in ERP implementation scenarios under the following conditions:

- Multiple ERP systems from around the world need to be consolidated into a single instance and a consistent, repeatable approach to consolidating the data is required.
- A reliable, attestable method is needed to ensure that as consolidation or upgrading occurs the data going into the new environment can be linked to the data going into the legacy environment.
- A large project, like many ERP projects, requires a consistent and efficient way to make decisions about how to integrate the data as the business groups go through their discussions on how to integrate or increase consistency of the business processes.
- A multiyear effort, as many ERP projects are, requires consistent data management processes as each phase is completed.

Sales force automation application implementation

Right ahead or right behind ERP projects, SFA projects are notorious for being complex and confusing. An SFA system is often the heart of managing sales activity. SFA applications often feed into sales and revenue reports, another source of urgency for the Playbook. SFA applications are also seen, perhaps incorrectly, as an authoritative source of the customer list and other master data. After all, the reasoning goes, everything starts with sales. It is also common to have multiple SFA systems in place at one time, sometimes based on geography. Multiple systems may also exist due to staggered deployment schedules for a new system or due to a preference by product lines to use an SFA application that better meets their needs.

A sense of urgency for deploying a Playbook is created in these scenarios under the following conditions:

- Multiple systems with similar information need to be attestably merged together to create one view of the customer base.
- Analysis of sales information requires consistent and efficient understanding of the data quality in the systems prior to use.
- Many SFA systems are implemented hurriedly, leading to conflicting and overlapping data within a single application and across applications. A better understanding of the data quality is needed both now and ongoing.

Data as a strategy

Some organizations know that their core business strategy relies on data services. For example, Acxiom, Experian, and IMS sell data. They carefully prepare and cultivate data sets for use by other organizations. They know that their value perception is based on customers' perceptions of data quality.

Many new startup organizations, especially Consumer Focus, understand the meaning of "data as a strategy." Facebook, for example, uses data to target ads. Google is the same. Their organizations revolve around data streams that feed their revenue model—advertising.

Other organizations are not sure if their data is a core part of their strategy. For example, an organization that provides durable medical equipment to their patients may care greatly about their reimbursement data, but they may not see the data as opportunities for expanding their business, eg, into fraud detection or general clinical analytics. Each company is different.

If your company is using its data as the primary factor in your company's revenue model, then "data as a strategy" applies to you. If you are a startup and handling customer or patient data, such as integrating into bank or healthcare data sources, you will need to ensure the data is properly governed.

A sense of urgency for deploying a Playbook is created in a "data as a strategy" organization under the following conditions:

- Rapid corporate growth can lead to expanded partnerships. Partners will want attestable proof that your company will manage their data.
- Rapid employee onboarding and corporate expansion can lead to rapid employee turnover. Consistency is needed as the organization's resources change.
- To reduce lawsuit risks, attestable data management practices are needed consistently in all departments in order to demonstrate that a negative event was not the result of negligence.

Performance management or metrics project

It is not uncommon to see data governance programs launched under the auspices of a performance management or metrics project. The approach to "managing by the numbers" or "you can only manage what you can measure" is very alluring. Most organizations already have a set of metrics in place, even if it is only financial metrics. In this case, a metrics project is usually an extension of existing capabilities.

Many of these projects are run by senior managers or executives who wish to have more "navigation" information when they make decisions or evaluate their business outcomes. Some metrics directly factor into compensation.

A sense of urgency for deploying a Playbook-based model is based on the following points of view:

- An attestable process is needed to ensure the data used to set baselines and perform ongoing monitoring and measurement is consistent and that standard procedures are being followed.
- You need line of sight into the information used to calculate the metrics so you can drilldown confidently and efficiently to understand the underlying reasons for deviations from targets.
- You know that the first set of metrics is only the beginning of the process. Additional metrics will be needed. You need an efficient method to ensure the definitions and understanding of the data are available on the schedule you need it to be.

CRISES AS A SOURCE OF URGENCY

While it is more common today to see data governance used as part of larger project implementation, a crisis is still a major motivation for rapid deployment. Unfortunately, in these scenarios, data governance is deployed rapidly without training or a much of a plan. In a crisis, senior management's directive is to quickly make things better and stop the bleeding.

Client-facing reports do not match

Business-to-business organizations may produce reports that describe their customers' status or state of relationship. For example, healthcare insurance companies produce clinical reports that describe the state of their employee population as part of a quarterly or annual review. Financial services companies produce financial reports describing the nature and status of various financial assets to its customers—the company that has employed them to manage their employees' pensions.

The client needs to use multiple types of reports to evaluate performance and expects your organization to produce them. Clients are confused or become upset when numbers in the reports do not match and they are unable to easily evaluate performance. If the inconsistencies are large or persistent, trust is lost and the relationship suffers.

If a senior leader is put into a position where inconsistent information is produced and they look poorly informed or the organization looks bad, the senior leader will escalate the issue. The escalation results in a scramble where both the business and IT are pulled into multiple hurried meetings and an action plan produced to try and remedy the issues. This is a common source of "data calls" where the organization disrupts its normal flow and tries to find and fix data issues. Unfortunately, even with this crisis, the fixes needed to create consistent, correct reporting may take a long time or be difficult to implement.

The opportunity for the Playbook in this crisis catalyst is to rapidly deploy it using a data sprint, a structured but agile way to start the Playbook-based data governance model. Then, in the heat of the moment when commitments may be easier to obtain, to gain commitment to successive data sprints as well as an ongoing Playbook-based data governance job model.

Implementation program failure

Implementation programs fail. In fact, they fail frequently. A project taking too long to complete or a project whose costs are escalating substantially higher than planned are good examples. Failure comes in many forms.

A large program failure usually results in a reshuffling or shelving of the project. Not all projects fail because of data-quality issues, but we have often seen higher cost and longer schedules in programs because they failed to account for the risk based on data-quality issues.

During debriefs and "lessons learned" sessions, there may be strong evidence that multiple programs fail for the same data-related reasons—poor data quality. It may seem obvious, but if multiple programs fail over time, then a data-focused program independent of the programs and with a structured set of processes designed to enhance knowledge and usability of data may be seen as a common-sense approach to reduce the risk of implementation failure. Since the Playbook-based model is designed to create reusable assets, reusable by project teams, a Playbook-based model can decrease each project's total cost.

AML/BSA and fraud

The Antimoney Laundering, Bank Secrecy Act and fraud are hot topics today because of increased federal and state scrutiny around financial and trade-based criminal and terrorist financing activity. As noted in an earlier chapter, the level and frequency of fines is increasing, some quite large. If your organization is audited or comes under regulatory scrutiny, regulators can shut down your business operations.

It is not uncommon today to see organizations put in place data governance program in response to regulatory consent orders. The justification for the program's cost is reducing overall financial and regulatory risk. However, a non-Playbook, data governance program will not reduce risk and be efficient. A Playbook-based model allows an organization to attest not only to the data but also to the process by which the data is managed. Having a process and attesting to its use with demonstrable artifacts creates a transparent and visible program that will support an organization's response to a consent order.

Restatement financial reporting

Financial restatement is often a source of crisis for a company. Financial restatements or issues in financial reports can cause investors to experience a dramatic loss of confidence in a company, which means stock prices may sag and sales decline. The reasons for restatement include updating accounting rules that were used improperly, financial fraud, or business fraud.

While this type of crisis may be caused by reasons unrelated to data, it provides a fertile ground for identifying the need for better data controls over financial data. Finance departments are highly receptive to data governance because their business is about managing the health of the company through financial data. During this type of crisis, it is much easier to justify a disciplined approach to data management. The Playbook offers a way to rapidly set up a set of processes and best practices a finance department can follow to ensure the data used will never be a source of financial-reporting problems.

Building another data warehouse—the last one failed because of data-quality issues

This type of crisis is surprisingly common. We have seen many data warehouse programs grind to a halt because of skyrocketing schedules and costs associated with integrating the data for a data warehouse. These negative aspects are some of the reasons you see ownership for data warehouses collocated into the same group as data governance.

If your organization has built multiple data warehouses and they are not used, it may be due to the lack of "trust" by business groups. You can use this "lack of trust" to justify a disciplined approach, the Playbook, to performing the data governance jobs. The Playbook model is designed to implement different resources both in business and IT groups. A Playbook model can identify ownership, roles, and activities that the different roles need to perform in order to be successful. Data warehouse projects fail for many reasons. When a project "restart" happens, you want to make sure the project does not fail because of data-quality issues.

URGENCY, PLAYBOOKS, AND EXISTING DATA GOVERNANCE PROGRAMS

You will have a harder time moving to a Playbook-based model if you have an existing data governance program but no catalyst.

Perhaps an upcoming set of application implementations, business group changes, or transformation programs are on the horizon. You may want to improve the efficiency of the groups dealing with data and who experience recurring issues. When the level of issues is constant but not thunderously loud or disruptive, consistency and efficiency become the primary catalyst you tap to create a sense of urgency. It is not as compelling as a crisis or large change program, and it may be difficult and take a long time.

To motivate a change in the current approach, you need to gather evidence, internal or external, to show the current approach needs to be changed. Internal evidence is the most compelling. There are several sources of "issues" that could motivate change:

- Quotes and notes from external clients indicating dissatisfaction or unhappiness with your services and products that is linkable to data-quality issues.
- Troubled ticket-request queues for changes to reports or analytical applications.

- Outstanding requirements that were not met in an application project.
- Pain-point lists gathered from business resources or a data sprint indicating that data is not "quite right" or requires substantial effort to perform a task.
- Pain-point lists gathered from IT resources indicating that they continue to run into issues surrounding a specific application or system.
- Direct quotes from business leaders indicating issues, perhaps not catastrophic issues, aligned with the catalysts described in the previous sections.
- Requirements and charters for projects that were rejected or deprioritized over the years.

These "data points" sources help you map out the true level of need. Perhaps the list is large, or maybe each element on the list is relatively small making the need hard to see. Aggregated together, the list may be more compelling. Sometimes you have to make the problem larger, not smaller, before a sense of urgency develops.

You can create a sense of urgency by running a data sprint. A data sprint is a short project designed to create outputs and conduct activities consistent with the Playbook but compressed into a much shorter timeframe. In our experience, it is fairly easy to obtain a list of issues from a data sprint that point to broader issues and concerns. A data sprint can be run internally with no additional funding or, as we have seen, some companies have end-of-year money that can be spent on improving operations and a data sprint is one way to determine what types of improvements and benefits could be obtained by improving data management capabilities.

When using a data sprint to create a sense of urgency, you need to do more than just profile data and discuss "found" issues. It is more compelling when you create durable artifacts out of a data sprint. Durable artifacts are the start of a Playbook-based data governance process. Creating these artifacts, even on a small scale, will show participants that a Playbook-based model is neither complicated and obtuse nor costly. Coupled with the data-profiling outputs, you will be able to show just cause for ramping the Playbook, continuing to use the Playbook model and addressing business issues.

IDENTIFY YOUR HIGHEST VALUE TARGET AREAS

To rapidly deploy the Playbook, first identify the highest value target areas that will benefit from a Playbook. In the previous sections, you saw many different situations that could provide a catalyst for a Playbook. In many cases, your organization may have multiple catalysts.

We can break down the approach into a series of steps (see Fig. 10.1):

1. List all the catalysts you have identified that could motivate a Playbook deployment
2. Identify the underlying causes for each catalyst
    a. Issues can be about specific data issues, inefficiencies, or the continued presence of issues over a long period of time.
    b. You may need to investigate the catalyst in order to directionally identify the underlying root cause. A data sprint is a fast approach to create an issues list and identify root causes.
    c. Catalog the underlying root causes
    d. Count and group the root causes
    e. There may be several common root causes that underlie an issue

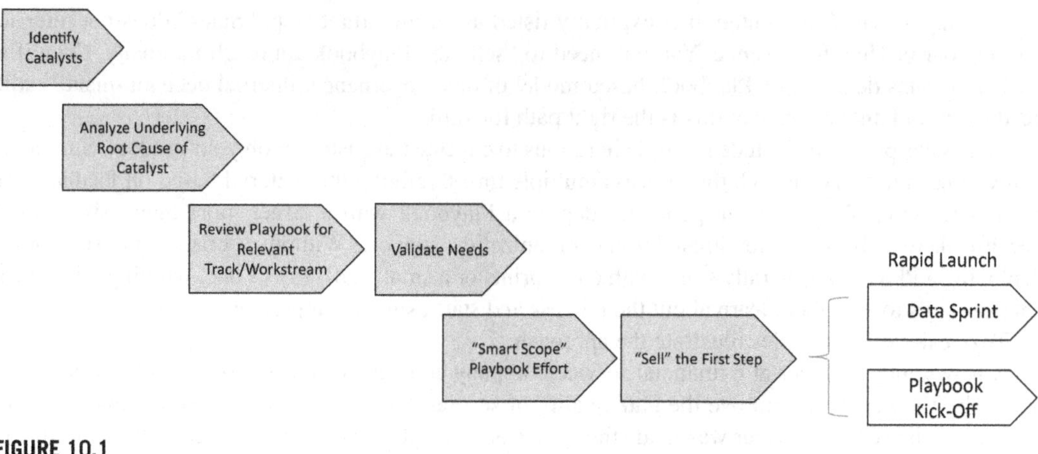

FIGURE 10.1

Rapid deployment process.

3. For each catalyst/issue
   a. Identify the business group
   b. List the "customers" that benefit from resolving the issues
   c. Identify through high, medium, and low the financial or operational impact of addressing the data issues. While ROI information may be available, it may not be accurate enough for other groups to agree with so high/medium/low may be more helpful at this time.
   d. Identify how many root causes contribute to the issue
   e. Link the catalyst to the Playbook value proposition as shown in the previous section
4. Create a "sales" presentation to call out needs
   a. Count and pie/bar-chart the catalysts and root issues
   b. Specific counts and pie charts are helpful to communicate the level of issues that exist and help motivate a sense of urgency
   c. Quotes from business and IT leaders
   d. Curated issues lists
5. Work with other business and IT stakeholders to validate and extend the list
   a. This can be performed offline through email or online in small to medium sized meetings.
   b. You will also want to work with leaders of the affected business groups to gain their perspective and obtain feedback on prioritization.
6. Review the Playbook for the relevant workstream or data sprint approach
7. Select and customize the Playbook deployment model including the:
   a. Business group to work with
   b. List of issues to address
   c. List of Playbook outputs to be created
   d. Ability to manage the critical success factors for the specific issues
8. "Smart scope" the Playbook deployment effort. Smart scoping is covered in the next section.
9. Update the "sales" deck and obtain organizational buy-in and agreement to proceed

Creating a "sales" presentation is explicitly listed as an important step. "Sales" does not refer to selling your product for revenue. You will need to "sell" the Playbook approach internally. Even if a crisis motivates deploying a Playbook-based model of data governance, internal decision-makers still need to be sold on the idea that this is the right path forward.

Most sales processes include multiple iterations to educate the customer on your product. Similarly, you will need to work through this process multiple times, refining the material based on feedback. If a crisis is the catalyst, you can generally deploy a Playbook with a larger more aggressive model because there will be greater financial and organization support. Without a crisis catalyst, rapidly deploying a Playbook generally starts with data sprints or a small staff, say of one, working with other data stewards to help them learn about the process and start using the approach.

Two real-world examples illustrate the approach.

A new senior manager at a financial service company enjoyed strong support from his vice president. The VP wanted to improve the data quality of several domain areas inside the company. At the same time, the senior manager was made the owner of a new data warehouse project. The senior manager knew that he wanted to improve data quality. He implemented an 8-week data sprint to gather metrics around data quality. Several systems were present that housed similar information, eg, customer lists and financial asset information. He identified that the data quality was low in certain data domains and created snapshots of specific data issues. He initiated data-quality reporting using a business-intelligence reporting tool starting with the baseline measurements.

After the data sprint, he initiated Playbook processes with some of the business units. Not all the business units wanted to work with him. So he chose the business groups and data domains that did support him. After 10 months of deploying the Playbook and addressing issues through technical and nontechnical fixes, he measured improvements to data quality by comparing current data-quality measures against the baseline. He was able to clearly show that where the business groups participated, there were improvements in data quality. Where business groups did not engage, the data-quality measures did not improve.

At another company, a vice president was asked by the CFO to create a data governance program due to ongoing issues around data quality, which affected their financial reporting. Financial reporting was becoming more difficult and there never seemed to be progress that improved the situation. The CFO asked the VP to take action. The VP realized that since there was not a crisis catalyst that would motivate a Playbook model, deploying the Playbook would take a few years before it became institutionalized in the analysts' behaviors.

The first step was to establish the Playbook process that was simple and easy. After delivering some training, analysts working on small projects were asked to work with the VP. The VP would step them through the Playbook process, provide examples of the types of outputs that were required, and work with the financial analysts to mentor them on the approach.

Over time, the list of documented and confirmed issues grew and the VP started planning what areas to proactively pursue as part of the Playbook program. Fixes for issues were consistently instituted inside various financial and technical projects. After 2 years, the Playbook was institutionalized across the finance group and the CFO continued to realize benefits from the program.

SMART SCOPING

Scoping your initial Playbook effort is a critical step. A badly placed first step can undermine credibility and result in slow interest in the initiative. The examples provided in the previous section suggest that narrowing the deployment effort to a manageable level of activity and outcomes is important to achieve demonstrable success. In those examples, a scope was crafted that was both reasonable and achievable. Although the timelines differed, each effort was purposeful and a careful selection of what activities would be performed was made and communicated prior to the effort. An important outcome of smart scoping is to control expectations of outcomes given the level of investment made.

The initial scope of the Playbook should be based on the specific catalyst but also include other dimensions. Some of these aspects are not present in other operational processes you find within your organization because a Playbook requires coordination across decentralized resources and has a higher "abstraction" level. While it is easy to make a customer order concrete, information about data is more complicated.

To decide what to pursue as your first project as well as the boundaries of your efforts consider the following factors:

- Are the catalysts already being addressed in other forums, programs and projects, or by other groups?
- Are the root causes of the catalysts related to data and data governance jobs?
- Is the initial scope set small enough to be accomplished by the available resources?
- Will the resources be dedicated or not?
- Does the Playbook scope require participation for certain roles in groups that you do not have oversight over or work with frequently?
- Can you calculate a hard or soft financial benefit to performing the Playbook activities?
- Do you have support for more than one cycle of effort?
- Is the support you have only for a single effort and future efforts will be evaluated after completing the first?
- Has the team working on the first Playbook effort worked with data before or understand the basic data governance jobs?
- Are those that would be involved in the project involved with other new, large or complex projects that would limit their time?
- Is there a strong business and IT sponsor?
- Is there existing application infrastructure that will make the job easier?
- Do you know who should be involved?
- Has a non-Playbook, data governance effort been tried before and failed or not had strong success?
- Are the power dynamics of the business and IT groups involved balanced between the groups?
  - Do the individuals involved wish to bury or cover up issues?
  - Are the individuals open to solving problems even if they were the cause of them?
  - Do the individuals in the different groups work together well? Has that been demonstrated on other projects?

Most of these dimensions (as shown in Fig. 10.2) have obvious positive answers. For example, if you have strong support from different groups, these groups have demonstrated that they work well together and their root causes are clearly data related, you can scope the Playbook effort to be larger and longer to accommodate these groups. However, if obvious answer to these scoping questions raises yellow flags because the answers are not clear or are "no," you will need to craft a smaller a more modest scope.

Who's Involved –	Problem Being Addressed –	Approach –
• Have the players involved worked together well before? • Will organizational dynamics play a negative role? • Do different people have overlapping responsibilities around this issue?	• Does anyone care about addressing the issues? • Have solution attempts been made before? • Can the Playbook address part or all of the issues?	• Do you need access to resources that are difficult to obtain? • What type of technologies might be involved? • How much education is needed in addition to the "doing"? • How much time is needed or required? • Can you scope small?

Most contextual factors, or critical success factors, are non-technical.

FIGURE 10.2

Contextual decision factors.

As an example, consider the following project scope for a data sprint in which a crisis had recently occurred. In addition to several other factors, there were data issues that were affecting business performance. A management plan was put in place to address issues. The management team wanted to see steps taken around the data as follows:

- Limited to one functional area of the company
- Duration: 7 weeks
- Scope of data: No more than 30 CDEs
- Limited data governance application support
  - Data-profiling tools were available and could be used quickly
  - Very few data catalogs and source systems descriptions were available
  - The majority of source systems were known but there were some that were unknown or not known to be in production
- Subject matter experts are easily identified
- Outputs included standard Playbook artifacts such as:
  - List of existing data controls
  - List of source systems (up to 20)
  - List of CDEs
    - Physical names, sizes, and locations
    - Mapping of the physical data location to the CDE
    - Definition by source system
  - List of issues produced from data profiling, by source system
  - Graphic diagram of data flows
- Intangible benefits desired:
  - Identify issues to be resolved in an implementation project to address crisis issues
  - Begin the deployment of Playbook-based data governance processes

This scope seems simple small, but it took nearly 10 involved individuals, working part-time, to execute this scope. In some organizations this is ambitious. In others, this work could be performed in days if not hours.

Although it was identified that most of the involved individuals had had some data governance training, there was confusion about the definition of CDE. Some thought it was a physical, target field in an application within the functional area. Others considered a CDE to be the source system's physical field. A CDE is actually a business definition for a business concept irrespective of its physical implementation in different source systems. In some cases a CDE matches one to one with a physical field in a database, sometimes not. These types of conversations are helpful for learning but it increases the duration of the data sprint.

Through smart scoping, you can identify where you will spend time in a Playbook deployment effort that may not otherwise be obvious.

GETTING HELP

The best sources of help for rapidly deploying a Playbook are the business and IT groups that would use it. They can provide guidance and feedback on the Playbook model and help you customize it for rapid deployment.

If you do not have buy-in to rapidly deploy a Playbook, then either you need to continue to gradually build a sense of urgency, wait for a crisis, or delay deploying a Playbook (or even data governance) until a more opportune time. Despite your best efforts, you cannot "push on string."

You can leverage external resources. External consultants can play an important role by bringing external viewpoint, motivations, and issue identification skills to your organization. For non-Playbook data governance programs, we think external consultants may not have the motivation to perform the jobs well. However, under a Playbook model, we think external consultants can be employed for many aspects of Playbook deployment and operational use. With a Playbook in hand, the objectives, activities, and outputs are well defined. Strong codification of the process is a good way to scale the model beyond yourself. Whether an internal resource or an external one is used, the Playbook's level of specificity gives you more resource options.

Professional organizations exist to help you including the following:

- DAMA: Data Management Association
- DGPO: Data Governance Professionals Organization

Industry and function-specific organizations can help you with topic-specific data issues you need to manage. For example, in the AML/BSA and fraud space the organizations below can provide insights into required data standards:

- ACFE: Association of Certified Fraud Examiners
- ACAM: and Association of Certified Antimoney Laundering Specialists
- FFIEC BSA/AML: Examination Manual

In additional to these professional organizations, analysts such as Gartner and Forrester can help you survey the landscape for tools to help deploy Playbooks-based data governance.

There are many websites with data governance content and we encourage you to review them. While they all have good ideas and many checklists to use, we have found that they lack specifics about how to perform the work—the area the Playbook addresses. Most professionals understand the basic ideas behind data governance. It is the specifics of making it actionable and sustainable that require Playbook-level detail to be successful.

Bibliography

[1] DW 2.0: The architecture for the next generation of data warehousing (Morgan Kaufman series in data management systems) Kindle Edition by W.H. Inmon (Author), Derek Strauss (Author), Genia Neushloss (Author) Morgan Kaufmann. 1st ed. July 28, 2010.
[2] Inmon WH, O'Neil B, Fryman L. Business metadata: Capturing enterprise knowledge. 1st ed. Morgan Kaufmann; October 11, 2007.
[3] Brestoff NE, Inmon WH. Preventing litigation: An early warning system to get big value out of big data paperback. Business Expert Press; August 28, 2015.
[4] Federal Reserve System Board of Governors; Federal Financial Institution Examiners Council Bank Secrecy Act Anti-Money Laundering Exam Manual 2014.
[5] US Department of the Treasury: Office of the Comptroller of the Currency, Comptroller's Handbook, 2011.
[6] Bank for International Settlements Basel Committee on Bank Supervision: Principles for Effective Risk Data Aggregation and Risk Reporting, January, 2013.

Background information from industry sources including: Internal Audit Institute (IIA), Information Systems Audit and Control Association (ISACA), American Telehealth Association, Global Association of Risk Professionals (GARP), Securities Industry and Financial Markets Association (SIFMA), Global Financial Markets Association (GFMA) and others.

Glossary of Terms

Glossary of Terms Activity A defined set f stakes related to a specific process that produce specific outcomes. Example: Defining critical data is an activity that includes multiple tasks and included a specific outcome.

Ad-hoc Occurring randomly or on demand, not given to periodicity.

Artifact A physical or digital result from an interaction or transaction. Example: a receipt is an artifact of a transaction.

Assessment The outcome of an evaluation of a process or event. Example: a scored exam constitutes an assessment of learning.

Attest Confirm and commit to the accuracy and integrity of the data.

Attribute Characteristics of an object we capture in a catalog or model for data management purposes. Example: last name is an attribute of a person.

Audit A disciplined approach to reviewing and ensuring appropriate controls and outcomes.

Bigdata A combination of facts and artifacts drawn from a myriad of sources and stored without regard to rational or normalized disciplines or structures. Example: bigdata about a customer shopping event might include files, web-click data and transactional data all stored in different formats, with redundant information.

Business case A compilation of costs and benefits associated with a planned project or investment.

Business glossary A technology repository that can contain many items or objects associated with a Business Term.

Call-for-papers A request for documentation related to a project or other initiative. Example: a bigdata project might issue a call-for-papers request for current bigdata requirements.

Capability A combination of working knowledge about a particular process or domain, and the capacity to apply that knowledge through action. Example: an accountant has the capability to produce financial reports.

Controls Manual or automated mechanisms to ensure events or activities are tracked and potentially limited in their scope or impact. Example: an airbag is a control intended to limit damage to an occupant in a collision.

Cost-benefit analysis A method of determining the expenses and impacts for a given investment. Example: a cost-benefit analysis will be used to determine whether we engage in a specific investment.

Critical data element A data element (*see data element*) is qualified or defined as critical based on criteria such as the financial impact of the data it represents. Example: net income is often considered a critical data element because it refers to financially impactful data.

Data Facts about events, objects, and associations. Example: data about a sale would include date, amount, and method of payment.

Data architecture The discipline, methods, and outputs related to understanding data, its meaning and relationships. Example: data architecture includes data models and dictionaries explaining the meaning and relationship of data.

Data catalog A collection of data elements along with their definitions and other metadata. Example: a business glossary used by data stewards to capture and define data elements.

Data cycle An approach that leverages an organizational unit or area to execute Playbook activities for its respective data in an ongoing manner. Example: the data cycle for finance will repeat as changes in data are noted.

Data dashboard A management-level online report capturing data conditions and trends. Example: a data-quality dashboard monitoring the quality status of critical data.

Data element A unit of data (fact) that can be uniquely defined and used. Example: last name is a data element that can be defined as the family name of an individual and is distinct from other name-related elements.

Data governance The discipline of applying controls to data in order to ensure its integrity over time. Example: we apply change and quality controls to critical data to ensure consistently accurate reporting.

Data lake A repository of data used to manage disparate formats and types of data for a variety of uses. Example: we will collect multiple formats of highly redundant data and maintain it in our data lake.

Data landscape A term often used to refer to the universe of data contents, structures, and systems in an organization or industry. Example: the data landscape in financial services is mixed, complex, and very dynamic.

Data lifecycle The series of stages that data moves though from initiation, to creation, to destruction. Example: the data life cycle of customer data has four distinct phases and lasts approximately eight years.

Data map A visual depiction of where certain kinds of data exist across an organization. Example: we have produced a data map showing where all customer data exists across our systems.

Data model A visual means of depicting data and its relationship to other data. Example: an entity relationship diagram is a data model depicting major data entities and their relationships.

Data officer A natural person assigned responsibility for a defined scope of data. Operates as an accountable party for change and quality control for their aligned scope of data. Example: Dan is the data officer for HR data and is accountable for its change and quality control.

Data profiling An automated method of analyzing large amounts of data to determine its quality and integrity. Example: profiling or customer data will help us determine how accurate it is and help to identify gaps and inconsistencies.

Data provider Either an internal or external entity who has agreed to provide you with data on certain terms and conditions. Example: Bloomberg is our data provider for market equities.

Data quality Refers to the accuracy, completeness, timeliness, integrity, and acceptance of data as determined by its users. Example: customer address information is of low quality because it is incomplete and inaccurate.

Data risk Refers to risk that accrues in an organization because of impaired data quality, or risk that occurs to data because of poor controls and governance. Data risk refers to the likelihood of a business problem occurring, not the likely severity of the problem. Example: we have high data risk in our finance area because we lack controls and governance.

Data science The discipline of analysis that helps relate data to the events and processes that produce and consume it for different reasons. Example: bigdata programs often engage data science in order to determine which data is of value and how to analyze it.

Data services Technical and business services related to providing data, ascertaining its quality and supporting its use throughout an organization. Example: our data service provides us with a data-quality dashboard to track the quality of our critical data.

Data sprint Defines, discrete series of actions taken over a specified period of time. Example: we will execute an agile data sprint to achieve a controlled level of maturity for a subset of our financial data over 30 days.

Data steward A natural person assigned the responsibility to catalog, define, and monitor changes to critical data. Example: The data steward for finance critical data is Dan.

Data warehouse A granular, time-variant, structured store of historical data in a neutral, nonredundant format for multiple uses. Its purpose is the reuse of data. Example: our enterprise data warehouse maintains our historical data in a neutral format supporting many users and formats.

Defensive lines Refer to the roles we have defined in the Playbook for officers as well as risk and audit specialists who detect and prevent major audits from data using Playbook controls and methods. Example: data officers and internal auditors can work together on a defensive line when detecting and addressing issues.

Demand management The defined process for accepting, prioritizing, and fulfilling demands for data services and outcomes. Example: the data demand management office accepts and prioritizes business demand for data services.

Detective controls Provide monitoring and assessment of data and analytic conditions to identify emerging issues and problems. Example: discovery profiling of data and rules-based profiling of data both provide detective controls for that data.

Discovery data profiling Uses automated profiling methods to analyze data based on its defined structure and other metadata. Example: we conducted discovery profiling against our finance data to determine where we were missing data, based on what the catalog determined was required.

Enterprise data Data that is shared by multiple people and organizations. The distinction is important because it establishes the scope of use or governance and control requirements. Example: finance data is used across the enterprise and must be governed using a shared governance model.

Executive sponsorship The support necessary to acquire human resources in order to define control data. Example: our executive sponsor for financial data is providing us with a budget and resources to define and control our data.

Exposure The potential impact a risk event can have if it occurs. Example: there is a 30% risk of a flood occurring in our area; if it occurs, we have a $10 million exposure at our data center.

Fact An observable or otherwise verifiable artifact of an object or event. Example: Dan is alive based on his current EEG results.

ISO An international federation of standardizing bodies, which collaborates to form international standards.

Maturity levels A measurement used to determine organizational performance with respect to data, the needs and expectations of the enterprise.

Metadata Artifacts of events and objects and contextual information that helps us understand the structure and meaning of data or facts. Example: the definitions of our data elements are metadata we store in the business glossary.

Offensive lines Refer to the roles we have defined in the Playbook for officers as well as risk and audit specialists who improve the quality and timeliness of data and analytics. Example: data officers and internal auditors can work together on an offensive line when improving data quality.

Playbook deployment The process of executing Playbook activities for a given scope of data using either a cycle or sprint approach. Example: we will deploy Playbook activities and capabilities for the accounts-payable finance data in a data sprint.

Risk The likelihood of a negative impact event occurring over a period of time, not to be confused with exposure. Example: there is a 30% risk of tornadoes occurring tonight.

Risk management The discipline and methods used to quantify, track, and reduce where possible various types of defined risk.

Standardization Using rules to conform data that is similar into a standard format or structure. Example: taking similar data, which originates in a variety of formats, and transforming it into a single, clearly defined format.

Index

'*Note:* Page numbers followed by "f" indicate figures.'

D

E

F

G

H

I

J

K

L

M

N

O

P

U

V

W

Printed in the United States
By Bookmasters